1 Corinthians

TEACH THE TEXT COMMENTARY SERIES

John H. Walton
Old Testament General Editor

Mark L. Strauss
New Testament General Editor

When complete, the TEACH THE TEXT COMMENTARY SERIES *will include the following volumes*:

Old Testament Volumes

Genesis .... Richard S. Hess

Exodus .... T. Desmond Alexander

Leviticus and Numbers .... Joe M. Sprinkle

Deuteronomy .... Michael A. Grisanti

Joshua .... Kenneth A. Mathews

Judges and Ruth .... Kenneth C. Way

1 & 2 Samuel .... Robert B. Chisholm Jr.

1 & 2 Kings .... David W. Baker

1 & 2 Chronicles .... Robert R. Duke

Ezra, Nehemiah, and Esther.... Douglas J. E. Nykolaishen and Andrew J. Schmutzer

Job .... Daniel J. Estes

Psalms, two volumes .... C. Hassell Bullock

Proverbs .... Richard L. Schultz

Ecclesiastes and Song of Songs ... Edward M. Curtis

Isaiah .... Frederick J. Mabie

Jeremiah and Lamentations .. J. Daniel Hays

Ezekiel .... John W. Hilber

Daniel .... Ronald W. Pierce

The Minor Prophets .... Douglas Stuart

New Testament Volumes

Matthew .... Jeannine K. Brown

Mark .... Grant R. Osborne

Luke .... R. T. France

John and 1–3 John .... David L. Turner

Acts .... David E. Garland

Romans .... C. Marvin Pate

1 Corinthians .... Preben Vang

2 Corinthians .... Moyer V. Hubbard

Galatians and Ephesians ...... Roy E. Ciampa

Philippians, Colossians, and Philemon .... Linda L. Belleville

1 & 2 Thessalonians, 1 & 2 Timothy, and Titus .... Philip H. Towner

Hebrews .... Jon C. Laansma

James, 1 & 2 Peter, and Jude .... Jim Samra

1–3 John .... (see *John*)

Revelation .... J. Scott Duvall

To see which titles are available, visit the series website at www.teachthetextseries.com.

TEACH the TEXT
COMMENTARY SERIES

1 Corinthians

Preben Vang

Mark L. Strauss and John H. Walton
GENERAL EDITORS

ILLUSTRATING THE TEXT

Kevin and Sherry Harney
ASSOCIATE EDITORS

Joshua Blunt, Rosalie de Rossett
CONTRIBUTING AUTHORS

BakerBooks

a division of Baker Publishing Group
Grand Rapids, Michigan

© 2014 by Preben Vang
Captions and Illustrating the Text sections © 2014 by Baker Publishing Group

Published by Baker Books
a division of Baker Publishing Group
PO Box 6287, Grand Rapids, MI 49516-6287
www.bakerbooks.com

Casebound edition published 2021
ISBN 978-1-5409-0238-2

The Library of Congress has cataloged the original edition as follows:
Vang, Preben, 1955–
    1 Corinthians / Preben Vang
        pages cm. — (Teach the text commentary series)
    Includes bibliographical references and index.
    ISBN 978-0-8010-9234-3 (cloth)
    1. Bible. Corinthians, 1st—Commentaries. I. Title. II. Title: First Corinthians.
    BS2675.53.V36 2014
    227′.207—dc23   2013033605

Baker Publishing Group publications use paper produced from sustainable forestry practices and post-consumer waste whenever possible.

21 22 23 24 25 26 27   7 6 5 4 3 2 1

Contents

Welcome to the Teach the Text Commentary Series

Why another commentary series? That was the question the general editors posed when Baker Books asked us to produce this series. Is there something that we can offer to pastors and teachers that is not currently being offered by other commentary series, or that can be offered in a more helpful way? After carefully researching the needs of pastors who teach the text on a weekly basis, we concluded that yes, more can be done; this commentary is carefully designed to fill an important gap.

The technicality of modern commentaries often overwhelms readers with details that are tangential to the main purpose of the text. Discussions of source and redaction criticism, as well as detailed surveys of secondary literature, seem far removed from preaching and teaching the Word. Rather than wade through technical discussions, pastors often turn to devotional commentaries, which may contain exegetical weaknesses, misuse the Greek and Hebrew languages, and lack hermeneutical sophistication. There is a need for a commentary that utilizes the best of biblical scholarship but also presents the material in a clear, concise, attractive, and user-friendly format.

This commentary is designed for that purpose—to provide a ready reference for the exposition of the biblical text, giving easy access to information that a pastor needs to communicate the text effectively. To that end, the commentary is divided into carefully selected preaching units, each covered in six pages (with carefully regulated word counts both in the passage as a whole and in each subsection). Pastors and teachers engaged in weekly preparation thus know that they will be reading approximately the same amount of material on a week-by-week basis.

Each passage begins with a concise summary of the central message, or "Big Idea," of the passage and a list of its main themes. This is followed by a more detailed interpretation of the text, including the literary context of the passage, historical background material, and interpretive insights. While drawing on the best of biblical scholarship, this material is clear, concise, and to the point. Technical material is kept to a minimum, with endnotes pointing the reader to more detailed discussion and additional resources.

A second major focus of this commentary is on the preaching and teaching process itself. Few commentaries today help the pastor/teacher move from the meaning of the text to its effective communication. Our goal is to bridge this gap. In addition to interpreting the text in the "Understanding the Text" section, each six-page unit contains a "Teaching the Text" section and an "Illustrating the Text" section. The teaching section points to the key theological themes of the passage and ways to communicate these themes to today's audiences. The illustration section provides ideas and examples for retaining the interest of hearers and connecting the message to daily life.

The creative format of this commentary arises from our belief that the Bible is not just a record of God's dealings in the past but is the living Word of God, "alive and active" and "sharper than any double-edged sword" (Heb. 4:12). Our prayer is that this commentary will help to unleash that transforming power for the glory of God.

The General Editors

Introduction to the Teach the Text Commentary Series

This series is designed to provide a ready reference for teaching the biblical text, giving easy access to information that is needed to communicate a passage effectively. To that end, the commentary is carefully divided into units that are faithful to the biblical authors' ideas and of an appropriate length for teaching or preaching.

The following standard sections are offered in each unit.

1. *Big Idea*. For each unit the commentary identifies the primary theme, or "Big Idea," that drives both the passage and the commentary.
2. *Key Themes*. Together with the Big Idea, the commentary addresses in bullet-point fashion the key ideas presented in the passage.
3. *Understanding the Text*. This section focuses on the exegesis of the text and includes several sections.
   a. The Text in Context. Here the author gives a brief explanation of how the unit fits into the flow of the text around it, including reference to the rhetorical strategy of the book and the unit's contribution to the purpose of the book.
   b. Outline/Structure. For some literary genres (e.g., epistles), a brief exegetical outline may be provided to guide the reader through the structure and flow of the passage.
   c. Historical and Cultural Background. This section addresses historical and cultural background information that may illuminate a verse or passage.
   d. Interpretive Insights. This section provides information needed for a clear understanding of the passage. The intention of the author is to be highly selective and concise rather than exhaustive and expansive.
   e. Theological Insights. In this very brief section the commentary identifies a few carefully selected theological insights about the passage.

4. *Teaching the Text*. Under this second main heading the commentary offers guidance for teaching the text. In this section the author lays out the main themes and applications of the passage. These are linked carefully to the Big Idea and are represented in the Key Themes.

5. *Illustrating the Text*. At this point in the commentary the writers partner with a team of pastor/teachers to provide suggestions for relevant and contemporary illustrations from current culture, entertainment, history, the Bible, news, literature, ethics, biography, daily life, medicine, and over forty other categories. They are designed to spark creative thinking for preachers and teachers and to help them design illustrations that bring alive the passage's key themes and message.

Abbreviations

Old Testament

Gen.	Genesis	2 Chron.	2 Chronicles	Dan.	Daniel
Exod.	Exodus	Ezra	Ezra	Hosea	Hosea
Lev.	Leviticus	Neh.	Nehemiah	Joel	Joel
Num.	Numbers	Esther	Esther	Amos	Amos
Deut.	Deuteronomy	Job	Job	Obad.	Obadiah
Josh.	Joshua	Ps(s).	Psalm(s)	Jon.	Jonah
Judg.	Judges	Prov.	Proverbs	Mic.	Micah
Ruth	Ruth	Eccles.	Ecclesiastes	Nah.	Nahum
1 Sam.	1 Samuel	Song	Song of Songs	Hab.	Habakkuk
2 Sam.	2 Samuel	Isa.	Isaiah	Zeph.	Zephaniah
1 Kings	1 Kings	Jer.	Jeremiah	Hag.	Haggai
2 Kings	2 Kings	Lam.	Lamentations	Zech.	Zechariah
1 Chron.	1 Chronicles	Ezek.	Ezekiel	Mal.	Malachi

New Testament

Matt.	Matthew	Eph.	Ephesians	Heb.	Hebrews
Mark	Mark	Phil.	Philippians	James	James
Luke	Luke	Col.	Colossians	1 Pet.	1 Peter
John	John	1 Thess.	1 Thessalonians	2 Pet.	2 Peter
Acts	Acts	2 Thess.	2 Thessalonians	1 John	1 John
Rom.	Romans	1 Tim.	1 Timothy	2 John	2 John
1 Cor.	1 Corinthians	2 Tim.	2 Timothy	3 John	3 John
2 Cor.	2 Corinthians	Titus	Titus	Jude	Jude
Gal.	Galatians	Philem.	Philemon	Rev.	Revelation

General

//	parallel
AD	*anno Domini*, in the year of (our) Lord
BC	before Christ
ca.	*circa*, about
cf.	*confer*, compare
chap(s).	chapter(s)
e.g.	*exempli gratia*, for example
esp.	especially
NT	New Testament
OT	Old Testament
v(v).	verse(s)
vs.	versus

Ancient Versions

LXX   Septuagint

Modern Versions

ESV   English Standard Version
HCSB   Holman Christian Standard Bible
LEB   Lexham English Bible
NASB   New American Standard Bible
NET   New English Translation
NIV   New International Version
NLT   New Living Translation
NRSV   New Revised Standard Version

Apocrypha and Septuagint

Sir.   Sirach
Wis.   Wisdom of Solomon

Old Testament Pseudepigrapha

2 Bar.   2 Baruch (Apocalypse of Baruch)
1 En.   1 Enoch
2 En.   2 Enoch
Pss. Sol.   Psalms of Solomon
Sib. Or.   Sibylline Oracles
T. Job   Testament of Job
T. Jud.   Testament of Judah
T. Levi   Testament of Levi
T. Naph.   Testament of Naphtali
T. Reub.   Testament of Reuben

Mishnah and Talmud

b.   Babylonian Talmud
m.   Mishnah
'Abod. Zar. 'Abodah Zarah
Ber.   Berakot
Qidd.   Qiddushin
Sanh.   Sanhedrin
Yebam.   Yebamot

Apostolic Fathers

1 Clem.   1 Clement
Herm. Mand. Shepherd of Hermas, Mandate

Greek and Latin Works

Aristotle

Eth. nic.   Nicomachean Ethics
Pol.   Politics
Rhet.   Rhetoric

Celsus

Med.   On Medicine

Cicero

Clu.   For Cluentius

Dio Chrysostom

Disc.   Discourses

Epictetus

Disc.   Discourses

Gaius

Inst.   Institutes

John Chrysostom

Hom. 1 Cor. Homilies on 1 Corinthians

Josephus

Ant.   Jewish Antiquities
J.W.   Jewish War

Justinian

Dig.   Digest

Philo

Moses	*On the Life of Moses*
Post.	*On the Posterity of Cain*
Virt.	*On the Virtues*

Plutarch

Advice	*Advice to Bride and Groom*
Mor.	*Moralia*
Rom.	*Romulus*

Quintillian

Inst.	*Institutes of Oratory*

Seneca

Anger	*On Anger*
Ben.	*On Benefits*
Dial.	*Dialogues*
Mor. Ep.	*Moral Epistles*

Suetonius

Cal.	*Gaius Caligula*

Tertullian

Apol.	*Apology*

Secondary Sources

ABD	*Anchor Bible Dictionary*. Edited by D. N. Freedman. 6 vols. New York: Doubleday, 1992.
ANF	*The Ante-Nicene Fathers*. Edited by A. Roberts and J. Donaldson. 10 vols. 1885–87. Repr., Peabody, MA: Hendrickson, 1994.
APOT	*The Apocrypha and Pseudepig-rapha of the Old Testament*. Edited by R. H. Charles. 2 vols. Oxford: Clarendon, 1913.
BDAG	W. Bauer, F. W. Danker, W. F. Arndt, and F. W. Gingrich. *Greek-English Lexicon of the New Testament and Other Early Christian Literature*. 3rd ed. Chicago: University of Chicago Press, 1999.
BDF	F. Blass and A. Debrunner. *A Greek Grammar of the New Testament and Other Early Christian Literature*. Edited and translated by R. W. Funk. 9th ed. Chicago: University of Chicago Press, 1961.
BIBD	*The Baker Illustrated Bible Dictionary*. Edited by T. Longman III. Grand Rapids: Baker Books, 2013.
EDNT	*Exegetical Dictionary of the New Testament*. Edited by H. Balz and G. Schneider. 3 vols. Grand Rapids: Eerdmans, 1990.
LCL	Loeb Classical Library
NIDNTT	*New International Dictionary of New Testament Theology*. Edited by C. Brown. 4 vols. Grand Rapids: Zondervan, 1975–85.
NPNF[1]	*The Nicene and Post-Nicene Fathers*. Series 1. Edited by P. Schaff. 14 vols. 1886–89. Repr., Peabody, MA: Hendrickson, 1994.
Str-B	H. L. Strack and P. Billerbeck. *Kommentar zum Neuen Testament aus Talmud und Midrasch*. 6 vols. Munich: Beck, 1922–61.
TDNT	*Theological Dictionary of the New Testament*. Edited by G. Kittel and G. Friedrich. Translated by G. W. Bromiley. 10 vols. Grand Rapids: Eerdmans, 1964–76.

Introduction to 1 Corinthians

The early Christian community was called forth by the proclamation of the risen Christ. The story of Christ came before the texts. Actually, not only did the story of how God established a new covenant in Christ become the interpretive key to Old Testament texts, but most significantly, it brought theological focus to what we now call Gospels and letters. Biblical texts exist to amplify the significance of the Christ story—a story that demands to be heard because, through the resurrection of Jesus, God guaranteed it as *the* true story for (and about) humankind (1 Cor. 15:12–28). Even before preachers could refer to chapter and verse of any New Testament book, evangelists called people to faith by pointing to Christ's resurrection (e.g., Acts 2:29–36). Paul, likewise, claiming to have received his apostleship directly from the risen Lord (Gal. 1:12), follows this tradition and summarizes his message in 1 Corinthians (15:3–8) with an unwavering resurrection focus:

> For what I received I passed on to you as of first importance: that Christ died for our sins according to the Scriptures, that he was buried, that he was raised on the third day according to the Scriptures, and that he appeared to Cephas, and then to the Twelve. After that, he appeared to more than five hundred of the brothers and sisters at the same time, most of whom are still living, though some have fallen asleep. Then he appeared to James, then to all the apostles, and last of all he appeared to me also, as to one abnormally born.

Paul writes to help his audience hear and understand God's Word. For Christians, Paul's letters are not mere historical documents exposing issues of a developing faith and its social consequences;[1] rather, they are Scripture: texts designed to speak *to* us and *for* God.

Some Important Background Issues

For the minister and the teacher who need to help others connect the biblical message to their daily lives, a commentary must focus on issues that illuminate rather

1

than obscure the meaning of the text. Since we are separated from the composition of the text by two thousand years of history and by vast cultural differences, some understanding of literary forms and genres, of historical and social contexts, and of religious and theological vocabulary proves necessary to exegete the text insightfully. Although such matters are background issues, they help us avoid reading our own culture and understanding *into* the text instead of allowing the text to challenge and correct our present understanding and culture.

Much has been said about Corinth (both from pulpits and in older commentaries) that suggests Paul came to the old Greek Corinth, a city more or less defined by a massive scale of temple prostitution and debauchery of every kind. This was not so, however. The Corinth Paul came to was a new city, proudly Roman—a city that saw itself as a significant and important province in the Roman Empire. Like Ephesus, Philippi, and other places where Paul visited and spent time, Corinth was a place that considered Roman citizenship a privilege and a virtue.

Geography and Trade

At the time of Paul, the city of Corinth was a prosperous international center for business connecting east and west. Although comparison to a modern situation remains difficult, the closest modern

Because of its location, the city of ancient Corinth prospered as a major trading center.

parallel may be Hong Kong. Surrounded by two harbors, Corinth became the favored place of exchange between traders from Rome to the west, Asia to the east, major Greek centers in both Achaia and Macedonia to the north, and the Peloponnese region (and North Africa) to the south. Trading vessels approaching from the west through the Gulf of Corinth harbored in Lechaeum, while eastern traders approaching through the Saronic Gulf harbored in Cenchreae (Acts 18:18; Rom. 16:1). Cargo was transported between the two harbors on the Diolkos, a paved road connecting the two harbors. Smaller, lighter boats were pulled across the approximately four-mile stretch on rollers, while cargo from larger vessels was emptied onto carts and transported to waiting ships on the other side. Whichever way it was done, Corinth made money on customs and taxes. Corinth's location as the intersection for international trade seemed firmly secured since sailing south of the Peloponnese around Cape Malea not only added six days of travel but involved a treacherous route merchants and sailors preferred to avoid.

Sport and Tourism

Every other year, Corinth hosted the Isthmian Games, which were second only to the Olympic Games in size and significance. Finds of ancient coins reveal visitors coming from near and far to participate in the festivities. Beyond the athletic games and races, competition developed between various artistic expressions, like music and poetry, making these events giant festivals. Corinth, in other words, was the hub for world-class entertainment, which in turn helped create a fast-growing business environment for a city that in Paul's time had not yet reached its peak. Paul's visits to the city overlapped the games in AD 51, giving him a unique opportunity for international impact in both ministry and business (cf. 1 Cor. 9:25–27). As a tentmaker he came to a city bustling with skilled workers of all kinds, and he quickly joined fellow tentmakers and Christian evangelists Priscilla and Aquila in their business (Acts 18:1–4).

Corinth was a cosmopolitan magnet for new commercial ventures, as tourists crowded the city to spend money not only on lodging and food but on a variety of products and services provided by a host of entrepreneurs. These in turn created employment opportunities, ranging from menial slave jobs to positions as personal bodyguards and accountants. Some of the athletes came to enjoy great fame and with it tremendous privileges. Witherington suggests that highly successful female athletes who had become accustomed to significant privilege and influence in society were creating a problem in the church.[2]

Wealth and Relationships

Corinth's prosperity naturally created extremely wealthy and influential individuals. Such wealth and influence came with rules and demands that can be rather difficult for modern readers to understand. What may look to us like nepotism and unfairness was in Greco-Roman antiquity the norm for social behavior. More discussion of this will be provided on specific texts, but a few initial comments will be helpful.[3]

Paul wrote in a situation where both he and his audience saw personal patronage as an essential part of life. Protection, employment, access to goods, and so forth depended on it. The relationship between patron and client, or gift giver and recipient, was rather well defined, even if rules often went unspoken (in fact, it still holds true that in many cultures the most important rules go without saying). The key word for understanding this patronage is "reciprocity." A granted favor required expressions of gratitude. Reception of a gift or a favor was thus never without strings (a situation that likely explains Paul's vehemence against accepting any support from the Corinthian church [e.g., 2 Cor. 11:9; 12:13–14; cf. 1 Thess. 2:9; 2 Thess. 3:8]). Among equals, or friends, such favor could take the form of merely granting access to another patron. Still, this was a favor granted, and the recipient now owed a debt of gratitude. Such unwritten rules of reciprocity created bonds of loyalty that could last for generations.[4]

It follows that friends and clients were to be chosen carefully. Seneca brings this out vividly, explaining that one has to be careful from whom one accepts a favor.

> It is necessary for me to choose the person from whom I wish to receive a benefit; and, in truth, I must be far more careful in selecting my creditor for a benefit than a creditor for a loan. For to the latter I shall have to return the same amount that I have received, and, when I have returned it, I have paid all my debt and am free; but to the other I must make an additional payment, and, even after I have paid my debt of gratitude, the bond between us still holds; for, just when I have finished paying it, I am obliged to begin again and friendship endures; and, as I would not admit an unworthy man to my friendship, so neither would I admit one who is unworthy to the most sacred privilege of benefits, from which friendship springs.[5]

Patron-client relationships, with their delicate social etiquette, were a significant undercurrent in Paul's relationships with his audience and churches. This societal reality must be understood, at least to some degree, by modern readers in order to fully appreciate Paul's arguments.[6] Truly wealthy Corinthians became public patrons. Public events—competitions, celebrations and festivals, entertainment, and so on—were usually given as gifts to the citizens by wealthy patrons, who might also guarantee both religious and secular improvements in the city.[7] The city, not individual citizens, was now in a debt of gratitude to the patron, a debt that most often was paid back with a bestowal of honors, like inscriptions and statues. Public benefaction could be granted by both men and women (cf. "prominent women" [Acts 17:4, 12]).

Grace and Patronage

Corinth's cultural environment was rather unusual in the ancient world. The new, fast-growing Roman city had become a place for self-promotion and upward mobility. Wealth in the Greco-Roman world usually remained in established families with established clients, but Corinth now had a new group of patrons without traditions and client relationships. This created both opportunities and challenges for the early church.

Modern Christians usually hear "grace" as a word that uniquely expresses an act of God toward believers. The Greek word for "grace," *charis*, explained as "unmerited favor," is often understood as a free-for-all gift made available through Christ's death on the cross (Eph. 2:8–9). Those who accept the gift by believing Christ died for their sins can be sure of their eternal destiny.

In the context of Paul's audience, *charis* relates directly to the reciprocal relationship between patron and client. Aristotle defines *charis* as "service to one in need, not in return for anything nor that the one rendering the service may get anything but as something for the recipient."[8] Seneca speaks of graces in plural—they come as three young sisters with interlocked hands: those granting the grace, those receiving the grace, and those returning the grace (simultaneously receiving and granting it). These sisters are young, Seneca continues, because the "memory of benefits ought not to grow old."[9] He goes on to encourage grace givers (benefactors) to imitate the gods and grant grace even to those who have proven unworthy, because "as a good farmer overcomes the sterility of his ground by care and cultivation," so can a second benefit win the heart of an ungrateful recipient.[10]

The point of Seneca and other ancient writers is that although grace should be given freely without expectation of return, it must still be met with gratitude, that is, reciprocal grace. Although patrons should give without consideration, they should still be careful to find clients who return the favor. This reciprocal nature of grace expressed itself as loyalty. A key word connecting loyalty to grace is *fides*, the Latin word for "faith" (Greek: *pistis*). Faith in this sense speaks of reliability or faithfulness. The patron needed to prove dependability (faith-worthiness) to the client, and the client commitment and trust (faith) to the patron. When grace is given

and received, a relationship is established that makes return to the "pre-grace" state impossible.[11] Grace as unmerited favor and faith as grateful and loyal response are thus interlocked in the mind of Paul's audience. Paul can therefore appeal to God as the graceful benefactor and expect his words to evoke a response of faithfulness in those who recognize themselves as beneficiaries of this grace. The *charis* (grace) that comes from God (the believers' patron) requires the believers (clients) to respond with *pistis* (trust and commitment) toward their grace giver.

Self-Made Corinthians

The vibrancy of Corinth and the prospect of social advancement for entrepreneurs generated a culture of self-promotion and pride that Corinthian converts found

The remains of ancient Corinth are visible in the foreground of this northern view from the Acrocorinth (acropolis). The proximity of the ancient city to the Gulf of Corinth can be seen. The exposed excavated area reveals the center of the city that Paul knew.

hard to separate from their Christian faith and their understanding of church. The system of patron-client relationships, where finding the right patron could secure and/or quicken promotion and prominence in the secular sphere, proved difficult to leave outside the doors of the church. If this system worked outside the church for social climbing, why not also use this system in the church to gain "spiritual" prominence (1 Cor. 1:11–13; 3:3, 18–19)? Since the church often met in the home of a (potential) patron, such conclusions seemed only natural.

Paul's chance to join an established trade in Corinth not only enabled him to preach his gospel free of charge (9:18); it gave him an opportunity to expose the Corinthian understanding of wisdom and knowledge as false and contrary to the gospel of Jesus Christ (2:6–8).[12] The gift of the Holy Spirit was not God's tool for Corinthian self-promotion, but enablement to understand God's plan and to make a proper use of spiritual gifts (2:12–13). Rather than personal gain, the Corinthians should strive for love. Paul's exposition of love in chapter 13 describes in the strongest way a contrast to Corinthian societal desires or entitlements (love is *not* impatient, unkind, envious, arrogant, boastful, or rude and does not insist on its own way).

Directly related to this is Paul's concern in 6:1–8 when he speaks about bringing lawsuits against fellow believers. Civil lawsuits were treated differently from criminal. Patrons with financial resources and social influence were able to sway judges.[13] For Paul the true problem was not the use of Roman law to settle issues; it was the underlying violation of the very message

of the gospel that happened when one "brother" could control another through social influence due to financial strength. In God's kingdom, power comes through weakness. In fact, to imitate Christ it is better to be wronged than to wrong (6:7). For an example, they need look no further than Paul (11:1).

The reality of a societal structure built around wealth and privilege proved difficult to disengage even in matters of worship. When Paul in chapter 11 speaks to church problems relating to the Lord's Supper (11:17–22), he likely refers to how wealthy church members used church gatherings in their homes for social promotion and division. A typical wealthy home would include both a *triclinium* and an *atrium*. The *triclinium* was an exquisite dining room designed for "significant" guests to recline on couches while eating. The *atrium* was a semi-outdoor courtyard designed to gather rainwater but useful as a gathering place for guests of lower social significance.[14] In line with conventional social patterns, therefore, it is more than plausible that when the church gathered for worship, the wealthier church members would be invited to the *triclinium*, where also the better food and wines were served, while poorer members would gather in the *atrium* to dine standing, eating lesser foods or leftovers. Such divisions within the church, Paul contends, may be acceptable in the society in general,[15] but they run contrary to the very nature of what it means to be the church.[16] The church is like a body, where the ear cannot tell the eye that it is more important (12:16). Self-promoting Corinthians will come under judgment when they consider themselves more important than the rest of the body of Christ (11:29).[17]

Rhetoric and Truth in Corinth

As Winter has amply shown, the Corinthians of Paul's day had moved beyond the classical patterns of rhetoric as taught by Aristotle and Cicero to a style of persuasion that was more interested in winning the argument than in presenting the truth.[18] While the classical rhetoricians were concerned with truth, society, and education, the so-called sophists gained their name from their ability to "secure a public following and attract students to their school."[19] Their focus was gaining admiration, and their methods were designed to turn the speakers into performers. Quintilian, a Latin contemporary of Paul, disapprovingly comments:

In the schools of to-day we see boys stooping forward ready to spring to their feet: at the close of each period they not merely rise, but rush forward with shouts of unseemly enthusiasm. Such compliments are mutual and the success of a declamation consists in this kind of applause. The result is vanity and empty self-sufficiency.[20]

But these creatures have another weapon in their armoury: they seek to obtain the reputation of speaking with greater vigour than the trained orator by means of their delivery. For they should on all and every occasion and bellow their every utterance "with uplifted hand," to use their own phrase, dashing this way and that, panting, gesticulating wildly and wagging their heads with all the frenzy of a lunatic. Smite your hands together, stamp the ground, slap your thigh, your breast, your forehead, and you will go straight to the heart of the dingier members of your audience.[21]

The Corinthians may well have been somewhat uncomfortable, and possibly even humiliated, by Paul's seemingly "nonprofessional" speeches; enough, at least, that Paul sensed a need to comment that his speech was not persuasive in the manner of the sophists' (2:1–2) since he did not come to proclaim himself (4:1–5).

With patterns that appear similar to the situation in the twenty-first century, first-century Corinthian sophists seemed concerned primarily with applause, power, and influence. In what could almost look like a precursor to postmodernism, the sophists seemed almost antifoundational, creating their own sociolinguistic world within which truth did not need to be rationally demonstrable, just convictionally persuasive.[22] Like sophisticated marketing campaigns of the twenty-first century, presentation and promotion trumped explanation and content. Distinctively different from Paul, who appealed to Scripture and reason for truth, the sophists appealed to the audience for recognition. As Moores observes, Paul does not think the truth of the message "is in any sense determined by what it means for those at the receiving end." Rather, for Paul, it is the identity of the audience that is revealed through their response, not the truth or quality of the message.[23]

Paul's Ministry in Corinth

Paul came to Corinth from Athens during what we now call his second missionary

This inscription is a copy of a letter sent by the Emperor Claudius in AD 52 to Lucius Junius Gallio, the proconsul of Achaia. From this the date of Paul's visit to Corinth can be determined, since Acts 18:12 mentions that Paul was in Corinth during the time Gallio held this administrative office.

journey (Acts 18:1–17). We are able to date this visit rather precisely because Acts 18:12 tells us that some from the Jewish community tried to persuade Gallio, the Roman governor, to imprison Paul. Since Corinthian inscriptions show that Gallio was governor in AD 51–52, Paul's stay must have overlapped this period.[24] His eighteen-month stay in Corinth (18:11) was considerably longer than his stay in any previous place, and it gives us a clear indication that Paul considered this city of the crossroads significant for the continued spread of the gospel as he pushed forward to reach the ends of the earth. Likely, the Corinthian church he started consisted of a number of house groups. A large Corinthian villa could accommodate up to fifty people. Given the significance of the Corinthian social structures (see discussion above), some factional problems the church faced (1 Cor. 1:10) may be rooted in contentions between patrons leading various home groups.

Paul's correspondence with the Corinthian church began with a previous letter (now lost) referred to in 1 Corinthians 5:9 in which he apparently had to deal with issues of immorality within the church.

The present letter was written around AD 54–55. According to Acts 18–19, after establishing the church in Corinth, Paul went to Ephesus, a city of considerable significance, and then on to Jerusalem. On his so-called third missionary journey he returned to Ephesus, where he stayed at least two years (Acts 19:10). First Corinthians 16:5–8 suggests Paul wrote this letter from Ephesus sometime before Pentecost (in May). At the time of writing, he intended to stay in Ephesus until Pentecost, then travel to Corinth via Macedonia, and perhaps stay the winter at Corinth.

The two immediate causes for writing 1 Corinthians were a visit from Chloe's people, who told Paul about issues of division in the church (1:11), and a letter (7:1) that may or may not have been brought by the same people (16:17). Apparently, this letter dealt with a litany of issues, to which Paul proceeds to respond one by one. Several of these issues may find their origin in well-known Corinthian slogans that new and misguided Christians used in order to address issues that arose after Paul left Corinth. As some of these slogans *could be* understood as similar to Paul's teachings on grace and freedom,[25] they may have seemed "relevant" and "useful" to the Corinthian preachers, but Paul sees them as contrary to his own message about Christ.

Introduction and "Hello"

Big Idea *Paul introduces himself as a fellow Christ follower and reminds his Corinthian friends that calling Christ Lord should generate life patterns that reflect such a relationship to Christ.*

Understanding the Text

The Text in Context

If anything strikes someone who begins reading 1 Corinthians, it is how Paul packs content into every word from the outset. When we realize how well he knows the Corinthian congregation even on a personal level and recognize that this is at least his second letter to the church (5:9), it is quite remarkable that even his opening "hello" reads like a thoughtful theological reflection. Not only does he broadly follow the conventions for a traditional Greco-Roman letter opening;[1] he subtly introduces the major perspectives that will guide his discussion in the coming sections of the letter.

Interpretive Insights

1:1 *Paul . . . an apostle.* Paul begins by identifying himself as "an apostle." Unlike in his letter to the Galatians, where the reference to his apostleship is an argument for authority (Gal. 1:1), Paul seems here more interested in announcing his allegiance to Christ.[2] He cares for the Corinthians because God has called him to do so. He is not driven by his own desire to have influence

in Corinth but is directed by the call and will of God to have influence for God's kingdom. It follows that his only desire in writing the letter is for the Corinthian Christians to recognize what it means to call Christ Lord and to worship the one true God (10:14–15). Christian believers are not free to determine right and wrong from what benefits themselves; rather, they must be shaped by the Christ, who surrendered his own desire in order to accept God's will on the cross (1:17–18).

by the will of God. The structure of the Greek text, where God's will functions as both the agency and the mode of being for Jesus's apostle (one sent by Christ), indicates that Paul understands Christian calling in trinitarian terms. The Father's will is recognized only in the life of the Son. Paul's Jewish background brings to bear an understanding of apostleship that is rooted in the Hebraic notion of *shaliah*—someone's personal representative who performs a specific task in the sender's name and in a manner that represents the sender.[3]

Paul's opening functions as a reminder both to those who know him and to new members in the church who know of him only from the testimony of other members.

Paul cares for the Corinthians not only as an itinerant philosopher sharing ideas but as a witness to the resurrection of Christ sharing life (1:30; 15:45). Although Paul is unworthy, his experience of the resurrected Lord has made him an apostle (15:3–11). This, and nothing else, is the basis for his missionary call to Corinth and all other places (Gal. 1:15–16; Rom. 11:13; Eph. 3:1–2).

and . . . Sosthenes. When Paul introduces the letter's co-sender Sosthenes as a "brother" (adelphos), it is more than mere shorthand for "fellow believer." It is an affectionate term that speaks to a kinship relationship that includes strong personal commitments—they come from the same spiritual womb (delphus), so to speak (e.g., Col. 4:7). Furthermore, it could be, as Thiselton suggests, that Sosthenes's inclusion in the letter opening[4] is a Pauline way of showing that he does not consider himself an isolated or "elevated" leader without the need for collaboration with other Christian leaders.[5] Paul, in other words, is a team player.

Sosthenes was a quite common name, and he could be anyone known to the Corinthian church. The use of the definite article in Greek (the brother), however, indicates that Paul speaks of a specific person already recognized by the Corinthians as his co-worker. Given this, it is at least possible that he is the former chief of the Corinthian synagogue spoken of in Acts 18:17. Sosthenes became

Key Themes of 1 Corinthians 1:1–3

- Paul introduces himself as a God-called apostle of Christ.
- Paul recognizes the Corinthians as the sanctified.
- Paul identifies the Corinthians as those called to holiness.
- Paul includes the Corinthians among those who call Jesus Lord.

a Christian listening to Paul's preaching in Corinth and as a result was beaten by the crowd when Gallio refused the charge brought against Paul by the Jews. A strong relational bond likely formed between the two following this event. If the former chief of the Corinthian synagogue indeed is the one cowriting with Paul here, he stands as a reminder to the Corinthian Christians of the gospel's power to overcome whatever pressure they now may feel to compromise their faith. Paul's inclusion of Sosthenes is not haphazard.

1:2 *To the church of God.* Still following the customary pattern of letter writing, Paul moves from an introduction of the sender to an identification of the recipient. Although the Corinthian church likely consisted of a number of smaller house groups, he addresses them with the singular noun "assembly" (*ekklēsia*).

The modern equation of *ekklēsia* with "church" (bringing buildings, liturgy, programs, and so on, to mind) was unknown to the early readers. *Ekklēsia* was a general term used for a variety of assemblies, political and otherwise. Moreover, many such assemblies belonged to wealthy patrons who could expect loyalty from their assembly's members, who in turn enjoyed the rights, prominence, and influence that came from being associated with that patron. The *ekklēsia* in Corinth, however, belonged to God, not to the patrons in whose homes it met or to the itinerant preachers who passed through it (1:12).

in Corinth. Paul qualifies the *ekklēsia* he addresses as "God's assembly" (NIV: "the church of God"). It was *not* meeting to honor a wealthy individual or to gain special social or spiritual prominence from being a part of this group. Neither wealthy patrons, empowered spiritual leaders, nor Paul himself could claim ownership of this assembly. The group Paul addresses has been called together by God and belongs to God as *his* community. It follows that its location in Corinth is a matter of mere geography. Paul spends no time, not a word, praising the "great city of Corinth"—a common practice in the city that many considered one of the most privileged in the Roman Empire. The church is there to bring witness to Christ, not to revel in their status as Corinthians.

sanctified. The Corinthian *ekklēsia* is further qualified as having been "sanctified in Christ Jesus." Their spiritual growth comes from Christ, who is the cause, reason, and power behind their sanctification (or, more literally, their "holyfication").

Paul addresses the church in Corinth as those "called to be his holy people" (1:2). Because they belonged to God, the Corinthian Christians needed to separate themselves from the worship of other gods. The temple to Aphrodite on the summit of the Acrocorinth (mountain in background), in ruins by the time of Paul, and the temple to Apollo (ruins shown in the right foreground) were two major pagan worship centers during Corinth's history.

Since they belong to God, their sanctification comes from Christ and no one else. He, not human leaders or spiritual guides, gives them a place in God's community.

called to be his holy people. In typical Pauline fashion, once he has established what Christ has done, he expresses what believers therefore should do. Since they have been sanctified in Christ, they are called to be holy—to live lives that portray their holiness ("saints" [NRSV] is a less useful translation here; see the sidebar).

together with all . . . who call on the name of our Lord Jesus Christ. The call to be holy is not just for the Corinthians but for all Christians everywhere. Holiness is the life that results from the confession that Jesus is Lord. To call Jesus Lord is not a mere theological confession but a statement of life allegiance. It is not a lofty, transcendent term, or a mere synonym for eternal salvation, but a practical expression of who you entrust your life to for survival.

In the context of the Greco-Roman world, it was even a radical political statement. Caesar's claim to be Lord, and the populace's acceptance of him as such, flowed from a quite practical consideration. He was their ultimate patron, to whom they should give their ultimate allegiance. After all, he was the one who gave all citizens the necessary peace on their borders for them to grow their crops, build their homes, and raise their families with confidence and security. He was the one who secured a "fair" justice system for all citizens. He built roads and infrastructure so trade could flourish and wealth could be generated. He encouraged entertainment and sponsored the regional athletic games.

Holiness and Sanctification

The Greek term *hagios* ("holy") is at the root of both "sanctification" and "saint." The key issue is holiness—likeness to Christ. Unfortunately, most word studies, text commentators, and preachers continue to advance the notion that "holy" primarily speaks of separation. To be holy, it is claimed, is to be separate, set apart. This makes the derived secondary meaning primary.

In Paul's use, the Greek *hagios* follows the meaning of the Hebrew *qadosh* ("holy"). *Qadosh* is God's exclusive adjective—God determines its meaning. Whatever God is, and does, is *qadosh*, holy. We humans cannot make up a list of attributes (pure, blameless, sinless, or whatever) and determine that these define what it means to be holy and then declare that since God is holy, he must fit this list. It is the other way around.

Since *qadosh* is God's exclusive adjective, the only way for anything in God's creation (things or beings) to become holy is to belong to God. *Qadosh* speaks of belonging. An ordinary bowl becomes a holy bowl when it is dedicated to God. An ordinary table becomes holy when it is dedicated to God. The spirit that is specifically God's is called the Holy Spirit. People likewise! A person becomes holy when he or she belongs to God, not from doing certain pious acts or from avoiding certain vices.

"Holy" is a relational word that speaks positively about belonging to God. Only as a logical consequence of this does it speak negatively about separation. By way of illustration we may say that when a man gets married, he belongs to his wife. It follows, logically, that this separates him from intimate relationships with other women. Still, the primary function of marriage is to define relational belonging. In similar fashion, Corinthians are "called to be his holy people," to prove they belong exclusively to God. Such focus leads to a separation from other gods.

1:3 *Grace and peace.* Calling Jesus Lord was saying that ultimate life security, both now and eternally, depends not on Caesar but on Christ. From him come both grace (see "Grace and Patronage" in the introduction) and peace. He alone should be trusted—a trust that proves itself in the Christian's decisions and patterns of life.

Theological Insights

To Paul the church is not a sociological gathering of the like-minded but a theological community whose aim is to portray the one true God, who revealed himself fully through his Son, Jesus Christ. Believers are relationally bound together by their common submission to the lordship of Jesus, who has called and sanctified them as *his* community.

Teaching the Text

Although this section on one level functions as a simple "hello, it's me, Paul, again," it is packed with theological content.

1. *Christian ministry must be guided by God's will.* Throughout Paul's letters we find a strong emphasis on divine calling. Paul serves not out of personal ambition but out of a necessity generated by God's will (9:16). The first would have led to defeat and given him an excuse to give up when things did not go his way; the latter called him to stay the course even when it was both unappreciated and dangerous (2 Cor. 6:4–12). Such focus brings about both humility and firmness. Not one without the other! Rather than using his position as an apostle as a platform for authority, he saw it as a charge to be faithful.

2. *The church belongs to God.* As much as it has become commonplace to hear both pastors and church members talk about "my church," it is useful to remember that for any assembly or fellowship to be Christian, it must be guided and instructed by God as he is known through Christ. Christian churches or groups must not be taken captive by wealthy or prominent members to serve their purposes or likes. Nor can they meet as a group to decide what they are to be about. God

has already determined the agenda! The task of Christian churches is to determine how to apply that agenda most effectively in their location and context.

It follows that there can be no pride in one's context or origin. Given the call from God to spread the gospel of Christ, the recipients' citizenship as "Corinthians" was not worthy of mention except to indicate their place of service. The same is true today. It makes no difference for the gospel that a church or a ministry is American or African, rich or poor. Nor is it significant to be a pastor or a member of a particularly prominent or influential church. The focus must remain on the will of God, the gospel of Christ, and the Christlikeness of the believers.

3. *Holiness is a life that flows from a relationship with Jesus.* It is not a list of acts to do or avoid any more than a marriage can be reduced to a set of rules and regulations. To call Christ Lord is to recognize that no one else is lord—not even oneself. As in a marriage, where a loving relationship generates a desire to do generous acts and to constantly find new ways

For the Corinthian Christians, to proclaim only Jesus as Lord was a potentially political statement because of the widespread practice of emperor worship. If Paul wrote this letter in AD 55, Nero would have been the emperor in Rome.

of affirming that love, holiness flows from a desire to show devotion toward God. The best way to test one's relationship to God is to check one's desire to do his will and find ways of expressing loving appreciation toward him. To be holy means to belong to God. Holiness flows dynamically from a life in his presence.

Illustrating the Text

Recognize the difference between a call to serve and a desire to gain prominence.

Quote: *Prophetic Untimeliness*, by Os Guinness.

For when society becomes godless and the church corrupt, the prospects of good people succeeding are significantly dimmed and the temptation to feel a failure is ever present. In today's world, this dilemma confronts us in the form of an added double bind. On the one hand, we are told by a myriad of Christian speakers that we should be thinking about our legacy—the clear knowledge of our contribution after our time on earth. On the other hand, we are told by countless other Christians that ambition is always wrong; synonymous with egotism, it is selfish and quite un-Christian.

Both of these positions are wrong. In fact, they are the opposite way around. For as followers of Jesus we can and should be ambitious, but we should never be concerned with our legacies. And the reason lies in the character of calling.[6]

God-given positions are a charge to faithfulness, not a platform for self-promotion.

Literature: *The Color of Blood*, by Brian Moore. In this small but profound novel, Irish author Moore (1921–99) tells the story of a cataclysmic change that occurs in the life of a cardinal in an unnamed Soviet Bloc country. When the man begins his career, it has never occurred to him that his life will have to be laid on the line for the God he loves. He is devoted to God and the church, is not particularly proud, and certainly is not evil. But he is detached and in no sense connected to the people he serves. He is more concerned about his people's stability than about their spiritual needs. He conducts his life on a higher level than they will ever attain. He asks to be called "Your Reverence"; he is given preferential treatment; his food is served to him, his vestments laid out. He has his own chauffeur, a private secretary, and a beautiful residence. The robes he wears set him apart, demanding obedience and respect.

Then, one day everything changes; he is kidnapped, escapes, and ultimately loses all the accoutrements of his position, becoming unknown among the destitute of society. Loneliness sinks deep into his soul until he understands his calling and knows he is not fit to be a leader. He knows that all he can do is pray, and he says to the Lord, "I have been blind to many things. My intellect is weak. I have not seen how many-sided is this world in which you have placed me in a position of trust. . . . I ask you to guide me now, to give me that strength and intelligence that I have failed to find in myself."[7] The novel is something of a thriller and has a marvelous ending and lesson.

Thanking God for His Work in the Church

Big Idea *Thanking God for his obvious presence in the church, Paul in effect says, "I am grateful that God's extraordinary grace toward you is not wasted. Remember, God is faithful. Being a part of his community secures your access to his eternal kingdom."*

Understanding the Text

The Text in Context

Contrary to traditional Greco-Roman letter conventions, and different from his own pattern in other letters (e.g., Phil. 1:3–11), Paul does not use the opening thanksgiving section in this letter to extol the Corinthians, either for who they are or for what they have done for him. Rather, he praises God for his faithfulness and grace toward the church.[1] Though modern readers may not pick up on this change, it would have stood out to the early audience. Clothed in the traditional language of an opening thanksgiving, this section functions to outline the major issues Paul aims to address in the letter.

Interpretive Insights

1:4 *I always thank my God.* Thanksgiving flows from a recognition that a gift is given and a debt of gratitude is owed. Such a clear sense of indebtedness to God made

thanksgiving the daily pattern of Paul's life. Paul may have been instrumental in planting the church, but it was God's nurturing grace that gave it root and made it grow (3:6). Thanksgiving was not diminished by the problems flourishing among the Corinthians; the problems were caused not by God's generous gifts but by the church's misunderstanding and misuse of these gifts.

because of his grace given you in Christ Jesus. The Greek construction here underscores that God's grace is not just the occasion for the thanksgiving; rather, grace is the undergirding foundation for every statement Paul makes and for every experience the church has. The grace Paul talks about is not from a human patron but from God, who grants his grace in Christ. Put differently, God's grace flows to those who are a part of the "in Christ" community.

To be "in Christ" is to be part of the community that belongs to Christ and recognizes his lordship.[2] The modern and Western individualized interpretation of Paul's use of the phrase "in Christ," which argues that personal faith can live without community participation, is foreign to Pauline texts. To Paul, the suggestion that one could be Christian without belonging to the Christ community would be as odd as to suggest that one could be a Jew without belonging to Israel. Furthermore, in the Greco-Roman context the notion of individual independence would seem odd. The very structure of social interaction was built on participation in communities that depended on goodwill from patrons (and loyalty from clients). This is why Paul consistently uses plural pronouns (speaking to the community, not the individual) when he speaks of being "in Christ."[3]

1:5 *enriched in every way.* Paul employs terminology about wealth to remind the church members that the riches that matter flow from their relationship to Christ. Even abilities they consider evidence of spiritual prominence and special endowment, their eloquence and insight, come as gifts from Christ and should therefore not give rise to boasting (1:29–31; 4:7). The reason Paul elevates "all kinds of speech" and "all knowledge" as primary examples of Christ's enrichment is that these two areas caused significant strife in the church. They are now introduced as reasons for

Key Themes of 1 Corinthians 1:4–9

- Thanksgiving is an essential part of the Christian life.
- God grants grace to those who are in Christ.
- Spiritual gifts are given to manifest Christ's presence while Christians are waiting for the Lord's return.
- Christians should not grow weary while they wait for his return.

thanksgiving, creating a positive base from which to explain their correct use later in the letter. God gave these as gifts to strengthen the church; the Corinthians have used them for self-promotion.

It is likely that the influence of the Corinthian sophists, who considered their ability to speak with conviction and fervor a point of pride and prominence, lies behind Paul's words. Paul probably does not have a specific kind of speech in mind at this point, like tongues or prophecy, but refers more generally to those who use mere eloquence to gain spiritual prominence (1:17; 2:1; 13:1). The same holds true for knowledge. Rather than referring to a specific spiritual gift, Paul here warns against using knowledge as a lever for self-elevation

Paul reminds the Corinthian believers that their relationship with Christ provides the riches that matter. They lived in a city where tariff income and trade provided opportunities for its citizens to become wealthy and influential. Corinth's strategic location, with two harbors and the Diolkos that connected them, allowed the city to become very prosperous. Shown here is a portion of the Diolkos, the portage road that connected the east and west harbors.

(8:1). Skilled speakers can sound wise yet be without the depth of knowledge that God's Spirit grants to those who are mature in Christ. The test of spiritual quality for both speech and knowledge is love (13:1–3).

1:6 *confirming our testimony about Christ among you.* The church was enriched because the members responded to Paul's proclamation of the gospel, not because certain members claimed superior speaking ability and knowledge. Paul's rare use of the forensic word *martyrion* ("testimony")[4] may be due to the rhetorical nature of this letter. By its use, he is setting the stage for judgment calls concerning the church's behavior based on the truth value of the gospel (cf. 6:1–11). He is grateful for the gospel's work in their midst, but this same gospel must now become the measuring stick for their life and conduct.

1:7 *Therefore you do not lack any spiritual gift.* Both the purpose and the result of God's enrichment of the church are that it does not lack any of the gifts God's grace provides (*charismata*; lit., "grace gifts").[5] The infinitival construction of the Greek text speaks to the purpose of God's gifts— why they lack nothing. As the church waits for Christ's return, God, as their patron, has provided everything. Paul's word choice speaks to several levels. Temporally, "not to lack" (*mē hystereisthai*; NIV: "do not lack") means the church will not be late or fail to be ready when Christ comes. Circumstantially, God's people do not lack any of his benefits or have any need his grace does not satisfy. In terms of significance, they are not inferior or unable to attain God's purpose.

Paul's deliberate play on the connection between intended purpose (present) and

Paul acknowledges that Christ has enriched the Corinthian church with "all kinds of speech and with all knowledge" (1:5) and will keep them "firm to the end," so that they will be "blameless on the day of our Lord Jesus Christ" (1:8). A *bēma* (shown here) has been excavated at Corinth. This was the place where oratory was delivered by public speakers, proclamations were made, and judgments may have been carried out by public officials as citizens appeared before them. During Paul's first stay in Corinth, some Corinthian Jews brought him to this spot so that the proconsul Gallio could rule on their complaint against Paul. Gallio refused to judge the case.

anticipated result (future) underscores the tension inherent in the church's life and mission. God equips his church in the present (1:5–6) to produce end-time results (1:7–8). Just as the revelation of the Lord will be visible and public (Rom. 8:19), God's present gifting of the church enables it to give visible and public evidence of, and testimony to, his grace.

1:8 *He will also keep you firm to the end . . . blameless.* The Greek term translated "blameless" (*anenklētos*) means "free from any accusation"; God's community will not be charged. This should change the rules for life and fellowship and take away the need for the divisive self-promotion so prevalent in the Corinthian society. Legal charges of all kinds may abound in Corinth, but those who live in God's eschatological community are protected against any ultimate accusation.

1:9 *God is faithful.* The church's protection does not come from its ability to prove its own worthiness. Rather, the God who lovingly and graciously has called them into Christ's fellowship, without requiring them to earn their right to his patronage, will faithfully keep them there. Their faith (see "Grace and Patronage" in the introduction) is a response to his faithful grace. Faithfulness is one of YHWH's identifying character traits (Deut. 7:9).[6] His people can rest assured that this covenantal love is steadfast (Rom. 8:38–39); his word and promises will not fail (Rom. 9:6).

Theological Insights

The church's greatness depends not on its own power and prominence but on God's endowment. Paul's trinitarian understanding of the church is clear—he

thanks God for the grace given through Jesus, which is evidenced through the gifts of the Spirit.

Teaching the Text

Compared to both traditional Greco-Roman thanksgiving sections and parallel sections in Paul's other letters, Paul's omissions in 1 Corinthians may speak as loudly as his words (see "Text in Context" above). His thanks is directed to God for his faithfulness, not to the Corinthians for their commitment to Christ.

1. *Thanksgiving is the breath of a living faith.* Thanksgiving refuses self-centeredness; self-centeredness eliminates thanksgiving. The focus of genuine Christian faith rests on God and his work. Although Paul is aware of many troublesome issues in the Corinthian church, his heart is overwhelmed by what God has done in their midst. God's blessings are obvious to those who are not confused by their own accomplishments. To church leaders this is a lesson on remembering their dependence upon, and indebtedness to, God. Paul can give thanks because he remains aware that the church is a result not of his effort but of God's grace. To church members this is a lesson on remembering that all things come from God and gratitude should be a natural reaction even when blessings seem to flow to others rather than to oneself. When thanksgiving ceases, it is because life no longer is understood as an experience of God's grace.

2. *The Christian life is community life.* The church is an alternative to the culture of secular society. Rules are turned upside down. Prominence comes from servanthood.

The weak deserve the most honor (12:22–24). The gifts that seem to allow individual recipients to portray themselves as "more spiritual than others" (e.g., certain kinds of speech) are the less significant.

God enriches the church—the community of believers. Individualism runs counter to God's kingdom purposes. In God's community, individuals find significance as members of a body (12:12–26). The whole is more than the sum of the individuals; in fact, individuals find meaning and significance in their relationship to the whole. Christians have been moved from an in-Adam existence, where sin has destroyed community, to the in-Christ community, where life is guided and determined by the members' commitment to the lordship of Christ (Gal. 2:20). It is a foretaste of life in the eschatological kingdom.

3. *God's gifts of grace are for the church to manifest Christ's presence while they wait for his return.* God has already poured out his Spirit and allowed the in-Christ community to experience the presence and gifting that belong to the kingdom. The end has already begun, though it has not yet fully come. As Paul explains later (13:9–10), the church's present experience may be partial compared to what will come when Christ returns to fill all in all (15:28), but its gifting is sufficient to demonstrate Christ's presence among them. Following Christ in the present may be marred with difficulty, but such difficulties are not due to a lack of gifting from God. As believers long to see Christ and eagerly await the time when every knee shall bow and every tongue shall call him Lord (Phil. 2:10), they should continue to imitate the one who called them in love. God's love builds up; human knowledge puffs up (1 Cor. 8:1).

4. *God is faithful.* Thanksgiving, like faith, begins and ends with an affirmation that God is faithful and trustworthy. He keeps his promises. The destiny of his church is already determined. Those who call Christ Lord will stand blameless on the day of judgment. Faith must dare to confidently trust God's grace. Doubt will cause humans to follow their own ways and will lead to strife and division (1:10).

Illustrating the Text

Thanksgiving and gratitude are consistent with Christian living.

Human Experience: With the art of saying "thank you" disappearing, gratitude may be a lost virtue. The thank-you note is a last bastion in what Mary Killen has called an "epidemic of discourtesy." Even with the ease of communication via email or text messages, fewer and fewer people seem to be taking the time to thank others. And this discourtesy seems only compounded by the move away from the personal touch of hand-written letters. The next generation seems content to live in a letter-free zone, confining themselves to various forms of electronic messaging, which can rarely be described as articulate, memorable, or thoughtful. According to one survey, a third of those under thirty-five have never sent a personal letter to a loved one in their lives, a statistic that is shocking for many who are older. The arrival of mail for the younger generation means bank statements, parking fines, junk mail, and offers for credit cards.[7] Amid such trends, thoughtful thanks can shape our hearts and speak powerfully to others. Gratitude expressed encourages grace-filled living, which goes a long way in holding back self-centeredness. And it is an inseparable part of being Christian—"give thanks in all circumstances" (1 Thess. 5:18).

Individualistic self-centeredness must be exchanged for self-giving for the sake of community.

Quote: **A. W. Tozer.**

It is not hard to see why the Christian's attitude toward self is such an excellent test of the validity of his religious experiences. Most of the great masters of the deeper life, such as Fenelon, Molinos, St. John of the Cross, Madame Guyon and a host of others, have warned against pseudo-religious experiences that provide much carnal enjoyment but fulfill the flesh and puff up the heart with self-love.

A good rule is this: Nothing that comes from God will minister to my pride or self-congratulation. If I am tempted to be complacent and to feel superior because of an advanced spiritual experience, I should go at once to my knees and repent of the whole thing. I have fallen a victim to the enemy![8]

Biography: **Vincent Van Gogh.** The first son of a Dutch minister, the great painter Van Gogh (1853–90) is not often associated with, as writer Kristopher Kowal puts it, "Christian conviction—let alone one with missionary and evangelistic aspirations." More often, biographers focus on the sensational sides of his personality. Nevertheless, at one period of his life, Van Gogh gained a reputation among very poor miners "for selflessly sharing their hardships and for his love of the unlovable. Anecdotes from this period illustrate the length to which he would go to practice the love of Christ." In one example, after a severe explosion in a mine, "he tore up his own clothing and linen, soaking the rags in wax and olive oil for use as bandages."[9]

1 Corinthians 1:4–9

Church Divisions and Confusion of Allegiance

Big Idea *Schisms and splits have no place in God's community. Paul says, "Forget what you know from the world around you. Christians are followers not of various patrons and human leaders but of Christ alone."*

Understanding the Text

The Text in Context

Paul's introduction continues. Verse 10 is his summarizing thesis for the rest of the letter, a thesis he will return to throughout the letter (e.g., 3:1–15). Whether Paul thinks of verse 10 in formal rhetorical terms as a *propositio*[1] or simply as a strong reminder to Christian friends who have lost their way[2] makes little difference for the issue facing the Corinthian church. Paul is not trying to assert his authority as an apostle they must obey but is attempting to remind his Christian brothers and sisters of the teaching of the cross.[3]

The thesis statement in verse 10 comes as a direct response to a report Paul received from people related to Chloe. Chloe was probably a patron in whose house a church group met. If not, she could have been a wealthy Corinthian businesswoman whose business associates were Christians.[4] Paul mentions her name simply to tell the church that he is responding not to rumors and hearsay but to a direct report from trustworthy church members.

Interpretive Insights

1:10 *I appeal to you, brothers and sisters.* Although there is much to be said for the use of *parakalō* ("I appeal") as a formal rhetorical device designed to place the orator in a position of authority, Paul's purpose here is not to claim authority but to speak urgently to "brothers and sisters"[5] concerning how the lordship of Christ should create unity among his followers.

in the name of our Lord Jesus Christ. It is not likely that Paul thinks of this phrase as a kind of healing formula that would repair the schisms.[6] Rather, as this is the tenth time Paul uses Christ's name in the first ten verses, he uses the phrase to once again chisel into the Corinthians' minds that they are a part of Christ's community and therefore should display *his* character. Their behavior affects the public image and reputation of Christ. They are Christ's community in Corinth and therefore *his* "clients." Their present manners seem to imitate something altogether different. They no longer represent their true patron.

that all of you agree. Paul frames the explanation for his urgent plea as a purpose statement.[7] The call to agreement (lit., "speak the same") refers not to doctrinal agreement but to the recipients' common testimony about Christ. The *schismata* ("divisions") were not so much caused by disagreements among individual members as they were the result of an errant focus. They had allowed the norms of secular Corinth to influence the thinking of the church.

that you be perfectly united. The word *katērtismenoi* ("be perfectly united") brings the sense of restoration to the context—putting things back to the order they were intended to have (cf. Mark 1:19). It may even contain a subtle reference to God's original plan for his creation (Heb. 11:3). What God intended from the beginning, and what Christ caused among you when you first received the gospel, should again be a reality among you.

in mind and thought. Having the "same mind" (NRSV; or "same understanding"; NIV: "united in mind") speaks to unity around the Christian message. The community called forth by the proclamation of the gospel is carried by a different understanding, a different

- Church splits and factions devastate the church's testimony.
- Christians have no business being separated by political, social, or racial divisions.
- The focus of the church should not be high-profile spiritual leaders and eloquent preachers but Christ and his gospel.

mind-set, than the Corinthian community at large. Along with a common mind-set comes a common purpose. In the Christ community, a united focus on restoration back to God's intended norm for his creation should instruct their thinking, inform their purpose, and inspire their decisions.

1:12 *I follow Paul . . . Apollos . . . Cephas . . . Christ*. That Greek uses genitives to express relationships (e.g., "I am of Paul") should not be misunderstood as an indication of possession. Genitive of possession is never used with reference to people except with slaves and, in certain situations, children. To translate this "I belong to . . ." is therefore not exactly right. Paul refers not to divisions among slaves of different masters but to strife caused by divisive alliances. Whether these alliances at their root were political, social, ethnic/racial, personal, or some combination thereof is impossible to determine with certainty from the text.[8] Whatever the precise cause,

In ancient Corinth, pupils were encouraged to show their loyalty to their teacher by promoting and defending him publicly. This mind-set may have transferred to the Corinthian church as they announced which church leader they would follow. Unfortunately, this led to divisions within the church. This fifth-century BC drinking cup from Greece shows a student with his teacher.

The Corinthian Cliques

Many suggestions have been given to explain the Corinthian cliques. Probably the most popular interpretation is that the divisions came from allegiances to various Christian leaders—favorite preachers and Bible teachers. Since F. C. Baur in 1831 suggested that conflicting theological convictions were at the root of the divisions, many scholars have asserted that doctrinal disagreements caused the factions. The Paul and Apollos parties affirmed a Pauline Christianity, emphasizing grace and freedom from the law, while the Cephas and Christ parties focused on the continued validity of the law. In other words, nothing was really solved at the meeting in Acts 15.

Scandinavian scholars like Johannes Munck and N. A. Dahl have since shown that such doctrinal division was unlikely. The factions, they claim, had more to do with "big personalities" gaining a following. Paul seems to have no particular interest in defending the group that bears his name (1:12–13), which would be strange if this had been a doctrinal issue. More recently, scholars like L. L. Welborn have reworked earlier suggestions, claiming the groups were political in nature. The power struggles and status competitions that flourished in all major Greco-Roman cities, and particularly in Corinth, had found their way into the church. Corinthian orators were well known for their inflated egos and their constant efforts to defame their competitors.[a]

The idea that the Corinthian schisms (*schismata*) were caused by church groups' disagreements with Paul originates from a dialectical method of interpretation where interpreters are preoccupied with the idea that every thesis must have an antithesis. Whatever Paul said, they claim, must have been a response to someone who was claiming the opposite. Nothing in the text indicates such a scenario, however. Rather, the various groups in the church were contending with each other, not with Paul. His reply is not one of self-defense (cf. Gal. 1–2) but a christological statement designed to reveal that their cliques run contrary to the undivided lordship of Jesus Christ (1 Cor. 1:10).

[a] For further discussion on the popularity of the sophist debaters, their followers, and their participation in the secular assembly (*ekklēsia*) in Corinth, see Winter, *After Paul*, chap. 2.

it was something everyone was caught up in. Rather than addressing the church as a group, as was his common pattern, Paul goes out of his way to say, "This pertains to every individual."[9]

Whether Paul lists all the cliques in the Corinthian church or whether these are selective examples, or even a list Paul made up

as a hyperbolic way to make his point, is not certain.[10] Any attempt to outline specific viewpoints or claims for each of the cliques is speculative (see the sidebar). Paul's concern is the troublesome reality of the splits, not the precise content of each group. In fact, he seems eager to underscore that he and Apollos are co-workers. Paul planted, Apollos watered (3:6). Concerning Peter, it is not certain he had ever visited Corinth, although his name obviously would be recognized by the congregation.[11]

In terms of content, interpreters generally agree that "wisdom" had become a code word that gave boasting rights and made groups claim that their particular wisdom gave them spiritual prominence. Paul's references throughout the letter to wisdom, boasting, and being spiritual are likely directly related to the cliques (e.g., 1:19, 29; 3:1–3).

1:13 *Is Christ divided?* The obvious answer to this question is "no!" But the Corinthian behavior makes it look as if the answer is "yes!" By allowing splits and cliques in Christ's body, they have created a situation that testifies against the very nature of Christ. Paul is so appalled that he uses his own name to put the absurdity of the situation in perspective. "Surely, you do not think Paul was crucified for you? Or that you were baptized into Paul's name?"

1:17 *Christ did not send me to baptize.* Given the competitive atmosphere in Corinth, it is quite possible that various patrons, in whose homes the church met, felt special allegiance to the one who led them to faith in Christ and baptized them. "Their preacher" was better and more significant than other patrons' preachers. To claim special relationship to Paul (or

Apollos or Cephas) had become a matter of competition and pride—a way to gain personal prominence and outcompete other Christian converts.[12] In other words, Paul's comment on baptism has nothing to do with baptism being insignificant, unnecessary, or even less important, compared to preaching.[13] Rather, it is a rebuke of those who muddy the water by giving honor to the one who performs the baptism instead of to the one into whose name they are baptized, Jesus Christ.

not with wisdom and eloquence. Paul's aim in this context is to highlight that cliques and divisions have a devastating effect on the gospel. When, therefore, he underscores that he is sent to proclaim the gospel but not with eloquent wisdom, he does not attempt to create a dichotomy between proclamation and wisdom (lit., "wisdom of speech") but tries to downplay the role of the minister. His point is to say

The members of the Corinthian church may have been competing with each other as they aligned themselves around the person who led them to faith in Christ and baptized them. Shown here are the remains of a baptistery from the fifth-century AD St. John Church at Ephesus. A similar baptistery has been excavated at Lechaeum, the western harbor of Corinth. It is connected to a fifth- to sixth-century AD basilica, although its orientation suggests it may have been built earlier.

that ministers who exalt themselves—even in the name of faith—do not proclaim the gospel. Paul's aim is not to gain a following for himself but to establish a Christ-empowered community.

Theological Insights

The problem with cliques and factions is not that they are "wrong," unbecoming, or a violation of a command. The problem is that they violate the very character of God. When a church is divided, it no longer portrays the Triune God.

1 Corinthians 1:10–17

Teaching the Text

The cliques in Corinth were anything but benign in Paul's eyes. They were caused by an alignment with the larger culture that downgraded the Christian faith to yet another religious expression in Corinth. Rather than allowing Christ to change Corinth, the church was allowing Corinth to change Christ.

1. *Christ is not divided*. Many churches go through difficulties caused by cliquish behavior. Whether these are caused by forceful personalities, political conviction, musical tastes, preference for certain church programs, theological catchphrases, or something else, they will eventually undermine the power of the gospel. If Christ, who came to break down the wall that separates (Eph. 2:14), cannot even remove cliques in his own body, the cross has lost its power (1 Cor. 1:17) and the church is left without a testimony.

2. *Unity and agreement*. To "speak the same" and have the "same purpose" does not translate into full agreement on all issues in the church. It does, however, rule out any notion of "I alone can be right." Personal agendas have no place and must give way to the greater purpose of creating a community that imitates Christ and exists to give him glory.

3. *Christ's power to transform*. It is always a danger for a church to downgrade itself to a mere religious expression of the culture that surrounds it. Although the purpose may be noble (to win more people to Christ) and biblical arguments may be found (e.g., 1 Cor. 9:20–22), the church ceases to be church in the true sense of that word when the larger culture around it sets its agenda and determines its methods. As

Martin Luther was upset when his followers were called "Lutherans." He did not want people to be devotees of the preacher but instead to follow Christ. This Martin Luther engraving by Fr. Müller is after a painting by Lucas Cranach.

a Christ community, the church must testify to a reformation of values and a reconstruction of priorities in order to accomplish its Christ-empowered purpose. In other words, the church is an alternative eschatological community in which Christ's transforming power makes the kingdom visible.

4. *Applause and spiritual leadership*. Reportedly, when the reformer Martin Luther heard his followers were called Lutherans, he was infuriated, saying, "What is Luther? The teaching is not mine. . . . How did I, poor stinking bag of maggots that I am, come to the point where people call the children of Christ by my evil name?" Disgusted with the vainglory of some pastors, he goes on to say, "May God protect us against the preachers who

please all the people and enjoy a good testimony from everybody. . . . Hearers should say, 'I do not believe in my pastor, but he tells me of another Lord whose name is Christ.'"[14] Today, as in ancient Corinth, competition for fame, honor, and a large following reigns supreme. Today, as then, it is easy for pastors and spiritual leaders (subconsciously?) to be caught up in the same pursuit. This text reminds us that in the Christ community, anyone other than Christ is a mere undeserving servant.

Illustrating the Text

Personal agendas and cliques must give way to a community centered on Christ.

Literature: **"Revelation," by Flannery O'Connor.** In this posthumously published short story, the great American writer O'Connor (1925–64) points out with dark, ironic humor the problem of grouping people. O'Connor was more concerned with pride than anything else. Her short stories, which appear bizarre to some readers, insightfully examine our need to be important and to make ourselves gods in our own worlds.

In "Revelation," her main character, Ruby Turpin, walks into a doctor's office in the South and thinks how she could improve the office and even the people. She begins to size up the occupants of the waiting room by the color of their skin or the clothes they are wearing. She even thinks about their shoes.

Without appearing to, Mrs. Turpin always noticed people's feet. The well-dressed lady had on red and gray suede shoes to match her dress. Mrs. Turpin had on her good black patent leather pumps. The ugly girl had on Girl Scout shoes and heavy socks. The old woman had on tennis shoes and the white-trashy mother had on what appeared to be bedroom slippers, black straw with gold braid threaded through them—exactly what you would have expected her to have on.[15]

Here O'Connor provides a vivid metaphor of the way we might quickly place people in groups without knowing them, an evidence of pride.

A church should never become a mere religious expression of its surrounding culture.

Quote: *Prophetic Untimeliness*, **by Os Guinness.**

By our uncritical pursuit of relevance we have actually courted irrelevance; by our breathless chase after relevance without a matching commitment to faithfulness, we have become not only unfaithful but irrelevant; by our determined efforts to redefine ourselves in ways that are more compelling to the modern world than are faithful to Christ, we have lost not only our identity but our authority and our relevance. Our crying need is to be faithful as well as relevant.[16]

Wisdom and Foolishness

Big Idea *Christians cannot use the commonly accepted wisdom that guides the surrounding culture as the standard for their thinking and living.*

Understanding the Text

The Text in Context

In the ancient world, "wisdom" was not an abstract concept unrelated to daily living. To the contrary, it was a way of living based on a given understanding of life's purpose and of what actions reasonably would accomplish such purpose. Various philosophers (lit., "lovers of wisdom") competed to gain a following for their particular brand of how-to-live.

Similar competition and pursuit of prominence lay at the core of the Corinthian cliques. Enamored with the "wisdom" and success of the professional speakers in the city, a number of house churches were using a similar approach to put them ahead of other church groups. Such behavior made it evident to Paul that they relied on human wisdom rather than God's. Paul's firm and uncompromising rejection of this behavior shows how strongly he considers this a direct attack on the gospel itself. Had they come to rely on their own "smarts" rather than God's grace, their own wisdom rather than God's wisdom? Apparently! They now trust the ways of Corinth rather than the way of the cross.

Verses 18–31 function as a climactic summation of verses 10–17, as an expansion of Paul's reason to come to Corinth in the first place ("to gospelize" [v. 17]), and as a transition to what follows in chapter 2. The section naturally falls into two paragraphs: verses 18–25 and 26–31.

Interpretive Insights

1:18 *the message of the cross.* Picking up on the connection made between "gospelizing"[1] and Christ's cross in verse 17, Paul summarizes the gospel as the "message [lit., 'word'] of the cross." In this context "word" functions as a synonym for preaching, while "cross" identifies the origin of the message. Paul's aim here is to show how Christ's cross should have a transformative effect on believers. Paul's proclamation reveals a wisdom that differs 180 degrees from human wisdom because it is generated by Christ's work on the cross.[2]

foolishness to those who are perishing, but to us who are being saved it is the power of God. Paul's deliberate play on grammar can easily be lost in translation. The force of the middle voice in the descriptive participle "perishing" is most likely reflexive, thus highlighting the effect of their own actions (those destroying *themselves*).[3] In clear contrast to this stands the passive participle describing those who are "being saved." The passive voice underscores that salvation is not self-caused but granted.[4] In other words, if Paul deliberately uses a reflexive middle, the grammatical construction throws the situation into the sharpest relief. The opposite of foolishness is not human wisdom but God's power. The contrast is between self-destroying pride and God-empowering transformation.

1:19 *the wisdom of the wise.* Using a quote from Isaiah 29:14 as a transition, Paul subtly argues that God has always shown his wisdom in ways that stultify human wisdom.[5] Human wisdom falters exactly because it looks to itself for guidance rather than to God.

1:20 *Where is the wise person . . . the teacher of the law . . . the philosopher of this age?* Paul's mention of these three groups may not have direct reference to specific cliques in the Corinthian church. It is probable, however, that he points to three

- Human wisdom is foolishness.
- God's "foolishness" is wisdom.
- The purpose of God's wisdom is to transform.
- Christ alone brings God's wisdom.

major sources of direct influence on the divisions in the church. The wise exemplifies those who were considered the great minds, the scribe exemplifies the Jewish torah expert, and the philosopher (or debater) of this age the sophist.[6] Together they make up the intellectual elite. Yet in light of God's wisdom they are nothing. Paul's rhetorical questions ("where are . . .") are designed to highlight their impotence (cf. Isa. 19:12; 33:18).

Has not God made foolish the wisdom of the world? Paul is careful never to reject wisdom as such. Rather, his purpose is to draw a sharp distinction between the results of worldly wisdom, led astray by depraved and self-serving human thinking, and Christian wisdom, guided by God's revelation of himself as exemplified in Christ (2:6–7). The first will eventually

"For the message of the cross is foolishness to those who are perishing" (1:18). This drawing etched into plaster was found on the Palatine Hill in Rome. It depicts a person with the head of a donkey hanging on a cross. To the left, another person stands with upraised arms. The Greek inscription reads, "Alexamenos worships [his] god." It is thought to be a caricature of a Christian worshiping a crucified god (ca. AD 225).

prove utter foolishness. Indeed, God has already shown it to be.

1:21 *the wisdom of God the world through its wisdom did not know.* Paul expands on the contrast between human wisdom and God's wisdom.[7] Humans have turned things upside down from what God intended. Because of this, God proves *his* wisdom by not making human wisdom an access road to the knowledge of God and salvation. The foolishness of human wisdom is exposed in the way it segregates people. God's wisdom, by contrast, is the greatest equalizer of humans. It gives every person equal access to salvation. Not only does the cross nullify the difference between Jew and Gentile, slave and free, male and female (Gal. 3:28); it eradicates any distinction humans may create between the trained and untrained, the eloquent and the babbler, the philosopher and the ignorant.[8] It may seem foolish to the wise, but God grants salvation to those who bet their lives that the gospel reveals the truth.

Like wisdom, the ancients did not consider salvation an ethereal issue unrelated to their daily experience of life. Rather, wisdom proved itself true when its message brought a salvific change in a person's life situation. In other words, the promise of eternal benefits did not render the temporal benefits insignificant.[9] When Paul speaks about knowledge of God and the salvation it grants, he refers to the life transformation that flows from it. God reveals himself in human history; the "wise" are foolish exactly because they do not recognize his deeds. Believers are saved because they do.

1:22 *Jews demand signs and Greeks look for wisdom.* To those who do not believe, the cross remains an affront. The Jews do not recognize it as a sign from God, and the Greeks do not understand its wisdom.[10] Paul's preaching, however, reveals that it is both.

1:23 *we preach Christ crucified.* *Kēryssō* ("preach," "proclaim") is a term more or less unused by ancient rhetoricians. Paul does not engage in a rhetorical dispute

Paul says, "But we preach Christ crucified: a stumbling block to Jews and foolishness to Gentiles" (1:23). Up until the sixth century AD, images of Christ on the cross were very rare. This ivory plaque from around AD 425 is one of the earliest crucifixion scenes.

attempting to show how his wisdom is better than the Greeks'. Rather, he is concerned with the content. The place and mode of the proclamation remain insignificant. Although often translated "I preach," *kēryssō* refers not to a pulpit sermon but to any explanation of Christ's work on the cross in whatever format and whatever avenue it may be given. The content of the proclamation is that Christ "has been crucified." This use of a perfect passive is deliberate. In Greek, the perfect tense expresses a completed action with lingering effects. Christ's cross may be an event in the past, but it continues to reveal God's power and wisdom in the present (1:24).

1:25 *the foolishness of God . . . the weakness of God.* Paul's argument has come full circle. Obviously, he is not suggesting that anything God does is foolish or weak; he is giving a climactic comparative statement on God and humans. The stage is now set for a direct application of his argument to the individual church members.

1:26–29 *God chose the lowly.* To recognize the truth in Paul's argument, the church members need to look no further than themselves. Why would God call *them*? By human standards, nothing about their pre-Christian situation qualified them for the relationship with God they now enjoy. With few exceptions, they belonged among those generally considered foolish, weak, or despised.[11] The *only* reason anything has changed is that God's wisdom effaces human wisdom. Their present cliquish conflicts are therefore senseless—a refutation of their own reality. Few of them have anything to boast about. If true wisdom and power could be gained through self-promotion, they would not be among the chosen. The status they now enjoy came as a gift from God. In fact, God chose them to shame those the world considered powerful and wise. They themselves are examples of how God's wisdom works contrary to the very "wisdom" they now seem eager to follow.

1:30 *righteousness, holiness and redemption.* Since the church exists "in Christ,"[12] God's wisdom is the only one to consider. Contrary to the wisdom that cultivated the status- and honor-driven culture of Corinth, God redefines wisdom as righteousness, holiness, and redemption. These are gifts from God leading to gratitude; they are not achievements or exercised virtues giving boasting rights.

Theological Insights

Worldly wisdom is usually oriented practically toward giving advice on how to do well (or gain prominence) in a certain culture. God's wisdom, on the other hand, focuses on *his* purposes for his creation. Often, therefore, it runs contrary to the common pursuits of worldly wisdom.

Teaching the Text

The seeker-sensitive desire to make the biblical text relevant to the surrounding culture faces the danger of taking over the categories and general thought patterns of the culture where it is located. The wisdom of the nation, so to speak, has more impact on Christian behavior, teaching, and decision making than does God's wisdom. That was exactly what happened in Corinth.

1. *Christian thinking must be rooted in the cross.* As much as we like self-help

books and need to help believers apply their Christian faith to daily living, we must be constantly aware of the disparity between secular wisdom and Christian wisdom. For example, the book *The Seven Habits of Highly Effective People* does not become a good Christian discipleship manual just because we add a scriptural proverb to each of the habits. The problem with the Corinthians was not that they did not "sound Christian" in their speech or lacked the ability to reinterpret their desires and find "spiritual" application. Rather, the problem was that in spite of eloquence and spiritual emphasis their behavior proved that their thinking was no more than a Christianized version of secular wisdom. The ground rules for their thinking had not changed.

2. *Wisdom and foolishness.* No one likes to be embarrassed or considered a fool. It is exceedingly difficult to call wise what others call foolish, and foolish what others call wise. This struggle has, as an example,

Paul contrasts Christ, "the power of God and the wisdom of God" (1:24), with the "wisdom of the wise" (1:19), the "wisdom of the world" (1:20), and "human wisdom" (1:25). This worldly wisdom was taught by the philosophers. Shown here on this sarcophagus relief is the deceased woman, standing with a child in the center niche and next to seated philosophers in the right and left panels. The figures hold scrolls, indicating an intellectual group (AD 230–40).

caused modern-day Christians to accept the secular notion that "providing for the family" is a purely financial expression—a notion that may sound wise but that proves devastating to God's purposes. When material wealth replaces spiritual wealth in significance, the time required to teach children godly wisdom may be neglected (cf. 2 Tim. 1:5). As a consequence, instead of a sense of rootedness and identity, Christian children often feel rootless and in search of meaning and identity. Similarly, when Christian businesspeople confuse godly and human wisdom, they feel able to make a distinction between their "business behavior" and their "ordinary behavior."

To Paul, all such examples are the result of human wisdom. God's wisdom, as expressed in the cross, changes everything and defies reduction to a mere doctrinal statement or relegation to a purely eschatological issue. To God, human wisdom is foolishness. God's wisdom calls for a new community where the ground rules for behavior in all spheres have changed. To nonbelievers, *that* is complete foolishness.

3. *Trusting in self-effort*. Self-effort leads to pride and gives opportunity to boast. As Paul so amply shows in 1 Corinthians, Christians are not immune to this, even on the spiritual level. Knowing more of the Bible than another, being more spiritually gifted than others, being a member of a certain church, following a certain Christian leader, faithfully serving in a church ministry, volunteering in social outreach, and so on can give rise to pride. Although out-and-out boasting exhibits poor social etiquette in contemporary Western societies (contrary to the situation in the Greco-Roman world), subtle ways still abound. Pride follows competition, and as Westerners we consider competition an incentive to succeed and do better. In Paul's teaching, however, there is no tension between striving for greater gifts (14:1) and recognizing that in God's kingdom gifts are given freely and grant responsibility rather than status (12:7).

Illustrating the Text

God's wisdom and human wisdom are profoundly different and must not be confused.

Personal Testimony: As a young man I (Preben) participated in a summer discipleship camp designed for the most dedicated young Christians—those who truly took their walk with Christ seriously. We were up early for personal quiet time, spent much of the day in Bible study, and were involved in evangelism and outreach during the late afternoons and evenings. All these things were good. I was struck, however, by some of the things the leaders considered "good Christian Bible teaching." For example, a full day was used to teach how to dress for success. Obviously, there is nothing wrong with knowing how to dress appropriately. However, how a culture's current norms for color coordination, tie knots, and belt width have anything to do with Christian discipleship remains a mystery, unless, of course, cultural wisdom is the guide to success. If that were the case (though it is not), all we would need to do is to "Christianize" secular self-help books and include a few Bible verses to back up our claims.

Christian Nonfiction: *Come before Winter and Share My Hope*, by Chuck Swindoll. Swindoll describes the nature of the eagle in human terms. "They are driving with this inner surge to search, to discover, to learn. . . . They're courageous, tough-minded, willing to ask the hard questions as they bypass the routine in vigorous pursuit of the truth." They are not, as he notes, like parrots who "stay in the same cage, pick over the same pan full of seeds, and listen to the same words . . . until they can say them with ease."[13] The suggestion is that to use human wisdom or water down divine wisdom is to be parrot people, while eagle people know the difference.

Applying God's Wisdom to Life's Issues

Big Idea *God's wisdom is understood only through the Spirit's revelation. Spiritual maturity comes from applying God's wisdom to all aspects of life.*

Understanding the Text

The Text in Context

Not only did the reality of the church members' inclusion in the Christ community directly demonstrate how God's wisdom was unusual (1:26–31), but Paul's own life and preaching were living proof that God's wisdom easily superseded any of the human wisdom being offered in Corinth. Although Paul avoids calling himself an *idiōtēs*, a term describing the common man who was not a philosopher (lover of wisdom),[1] he does describe his entry onto the Corinthian scene as an illustration of how God uses the ordinary. Like the Corinthians when they were called, Paul was nothing in the eyes of the world.[2] Contrary to the Corinthians, however, Paul had no desire to display his own accomplishments. He had come solely to proclaim Christ.

After these reminders of the church's beginning, Paul expands his discussion to include favorite catchwords from the Corinthian cliques. The Corinthian Christians are misusing terms like "maturity," "wisdom," "knowledge," and "spirituality." The terms themselves are not wrong, but they must be reinterpreted in light of God's wisdom.

Interpretive Insights

2:1 *the testimony about God.* Several significant biblical manuscripts read "mystery" (*mystērion*) rather than "testimony" (*martyrion*) of God.[3] In this context, however, the difference in meaning between these readings seems minor. Paul's point is clearly that the content of his proclamation came as revelation from God and did not originate in human thinking. God's testimony to the world, his salvation through Christ, remains a mystery to human wisdom (2:7) that the unspiritual do not understand (2:8, 13).

2:2 *nothing while I was with you except Jesus Christ and him crucified.* As the rest of the letter amply shows, this statement is neither absolute nor doctrinal—as if the only thing Paul talks about, or the only doctrine he expounds, is Christ's death.

Rather, Paul's intention is to highlight the distinction between his "lowly" message and the philosophers' "lofty" (*hyperochēn* [2:1]) message (NIV: "eloquence").

2:3 *in weakness with great fear and trembling.* The Corinthians' acceptance of Paul's message was not due to his personal strength and conviction. Rather, God proved the content of his message by using a physically weak person like Paul (Gal. 4:14; 2 Cor. 10:10). Paul's appearance exemplified Christ's victory through weakness (1 Cor. 4:16; 11:1). His fear and trembling were caused not by a sense of inferiority toward the "eloquent" but by a concern that both his message and his life faithfully portray Christ.

2:4 *not with wise and persuasive words.* This statement should not be misunderstood to suggest that Paul favors inept preaching or poorly presented speeches. His point is that he does not rely on the clever rhetorical devices used by the public speakers whose aim is to make themselves famous.

a demonstration of the Spirit's power. Paul came to Corinth to demonstrate not his own strength but the power of God's Spirit in human weakness. The mismatch is now exposed in the strongest way. In contrast to human cleverness and persuasive ability stands a demonstration of God's presence and power (4:19–20). Paul's language is deliberate. Using the language of the rhetorical schools (persuasion,

demonstration, power), he erases any notion that God's demonstration in some way should be less persuasive than the speeches made by human rhetoricians. As Aristotle taught four hundred years earlier, persuasion (*pistis*) "is clearly a sort of demonstration, since we are most fully persuaded when we consider a thing to have been demonstrated."[4]

2:5 *so that your faith might not rest on human wisdom, but on God's power.* It is not human wisdom that leads to faith (*pistis*) but God's power. If Paul uses *pistis* in its technical rhetorical sense, referring to "demonstrated proof" (as opposed to its theological use

Paul's message relied on the power of the Holy Spirit, not "wise and persuasive words" (2:4). This is in contrast to the sophists of the day, who used elegant oratory and clever words to attract followers. Herodes Atticus, whose bust is shown here, was a wealthy and distinguished sophist of the second century AD.

referring to Christian commitment to God), his point is even stronger. The proof the Corinthians are seeking is found in the power of God, not in human argument. Given the context, Paul may even deliberately be playing on this double meaning of *pistis*.

2:6 *wisdom among the mature*. Between two weighty "I" sections, Paul now switches to "we" to give a broader statement about his teaching in general (2:6–16). The wisdom Paul teaches wherever he goes is understood by mature Christians. The Corinthian church should have been able to understand it, but their actions show they do not. They are mere babes who still need baby food (3:2). Contrary to what the Corinthians apparently thought, "maturity" does not divide the church into "primary" and "secondary" Christians. There is no talk of spiritual status but only of application of God's wisdom. The mature are those whose understanding and actions are changed by Christ's cross. The immature are those who continue to live on the basis of human wisdom and merely add special experiences and theoretical points of teaching to their way of thinking. Their actions have not changed; they are like those who reject the cross.

2:7 *God's wisdom, a mystery that has been hidden*. The perfect passive participial form "has been hidden" explains God's wisdom as a wisdom that has been hidden through the ages and to some extent still is.[5] It is not a new, transient wisdom but one that has been true since before time began. Even then, God willed for it to be revealed in Christ.

2:9 *What no eye has seen, what no ear has heard*.[6] Human senses may instruct human judgments, but they are not reliable alone as instruments for understanding God's heart and will.

2:10 *things God has revealed to us by his Spirit*. For Paul, as for all Christians, life guidance comes from God's Spirit, not from human orators. Only God's Spirit can grant the power needed for a person to live a life that demonstrates God's wisdom (2:4).

The Spirit searches all things, even the deep things of God. The neuter noun "deep things" can be translated "depths," "areas," "thoughts," or "concerns." Humans may search for wisdom in many areas, but only the Spirit can search the depth of God's heart and reveal it to humans. That should not surprise anyone; the same holds true with the spirit of a person (2:11). No one but the person knows his or her own deepest thoughts.

2:12 *the Spirit who is from God . . . what God has freely given us*. God was deliberate in granting his Spirit. Although the church used the language of the Spirit, it seemed to have lost sight of why God sent his Spirit. God gave his Spirit not as a reward to the "wise" but to enable all believers to comprehend the magnitude of God's gift through Christ. Those who are truly spiritual are those whose lives evidence that they have grasped God's wisdom.

2:13 *explaining spiritual realities with Spirit-taught words*. Using a simple shift of gender between two otherwise identical words,[7] Paul restates that the purpose of the Spirit's teaching is to help the church recognize and understand the spiritual nature of reality. God's Spirit is the interpreter of God's wisdom.[8] Those without the Spirit, the unspiritual (*psychikoi*), cannot fathom God's purposes, and they misunderstand what God is doing (2:14).

2:15 *The person with the Spirit makes judgments about all things.* Paul's point is not that a person who has received the Spirit is above reproach in all matters. Rather, he is bringing his rhetorical argument to its full conclusion. If someone is truly a mature spiritual person, the wisdom of the cross will guide every decision and influence every attitude. No higher criterion is given, and no human wisdom can outrank it. Those who are spiritually mature are guided by the Spirit, who searches the depths of God and reveals the mind of Christ (2:16).

Theological Insights

Because God's wisdom has a different aim from human wisdom, sinful human nature cannot recognize it and will not accept it. It must be revealed to the believer by God's Spirit. Only God's Spirit can open the believer's eyes to God's wisdom and ways.

Teaching the Text

By allowing the surrounding culture to set the agenda for their thinking, the Corinthian Christians had come to reinterpret the very message of the gospel in ways that made it look more like human wisdom than God's wisdom. Even their understanding of spirituality and Christian maturity had become warped.

1. *Christians should be more concerned with adherence to the message of the cross than the attractiveness of the preacher.* It is nothing new that charismatic personalities attract large crowds with greater ease than those less inspiring. Our present infatuation with speakers able to excite their audiences beyond the usual is well illustrated by the old phrase "he can preach squirrels down from trees." Such an idiom would have made much sense in Corinth. Eloquent expositors of wisdom were rated on their

Paul spoke to the Corinthians "not in words taught us by human wisdom but in words taught by the Spirit" (2:13). Paul's words were not like those of the orators of the first century AD. The primary focus of these rhetoricians was the presentation of speeches that were eloquent, persuasive, and clever. Content became secondary. Shown here is the *ōideion* in ancient Corinth, a venue for oratory, music, and poetry events.

ability to "preach squirrels down from trees." With this backdrop, Paul reminds the Christians to be careful not to confuse the gospel's content with the attractiveness and popularity of the preacher. Those who are merely adding Christian verbiage to human wisdom are not preaching the gospel. Their faith ultimately rests on human wisdom rather than on God's power.

2. *Christian spirituality cannot be reduced to human reflection on life*. It has become rather commonplace to exchange terms like "Christianity," "faith," "discipleship," and so on with the broader term "spirituality." After recognizing the bankruptcy of secular materialism, younger generations now recognize their need for spirituality. Similar to the situation in ancient Corinth, it has become hip to be interested in spiritual matters and engage in spiritual exercises. It is, of course, a good thing when people take time to reflect on the meaning and purpose of their lives; but, as Paul warns the Corinthians, such does not equate with authentic Christian faith. Paul is quite adamant that although many spiritualities (human wisdoms) are offered and followed, only God's wisdom, as revealed on the cross, has the power to save lives both here and eternally.

The Spirit empowers Christians to follow God's wisdom. In Christian art and architecture the presence and activity of the Holy Spirit are often depicted by a dove. Shown here is the alabaster window above the Altar of the Chair of St. Peter at St. Peter's Basilica in Rome, designed by Gian Lorenzo Bernini in the seventeenth century AD.

3. *Christian maturity is demonstrated through life application of God's wisdom*. Now, as then, people confuse giftedness with maturity. Paul's point in this text, however, is to make the Christians aware that they have fooled themselves if they think they are mature because they have certain spiritual experiences, know certain things, or can speak with conviction and eloquence. Such things have little to do with Christian maturity. To the contrary, Christians evidence their maturity when they exhibit the mind of Christ—that is, when their whole perspective on life is so guided by the message of the cross that their attitudes and actions are changed by it. To be a Christian is to be filled by God's Spirit, the Spirit that reveals and interprets God's heart and purpose to his people.

4. *The Spirit gives power to overcome the temptation to act according to human wisdom*. Habits are hard to break. It is difficult to swim against the current. It can be dangerous to stand out in a crowd. Such expressions illustrate the difficulty of living a life that follows God's wisdom. The temptation to make little or no lifestyle change after becoming a Christian is enormous. In light of the cultural pressures from our surroundings, and from

other church members, it proves easier to follow the crowd and reduce faith to an additive—something that adds yet another nuance or flavor to life. To act like Christ, to consider others greater than oneself, to give up personal rights, to accept suffering when there could or should have been praise is no easy matter. But, as Paul argues in this text, God's Spirit empowers the Christian to overcome these fears and difficulties. The Spirit empowers Christians to follow God's wisdom.

Illustrating the Text

The Christian life is organic: what one believes and how one lives are inseparable.

Quote: **"Religion and Literature," by T. S. Eliot.** Eliot (1888–1965) believed that everything we do affects us, particularly what we do in our leisure. As he said in this wise essay about literature, "what we do 'purely for pleasure' may have the greatest and least suspected influence upon us. It is [what we do] with the least effort that can have the easiest and most insidious influence upon us." He continues by remarking that

> we need to be acutely aware of two things at once: of "what we like," and of "what we ought to like." Few people are honest enough to know either. . . . It is our business, as Christians, as well as readers of literature, to know what we ought to like. It is our business as honest men [and women] not to assume that whatever we like is what we ought to like; and it is our business as honest Christians not to assume that we do like what we ought to like.[9]

Study Scripture for the sake of your life, not just for the sake of doing biblical study.

Quote: *A Little Exercise for Young Theologians,* **by Helmut Thielicke.**

> The man who studies theology, and especially he who studies dogmatics, might watch carefully whether he increasingly does not think in the third rather than the second person. You know what I mean by that. This transition from one to the other level of thought, from a personal relationship with God to a merely technical reference, usually is exactly synchronized with the moment that I no longer can read the word of Holy Scripture as a word to me, but only as the object of exegetical endeavors.[10]

Christian spirituality cannot be reduced to human reflection on life.

Quote: **Dorothy Sayers.** British scholar and writer Sayers (1893–1957) was particularly concerned about language and that the teaching of theology not be put in the hands of amateurs. She was afraid that people could be led astray. In 1939 she wrote to a member of the clergy about "books published under devout titles":

> For one thing, most of it isn't well enough written, the thought is often all right, but it's tied up in dull words. If they want to say "Brood of vipers," why the blazes don't they say "Brood of vipers"? Christ didn't say "a whole community infected by an unsound ideology"—He said "vipers" and meant "vipers." If they mean that the Church must either be crucified or disappear, why not say so? It's no good saying that "a time of trial is possibly in store for us."[11]

1 Corinthians 2:1–16

Christian Maturity

Big Idea *Mature Christians recognize that Jesus Christ must remain the church's only foundation. The existence of church cliques testifies to infantile behavior, and God will expose those practicing it.*

Understanding the Text

The Text in Context

Although Paul has made it clear that those who rely on human wisdom and rhetorical inspiration are doomed to become nothing (2:6), he is not opposed to effective communication. Paul's use of metaphor and simile to drive home his point aligns well with ancient rhetorical conventions,[1] and he can use rhetoric as effectively as anyone—even to chastise those who consider themselves spiritually mature (*teleiois* [2:6]). Since the Corinthians are claiming allegiance to various human leaders, their understanding of maturity demonstrates more influence from the popular Corinthian sophists than from God's Spirit.[2] They may claim grand spiritual experiences, but their behavior proves they have not grasped God's wisdom. Spiritually speaking, they are more like infants than adults. Had

they understood God's wisdom, cliques would not have formed among them. They would have recognized that human leaders are no more than builders, co-laborers put to work on the same project by God.

Interpretive Insights

3:1 *I could not address you as people who live by the Spirit.* The Corinthians have not become the Spirit's people (*pneumatikoi*) as Paul expected. This realization forces him to start over, so to speak, and address them as immature infants who need to be taught about trivial matters.[3] The content of the term *pneumatikoi* has been much debated through the years,[4] but in this context, where Paul focuses on the contrast with God's wisdom, he uses the term to explain how their

Because of their lack of spiritual maturity, Paul says to the Corinthians, "I gave you milk, not solid food" (3:2). Here is a pottery piece with a nozzle through which infants were fed (Hellenistic period).

behavior lacks any indication that they belong to God's Spirit and have learned his ways.

3:3 *You are still worldly.* To be worldly, or carnal (*sarkikos*, "fleshly"), is to be infantile. "Carnal" must not be misunderstood to indicate impermissible sexual behavior. Rather, it speaks to the origin of their thinking (cf. Rom. 12:1–2). *Sarkikos*, like *sarkinos* in 3:1, speaks to that which comes from human nature rather than from God (9:11; 2 Cor. 1:12; 10:4; Rom. 15:27).[5] The Corinthians were infantile because their thinking had not been transformed by the Spirit but remained merely human (*sarkikos*).

jealousy and quarreling. The Corinthian culture excelled in competition, and the followers (called disciples) of the various orators spent much of their time ridiculing rival teachers and attempting to create jealousy and strife.[6] Paul picks up these two words precisely because they perfectly compare the Christians who claim special allegiance to a specific teacher with the disciples of Corinthian sophists. It is Paul's shorthand for "you have become like the surrounding culture" (cf. Rom. 13:13; 2 Cor. 12:20; Gal. 5:20). They are following not God's will but their own desires.

acting like mere humans. The Greek verb translated as "acting" (*peripateite*) literally means "walking." If Paul pours Hebrew meaning into Greek words (common for bilinguals), the Hebrew *halakah* (lit., "walking") undergirds his word choice here (see the sidebar "Walking in the Way of God").

3:5 *What, after all, is Apollos? And what is Paul? Only servants.* Paul's use of the neuter "what" as opposed to the masculine "who" reduces them to the level of

instruments or tools.[7] Paul and Apollos are not competing as if they were patrons of the Corinthian church groups. They do not have or seek social status as patrons. Rather, they are mere servants commanded to work on God's field (3:9). The patron is God; he alone gives the increase (3:6–7). Whatever status they might have comes exclusively from their Christ-granted relationship to God. Because they were servants of the Lord, the Corinthians came to faith in Christ (3:5), not in Paul or Apollos.

3:6 *but God has been making it grow.* In Koine Greek the aorist tense was the default tense. It was used simply to describe what happened with no further ado. When an author used a different tense, it was intentional and aimed to highlight a special verbal aspect. This is significant here. Paul and Apollos simply planted and watered (aorist tenses). God, however, continued to give increase (imperfect tense, underscoring the ongoing quality of his action). All of the emphasis is on God's continuous action. Paul's farming metaphor completely undercuts the cliquish behavior of the Corinthians. The ones planting and watering must, obviously, work together; yet both of them are powerless without the one causing the growth (cf. Mark 4:26–28).

3:8 *each be rewarded according to their own labor.* Although ultimately Paul, Apollos, and any others working among the Corinthians are mere employees (or slaves) of God, they are not without responsibility. They will be held accountable to God, their

patron, for how and what they plant and water.

3:9 *we are co-workers in God's service.* Paul's use of the genitive construction, literally "co-workers of God," could give the impression that Paul intended to suggest that he and Apollos were co-workers with God. However, it is far more likely that he considered them co-workers with one another, both serving God. "Co-workers of God" is a possessive genitive highlighting their relationship to God as his servants. They are employed not by any Corinthian patron but by God. They are working "God's field" in Corinth, and the Corinthian church is "God's building." The string of possessive genitives is designed to underscore, once again, that none other than God can demand their allegiance and loyalty. The Corinthian believers are not many buildings but one. Although they meet in the homes of different patrons and have listened to different teachers, they are one community, one house belonging to God.[8]

The foundation for the church at Corinth was Jesus Christ. This metaphor had meaning because of the strong foundations that the Romans used in their building projects. The foundation for this temple at Corinth was initially laid in the early first century AD. The remains seen here are from renovations done in the late first century AD when it was dedicated to Octavia, the sister of Augustus.

3:10 *I laid a foundation as a wise builder.* Although the Greek word *sophos* ("wise") is well covered by the English "skilled" (see, e.g., ESV, NET, NRSV), the wordplay connection to Paul's preceding discussion of wisdom must not be lost. The word *architektōn* refers to the chief (*archi-*) woodworker or stoneworker (*tektōn*) on a building site. According to Shanor, small teams usually led even large building projects, and the most skilled member on a team became the *architektōn* for the project.[9] By using this word, Paul acknowledges the contribution of Apollos and others while holding on to his own special appointment in Corinth. The foundation he laid was God's wisdom revealed through Christ's cross (3:11). Any work that did not fit that foundation was automatically doomed.

3:12 *gold, silver, costly stones, wood, hay or straw.* Paul's list of building materials is, of course, not factual but a metaphorical setup for his imagery of testing through fire (3:13). Some building materials do not pass the quality test. Clearly, whoever has caused the divisions in the church used building materials that could not stand the test. Those who are still building should consider very carefully how well their work fits the foundation.

3:13 *the Day will bring it to light.* Different from whatever human wisdom the Corinthians may find attractive, God's wisdom has eternal effect and will stand as judge over everyone and everything else. Paul's eschatological focus is never far from the surface of his discussion. God has gifted his church in order to enable and protect believers as they wait for Christ's return (1:7–8). When that day comes, God will reveal how everyone has used what he has

given him or her (cf. Matt. 25:14–30). The apocalyptic imagery of test, fire, and reward[10] functions as a strong exhortation and warning to enhance Paul's building metaphor. A builder will be paid only if the work proves acceptable to the patron; if it does not, the builder will not be paid but will pay a penalty (3:15).[11]

3:15 *the builder will suffer loss but yet will be saved . . . escaping through the flames.* As if to make sure no one misunderstands his metaphor, Paul underscores that he is not giving a soteriological statement. Salvation is obtained by God's grace and cannot be lost by saying the wrong thing or misrepresenting God's wisdom or gospel. However, building one's own "house" rather than God's comes with a price. Such builders will miss out on the joy and blessing from God's affirmation. They will, in the words of Amos 4:11, be "snatched from the fire" in the last minute.

Theological Insights

Not everything that glitters is gold. The absence of maturity becomes clear when Christians are busier, and more concerned, with their own enjoyment and benefit than with building an alternative, Christ-empowered community where the presence of God's wisdom is evident.

Teaching the Text

Christian maturity is often measured against criteria that have little or nothing to do with the gospel of Jesus Christ. As a result, wealth and human leadership ability can place even infantile Christians in church leadership positions where they gain a personal following. The result can be an organization that, while called church, is devoid of a genuine testimony to the cross of Jesus Christ.

1. *Infantile faith*. To be called infantile and unable to digest "regular food" can be hard for anyone. It only becomes worse if one's self-perception is the opposite. According to Paul, however, the proof of the pudding is in the eating. In spite of claims of personal experiences, even grand spiritual experiences, Christians whose decisions and behavior seem unchanged by God's Spirit remain infants in Christ. Not only do they not recognize the gospel's impact on every aspect of life; they accept the surrounding culture's explanations and excuses as valid. When the Christians do nothing but baptize their personal desires in God language, they remain infantile. When churches no longer concern themselves with how well they reflect the life and teaching of Jesus, they remain infantile.

2. *The challenges of Christian leadership*. Christian leaders face two opposite challenges. On the one side, church members sometimes struggle to find the right balance in their appreciation of their pastor or ministry leader. Some ministers are treated poorly and seem to face nothing but opposition, while others are adored and treated like they alone hold the keys to the kingdom. This passage speaks to a proper balance between these two. On the other side, Christian leaders can never lose sight of their own responsibility before God, regardless of their situation (2 Cor. 11:23–28). James's warning against eagerness to become a spiritual leader (James 3:1) runs parallel to Paul's teaching here. The lure of success and human acclaim is strong. It is quite possible for greatly loved leaders and effective communicators to build with "hay and straw."

3. *Finding superior building materials*. Just as accredited schools and universities are required to document learning outcomes for students, Paul exhorts the church to build its ministry in such a way that Christians actually mature. A transformational outcome among the believers gives evidence of quality building materials. When the Spirit's work among believers is reduced to momentary inspiration and lacks evidence of real transformation, the building materials are poor. God's call is for the church to become the Spirit's community—a community whose life, decisions, fellowship, care, and so on verify the Spirit's guiding presence by demonstrating the wisdom of the cross. Anything else will prove insufficient and burn up.

Paul says in 3:6, "I planted the seed, Apollos watered it, but God has been making it grow." Just like farmers working in the fields around ancient Corinth, Paul and Apollos were mere workers in God's field, the church. God alone provides what is necessary for growth. This view from the Acrocorinth shows modern areas of cultivation that were probably also used for farming in ancient times.

4. *Oneness and individual responsibility.* Paul addresses the church as community. The church, not the individual, is God's building. Christ is the foundation for the church. This emphasis, however, does not remove the individual's responsibility. Two things become clear. First, there is no room for individualism; individuals must see themselves as co-workers on God's field. No one has higher status than anyone else; God alone is the patron who employs everyone with different gifts for the same task. Second, the individual cannot hide as if only the group as a whole will be tested. God will test the quality of each member's work (3:13). Each one is responsible for utilizing his or her gift(s) to build God's building on the foundation of Jesus Christ (12:7).

Illustrating the Text

Christians whose decisions and behavior seem unchanged by God's Spirit remain infants in Christ.

Human Experience: Compare the behavior of infants and toddlers with the behavior one expects of a growing child, a teenager, and then a young adult. Infants cannot live beyond their most primitive needs; they must be fed, bathed, and changed and sleep on schedule, or they will be miserable and unwell. They are unable to delay gratification or to discipline their needs. Slowly but surely, parents must teach young children to manage their needs and emotions, to be patient, to learn to share, not to interrupt, to obey. If some of these disciplines are not in place by the time these children start school, their lives will be difficult, and

the lives of those around them will be disrupted. So too growing Christians learn to put self-centeredness and worldly ways behind them and instead curb their desires and conform them to Christ.

The church's ministry should help Christians to mature and to exhibit lasting transformation.

Human Metaphors: Paul's illustration about finding quality building materials presents many accessible present-day parallels. For example, all the building codes were changed in South Florida after Hurricane Andrew's terrible destruction in 1992. Then the codes were changed again a couple of times after that—always after a strong hurricane blew in, exposing considerable weakness in the building materials and processes. In major cities where many new apartment and condo buildings go up, all appearing cosmetically refined, some will eventually reveal that they were constructed using shortcuts and inferior materials, flaws that inevitably plague their owners.

Success and leadership need to be redefined in communal categories.

Personal Testimony: When one of my (Preben's) family members was in the hospital in a two-person room, his friends and family kept filing in repeatedly over a two-week period. His roommate suddenly broke down. "You are one lucky guy," he said. "No one comes to see me. I have spent my life focusing on me—I became wealthy, know a lot of people and have been married four times—but I have no one who cares to come see me."

Leadership and Servanthood

Big Idea *Christian leaders must remember they are mere servants who are expected to be trustworthy and eager to enhance the mission and message of their master.*

Understanding the Text

The Text in Context

First Corinthians 3:16 and 17 function as a bridge connecting two sides of the same argument. Still addressing the secular nature of the church's behavior, Paul concludes his exhortation to use superior building materials with a reminder that the Corinthians are building God's holy temple. This reminder becomes the launching pad for his rejection of Corinthian ideals. They have polluted the church's thinking and kept it spiritually infantile.

Interpretive Insights

3:16 *you yourselves are God's temple.* Modern readers of English translations can easily miss the force of Paul's language here. The common Greek term for temple was *hieros*. It referred to the whole temple complex, naming the place where people went to sacrifice and worship God (or a god). Paul's word here, however, is *naos*. *Naos* (lit., "dwelling") refers to the most sacred area in a temple—the particular room where God (or a god) was thought to reside.[1] The church is not a social gathering

"You yourselves are God's temple" (3:16). Jewish believers would have thought of the temple in Jerusalem and the holy of holies, God's dwelling place in the temple complex. Shown here is a model of the temple building, which housed the holy place and the most holy place. This model is part of the 50:1 scale reproduction of the first-century AD city of Jerusalem now on display at the Israel Museum in Jerusalem.

of the like-minded but the sanctuary where God reveals his presence.

God's Spirit dwells in your midst.[2] The place for God's dwelling is the church body. Together the believers are the sphere in which the Holy Spirit reveals his presence and power.

3:17 *If anyone destroys God's temple, God will destroy that person.* The Greek has several classes of conditional sentences, each used for different purposes. By choosing a first-class conditional sentence here, Paul shows he expects the "if" statement to be a reality. In other words, he is not speaking hypothetically but gives direct reference to those causing the church divisions. Clique-creating competition and self-promotion may find approval among Corinthian philosophers, but these things defile God's sanctuary. God, of course, does not allow such blasphemy (cf. Acts 5:1–11).

3:18 *become "fools" so that you may become wise.* Paul brilliantly exposes how upside down the Christians have become in their thinking. They have given in to both deception and self-deception. Two imperatives define the rhetorical structure of this verse, expressing what to avoid and what to become: "do not be fooled . . . become a fool" (NIV: "Do not deceive yourselves . . . you should become 'fools'"). Those who strive for recognition as "wise" according to worldly standards reveal a foolish self-deception. A true disciple of Jesus accepts that although following God's wisdom looks foolish to non-Christians, it actually is the only way to become truly wise. Contrary to common human thinking, God considers the world's wisdom foolish (3:19).

Key Themes of 1 Corinthians 3:16–4:5

- The church is God's temple, the place where he resides.
- Christians should not boast about human accomplishments and relationships; everything is a gift from God.
- Christians and Christian leaders should consider themselves mere servants.
- Christians should strive for praise from God.

3:21 *no more boasting about human leaders!* Christian faith is not about human leaders, who are mere mortals, but about God (1:31; Gal. 6:14). When Christians follow God and his wisdom, they will become keenly aware that both their human leaders (Paul, Apollos, Cephas) and their victory over their human concerns (world, life, death, present, future) have been granted as gifts from God (3:22). All this belongs to Christians already since they belong to Christ and Christ belongs to God (3:23). Put differently, boasting about human leaders reduces Christian faith to provincialism and deprives Christians of their Spirit-empowered vision of God's truth.

4:1 *as servants of Christ and as those entrusted with the mysteries God has revealed.* Exemplifying the contrariness of the cross's wisdom, Paul asks the Corinthians to view him as a servant and not as one with prominence.[3] It is a subtle way of saying, "Consider me the opposite of what you apparently now wrongly adore." Enhancing his reproof even further, Paul chooses a "servant" term with significantly low-class connotations. In classical Greek a *hypēretēs* was a rower of the lowest rank. Although the term had a more general application at the time of Paul, it still clearly referred to a subordinate. In God's economy, an insignificant servant of Christ ranks higher than a patron of humans.

Both "servants" (*hypēretai*) and "those entrusted" (*oikonomoi*) could refer to trusted helpers or estate managers (cf. Gen. 39:4). They are managers of God's mysteries. Paul, here as in other places, uses the phrase "mysteries of God" (NIV: "mysteries God has revealed") as a synonym for the gospel—the cross message, God's wisdom (e.g., 2:7; 14:2; Eph. 1:9; 3:3–10). It is a "mystery" not because it is designed only for a few divinely initiated, as in the mystery religions, but because it runs contrary to human wisdom and therefore is available only through God's revelation in the cross and resurrection of Christ. What humans cannot discover for themselves, God has revealed through his Son, Jesus Christ. The task of the Christians is to make this mystery, or wisdom, known and visible to the world around them.

4:2 *those who have been given a trust must prove faithful.* Estate managers become useless (and unusable) unless they are trustworthy and administer what they have been entrusted with according to their master's design. By the same token, Christians must not use what Christ has entrusted to them for their own self-promotion but must be faithful to the wisdom of the cross. The illustrative parallel could not be missed by the Corinthians, who all recognized the consequences of unfaithful management of a patron's estate. Applying this general, common-sense truth to the church situation, Paul switches his language from plural to singular. He is no longer speaking about something that generally should be true but pointing directly to each church member: among administrators *each* individual must be found faithful (or trustworthy).[4]

4:3 *I do not even judge myself.* Since Paul is nothing but an administrator of God's mysteries, he is not in a position to judge himself. Nor can he be judged by the Corinthian church or any other human individual or institution.[5] Only God, his patron, is in a position to judge Paul. And he will! What is true about the Christians in general is true also about Paul. He must be found faithful as an administrator of God's mysteries.

4:4 *but that does not make me innocent.* Although Paul is unaware of any personal missteps regarding his faithfulness toward the gospel about Christ, he cannot be his own judge. What matters is not what he considers right and good but God's evaluation of his servant's faithfulness. The same will be true about other Christian leaders and the Corinthians themselves. No eloquent rhetoric or claims of superior spirituality can make people judges of themselves or of God's servants, nor will such claims justify them before God. Everything must be measured against its fidelity to God's wisdom, the gospel of Jesus Christ.

4:5 *what is hidden in darkness . . . the motives of the heart.* Paul concludes this section by summing up ultimate reality. Human judgments and opinions may abound; criticisms and adorations may seem relevant in the present moment. But since only God knows the deepest motivations of a person's heart, Christians should not hasten their judgments. At the Lord's return, even what is now hidden will be revealed, and each person will receive the recognition that he or she deserves (cf. *1 Clem.* 30.6).[6]

"What is hidden in darkness" can refer either to "unconscious plans and motives," as Theissen suggests,[7] or to a consciously hypocritical concealment of personal intentions and immoral actions, as Paul refers to in other places (2 Cor. 4:2; Eph. 5:11–12).

Theological Insights

Christian leadership remains middle management. Even leaders are servants. Only God is in charge and can determine the agenda. The purpose of Christian leadership is to lead the church to accomplish *God's* purposes.

Teaching the Text

The inherent danger of all leadership is to forget the importance of accountability. This is true especially when someone who holds a top leadership position begins to feel a sense of special ownership. Even among Christian leaders such a sense of entitlement and prominence can turn "servant" language into mere nomenclature. Sentences like "I'm just here to serve" can sound rather hollow in some situations, and self-proclaimed "servant leaders" can easily be tempted to reduce the servant part of that equation to a language game. Paul's warning in this text is that God *will* hold each Christian accountable. He alone holds ownership of his church.

1. *God resides in the Christian community.* In chapter 12, when Paul describes the church as a body, he again takes up the question of Christian unity. The language here, however, crystallizes the importance of community in the strongest terms. The Christian community, the church, is God's temple—the place where he dwells and reveals himself. Any notion of individualism

In 3:17 Paul tells the Corinthian church that, as a community, they are God's temple, the place where God dwells and through whom God reveals himself. This temple imagery would have resonated with both Jewish and Gentile believers. Towering over the forum in Corinth stood the temple to Apollo; its archaeological remains are shown here.

that gets in the way of God's "common-unity" is in the process of destroying God's holy space. It follows that when someone introduces a wisdom among God's people that runs contrary to the wisdom of the cross, God's holy temple is blasphemed. Both of these scenarios engender God's wrath.

2. *God does not use worldly standards to evaluate ministry.* As the famed preacher of the fourth-century church John Chrysostom reminded his congregation, God's rubric for evaluation is christological and soteriological in character (*Hom. 1 Cor.* 10.2). Fidelity to the wisdom of the cross must be the measuring stick for any and all Christian activity. Paul's emphasis in 3:18 on becoming a "fool" is designed not to encourage ignorance or a lack of refinement but to remind the Christians that the agenda for the church is imitation of Christ. When the church's agenda, and its measurement for success, is set by the world, churches and Christians have gone awry. It proves they are more interested in the praise of other humans than in the praise of God.

3. *It is one thing to claim to be a servant; it is quite another to actually be one.* As Paul teaches here, true servanthood springs from a person's mental attitude. Physical ability enables everyone to do acts of service. True servants, however, do not just do service; they recognize their position as servants and act accordingly. They do not consider serving to be paying a price. Rather, being asked to serve is like "gaining a price"—it is an unexpected honor, a demonstration of "worthiness" to serve in Christ's community. True servants think themselves unworthy of honor and are

genuinely surprised when given praise (cf. Luke 14:10; Matt. 23:1–12).

4. *If anything gives rise to pride and a sense of entitlement in modern Western societies, it is personal accomplishments.* When we have worked hard for something and have attained it, we owe ourselves thanks and expect others to add their approval and recognition. The ability to count prominent people in one's circle of friends can afford the same sense of significance. The frequency of name dropping makes that abundantly evident. Paul speaks to that exact situation when he reminds the Corinthians that bragging about such things does nothing but reveal how they have missed the gospel (3:21). A proper understanding of accomplishments and relationships recognizes that all things come as undeserved gifts from God. Among Christians, therefore, there is no room for boasting or bragging (Eph. 2:6–10).

Illustrating the Text

The Christian community, the church, is God's temple, where he dwells and reveals himself and where its members receive a new identity.

Personal Testimony: The Western highlighting of individualism has obscured the understanding of community, causing it to be understood simply as a gathering of individuals. The notion that a community *defines* us is almost gone. I (Preben) once traveled to Europe with a group of American students, all with US passports, which required their standing in line to be checked. With a European passport, I was allowed to go through another line more quickly and easily. Although I lived where they did, I belonged to a different

They [leaders] have imitated the world, sought popular favor, manufactured delights to substitute for the joy of the Lord and produced a cheap and synthetic power to substitute for the power of the Holy Ghost. The glowworm has taken the place of the bush that burned, and scintillating personalities now answer to the fire that fell at Pentecost.[8]

True servants serve unself-consciously and are genuinely surprised when given praise.

Christian Nonfiction: *The Practice of the Presence of God,* **by Brother Lawrence.** In this collection of letters and conversations, French Carmelite monk Brother Lawrence (1614–91) expresses the constant companionship he feels with God. He was known to pray more in the kitchen than in the cathedral, saying, "Lord of all pots and pans and things . . . / Make me a saint by getting meals / And washing up plates!" He also was heard to say that "he was pleased when he could take up a straw from the ground for the love of God, seeking Him only, and nothing else, not even His gifts."[9]

community in the eyes of the authorities. Each of us was defined by his or her "community." Paul similarly sees the Christian community as identity giving.

True leadership and having a following (celebrity) are different and should not be confused.

Quote: *Of God and Men,* **by A. W. Tozer.**

We may as well face it: the whole level of spirituality among us is low. We have measured ourselves by ourselves until the incentive to seek higher plateaus in the things of the Spirit is all but gone. . . .

Christian Success and Christlikeness

Big Idea *When the Christian faith is reduced to a mere complement to cultural norms, churches come to affirm the very things they should despise and despise the very things they should affirm.*

Understanding the Text

The Text in Context

First Corinthians 4:6–13 ends Paul's response to the deeper and broader issues in the report coming from Chloe's household. Paul brings the tension between Corinthian ideals and true Christian ideals into their sharpest contrast yet by pointing to his own situation. Everything about Paul, both his appearance and his behavior, exposes the incongruity of worldly ideals with the Christian faith.

Interpretive Insights

4:6 *Now, brothers and sisters.* Paul indicates he is ready to summarize his teaching by his use of the inclusive *adelphoi* ("brothers and sisters"). He is speaking not to anyone in particular, or to a specific group, but to the whole Christian family in Corinth.

I have applied these things to myself and Apollos for your benefit. The Greek word translated "applied" means "change the arrangement of" or "transform" (cf. Phil. 3:21). As several commentators point out, Paul's intention is to show the Corinthians how he has used himself and Apollos as examples in order to avoid calling out specific names in the church.[1] Paul takes for granted that both he and Apollos (and Cephas) are held in high esteem. To pitch them against each other would be unthinkable. Since that

The interpretation of the phrase "not beyond what is written" is debated by commentators. Some suggest it refers to penmanship practice by schoolchildren, who would copy what their teacher had written. This wax board is a pupil's practice tablet containing a Greek inscription.

is true, the Corinthians should realize that it is just as foolish to do it with other Christian leaders. What are *they* (3:5)? In other words, Paul is a shrewd communicator who avoids alienating his listeners—thereby enabling them to hear his message. After all, his point is not to shame them (4:14).

Do not go beyond what is written. Paul's phrasing makes it sound like he is quoting a specific Old Testament text. Since no such text exists, interpretations of this phrase have varied widely. Is Paul quoting an idiom that means "stay within the rules"? Is he referring to a penmanship practice known among children (3:1) where they, while learning to write, trace letters written by their teacher? This latter suggestion could fit his encouragement in 4:16, "Imitate me." Does he refer to a document on church practice that is now lost (a "letter of intent" of sorts)? None of these suggestions are impossible. Given his usual use of *gegraptai*, however, as a formula to introduce Old Testament texts, it is quite possible his real aim is to remind the Corinthians of the specific Old Testament texts quoted earlier in this letter (1:19, 31; 2:9; 3:19, 20). Held together, those texts function as a summary of Scripture's teaching on boasting and destruction of unity. As Garland summarizes, "Instead of boasting only in the Lord, the giver of the gifts, they boast in humans, the recipients of the gifts, and create factions and dissensions."[2]

4:7 *For who makes you different from anyone else?* As if to eliminate any remaining uncertainty about the foolishness of their boasting and cliquish behavior, Paul raises three rhetorical questions whose answers squelch objections rising even from human wisdom. Corinthian culture was

replete with evidence that everything a person had came from someone else—status, wealth, opportunity, and so on. There was always a patron "above" whose grace had enabled a person's life situation. Even those of noble birth, who were less dependent upon "above patrons," recognized their debt to ancestors who functioned as their "before patrons."[3] Ultimately, therefore, no one had bragging rights. Everyone owed his or her life to someone else. Since all Christians depend on the same patron (the *Kyrios*, Jesus Christ) and remain completely in his debt, none have bragging rights to claim special distinction. The force of Paul's language is enhanced even further by his switch to singular ("you") in this verse alone.[4] What he says applies to every single individual, not just to the group.

4:8 *Already you have all you want! Already you have become rich!*[5] Sarcasm drips from this verse.[6] Those applying non-Christian philosophy to their Christian experience have reinterpreted their eschatological anticipation and concluded that they already now have rights as kings and patrons in the church.[7] Like kings and emperors, they claim that all things are permissible to them (6:12; 10:23).[8] Their pride has run amok. They have come to fit Philo's description of the proud (Greek: *hybris*), thinking of themselves "as the most

"For it seems to me that God has put us apostles on display at the end of the procession" (4:9). Here Paul may be alluding to the Roman practice of parading prisoners of war as part of the triumphal march by the conquering hero. In this Roman relief, two captives are on display as part of a triumphal procession (first to early second century AD, Italy).

wealthy, the most distinguished, the most beautiful, the strongest, the wisest, the most prudent, the most righteous, the most rational, and the most learned of all men," looking upon "all the rest of mankind as poor, of no reputation, dishonoured, foolish, unjust, ignorant, mere dregs of mankind, entitled to no consideration."[9]

You have begun to reign—and that without us! Rhetorically, "without us" parallels "already" in the first two statements, forcefully underscoring that the Corinthians' thinking and actions do not reflect anything they have learned from Paul or Apollos. They may crown themselves as kings, but true Christians understand themselves to be servants of the King (15:25; 1:26).

How I wish that you really had begun to reign. The irony is as thick as it can get. If the Corinthians had indeed been kings, maybe Paul and Apollos could have been their co-kings. After all, Paul is their spiritual father. However, as it is, God made Paul and Apollos theatrical displays for ridicule (4:9). The Corinthians could not be any more different from Paul. They thought themselves rich while making others poor; Paul was "poor, yet making many rich" (2 Cor. 6:10). Moreover, in contrast to Corinthian thinking, though Christ was rich, "yet for your sake he became poor" (2 Cor. 8:9).

4:10 *We are fools . . . weak . . . dishonored*. Three stark contrasts deepen the chasm between Paul's and their behavior even further. (1) For the sake of Christ, Paul is ridiculed as a fool, while they hail themselves as wise. (2) Following the teaching of Greek philosophers, they work intensely to portray themselves as strong, while apostles are exposed as weak. (3) The apostles are dishonored. The ultimate humiliation of the "dishonored" in Corinth would be death in the arena. This would happen while the "honored," certain Corinthian church members, would be cheering in the crowd. Paul's irony stung! According to the wisdom of the cross, which Paul preached, all this is reversed. Here the wise become fools, the weak are the strong, and the dishonored will become the honored.

4:11–13 *we go hungry . . . we are in rags . . . we are homeless.* To emphasize the contrast between gospel wisdom and human wisdom, Paul describes himself in the very terms Corinthian culture would consider contemptible.[10] Gospel wisdom imitates Christ; Corinthian wisdom does not. Paul is hungry and thirsty; they are satiated (4:8). He is dressed like the poorest[11] and treated like a slave;[12] they strive for prominence and honor. Like Christ, he blesses when abused, endures under persecution, and returns kind words (lit., "encourages") when slandered. In spite of hard work, he remains like an outcast without a place to call home (cf. Matt. 8:20).

We work hard with our own hands. Paul's somewhat awkward reference to his personal participation in manual labor is likely designed to contrast him with the sophists and others who considered manual labor beneath them and a sign of unworthiness. Opposite those who charged for their "wisdom," Paul behaved like a godly rabbi, exercising a trade that enabled him to share God's wisdom for free (2 Cor. 11:7). How much of the actual sewing Paul did as a leatherworker is somewhat uncertain. The word used here refers to strenuous work, but Paul's relationship to Priscilla and Aquila as their associate (16:19; Acts 18:1–3) makes it unlikely he did the work traditionally performed by slaves. He may have had the ungrateful job of dealing with customers in the marketplace, night and day (1 Thess. 2:9; 2 Thess. 3:8).

Theological Insights

The church that learns more from Madison Avenue than from the Via Dolorosa has lost its footing and will ultimately lose its crown. When the desire for societal prominence and acceptance steals a church's focus on self-giving and pursuit of Christlikeness, the church will ultimately lose its power and become self-indulgent.

Teaching the Text

As Paul is drawing his overarching argument to a close, he is sharpening his rhetoric to expose the contrast between the Christian message (and lifestyle) and the one of the surrounding culture. Irony and sarcasm cut like a sharp knife and allow him to say about as much between the lines as he does on the lines.

1. *Scripture is more than a springboard for ideas "that will preach."* As Paul has shown throughout these first four chapters, the Christian faith cannot be reduced to a mere complement to the dominant philosophy of the culture. When it is, the believer becomes the arbiter of its content. God becomes the servant, the believer the Lord. Jenkins has skillfully shown[13] that even those attempting to do faithful exegesis stand in danger of doing cultural eisegesis of the biblical text. This danger is enhanced manifold when someone treats the Bible as one large book of proverbs that can be linked in whatever sequence seems to best further a personal conviction. As Paul points out, Scripture's purpose is primarily transformation, only secondarily inspiration.

2. *The cultural emphasis on fame, prominence, and wealth can be detrimental to the*

Christian witness. Nothing can twist Jesus's message more than human pride and desire for prominence. Whether it is Jesus's disciples asking for the seats of prominence in heaven (Matt. 20:21; Mark 10:37), Corinthian Christians wanting to mimic their cultural elite, or modern Christians who see fame and fortune as a significant life goal, they have all made themselves, rather than Jesus, the centerpiece of their testimony. It is easier to adore Mother Teresa than to imitate her. It is easier to apply the culture's success norms to ministry than to risk a "lack of success" for the sake of one's witness to Christ.

3. *An overemphasis on DIY (do it yourself) puts Christians in danger of being self-dependent rather than God dependent.* Because "success" is so tied to cultural norms, it follows almost automatically that innovative and culturally relevant ministry looks to business models to learn how to be effective. When approaches following such models then work, it proves hugely tempting to equate human success with divine approval. Who, after all, can argue against "success," even Christian success? Paul's approach runs contrary, however. Refusing to rely on his own creative abilities and ingenuity, he trusts his imitation of Christ to yield stronger long-term results for God's kingdom than approaches that draw immediate applause. What looks like "anti-success" to the culture, and to many in the church, is Paul's example of what it means to follow Christ. Self-dependence will ultimately prove to be gospel defeating (1:22–25)—even when dependence upon God seems to lack all indicators of success (4:11–12a).

4. *God's promised crown for his church is inseparably connected to a lifestyle of the*

In 4:9 Paul says that the apostles have been put on display and made a spectacle "like those condemned to die in the arena." What little remains of the amphitheater at Corinth may be seen here. Over the course of its history it underwent many alterations to accommodate different functions. During the first century AD it was converted into an arena. It once held fourteen thousand people, and its uses included gladiator contests and wild beast shows. It was even flooded for water-battle productions.

cross. That Paul considered suffering an inseparable part of imitating Christ proves difficult, if not impossible, to dispute (e.g., Rom. 8:17; 2 Cor. 11:23–27; Phil. 3:10; cf. 1 Pet. 4:13–14). In fact, Paul understood his suffering as a direct continuation of Jesus's sufferings, even seeing it, in some way, as completing Christ's work for the church (Col. 1:24). He had heard Jesus's word that a disciple should expect to be treated like his master (Matt. 10:24–25). The experience of (post)modern Western Christians seems, like that of the Corinthians, to stand in stark contrast with this perspective. Cultural pressures may make us adore those who are willing to suffer for others, but personal suffering is usually to be avoided as a curse rather than accepted as a blessing. At best, the phrase "the cross comes before the crown" translates into something like "we must accept that things can be hard before they become good." To Paul, the Christian message and lifestyle bring a 180-degree correction to secular understandings of success. The cross calls for his willingness to crucify personal desires (1 Cor. 9:19–22) and wait for the crown till Christ calls him home (2 Tim. 4:8).

Illustrating the Text

The Bible is not a treasure trove of unrelated sayings to be used however we find convenient.

Anecdote: A familiar story tells of a distressed man who was seeking a word from the Lord by closing his eyes, opening the Bible, and reading the first verse his finger pointed to. His finger landed on "Judas went and hanged himself." Very confused, he repeated his attempt. The next verse said "Go ye and do likewise." Out of his wits, he tried a third time and read, "What you must do, do immediately." Although everyone might laugh at the absurdity of this old illustration, Christians and preachers looking for "power verses" to claim (or preach) often use similar approaches. Scripture's purpose is transformation, not just inspiration or confirmation.

Having effective and innovative ministry can lead to equating human success with divine approval.

Quote: *No God but God: Breaking with the Idols of Our Age*, by Os Guinness.

> If Jesus Christ is true, the church is more than just another human institution. He alone is its head. He is its sole source and single goal. . . . What moves the church is not finally interchangeable with the dynamics of even the closest of sister institutions. When the best of modern insights and tools are in full swing, there should always be a reminder, an irreducible character that is more than the sum of all the human, the natural, and the organizational.
>
> The church of Christ is more than spiritual and theological, but never less. Only when first things are truly first, over even the best and most attractive of second things, will the church be free of idols, free to let God be God, free to be itself, and free to experience the growth that matters.[14]

Role Models versus Role Players

Big Idea *There has never been a shortage of "spiritual guides." Paul recognizes that many are designing their appeal to maximize personal gain. Christians must therefore be careful to choose guides whose messages and lifestyles exemplify Christ. They should look for Christlike role models worth imitating.*

Understanding the Text

The Text in Context

These summarizing verses follow a rather stern passage outlining the stark differences between Paul's lifestyle and the "cultural success norms" that have attracted some church members. This passage also functions as a bridge to a new, large section of the letter dealing with specific moral issues (chaps. 5–6). What Paul said above was not to shame the church but to encourage the church to reset its focus on Christ. What he is about to say in the chapters that follow is the message he teaches in all churches everywhere.

Interpretive Insights

4:14 *not to shame you.* In an honor-shame society like Roman Corinth, "shaming" related directly to public status and recognition.[1] Paul has no desire to "defame" the Corinthians but wants to help them refocus their perspective on honor and shame. Rather than considering suffering and ridicule a status-robbing experience,

the Corinthians should consider being treated like their Lord, Jesus Christ, a status-enhancing experience. In other words, Paul uses their hunger for status to remind them that the status that matters, the one God recognizes, comes from Christlikeness.

but to warn you as my dear children. In Paul's mind, the church members are his spiritual children; he writes to them with the love of a father, who is responsible to admonish, warn, and instruct. As their only father, he feels obligated to counsel them on what to avoid and how to properly respond to various temptations in life. Like any worthy and loving father, God is truly concerned with their path to maturity, not their immediate pleasure or desire for public recognition. Paul's perspective on this most likely comes from his rabbinical tradition, where, during the circumcision ceremony, the father committed to nurture his son by making sure he learned the Scriptures, found a good wife, and performed good deeds.[2] To have taught the Scripture to someone else's child was like having that child added to one's family, like a son or daughter.[3]

4:15 *Even if you had ten thousand guardians in Christ, you do not have many fathers.* As a father, Paul has no interest in shaming or threatening, as an angry patron who is dissatisfied with his clients (contrast 2 Thess. 3:14; cf. Ps. 35:26). Paul draws a clear distinction between a tutor (*paidagōgos*, "pedagogue"; NIV: "guardian"), of whom a child could have many, and a father, with whom a child has a unique and singularly devoted relationship.[4] Pedagogues were usually slaves who followed children to school and who made sure they did their work. They were often little more than strict disciplinarians, but they could have great significance as guides and teaching aids. Whatever their function in a child's life, they were not to be confused with the teacher (*didaskalos*) or the father himself.[5] What Paul does not say directly, but clearly implies, is that the Corinthians are not mature but children—even unruly children who apparently need many guides.

4:16 *I urge you to imitate me.* Paul's language here allows him to bring the discussion he has carried since 1:10 to a conclusion. After urging the Corinthians in 1:10 to end their cliquish behavior, Paul has spent the next four chapters spelling out the unfortunate reasons for, and effects of, this behavior. Now, in the tersest way possible, he restates his original appeal in a three-word solution clause that solves the issue outlined in 1:10: "Become my imitators" (NIV: "imitate me").

Although some have understood this statement as Paul's attempt to claim or regain a special and privileged place of authority among the Corinthians, this is

Key Themes of 1 Corinthians 4:14–21

- Immature Christians confuse spiritual depth and personal recognition.
- Younger Christians should seek more mature Christians as role models.
- Mature Christians live lives worth imitating.
- Role modeling should be parentlike.

not likely.[6] More likely, Paul is genuinely concerned about the church's identity, and his statement here should be understood in light of his fuller statement in 11:1—be imitators of me, as I am of Christ. His self-description in 4:9–13 is designed to make this point. Put differently, it was because Paul's life so clearly reflected that of Jesus (4:9–13) that he was able to call the church to imitate him. Other patrons (or sophists) the Corinthians may have looked to

Paul can admonish the Corinthian believers because he considers himself their "father through the gospel" (4:15). Paul makes a distinction between his position and the role of other Christian leaders teaching in the church by referring to them as guardians or pedagogues. In wealthy Greek families, a pedagogue might be hired as a guardian, tutor, or companion to children and would practically raise them. This funerary relief recognizes a young man named Hermēs who might have played this role. The translated inscription reads in part, "Thrasōn, son of Diogenes, erected this funerary stele for his two sons, Dexiphanes, age 5, and Thrasōn, age 4, and for Hermēs, age 25, who brought them up."

as worthy of imitation apparently did not imitate Christ. If the Christians needed a human example of what it meant to imitate Christ, they needed to look no further than to Paul.

The broader issue Paul faced was Christian identity. The cliques demonstrated a degree of independence and autonomy that threatened the unity of the Christian church and message. Paul seems unconcerned with uniformity and gives no outline of what it specifically means to imitate him. He includes no encouragement to reject other apostles and co-workers in order to boost his own image. Rather, his concern is that Christ's cross and resurrection remain central to all Christian thinking and endeavor. The cross is the measuring stick used to scrutinize all Christian ministry, including his own. There may be many churches (or Christian house groups), but there can be only one people of God—those guided, taught, and empowered by Christ's Spirit to reflect Christ's life. Without the evidence of a cruciform lifestyle, the Christian faith is reduced to otherworldly speculations, and Christian churches become centers for self-glorification. To Paul, the centrality of Christ's death and resurrection is the sine qua non of the Christian faith, as indeed he is teaching in every church everywhere (4:17).

4:17 *For this reason I have sent to you Timothy.* Paul sent Timothy, not to remind them that he (Paul) was their father, but to show them what a true disciple looks like.[7] Not only was Timothy Paul's beloved child; he was also to be trusted ("faithful in the Lord"). The reminder that Timothy was to bring was not a repeat explanation of Paul's teaching but a living example of his

lifestyle—the application of his teaching, so to speak. The imitation Paul encourages is visible in Timothy.

remind you of my way of life in Christ Jesus. It is not likely that Paul envisioned his reminder would solicit an "aha" moment among the Corinthians, as in, "Oh, now we remember—sorry we forgot." Rather, as in 11:24, where the same word is used ("do this in *remembrance* of me"), the expression functions as a corrective designed to refocus attention on the central point. In a similar fashion, Paul's use of "my way" is not a pre-Sinatra reference to how he prefers to live. Instead, he uses this as a direct Greek parallel to the Hebrew *halakah* (lit., "walking"), which is the Hebrew word used to describe a person's lifestyle in relationship to God's law (see the sidebar "Walking in the Way of God" in the unit on 3:1–15).

everywhere in every church. Paul is not singling out the Corinthians for special correction; he is simply sharing the Christian faith as he teaches it in every church he starts or visits. When the Corinthians recognize his teaching as truth they need to follow, they identify with Christians everywhere. When they do not, they sidestep the Christian faith and lose their identity as Christians.

4:18 *Some of you have become arrogant.* Rather than recognizing the Christian teaching that is universally taught in all churches, some members of the Corinthian church felt entitled to make up their own gospel. As we have already seen, pride ran high in Corinth. Paul's word choice is somewhat picturesque—to be blown up, full of hot air—and designed to remind his audience that genuine Christian faith has power. Opposite the powerless "air" of the inflated Corinthians, Paul will soon come and reveal the powerful "wind" of God's Spirit (4:19; cf. 2:1–4). The true test of those belonging to God's kingdom[8] is not their ability to talk but their empowerment by God's Spirit. Those who truly belong to God's kingdom evidence God's presence; their pride is in Christ, not in themselves.

4:21 *with a rod of discipline, or . . . in love.* Paul now turns his reminder in verse 15, that they have a multitude of tutors (*paidagōgos*) but not many fathers, into a choice. How do the Corinthians want him to come when he returns for a visit? As a disciplinarian tutor who uses a rod[9] to enforce his instruction, or as a father who instructs his children out of love? The father need not use the rod, because his children recognize that when he admonishes (4:14), urges (4:16), and reminds (4:17), he does so out of love. The discipline from the pedagogue, on the other hand, is designed to enforce his own authority rather than to express love for the students.

Theological Insights

The Christian life cannot be reduced to mental conviction or mere words of confession. Paul's call is not merely for them to memorize certain words of Christ, or to learn new patterns of worship, but to live lives that are transformed by the imitation of Christ.

Teaching the Text

Paul is drawing his opening and foundational argument (1 Cor. 1–4) to a close. Rather than imitating the world around them, which so obviously destroys their Christian identity and Christlikeness, they should imitate Paul. When certain church leaders set themselves up against Paul and do not recognize the teaching that is foundational in all Christian churches, the Corinthians should ask themselves whom they trust more—those whose aim is to inflate themselves or the one who speaks with the love of a father.

1. *Status and recognition.* The minimal significance of honor and shame in a typical Western society makes it difficult to understand its significance in Paul's Corinth. However, its siblings, recognition and ridicule, are well-known concepts in Western culture. People are still driven by a desire for recognition, and it can be exceedingly tempting to reinterpret and refit the gospel into categories more palatable to modern societies. Paul's reminder remains important: the only status or recognition that matters is

Paul urges the Corinthian church to imitate him (4:16) as he imitates Christ (11:1) rather than imitating the philosophers and orators of the day. Centuries later, Thomas à Kempis would publish *The Imitation of Christ*, in which he says, "Learn to obey, you who are but dust! Learn to humble yourself, you who are but earth and clay, and bow down under the foot of every man! Learn to break your own will, to submit to all subjection! Be zealous against yourself! Allow no pride to dwell in you, but prove yourself so humble and lowly that all may walk over you and trample upon you as dust in the streets!" (*The Imitation of Christ*, 125). This statue of Thomas à Kempis is from Kempen Castle, Germany.

1 Corinthians 4:14–21

the one that counts before God. The thing that people outside—and maybe even inside—the church ridicule may be the very thing that God recognizes as true prominence before him. The gauge that should guide Christians striving for prominence and status is Christlikeness—or, maybe clearer, Jesus-likeness—a willingness to serve, even suffer, without the expectation of repayment or even expressions of gratitude. Thomas à Kempis says, "My child, he who attempts to escape obeying withdraws himself from grace. Likewise he who seeks private benefits for himself loses those which are common to all."[10]

2. *Imitation.* Paul's word about imitation may strike us as odd; maybe even as somewhat arrogant or haughty. Paul's statement, however, is designed not to put himself on a pedestal but to show newer (or weaker) Christians that it is possible to live life in such a way that it resembles Christ. The text, therefore, becomes an encouragement for Christians to live as role models. Modern Christians may shy away from using "imitate me" language because the lifestyles they live do not exactly exhibit Christlikeness. Paul's word here is therefore both a challenge for Christians to make sure their lives resemble Christ's and a charge to every serious Christian to become an active role model for other Christians, a deliberate mentor who teaches as much by example as with words.

3. *Finding a role model.* For newer or weaker Christians, this is a charge to search for role models whose lives are worth imitating and then to request their help as mentors and Christian guides. If the immature Christians in Corinth had looked to Paul instead of to those who were puffing themselves up, they would have recognized the error of those they were now following. Role modeling is as much a charge to those who are observing and learning as to those who are sharing their lives. In a healthy church, all members will be in both camps at the same time—role modeling to others while finding more mature Christians to be their own role models.

4. *Learning to imitate.* Learning from a role model means not mechanically repeating every detail of another person's life but recognizing patterns of behavior, ways of response, guidelines for decision making, emphasis on spiritual devotion, commitment to Christlike service to others, and so on. Those who actively share their lives as role models must be alert for the temptation to confuse shaping with controlling. Paul uses parental language when speaking of imitation. A good parent approaches a child with love and a gentle spirit, guiding and exemplifying with word and life. Any growth process must make room for mistakes and create an atmosphere that continually makes restoration possible. Grief, pain, sorrow, and confrontation may be involved in the process, but the love and genuine concern of the "parent" must never be put in question. The disciplinarian wants his or her way; the good parent always focuses on the formation of the child.

Illustrating the Text

Accept recognition and ridicule from the right people and for the right reasons.

Popular Sayings: A "backhanded compliment" is an insult disguised as a compliment. For example, "You're smarter than you look," or "I didn't recognize you all dressed up and looking so good." When we live too much in line with our culture's values, unbelievers can end up giving us spiritually backhanded compliments, like, "Wow, you are a lot more fun to party with than most Christians I know," "You're not all wimpy like other Christians in this office—you go for the jugular," or "Most Christians I know never quit talking about Jesus, but you always make me feel comfortable." It is tempting to want to pursue this kind of praise from the world, but if we really look at these kinds of comments, they may actually reveal that we have failed to exhibit the integrity, witness, and compassionate honesty our faith demands. When we live our faith authentically and consistently, we will often face the opposite phenomenon, front-handed insults, like, "C'mon, man—you make everything about Jesus," "Shhh—don't gossip about Bob in front of 'Mother Teresa' over there; she'll just go all bleeding heart and tell us to pray for him again," or "Well, I think you're a fool for believing all that, but at least I appreciate your sincerity."

Sports: There is a significant difference between sumo sports culture in Japan and gymnastics culture in the West. If a sumo wrestler were to adopt the same diet and training regimen as a Western gymnast, he might win approval and recognition from Westerners for weight loss and a svelte physique, but he would utterly fail at bouncing other sumos out of the ring. He would have won praise in a foreign culture but been exposed to utter ruin and ridicule in the arena in which he was pledged to compete. (The reverse would be true for a gymnast who adopted a sumo training regimen and ate over twenty thousand calories a day!) In the same way, believers who seek the approval of this world and its cultural systems may end up being praised in a foreign culture but being exposed to utter ruin and ridicule in the arena of holiness and worship to which they have pledged themselves. (If you really want to go all in on this one, you could rent a pair of those big, padded sumo suits and bounce a volunteer or two around on the stage!)

Be illustrators of Christ's character and imitators of other people's godly examples.

Human Experience: Ask listeners to consider an organization in which they have participated that involves advancement through ranks, such as scouting, martial arts, or various service clubs like the Rotary or Kiwanis. While many focus on the top and bottom ranks (like white belts and black belts in Karate), the really interesting growth happens in the middle ranks. This is where participants are looking up to the teacher and advanced students above as well as modeling skills to less-developed initiates below. These middle ranks exemplify the calling and dual responsibility we have as Christians to look up to and copy Christ as well as to represent him accurately to others looking up to us. We all help one another in this way, since we need a vision of the ultimate goal (Christ), examples of others who are quite advanced (seasoned saints), peers who are just a little ahead of or behind us, and new learners looking up to us whom we seek to serve and develop. We have a responsibility to identify and imitate good role models and then to do the same for others.

Separation of Faith and Life

Big Idea *The desire to gain cultural acceptance, significance, and influence can lead a church to lose its Christ focus and make it blind to even the most blatant violations of the Christian message by its prominent members. Genuine disciple making, then, becomes impossible and even unnecessary.*

Understanding the Text

The Text in Context

A major shift occurs here. The theological discussion of the first four chapters dealing with the church's cliquish behavior, pride, and attachment to secular culture now moves to a head-on confrontation of specific community issues. The connection between chapters 1–4 and chapters 5 and 6 must not be missed, though. Because the community of the Corinthian Christians looks nothing like a true Christlike community, their vision has become so blurred that they cannot evaluate and judge even the most obvious and explicit moral issues from a "Christ perspective." When a church looks and functions as described in the first four chapters, it invariably leads to the behavior of the next two chapters. First Corinthians 5:1–13 opens this section with the most unconscionable issue imaginable. The most likely scenario is that the church had become so enamored with the significance of prominence that they had allowed a wealthy member, from whom

they benefitted, to set aside even the most basic moral guidelines.

Interpretive Insights

5:1 *It is actually reported*. From his broader discussion in chapters 1–4, Paul now addresses specific issues reported by an unnamed source.[1] The expression indicates shock and dismay.[2]

sexual immorality. The Greek word *porneia* is a broad word referring to illicit, unlawful, or unsanctioned sexual relationships of any kind. As this verse so explicitly portrays, context reveals the particular kind. The kind (*toiautē*) referred to here is among the very worst—unimaginable even among those who have no commitment to God.[3]

that even pagans do not tolerate. Ethnē ("pagans") is usually translated "Gentiles" or "nations," but in this context Paul clearly refers to the Corinthian society in general—unbelievers, who are not a part of the Christ community. A number of those in the Christ community were, obviously, Gentiles.

- Societal recognition should not influence Christian behavior.
- Sexual immorality is one of many Christ-quenching sins.
- Pride and boasting lead to arrogance, not to true Christian significance.
- Church discipline is part of church "discipling."

A man is sleeping with his father's wife. The present tense form of this expression ("is sleeping with"; lit., "is having") indicates that this was an ongoing reality. Reference to a one-night stand would have called for an aorist tense. Given Paul's argument in 5:11–13, that the church should judge those "inside" and not those "outside," Paul's silence about the woman clearly suggests that she is not a Christian. The same probably holds true about the son's father.[4]

5:2 *And you are proud!* Since this was a crime of considerable magnitude, it is not likely that the church flaunted the event or bragged about it publicly as an expression of Christian freedom.[5] The arrogance and the boasting probably relate to the son's prominence or social status. They proudly counted him as a member of their community while overlooking his immoral behavior. Instead of being eager to socialize with a son of status, they should have been hesitant to fellowship with a son of immorality. Paul's reference to the Passover meal (Lord's Supper) in 5:6–8 bluntly makes this point. Dinner fellowship was the strongest expression of social interaction and approval; at Christian assemblies it was furthermore a pivotal moment for worship, as this was the setting for the Lord's Supper. Their eager inclusion of this son devastated their very worship of God's Son (cf. 5:7–8). They had taken over the standards of the Corinthian community, where different rules applied to the elite and nonelite, and thereby failed as a community of Christ.

5:3 *I am not physically present, I am with you in spirit.* Paul's language here does not suggest a dualistic contrast between body and spirit—as if part of him was there but not all of him. Nor should this be reduced to a somewhat flippant or superficial statement.[6] Rather, Paul sees himself as a significant part of God's holy temple in Corinth, the community created by the Holy Spirit, which is now in the process of being destroyed. In the power of God's Holy Spirit, who empowers Paul's ministry and sanctifies

Because of scriptural and apostolic teaching on sexual behavior, certain sexual practices were considered sinful, and the Christian community was admonished to avoid sexual immorality. Greek and Roman pottery often portrayed scenes of the sexual promiscuity that was part of the pagan culture. The painting on this Greek *kylix* (drinking cup) is more suggestive than explicit and shows a drunken banqueter with a lovely female musician (510 BC, Attica).

God's community, Paul has already passed judgment on this son of incest.[7]

5:5 *hand this man over to Satan.* The parallel to Roman law seems obvious (see the "Additional Insights" section after this unit). He is to be exiled from the community where Christ reigns and be stripped of the spiritual possessions, citizenship, and privileges afforded to members of that community.

destruction of the flesh. That Paul envisions physical death by this expression, as many commentators suggest, does not seem likely. Rather, in light of Paul's rhetoric, paralleling this to a legal judgment of exile from community and citizenship, the destruction of the flesh envisioned here is the incestuous relationship. Paul envisions that the man's removal from Christ's presence, or the sphere of the Holy Spirit's power, will remove the spiritual protection he enjoyed within the community. This "stripping" will place the man in a situation that will lead him to repentance.[8]

so that his spirit may be saved on the day of the Lord. It is not clear from the text whether Paul here refers to the man, the church, or both. Paul is neither a dualist nor a Platonist. He does not suggest that the killing of the man's flesh will enable his disembodied spirit to find eternal salvation on its own. So, is Paul expressing concern for the church itself? Is he suggesting that leaving the "leaven" as a part of the community (5:6; NIV: "yeast") eventually will lead to the community's destruction? This could be, but it is more likely that Paul has both the man and the church in mind. By exiling the man to Satan, the church will be strengthened by refocusing on Christ, their true patron, and the man will be brought to repentance, his incestuous relationship destroyed, and he himself restored to the community—not as patron, but as a client (servant) of Christ. In this way, the spirit is saved; the full community will remain strong and vibrant in the day of the Lord.

5:7–8 *Get rid of the old yeast.* As Mitton points out, making a distinction between yeast and leaven proves helpful for this passage.[9] Whereas yeast is a distinct substance added to bread dough to make it rise, leaven is a piece of dough left over from a previous baking of bread. The leftover dough will ferment and, when added to the next batch of dough, cause it to rise.[10] This is an effective practice, but in the ancient world such lumps of leaven could become filled with disease, dirt, and other unpleasant things and, when added to the new dough, would pass on the bacteria to the next loaf.

Paul's metaphor in this verse relates to the Jewish practice of once a year breaking the process and starting over with fresh, unleavened dough.[11] In fact, Paul

Paul uses bread-making imagery in 5:6–8. "Yeast" refers to the leaven, bits of fermented dough that were held back before baking so they could be used to start a new batch of bread. This figurine shows bread dough being kneaded as part of the bread-making process (ancient Medma, 490 BC).

strengthens this imagery even further: you are unleavened. The Christ community is the unleavened bread fitting for the festival where Christ himself is the paschal lamb. Since the Holy Spirit has cleansed the community, empowered them to start afresh as unleavened bread, without the impurities of the old leaven, they should celebrate as those who have cleaned out the old leaven (5:8). A paschal celebration does not begin until after the old leaven has been cleaned out.

5:9–12 *not to associate with.* The Greek infinitive *synanamignysthai* does not suggest that Christians are to avoid any contact with immoral people; rather, they are to discriminate within the church for the sake of their identity as a Christ community. They are not to judge those who are "outside" but to be protective of their corporate testimony as a community directed and defined by its relationship to Christ (5:12). What Paul encourages is not isolation from the world but identification with Christ (5:10). The community should recognize that identity with Christ excludes them from identification with those who exemplify sexual immorality, greediness, idolatry, abusiveness, drunkenness, or theft (5:11). As dining signifies social closeness and inner-circle friendship, if not direct community participation, they should not even eat with such people (5:11).

Theological Insights

Sin's primary roommate is pride. Sin separates people from God; pride comes before fall. Paul's theological point is that where sin can live unhindered, the church remains a social gathering and has not become a community empowered and sanctified by Christ.

Teaching the Text

1. On the surface, the scene in Corinth seems despicable to any decent human being and certainly to normal Christian sensitivities. However, the underlying issue may be all too well known in Christian churches today. Both larger and smaller churches are well acquainted with what looks like "special rights" of prominent members. Sometimes church members (or pastors) are proud that such wealthy, well-known, or culturally recognized people are members of their congregation, and they allow for lifestyles that impede rather than enhance the church's Christian testimony. Other times, a congregation brings itself into a situation where it becomes dependent (financially or otherwise) upon the goodwill of such people. The situation in Corinth was very similar to that, and Paul calls the church to rely on no one but Christ. As many high-profile examples have shown in recent years, the opposite can bring the church to accept behavior so abhorrent and unethical that even the surrounding society considers it criminal.

2. The text deals broadly with sexual immorality and more specifically with the issue of incest and adultery. Paul's response proves a helpful guide to any Bible teacher or preacher who prepares to teach on sexual ethics. (1) Paul does not disconnect his discussion from the Christian testimony or the Christian community. Paul's desire is to call the church back to identity with Christ, to restore both the individual and the collective testimony of the believing

Paul tells the Corinthian believers, "But now I am writing to you that you must not associate with anyone who claims to be a brother or sister but is sexually immoral or greedy, an idolater or slanderer, a drunkard or swindler. Do not even eat with such people" (5:11). Some of the practices described here were common for those who engaged in the worship of Bacchus or Dionysus, the Roman and Greek gods of wine, where overindulgence led to carousing. Shown here is a mosaic depicting the head of Dionysus from a Roman Villa excavated at Corinth (second to third century AD).

community. They may live in Corinth, but their primary community is the Christ community—a community that should be guided exclusively by allegiance to Christ's message. The church is a body of believers encouraging and instructing one another in their joint pursuit to reveal Christ. (2) Paul does not judge Corinth or the Corinthians in general. He is convinced that outside the sphere of the Spirit's power, people are outside the church's "jurisdiction," although they always remain responsible to God. (3) Paul does not single out sexual sins as the only Christ-quenching sins. Greediness, abusiveness, theft, and so forth belong in the same drawer and must be dealt with likewise (5:11).[12]

3. "Pride comes before destruction, a haughty spirit before a fall," Proverbs says (16:18; cf. 11:2; 16:5; 18:12; 29:23). Christian pride and arrogance come in many colors and flavors. The trouble in Corinth was not necessarily that they boasted—Paul himself can be found boasting—but what they boasted about. Rather than boasting in their unworthiness and dependence upon Christ, they boasted about their relationship to the social elite and their acceptance by them. They had come to confuse false and true significance and now boasted about their own accomplishments rather than the accomplishments of Christ and their relationship to him. Pride leads to arrogance and self-sufficiency, boasting in Christ to humility and Christ dependency.

4. The importance of Christian discipleship and church discipline easily comes to the fore in this text. In Western societies especially, Bible-guided church discipline has all but disappeared. Many reasons for this can be given, some of which are rather obvious. The extreme focus on individualism and personal rights has seriously hampered a community's ability to exercise spiritual authority. Misguided efforts from years gone by, where church discipline looked more like a pursuit of self-righteousness by the few than the pursuit of Christlikeness by the many, have made the very concept of church discipline distasteful. In yet other situations, the very notion of community membership has disappeared: the church is a place to attend and receive spiritual inspiration, not a community that requires allegiance and can demand serious spiritual engagement.[13] As a result, churches have become complacent about the Christian devotion and lifestyles of their members. In this text, Paul charges the church to take their corporate testimony seriously. There can be no real distinction between salvation,

testimony, and discipleship—either for the individual or for the community. Church discipline is best done through church discipleship. It is the responsibility of the community to foster Christlikeness and bring guidance to the lifestyle testimony of its members, and the responsibility of the members to strengthen the corporate testimony of the Christ community.

Illustrating the Text

No one is above God's law—those in authority must submit to God's standards more, not less.

Quote: Theodore Roosevelt. Roosevelt once said, "No man is above the law, and no man is below it: nor do we ask any man's permission when we ask him to obey it." In other words, neither great stature and power, nor weakness and poverty, can remove a person's obligation to follow the law. Moreover, Roosevelt is asserting that laws are intrinsically authoritative and binding, in that they reflect self-evident values to which we are accountable whether we choose to accept it or not. If this is true of a nation's laws that are adopted by representatives of the people, how much more when we think of the way God's divinely given laws govern the affairs of his church? If the representatives who govern a nation cannot be above the laws they write, how can leaders in Christ's body claim to be above laws they have received from their divine Lord and master? Anyone who does so must be disciplined for God's honor and even for one's own healing.

News Story: This text provides an opportunity to talk about the kinds of breaches in trust that have plagued many churches and denominations. Sadly, there is ample fodder to illustrate the fact that excessive power and influence can tempt or corrupt leaders, even in the family of God. When this happens, it highlights the fact that people are trusting their leaders to uphold and exemplify God's standards and laws more meticulously than others; cavalier treatment of God's laws discredits the witness of the church and can be repaired only by public discipline that leads to repentance. Point listeners to resources that assure them of your congregation's policies and boundaries so they can know some of the steps you are taking to ensure your leaders are accountable and above reproach.

What we do with our bodies is part of our testimony to outsiders.

Popular Culture: One (hopefully passing) fad in our culture involves tattoo advertising. In this marketing ploy, advertisers pay large sums of money to have their logos and brands tattooed on a person's face, head, or other prominent body part for display. The issue is not whether tattoos are allowable or moral but how what we do with our bodies communicates to others around us. Advertisers know that observers will react strongly to the idea that a person is willing to have a brand or product become part of his or her body and present it to the world. In the same way, people react strongly and take note of how we do or do not care for our bodies, protect our bodies, expose our bodies, advertise our bodies, and so forth. When we care about Jesus enough that love for him and stewardship of his property begin to govern our use of the body, people take notice, and we have an opportunity to deepen our testimony to them.

Corinthian Law

In order to avoid a superficial reading of 5:1–13 informed mainly by our modern sensitivities, a brief introduction to the Corinthian laws that guided these situations will prove helpful.[1]

Our modern notions of fairness and equality run contrary to the judicial system in Roman Corinth. In Corinth, the "county seat" of Achaia, the governor was responsible for hearing criminal cases, while it was the responsibility of the local magistrate to hear civil and financial cases. These aediles were in charge of city finances and responsible for the upkeep of public buildings. Their responsibilities included regulations related to public festivals, which in Corinth included the Isthmian Games. Along with this came the authority and power to enforce public order. Erastus, mentioned as a prominent fellow believer in Romans 16:23, was an aedile.[2]

Prosecutions were private rather than public, and only the privileged were allowed to institute legal proceedings. A person could sue "down," but not "up"—children could not sue parents, clients not patrons, private citizens not magistrates, lower ranks not higher ranks, and so on.

Adultery could result in criminal charges, but a man could sue his wife only *after* he had divorced her. If after the divorce the woman became the wealthier of the two, he could not bring charges against her. A charge of incest *could* be brought against someone who married his stepmother, the widow of his deceased father, but leniency was usually shown.[3] If, however, a man was indicted for the combined crime of adultery and incest, Roman law showed no leniency. In such cases, both the man and the woman involved would be sentenced to permanent exile, which included a stripping of citizenship and a loss of all property. This combined charge was considered so

Local magistrates known as aediles served as judges, hearing civil and financial cases. Erastus, a Corinthian believer mentioned by Paul in Romans 16:23, was an aedile. This inscription, found on a paving stone near the Corinthian theater, links Erastus to this public office, in which he served under the emperor Nero.

serious that the usual statute of limitations did not apply.[4]

Roman law, in other words, distinguished between adultery and incest as two separate violations and adultery/incest as a combined crime. Paul's reference in 5:1 to immoral behavior of a kind not even tolerated among unbelievers (*ethnē*) may be a deliberate play on this distinction. If so, Paul charges that Corinthian believers are showing leniency toward a kind of immorality that even unbelievers consider a crime so heinous that no leniency should be shown. A son has been having sexual relations with his stepmother while his father is still alive. Paul's suggestion in 5:2 that they should "exile" the transgressor from the Christ community, and thereby strip him of the kingdom "citizenship" and rights (5:5), parallels the forensic realities of the Roman law in such situations. The person Paul refers to may not yet have been charged, indicted, and exiled from the city of Corinth (under Roman law, only the father could bring charges against his son for the first sixty days), but he should already have been exiled from the Christ community.

As Paul will spell out just a few sentences later, in 6:9 (see comments below),

the Corinthians deceive themselves (*planasthe*) if they think *pornoi* ("the sexually immoral," "fornicators") and *moichoi* ("adulterers") will inherit the kingdom of God. *Pornoi* often references premarital sex; *moichoi* includes extramarital sex and incest. The person in question here fits under both terms.

The inner workings of ancient Roman societal structures are intricate and not immediately understandable to modern Western society. In an honor-shame society, a husband, or a father, may be hesitant to bring marital matters to court, in order to avoid public humiliation. It could expose him as an incompetent *paterfamilias* (the head of the household) and thereby shame him into a loss of dignity.[5] Put differently, he may have chosen to accept even severe ethical violations within his own family to keep his public dignity. In the church, Paul says, the only dignity that matters is dignity before God. By allowing the person a seat around Christ's table, the Corinthian Christians were announcing that they were more concerned with their acceptance and honor in Corinth than with allegiance to their true patron, Christ. The issue cut to the core of their identity as Christ's community.

Being Wronged versus Claiming One's Right

Big Idea *The church must be vigilant in protecting its identity as a Christ-empowered community and recognize that it is more Christlike to accept being wronged than to pursue retaliation through means that contradict Christ's teaching. In the community of Christ, no interpersonal differences should be irreconcilable.*

Understanding the Text

The Text in Context

In a second practical example of the troubles arising from the behavior and wrongheaded allegiances discussed in chapters 1–4, Paul confronts a situation where one member of the Christ community has brought another member of the Christ community before a court in the community of the unbelievers. Apparently, church "insiders" drew "not only their assumptions about 'wisdom' and 'rhetoric' (1:10–4:21), but also their standards of self-gratification, morality, and manipulation from the secular culture of 'outsiders' at Corinth."[1]

Historical and Cultural Background

If the fairness of the Roman criminal system was somewhat questionable,[2] the courts of the local magistrates were downright rigged against the poor and the weak.

Magistrates (Latin: *aediles*) were elected by the elite to preside over commerce disputes. Their jurors, likewise, were required to be wealthy, having a net worth that exceeded 7,500 denarii.[3] In the Roman provinces, Roman jurors were preferred above other prominent citizens.

Not everyone was allowed to prosecute—no one could sue someone of a higher rank or level of wealth. A person's public status usually determined the veracity of that individual's testimony. The system was somewhat designed for wealthy patrons to manipulate the outcome through bribery, application of social pressure, utilization of powerful friendships, and so forth. If a wealthy patron from the church brought a poorer church member to such a court, the less fortunate would have no chance of a fair hearing. If two patrons of similar wealth (leaders of two different Christian house groups, for example) faced off in such a court, they would need to rely on their ability to publicly discredit their opponent in an attempt to bring dishonor to their *paterfamilias* (and church group). To Paul, this looked like the feud between two political *ecclesiae*, where friends, clients, and followers, regardless of the issue, became actively involved in shaming their patron's opponent. When believers approached disagreements this way, the church's very testimony to Christ was at stake. To win their case, the parties would be forced to resort to the "ways" of secular Corinth. The Christ community would lose its identity—their very actions would demonstrate that they considered the norms and methods of the culture more significant and powerful than the teachings and power of Christ.

Interpretive Insights

6:1 *do you dare to take it before the ungodly . . . instead of before the Lord's people?* The first word of this section, *tolma*, introduces a "dare."[4] To "dare" the enabling power of God by trying in the court of the ungodly a case that should have been handled in the court of God's Spirit is an outrage to Paul and a provocation against Christ.[5]

Although the Greek phrase *pragma echōn* (lit., "having an issue"; NIV: "has a dispute") clearly refers to a lawsuit, Paul's language suggests a smaller civil matter,

not a major criminal case. It is not clear whether his naming of the court officers as "unrighteous/unjust" (*adikoi*; NIV: "ungodly") is deliberately descriptive of the magistrate's judges and jurors[6]—in contrast to his use of "unbelievers" (or "Gentiles" [*ethnē*]; NIV: "pagans") in 5:1—or simply a general reference to those outside the Christ community (i.e., pagans). It may be a play on both. Whatever the intimation, this adjective plainly functions as the antonym to the saints (*adikoi* vs. *hagioi*). Whereas Christ should characterize the *hagioi*, the self-promoting Corinthian culture characterizes the *adikoi*. Verse 9 spells out the contrast: *adikoi* will not inherit God's kingdom.

6:2 *the Lord's people will judge the world.* *Hagioi* ("holy ones," "saints"; NIV: "the Lord's people") is Paul's preferred word for the Christians. Although Paul uses the term as a name for the Christ followers, his deliberate choice of this somewhat audacious nomenclature suggests that the name retained the importance of

The courts over which local magistrates (*aediles*) presided favored the wealthy and the elite. This inscription from the remains of the Babbius Monument at ancient Corinth identifies Cnaeus Babbius Philinus as an aedile and the one who paid for the monument to be erected. He served during the reign of Augustus.

its meaning. *Hagioi* describes the group of those who belong to God, who alone is holy. They have become holy because they are his, not because of certain "holy" behaviors. Translated from the Hebrew *qadosh*, "holy" is a term of belonging.[7] The Christ community, the *hagioi*, will judge the world, not because they have deeper insight or higher righteousness, but because they, as the people who belong to the one who rules the earth, will participate in the final judgment (cf. Rev. 2:26; Dan. 7:22; Wis. 3:8).

competent to judge trivial cases. Paul's argument runs contrary to the traditional rabbinical approach. Rather than arguing from the minor to the major (as in Jesus's teaching on worry [Matt. 6:25–33 // Luke 12:22–31]),[8] he argues from the major to the minor. Those considered worthy to judge in the highest of courts are also worthy to judge in the "small claims" court. Moreover, Christ followers will be judges with God over all creation and all created beings, even the angels (6:3).[9]

6:3 *the things of this life.* Paul's more general statement in 6:2—"trivial cases," or insignificant matters—is specified in 6:3 as "matters pertaining to life" (*biōtika*; NIV: "the things of this life"). The irony stings! Those who are to rely on God's guidance as judges of the universe do not trust his guidance in judgments relating to small matters of daily life.

6:4 *do you ask for a ruling from those whose way of life is scorned in the church?* Paul describes the magistrate's judges with the strongest disdain. The word he uses (*exouthenēmenous*) refers to those who are considered to have no merit or worth—those who should be beneath consideration.[10] The perfect tense only exacerbates

this perception.[11] Paul's irony may continue here. Whereas many of the Christ followers are poor and consequently looked upon with disdain by the Corinthian elite (and by the magistrate's court), things should be completely different in the church. God makes important what the world despises and despicable what the world honors (1:26–29).

6:5 *I say this to shame you.* Contrary to 4:14, where Paul did not intend to shame the church members, his purpose here is to do so. Here as in chapter 4, it is a mistake to understand this as a mere corrective remark in the traditional Western understanding (as in "shame on you"; see comments on 4:14). To be publicly shamed is to lose standing; it can be an identity-changing event. When Paul shames the church, he exposes them as being "not worthy" of their standing as Christ followers. Whether the situation has to do with a feud between two church patrons, or between a Christian patron and client, the spiritual devastation paraded by the church when asking the *adikoi* to arbitrate between them brings shame to the whole *familias* (household) of God. It is an identity changer—among the outsiders, the Christ *ekklēsia* proves no different from any other political *ekklēsia* in Corinth.[12]

nobody among you wise enough to judge a dispute between believers? Hearing cases privately was a well-known process in Corinth. Once a year, the city appointed an arbiter for the very purpose of hearing private cases. Those making use of this avoided the public embarrassment, expense, and potential loss of dignity. The church could have made use of such, or better, as Paul seems to suggest here, chosen one from their midst. Instead, they chose a public trial designed to glorify the "winner" and destroy the "loser."[13]

6:6 *one brother takes another to court.* As the argument builds, Paul erupts in disbelief. Paul's choice of "brother" is hardly coincidental. No Roman would ever call someone outside the bloodline "brother"—except in cases of formal adoption.[14] And it was unheard of to sue a member of one's own *familias*. In fact, it was the responsibility of the *paterfamilias* to decide between brothers when disagreements and disputes arose. Paul's use of "brother," then, adds further indictment. Who can even fathom that a brother sues a brother? Could it be that fellow church members no longer consider each other brothers in Christ? If so, their identity as a Christ *familias* has been shattered.

in front of unbelievers! Those Paul earlier called "unrighteous" (6:1; NIV: "ungodly") and "despised" by the church (6:4; NIV: "scorned") he now defines as "unbelievers." The purpose of this change is to sharpen the contrast between brothers (fellow believers) and unbelievers.[15] They are letting those outside the *familias* judge those inside the *familias*. Even secular Roman etiquette said, "Reprove your friends in private, praise them in public."[16]

Theological Insights

A central theme of the Christian faith is Christ's willingness to be wrongfully sentenced and killed on the cross. Christians, therefore, should realize that it is more Christlike to accept being wronged than to seek retaliation.

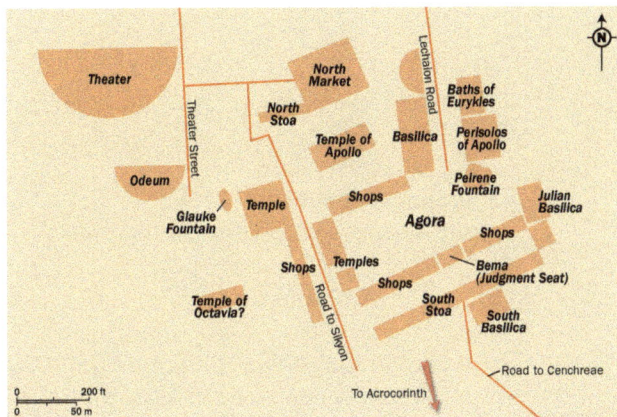

There were several law courts in ancient Corinth. The Lechaion Road Basilica, the Julian Basilica, and the South Basilica were probably locations where disputes were brought to be settled by the local magistrates.

Teaching the Text

1. Paul's overarching concern in these verses is the *Christian* identity of the church. When the church uses the same means to settle their disputes as non-Christian fellowships, there is no real difference between them and any other interest group. The occasion in Corinth is exacerbated further by the church's acceptance of a system that allows political and financial favors to play a role in the decision making. Rather than looking to Christ for guidance on how to approach a dispute, they have turned to lawyers outside the church, whose aim is to maximize one party's personal gain regardless of what the outcome does to the other party or what testimony it brings to the world. Paul's answer to the individual Christian is that it is better, and more Christlike, to be wronged than to sacrifice one's testimony. Paul's answer to the church is that when members seek means to resolve conflict that violate their identity as Christians, it reveals that the church as a community has lost its spiritual authority. They

1 Corinthians 6:1–6

all need to recommit to a deeper Christian walk so the Spirit's power again becomes apparent in their midst.

2. Should modern Christians sue each other? The answer to this question is not a clear "yes" or "no" but "it depends." Clearly, the situation in Corinth is not directly applicable to our modern legal systems. The Corinthian courts were corrupt to the core and made difficult what we would consider a fair trial. We like to think our modern Western court systems are better (although "fairness" may still be easier to find for deeper pockets). Furthermore, there is hardly a society in history that has been more litigation-happy than ours. Christians are no exception to this pattern—even denominational disputes are now settled in secular courts. Paul's teaching seems to set up the following criteria to guide a decision on whether to litigate:

A. Is there any way the matter can be mediated outside a court system? Churches and denominations may be wise to study alternative dispute resolution and seek applications for this approach that fit the Christian setting.
B. Will a given litigation be harmful to the Christian testimony? Will those "outside" conclude that this is the "Christian way" to approach such matters? Or do they conclude that Christ makes no difference in the life of those suing (cf. 6:9–10)?
C. Is the aim to be personally vindicated or to settle a matter in order to create peace and unity? Claiming personal rights is such a common modern theme that Paul's emphasis on giving them up (being wronged and defrauded) almost

seems naive, if not foolish. Yet that is the response Scripture calls for.

3. Should a church or a Christian denomination hide their crime by keeping it "in-house"? Is it biblical to claim that a country's legal authorities should stay away from any and all church issues? The answer from 1 Corinthians 6 is clearly no! A case in point could be the issue of pedophilia that continues to mar some churches and denominations. Paul's concern is civil cases, not criminal. He continues to trust governmental legal authorities to determine criminal laws and the punishment for their violation (Rom. 13:1–7). That being said, the church should be more vigilant in its care and discipline of its leadership and members (cf. 1 Cor. 5:1–2).

Illustrating the Text

It is better to lose an argument than to lose your testimony.

Personal Stories: If you are willing to do a little confessing, tell a story about a time when a debate, disagreement, discussion, or feud between you and another believer confused or discouraged an unbeliever or new Christian. Perhaps you were having a long-winded and esoteric theological debate at a restaurant and the server felt uncomfortable, or maybe as you tried to explain a quarrel in the church to a spiritually weaker family member, that person became embittered or lost heart. (Be sure not to get into the details to the point that you risk discouraging the congregation from actually listening to you and add to the transgression!) Explain that the point is not who was right or wrong in your dispute; the point is that you look back with regret and would rather have chosen to lose the debate or be wronged in the quarrel than to have left a bystander convinced that Christians are petty and obtuse.

Believers should exemplify healthy conflict resolution and seldom use civil courts.

Bible: Matthew 18:15–20. This is a great opportunity to highlight the beauty of this passage on dealing with sin in the church, and to hold it up as a pattern that helps us to set a winsome, effective, and repeatable example of conflict resolution to the world around us. Teach that the process is for issues of sin, not simple differences of perspective or opinion; we are not meant to waste one another's time and energy debating preferences. Point out Jesus's consummate wisdom in commanding us to use a form of confrontation that begins discreetly and directly without room for gossip, dragging others in prematurely and enflaming misunderstandings. It then escalates incrementally, involving witnesses and the church only if repentance is not achieved in earlier stages. It saves severance of fellowship as a last resort, only ejecting the sinning person if he or she rejects the wronged party, a witness, and the admonition of the church itself. Even in the end, there is the hope that the separation will lead to restoration, since treatment as a tax collector or sinner does not preclude the church from reaching out through fresh evangelism and grace—it simply protects the public witness of the church and keeps the sinner from self-deception through unchecked and open hypocrisy. Challenge your listeners to avail themselves of Matthew 18:15–20 to approach one another, and make it clear what "witnesses" and "tell it to the church" look like within your particular tradition and polity.

Paul's teaching is about civil cases, not criminal ones.

Church Government: It will be very important to clarify this point, especially for the sake of any victims of abuse who may be present in your congregation. It is essential that they understand where your polity and policy stand on how to approach criminal issues, and what commitment you, your board, and your denomination have made regarding the prevention of abuse. It is essential that you stress the difference between the situations Paul is addressing (civil and fiscal disagreements like a feud over a property line or a severance package) and the kinds of dangers posed by abuse (drunk driving, battery, molestation, drug trafficking, gang violence, and so on), in which you and your leaders will fully support and encourage members who must appeal to civil authorities to prevent harm. It would also benefit you to briefly clarify any of your church's specific policies regarding pastoral confidentiality when dealing with criminal matters (priest-penitent privilege) and laws in your area that may require certain church staff to act as mandated reporters in cases of suspected child abuse. This may not be the easiest illustration to give, but even pointing out these interpretive distinctions may expose gross distortions of Scripture that have held victims in your congregation captive to false guilt and isolated from help.

Highlighting the Transformation Christ Causes in Attitude and Action

Big Idea *When those who claim to be part of the Christ community live like those who will not inherit the kingdom of God, the church must be reminded of its identity and be willing to protect its testimony as a Christ-empowered community.*

Understanding the Text

The Text in Context

Having shown that the way the Christ community settles matters of dispute reveals their identity, Paul brings the discussion to a climax. The way the church and the individual members have approached this matter gives no evidence of their identity as Christ followers. Rather, it makes them look like those who will not inherit the kingdom of God. Put differently, rather than being clients of Christ, they act as if they follow the same patron as the wrongdoers, whose actions so clearly reveal an identity foreign to Christ followers (6:9b–10).

The change that should have happened apparently has not (6:11).

Interpretive Insights

6:7 *you have been completely defeated already.* Paul's outburst underscores, as Conzelmann comments, that even a "Christian court of arbitration is only a concession."[1] If they had considered each other higher than themselves (Phil.

Rather than demanding their rights and taking disputes to court, the Corinthian believers should have followed Christ's example. Christ was deprived of his rights and treated unjustly. These fourteenth-century AD marble statuettes depict the flogging of Christ.

2:1–4) and, like Christ, accepted being unjustly treated (*adikeō*), even defrauded (*apostereō*), there would have been no need for arbitration of any kind.

6:8 *Instead . . . you do this to your brothers and sisters.* The contrastive "but" (*alla*; NIV: "instead") emphasizes how their behavior stands as a sharp contrast to Christ's. He accepted being unjustly treated and deprived of his rights; the Corinthian Christians have not. Rather, they have thought nothing of actively causing the same kind of harm to others as was caused to Christ, even to members of their own Christian household (*adelphoi*).

6:9–11a *wrongdoers will not inherit the kingdom of God.* Paul's argument climaxes with unquestionable clarity. The members of the church who are engaged in bringing this matter before the unjust (*adikoi*; NIV: "wrongdoers") have themselves become like the *adikoi*. Common to all *adikoi* is that they do not inherit the kingdom of God. Paul's point is clearly not that adherence (or the lack thereof) to a specific set of moral requirements or laws will secure (or hinder) entrance into God's kingdom. Rather, the very evidence that someone has become a Christ follower is that his or her value system and perspective on life's purpose have been transformed by Christ's teaching. Paul expects willing submission to the Spirit's guidance, not sinless perfection. The behavior of these Corinthian "Christians" parades a blatant disregard for what it means to imitate Christ and be a member of his community. Thus, they have placed themselves among the *adikoi* and proved to be no different from them.

As if to remove any doubt that *adikoi* ("wrongdoers") have a different identity

Key Themes of 1 Corinthians 6:7–11

- In the court of the Spirit, it is better to be defeated than to wrong a fellow believer.
- Wronging a fellow believer using secular means is a rejection of God's involvement in believers' lives.
- Certain actions and attitudes have no place in God's kingdom.
- The life of a true believer should bear evidence of Christ's transformational work.

or set of values from the Christians, Paul lists a series of vices that characterizes their lifestyle patterns (see the sidebar). The list is neither exhaustive nor designed to list only the "Corinthian sins" (cf. Gal. 5:19–21; Rom. 1:29–31; 1 Tim. 1:9–11). Vice lists were common and used also by Diaspora synagogues to distinguish Hellenistic Judaism from its Gentile society surroundings. According to the Wisdom of Solomon, immoral lifestyle is the result of idolatry (Wis. 14:22–26). Paul seems to follow this line of thinking (cf. Col. 3:5). Still, Paul's present list is precise enough for him to refer to it as a list of lifestyle examples some of the Corinthians followed before they joined the Christ community (6:11a). The list reminds them that although their actions may have changed in some areas, their present behavior in settling disputes gives evidence that their identity as Christ followers is anything but clear.

6:11b *But you were washed, you were sanctified, you were justified.* No theological point should be made of the sequence to these three verbs. For Paul, the Christian life involves all three—none exists without the others. The neat ordering of these by later systematic theologians goes beyond Paul's interest in this text (cf. his sequence in 1:30).

1 Corinthians 6:7–11

List of Vices in 6:9–10

- "Sexually immoral" (*pornoi*) refers to any kind of illicit sexual activity, although often it refers to premarital sex.
- "Idolaters" functions as a broad term that explains the reason for the rampant nature of immorality.[a]
- "Adulterers" (*moichoi*) usually refers to those who engage in extramarital sex.
- "Men who have sex with men" translates two Greek words: (1) *Malakoi* means those who are "effeminate" or "soft" and usually refers to men or boys who are sodomized by other males (the passive partners in same-sex relationships). (2) *Arsenokoitai* refers to the active partners in same-sex relationships (cf. Lev. 18:22; 20:13; LXX uses *arsenos*).[b]
- "Thieves" were a prevalent problem in the ancient world; this allowed the New Testament writers to use them in a variety of picturesque applications.[c]
- "The greedy" claim more than they are due.
- "Drunkards," along with the greedy, often show up in lists of wickedness.
- "Slanderers" (*loidoroi*) refers mostly to verbal abuse.
- "Swindlers" (*hapages*) carries the idea of ravenous wolves (e.g., Gen. 49:27; Matt. 7:15) to the sphere of violent human crime (robbery). It relates to greediness (cf. Luke 11:39; Heb. 10:34).

[a] "For the worship of idols not to be named is the beginning and cause and end of every evil" (Wis. 14:27).
[b] For more information about active and passive partners in the Greco-Roman world, see Halperin, "Homosexuality," 720–21.
[c] E.g., Matt. 6:19; 24:43; Luke 12:33, 39; John 10:1, 8, 10; 12:6; 1 Thess. 5:2–4; 1 Pet. 4:15; 2 Pet. 3:10; Rev. 3:3; 16:15.

That Paul chooses "washed" rather than "baptized" likely indicates that he refers to the Spirit's transforming and empowering work in the believer rather than to the act of baptism—although Paul's thinking likely includes baptism as the initiating occasion of the Spirit.[2] "Sanctified" follows naturally in this short list. The cleansing filling by God's Spirit changes a person's relationship to God and moves her or him from the community of the *adikoi* to the community of the holy God—the *hagioi*. Much is made of "sanctification" as a term expressing separation (to be holy is to be "set apart"; see the sidebar "Holiness and Sanctification" in the unit on 1:1–3). Such emphasis is wrongheaded and has created much confusion as to the character of sanctification.[3] The Corinthians are holy because they belong to God, not because they have been separated from Corinth. Separation is the secondary reality that flows from exclusive belonging.[4] Paul's emphasis is on their relationship to God through his Son, Jesus Christ. They now belong to a different community, and because they relate differently to God, they should relate differently to each other.

The passive force of *edikaiōthēte* ("you were made righteous"; NIV: "you were justified") conveys the same relational emphasis. Paul's understanding of righteousness is relational rather than strictly moral. The Corinthians were made righteous through faith in Christ, not by avoiding the things on Paul's list in the previous verse. The relationship between the gift giver and the gift recipients, established through faith, is at the core of Paul's thinking.[5] The change of moral behavior flows from their change

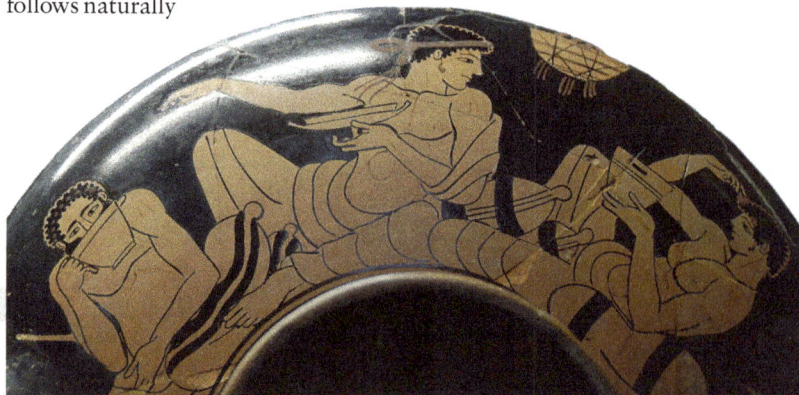

Drunkards are on Paul's list in 6:9–10 of those who will not inherit the kingdom of God. One of the artistic themes on Greek pottery is that of the Greek symposium or drinking party. Pictured on this cup from 490–480 BC are banqueters relaxing and enjoying their wine.

in relationship. Their aim (and salvation) is to live a life that pleases their true patron, Jesus Christ. Their current behavior is a direct violation of their new relationship—they act like clients who refuse to consider the wishes of their patron.

in the name of the Lord Jesus Christ. Their salvation (washing, sanctification, justification) is guaranteed on the authority of their *kyrios* ("Lord"), Jesus Christ. Their own names carry no authority with regard to salvation. To gain access to the kingdom of God, they must be able to present themselves as clients (community members) of the patron (*kyrios*) Jesus Christ.

by the Spirit of our God. The agent that empowers their washing, sanctification, and justification is God's Spirit. The Spirit that carries the presence of God not only reveals his character but empowers his people to conform to a lifestyle that reveals God's character.

Theological Insights

Christian identity is at stake when the behavior and attitude of Christians reflect the prince of this world more than the God of the kingdom inaugurated through Christ.

Teaching the Text

1. What story guides your life? Everyone's life consists of an uncountable series of events and experiences that impact thinking and decision making. All of these individual stories are understood (consciously or subconsciously) in light of a major story—a metanarrative—that has become the interpretive grid for how we put life together. Usually that story is guided or defined by culture. Events and experiences in a person's life are made sense of in light of cultural norms and the overarching way we have been taught to think about reality. Americans therefore will think differently about matters than Kenyans, and Kenyans differently than Indonesians (and so on). Again, decisions and conclusions are made according to the grand stories that guide us.

Individualism develops to a large extent from how our personal stories cast a special light on this grand story. An example of a grand story (metanarrative) is the "survival of the fittest" narrative—it is a "winner takes all" kind of story. The biblical story runs contrary to that—it is a story of redemption and restoration. It is this exact contradiction that concerns Paul here. When the Corinthian Christians sued each other, it became evident that they were still guided by the Corinthian narrative rather than the Christ narrative. In the Corinthian story, winners take all by elevating themselves above others; in the Christ story, "winners" show their strength by considering others higher than themselves. In the court of Christ's Spirit, it is better to be defeated than to do wrong against a brother or sister in Christ.

2. The extension of the Corinthian "identity crisis" is highlighted even further by their use of secular means to settle disputes between fellow Christ followers. In Paul's thinking this amounts to a rejection of God's particular involvement in the lives of the Christians. Rather than seeking God's will (or justification) and trusting that the Spirit will reveal it, the purpose has become self-justification. Put differently, some Corinthian Christians are seeking to be "declared righteous" (justified as right)

by the pagan society rather than by God. By doing so, they are violating their identity as Christ followers.

3. Paul's listing of vices that characterize the surrounding society highlights the troublesome nature of their action. It may seem as if "there is nothing contrary to Christ's teaching" in the way they bring each other to court. But, as Paul would say, that is because they do not get the bigger picture. The individual vices listed are indisputably actions that have no place in the kingdom of God. All the Corinthians would "amen" that. What they have failed to see by bringing their issues to the secular settings like this is that their thinking is still rooted in idolatry. They put two and two together, so to speak, in the same way they did before they became Christ followers. They have again aligned themselves with the wrongdoers, whose actions run contrary to what should characterize the people who belong to the kingdom of God. Their lives lack the evidence of a transforming work of Christ's Spirit—a demonstration that they belong to the kingdom of God.

Illustrating the Text

The story in which we frame our lives will determine how we define winning and losing.

Film: Pick one, two, or three current movies, the genre and plot of which will be familiar to a majority of your listeners. (You could do this illustration with only one example, but the point gets stronger if you have time to cover a small variety.) Pick ones that are vastly different in genre and style, like an action/adventure or war movie, a romance or moody drama, and perhaps a comedy or children's adventure. If you have projection capabilities, consider creating slides with the logo or poster from each, or even consider short clips or soundtrack snippets to help establish the mood. Move through them one at a time, asking your congregation to consider (and perhaps call out their answers) how they would define success and failure or winning and losing if they were the main character in each film. In the action movie, success or winning might be surviving a crisis or defeating one's enemies,

Idolaters are on Paul's list of those who will not inherit the kingdom of God (6:9). In Corinth a temple was built for the worship of the goddess Tyche. The head from a statue to honor her is shown here (late first century AD).

and losing might be death or miscarriage of justice. In the romance, winning might be wooing the right guy or girl and discovering true love, and losing might be ending up alone. In the comedy, success might be making others laugh and being the life of the party, and failure might be taking yourself too seriously or being a killjoy. Now invite them to silently ask themselves how they would define success and failure in their line of work, in their family, in their marriage, or in their friendships. Finally, ask them how they would define success or failure as a disciple of Jesus Christ and a member of his church; pause and then proceed to exposit the passage's content.

Quote: Voltaire. Voltaire once said, "Each player must accept the cards life deals him; but once they are in hand, he alone must decide how to play the cards in order to win the game." Point out to your listeners that before the player can do so, he or she must also determine what the game even is and who defines its rules. So often, we are taking the cards God deals us in his providence and using them to play a game he never intended. We need to saturate our minds with the Bible and stay connected with his community, the church, in order to understand the cards God deals us and how to play them in a way that pleases and glorifies him.

The gospel must totally transform our understanding of life and our way of living.

Popular Saying: Reference the popular phrase "rearranging deck furniture on the *Titanic*." It is usually used to describe a futile or pointless course of action in the face of certain destruction. However, it can also be adapted as an illustration of what happens when believers attempt to pursue holiness within the surrounding culture without first being transformed by the Spirit. The Corinthians were attempting to be holy and set apart from the surrounding culture morally, but they were still seeking to be justified and win approval from the pagan culture in its courts. This behavior would be like the *Titanic*'s first-class passengers milling about on deck in their fine clothes, listening to fine music, and rearranging the deck furniture as the ship sank. They may have imagined themselves separate from the other classes on the ship, but all were equally in need of rescue. The only way for a believer to truly be set apart for Christ is to fully jump ship and allow the Spirit to transform his or her mind to be like Christ's. He or she must completely forsake any claim to prominence, rights, or advantage the culture may afford and cling to the gospel. Otherwise, even the best behavior is just "rearranging deck furniture on the *Titanic*."

Unity of Life and Faith

Big Idea *Spiritual life cannot be separated from the material. Rather than being spiritually irrelevant, the body is the sphere of worship—a place for God's presence to be revealed. Christian identity and Christian lifestyle are interlocked.*

Understanding the Text

The Text in Context

Following his vice list in 6:9–10 and getting ready for his teaching on marriage in chapter 7, Paul now revisits and broadens his discussion on sexual immorality from chapter 5. Whereas chapter 5 and 6:1–11 dealt with particular and somewhat narrow issues, these last verses of chapter 6 give a broader theological statement on Christian lifestyle using the practices at Corinthian dinner parties as a launching pad. The way Christ followers use their bodies and their material situations reflects their relationship to Christ. Christian faith makes no room for a separation of body and Spirit. The three-legged stool of gluttony (drinking, eating, and sexual immorality) so proudly exercised at Corinthian dinner banquets is irreconcilable with calling Christ *Kyrios* ("Lord"). Christian identity and Christian lifestyle go hand in hand. Christian identity becomes evident in a lifestyle that embodies Christ's *incarnational* teaching.

Interpretive Insights

6:12 *"I have the right to do anything," you say.* The NIV adds "you say" to make it clear that this is a Corinthian slogan. That Paul quotes a slogan common among the Corinthian elite indicates that church members were accepting, even advancing, an anthropology that was foreign to Christian teaching and destructive to Christian living. The more literal rendering "all things are lawful for me" highlights the level of self-love among the wealthy that separated them from other members of the Christ community. Certainly, none of the poor members of the church would have been able to say, "I have the right to do anything." Even beyond the immorality of the elite's gluttonous behavior, therefore, the egotistical nature of the statement itself militated against the unity and identity of the community. Since absolute freedom by necessity involves other people, those demanding unlimited freedom must expect the submission of others in order to obtain their own experience. Such pursuit militates against Christian identity and unity (e.g., 12:7).[1]

but I will not be mastered by anything. Paul turns the freedom argument on its head. Playing on two Greek words (*exestin, exousiazō*), he declares that true freedom comes not from permission to do everything but from not being enslaved by anything. Giving in to the desires of the flesh (gluttony) proves to restrain freedom rather than enhance it.[2] As Paul further argues in Romans 8:13, only the power of Christ's Spirit can overcome the enslaving power of the human flesh. Rather than claiming their rights as Corinthian individuals, they should focus on what is helpful (*sympherei,* "bringing together"; NIV: "beneficial") for Christ's community (cf. 2:13–16).

6:13 *You say, "Food for the stomach and the stomach for food."* When Paul quotes Corinthian slogans, it is not to say he agrees but to display their incongruence with the Christian gospel. This is his aim in verse 13. The Corinthians have taken the freedom to eat any kind of food (cf. Matt. 15:17), joined that with the Platonic notion of separation of body and spirit, and drawn the broad conclusion that whatever has to

- Christian identity and Christian lifestyle are inextricably linked.
- Culturally acceptable actions may militate against Christian ethics.
- Christian thinking shapes Christian living.
- Sexual immorality expresses ignorance of the most foundational Christian tenets.

do with the sphere of the "body," including sexual immorality, is without eternal significance since God will eventually destroy it (see the sidebar).

The body, however, is not meant for sexual immorality but for the Lord. Paul's objection to this kind of reasoning comes without hesitation. God is the author of both the material and the spiritual, and the two are not separable. Paralleling the Corinthian slogan, Paul counters, "the body for the Lord and the Lord for the body." In line with the holistic thinking of the Hebrew Scriptures, Paul highlights that Christ's lordship relates directly to ethical behavior. The body belongs to the Lord, not to the individual. The relationship between Christ and the believer finds expression in this world. Moreover, the eschatological hope for the Christian is a bodily hope (15:35–49). The body is not a mere shell for the spirit to be destroyed at the end of bodily life. The human being is one unit, all of which will face judgment and redemption.

In 6:13 Paul quotes a Corinthian slogan, "Food for the stomach and the stomach for food, and God will destroy them both." Banquets were often a part of important social, business, religious, and political activities in the Greco-Roman world. This banqueting scene is on a funerary stele from the fourth century BC.

1 Corinthians 6:12–20

Food and Sex

What may seem like a strange argument for modern readers, reasoning theologically by paralleling food and stomach to body and sex, is Paul's profound way of dealing theologically with yet another practical issue facing the Christian community. Paul's issue with the Corinthians is probably not, as Fee suggests, that church members were "going to prostitutes,"[a] but that they were participating in the Corinthian dinner parties where sexual immorality was part of the dining experience. As Winter observes, on the grounds of a first-century Platonic anthropology, Corinthian Christians were able to argue that because food is for the stomach and the stomach for food, sex (Greek: *porneia*, "sexual immorality") is for the body and the body for sex.[b]

[a] Fee, *First Corinthians*, 251.
[b] Winter, *After Paul*, 88.

6:14 *By his power God raised the Lord from the dead, and he will raise us also.* Christ's bodily resurrection forms the foundation for Christian hope and the Christian teaching on discipleship. The resurrection of Christ is not unrelated to the daily experience of the Christ follower. Rather, Christ's resurrection introduced a new eschatological reality to the sphere of history that opened the door for humans to have an "already" experience of the power that reigns in God's kingdom.

6:15 *Do you not know that . . . ?* Paul is flabbergasted that he has to correct even basic matters—huge foundational issues of anthropology—that should be known to everyone.[3]

Shall I then take the members of Christ and unite them with a prostitute? The abhorrence of taking holy vessels (that which belongs to Christ) and using them in the service of the unholy (*pornē*, "prostitute") is to Paul self-evident. His triple use of "members" (*melē*) is to highlight the relational quality of the Corinthian believers' actions—they are taking the limbs (*melē*)

of Christ's body and making them limbs of a prostitute.[4]

Never! Paul answers his own question with the strongest negation possible—*mē genoito!* The best modern English translation may be "no, not ever!"; "that's insane!"; or simply, "heck no!"

6:16–17 *he who unites himself with a prostitute is one with her.* Now, for the seventh time, Paul says, "Do you not know?" Reaching back to the creation narrative itself (Gen. 2:24), Paul reminds the Corinthians of some of the most basic Christian teaching on anthropology and relationship. Having sex with a prostitute—even as a well-accepted part of a common dining experience, maybe even while other Christians are present at the dinner, and maybe even in the home of a Christian patron—is not an inconsequential matter (see the sidebar "Food and Sex"). One who does this becomes "one with her in body" and will be no different from her at the time of the resurrection. Those who belong to Christ are part of his body and have become "one with him in spirit." These are two opposite, mutually exclusive spheres of belonging.[5]

6:18 *whoever sins sexually, sins against their own body.* As several commentators have pointed out, the expression "All other sins a person commits are outside the body" is a Corinthian slogan based on their dualistic anthropology, which made the body morally irrelevant.[6] Paul clearly rejects such notions and responds by emphasizing that "whoever sins sexually, sins against their own body."[7] His point is not to express a negative view of sex, as Nietzsche and others would charge against him, but to highlight that the body cannot be separated from a person's relationship to God. Body and spirit are not separable. What happens in the body impacts the spirit and vice versa.

Sandwiched between verses 17 and 19, verse 18 connects the spirit and the body in the worship of Christ and the believers' experience as a Christ community. How well the Corinthians were acquainted with the Old Testament prophetic literature remains uncertain, but it is likely that the covenantal story of Hosea and Gomer may form the background for this passage, at least in Paul's own mind. The one who sins sexually sins not against the prostitute but against his own body. Sexual immorality makes the body unholy and thereby unfit as the temple for God's Spirit.

6:19 *your bodies are temples of the Holy Spirit.* As the sharpest of contrasts to a Platonic dualistic interpretation of anthropology, Paul brings his discussion to a crescendo by stating it as a point of foundational Christian knowledge ("Do you not know?") that the body, far from being morally irrelevant, is the very seat of God's presence. Although Paul obviously references the body (or flesh) of the individual in this context, his consistent use in this verse of plural pronouns with singular nouns (body, temple; contrast "bodies" in 6:15; Rom. 12:1) makes his point a community matter as well. Paul's concern is not just the individual but the impact this behavior of members (*melē*) has on the whole body (*sōma*).[8] The identity of their body as the residence/temple of God's Spirit is at stake. As pagan temples reveal their gods through images to everyone who enters, Christ's body must

The Body and the Soul

Plato's teaching on the separation of body and soul (mortal body, eternal soul) had in the first century turned into an anthropological ethics that gave the elite a philosophical argument for hedonistic indulgence. Sophists (see "Rhetoric and Truth in Corinth" in the introduction) argued that since the body was the house of the soul, it was the duty of humans to make sure this house was extravagantly cared for. They asked, "Are not the eyes and ears and the band of other senses body-guards and courtiers, as it were, of the soul?"[a] Put differently, since human senses exist for this lifetime only, they are given by nature to be exploited for the greatest pleasure. The slogan "all is permissible to me" expressed such perception with succinct clarity. Human senses were "friends" given for the time the soul was housed in the body. Human life was designed for people to become *philautoi*, "self-lovers."

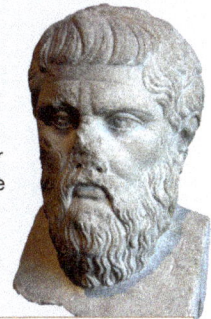

The hedonistic practices that Paul preached against were being justified philosophically because of Plato's teaching on the separation of body and soul. A bust of Plato is shown here (perhaps second century AD).

[a] See citation in Winter, *After Paul*, 78.

evidence God through the presence of his Holy Spirit.

6:20 *you were bought at a price.* The claim of the elite that no one has any rights over them and that therefore "all things are permissible" to them does not apply to the Christ followers. They are not their own but servants of Christ, bought at a price. Paul's logic cannot be missed. Slaves, those bought for a price, cannot be "self-lovers" but are expected to be "virtue lovers" who honor their patron. Since the Christian body (individually and corporately) functions as the shrine for their patron, God, Paul's command is clear: "honor God with your bodies." The body is not morally irrelevant; rather, it is the locale for worship.

Theological Insights

God created humans in his image as whole beings designed to worship him. No separation can be made between body and soul that suggests that one part is less relevant for worship. Anything a human does, with any part of his or her being, is an expression of worship (or the lack thereof).

Teaching the Text

1. Although Paul deals with the specific issue of sexual immorality in this text, he does so from the broader perspective of Christian identity. By doing this, he makes impossible the very notion that faith in some way can be reduced to mental assent. The grace shown by God, the ultimate patron of Christ followers, transforms their identity. They no longer depend on, belong to, or find life instruction from human patrons. They have been moved from the community of the world to the community of Christ. Since, however, identity and community relationship go hand in hand (as anyone who has traveled even a little bit recognizes), a person's lifestyle, preferences, likes, and so forth reveal her or his true identity. Faith is the human response of loyalty toward the grace shown to that person by the patron.[9] Both grace and faith are relational expressions. What is at stake, therefore, when Christians reduce faith to mental assent and feel free to live in a way that violates the very character of Christ is the destruction of their identity as Christians.

Paul writes, "By his power God raised the Lord from the dead, and he will raise us also" (6:14). The Gospel writers tell us that Jesus's body was placed in a tomb and a stone rolled across its entrance. Three days later Jesus arose. Here is a first-century AD rolling-stone tomb from lower Galilee.

2. It follows from the above that Christian ethics flows from Christ's character and teaching. Because the historical impact of Christianity and the proliferation of churches, especially in the Western world, it proves almost natural to consider one's cultural preferences and patterns as more or less synonymous with Christian behavior. Certain things may be suspect, but if everyone does it, it cannot be "altogether wrong." The sexual immorality that occurred at regular dinner banquets among the elite in Corinth would be rather repulsive to most people today—Christian or not. However, on the background of their cultural patterns, the teaching of their philosophers and politicians, and their understanding of anthropology, the Corinthians easily found room for this alongside their Christian faith. Modern Christians and churches, therefore, must constantly ask questions about how their actions align with the model given by Christ, not just in questions of sexual immorality, but in all questions of human relationships. Faith, again, is the human response of loyalty to the character and teaching of Christ.

3. The countercultural nature of Paul's teaching flows from his unwillingness to separate Christian thinking and Christian lifestyle. To Paul, theology shapes Christian lifestyle. Our modern "quickly, tell me how" attitude has allowed us to sidestep reflection and turn our Bible reading into

a search for daily power verses (pure inspiration) or for specific corrective statements (direct instruction). When both the inspiration and the instruction are reinterpreted in light of contemporary culture, they easily come to function as endorsements of, rather than a challenge to, present behavior. In such scenarios, questions that do not receive specific treatment in the text seem unrelated to the Christian faith. First Corinthians 6:12–20 helps us see how the Corinthians used their contemporary understanding (separation of body and soul) to conclude that sexual immorality does not relate to Christian faith. Paul's response is to help them reflect on their faith and from this come to conclude that their actions must change. Two theological or anthropological realities should guide their thinking here. (1) When God created human beings he made no separation of body and soul—bodily sexual intercourse joins (generates a oneness between) the partners (6:16). (2) The body has eternal significance. In fact, the resurrection of the body, guaranteed by Christ's resurrection, is the climax of the Christian hope (6:14). Christians must learn to think theologically and christologically to find guidance on how to live as true Christ followers. When they do not, culture rather than Christ becomes their true patron.

Illustrating the Text

Rather than reading the Bible through the lens of culture, read culture through the lens of God's Word.

Object Lesson: Bring a topographical or trail map and discuss navigation when hiking. Point out some features on the map, such as trees, slopes, creeks, and the trail itself. Then ask whether the best way to navigate is to interpret the map according to one's surroundings or one's surroundings according to the map. In order to explain, act both options out, first orienting yourself based on matching landmarks to the map and second by turning the map simply to point the direction you're already going. The Bible is similar as it relates to our cultural landscape. Many people think, "I am already heading this way along with the culture, so let me twist the Bible around until it confirms my current course." Instead, we ought to stop and see how the various landmarks in our culture (ideas, values, worldviews, and allegiances) line up with the Bible's landscape, then repent and adjust until we are safely on the path marked out for us by Jesus.

Sexuality is inseparable from spirituality, since it happens within the temple of the Holy Spirit—our bodies.

Human Metaphors: Ask what would happen if a person were to walk to the front of the church and start doing heroin on the altar, drowning an enemy in the baptismal font, or spray-painting obscenities on the pulpit? If, in the face of horror and outcry from the congregation, the person asserted, "This is my church—what I do in my church is none of your business," how would church leaders respond? Church leaders would say that the building is a space that belongs to God and is both set apart for his worship and shared by others who also have a stake in its upkeep and purity. In this passage, Paul is saying that we must look at what we do with our bodies in the same way: our bodies are set apart for God's worship and may be shared by a spouse, who also has a vested interest in our health and purity.

Marriage, Sexual Intimacy, and Spiritual Devotion

Big Idea *Husbands and wives must protect each other from sexual temptation and recognize their obligation to take care of each other's sexual needs. They are co-owners of each other's bodies.*

Understanding the Text

The Text in Context

Although Paul's discussion on sexual immorality in chapter 6 makes the transition to his discussion on sexual obligations in marriage smooth, chapter 7 introduces a new section that continues through 11:1. After his extended discussion of the Corinthian Christ followers' troublesome allegiance to their culture in the first six chapters, Paul will now address specific questions and issues that have come to him in a letter from the Corinthian church (7:1). He moves from a rather stern corrective, reproaching tone (they should have known better) to a pastorally informative tone. Put differently, Paul is moving from pointing out significant errors in their thinking to dealing with issues that are not necessarily black and white but require deeper spiritual insight and pastoral guidance.

Historical and Cultural Background

Most Roman marriages were arranged by families for the purpose of enhancing status and family wealth. Social distinction mattered for a "good marriage," and financially and politically helpful arrangements made much sense in Roman Corinth. Gaius, a Roman jurist writing approximately seventy-five to a hundred years later than Paul, states: "In marriage by coemption, women become subject to their husbands by mancipation, that is to say by a kind of fictitious sale; for the man purchases the woman who comes into his hand in the presence of not less than five witnesses, who must be Roman citizens over the age of puberty."[1] Because a husband was often considerably older than his wife, the husband usually was the dominant authority figure in the marriage.[2] The relationship between the two did not often resemble that of most modern marriages in the West. Rather than love and affection, the emphasis of a good Roman marriage was *concordia*, harmony, between the spouses.[3] Marriage ceremonies were not uncommon, but they were not required. The same held true for divorce. A marriage could end simply by the husband telling his wife to leave the house.[4]

Interpretive Insights

7:1 *Now for the matters you wrote about.* Paul refers to an unknown letter from the Corinthian church to him, possibly received as a response to his earlier letter mentioned in 5:9 (see "Paul's Ministry in Corinth" in the introduction).

It is good for a man not to have sexual relations with a woman.[5] Taken as a firm and clear assertion of Paul's own understanding, this clause has generated much impassioned discussion throughout the history of interpretation and been a key verse in arguments favoring celibacy. The discussion is only made more difficult by the fact that the Greek word *gynē*, "woman," also translates as "wife" and clearly does so for the rest of this paragraph. Did Paul really mean to say that sexual intercourse should be avoided even in the marriage? Was this Paul's way to agree with the ascetics against the libertines?[6] Such a view, however, would place Paul in the unlikely situation of an adversary to his own Pharisaic tradition, which, on the basis of Genesis 2:18, saw marriage as God ordained, if not God commanded.[7]

The more likely scenario, as a number of more recent scholars have pointed out, is that the statement is a Corinthian slogan Paul rejects. In like fashion to the slogans quoted in 6:12–20, Paul aims to correct the

Corinthian sayings that have misguided the church. The letter from the Corinthians apparently included the question about marriage and sex, indicating that some in the church used the slogan to further a kind of sexual asceticism that paralleled the cult of Isis, teaching of the Cynics, or another popular movement in first-century Corinth.[8] Paul responds with a rejection: "you wrote . . . : 'It is good . . .' But since sexual immorality is occurring . . ." (7:1–2). Put differently, rather than confirming celibacy or sexual abstinence, Paul emphasizes that sex is good, it must be experienced only between a husband and wife, and in this setting it functions as an antidote against sexual promiscuity.[9]

7:2 *But since sexual immorality is occurring.* Paul's counter to the question of celibacy is tied to his understanding of fornication and unity. To minimize the temptation to engage in fornication and thereby destroy their Christian identity as "united with Christ," Christian couples

Most marriages in the Greco-Roman world were arranged by the families. Here is a Greek marriage contract from 310 BC.

are sexually responsible to and for each other. Such emphasis on the equality and mutuality between husbands and wives is striking. In the Corinthian situation this would have been heard both as a rejection of privileges claimed by some men (see comments above on 6:12–20) and as a redemptive emphasis on a privilege that should be claimed by all Christian wives.[10] The woman, as much as the man, should expect that her spouse will fulfill her need for intimacy and hers alone. This stress on equality and mutuality continues throughout this paragraph—even requiring a mutual decision for short periods of sexual abstinence.

7:3 *The husband should fulfill his marital duty to his wife . . . the wife to her husband.* Paul's use of "obligation" (NIV: "marital duty") should in this context be understood as relational rather than legal. He is not referencing "rightful claims" but speaking pastorally about the significance of spousal intimacy and the protective quality this yields in a society where sexual temptations run rampant. Along with the marriage vow come spousal responsibilities. Intimacy ranks high on such a list.

Spousal responsibilities come along with the marriage vows. A bride and groom decorate this piece of Greek pottery (440–420 BC, Athens).

7:4 *The wife does not have authority . . . the husband does not have authority.* Again a statement expressing equality and mutuality! Paul's argument moves toward a climactic refutation of the Corinthian slogan. With the words of 6:19–20 still ringing in their ears ("You are not your own; you were bought at a price"), Paul draws a direct parallel to the marriage partners. They have become one; their bodies, therefore, no longer are just their own but belong to the other. What Paul says about the rights of Christ over the members of his body (6:15) applies to the marriage relationship—equally (*homoiōs*) to both the husband and the wife. Their freedom is limited by their belonging to each other.

7:5 *Do not deprive each other.* Paul chooses the imperative of a rather strong word, *apostereō* ("defraud," "steal," "rob"; cf. 6:7–8; James 5:4), to match his language of authority in verse 4. Since the body belongs to the spouse, withholding intimacy in the marriage, even for spiritual purposes, would be taking for oneself what rightfully belongs to both. Such decisions, rather, require mutual consent.[11] Even then, Paul seems almost hesitant to encourage such exemption. The Greek *ei mēti an* is best translated as "except maybe, if you have to"—and then only "by mutual consent and for a time" (lit., "time of agreement"). Paul's concern is those who, in the name of spirituality and on the basis of a Corinthian slogan, or for whatever reason, claim they have the right to abstain from sexual intimacy with their spouse. He is not arguing that either spouse has the right to force the other to fulfill whatever sexual fantasy can be dreamed up.

The exception of an agreed-upon time connects to a purpose statement, "so that," followed by a plural subjunctive, "you may devote yourselves to prayer." Paul does not use a new imperative (e.g., "pause for prayer") to parallel the previous verb; rather, he concedes that periods of intense spiritual devotion may require a short period of sexual abstinence. The plural "devote yourselves" (or "busy yourselves with") seems to indicate that Paul envisions the period of spiritual devotion to be engaged in by both.

When the agreed-upon time for intense spiritual devotion is up, sexual intimacy—which includes spiritual union (cf. 6:15–17)—should resume. The reason and purpose for this is to avoid satanic temptation. Unless sexual intimacy resumes, the renewed spiritual depth and fervor attained during the time of special devotion may be quashed and invalidated by Satan's temptation. Since the Corinthians lack self-control, and some even have found arguments to spiritualize and sanction their incontinence (6:13), sexual intimacy between spouses functions as a guard against Satan's attempt to devastate their unity with Christ by leading them into sexual immorality.[12]

7:6 *as a concession, not as a command.* Paul emphasizes that his word about abstinence is only a concession. When spouses agree upon it, sexual abstinence for a short season of focused spiritual devotion is okay. Several commentators have connected this verse with the following verse (rather than the preceding one) and argued that Paul's "concession" is marriage and sex itself. As their argument goes, Paul is compromising because not all are able to remain unmarried and celibate like himself—although

that would be better. Such an argument, however, does not fit the text or context very well. Rather than introducing a new thought, the Greek postpositive conjunction *de*, "but," sets up a soft contrast, or qualifier, to the preceding verse. The Corinthians should not hear what he has just said about abstinence as a command.[13]

7:7 *I wish that all of you were as I am.* The Greek construction expresses a genuine desire on Paul's part and sets the stage for the following acknowledgment that celibacy is a particular gift from God that he has received. Others have received other gifts. The point is not that he wills (*thelō*) for them to become like him but that, although his situation grants him more freedom to serve Christ (7:32–33), he recognizes that his gift is not theirs. To Paul celibacy is not a forced act of sexual abstinence but a spiritual gift (*charisma*) from God that sets the recipient free from the desire and need for sexual intimacy.

Theological Insights

Because body and soul cannot be separated, physical and spiritual intimacy are inseparable as well. Because the unity of marriage reflects God, adultery is a violation of the very character of a Christian marriage. Each spouse is thus charged with the responsibility to remain intimate—physically and spiritually—with the other.

Teaching the Text

1. The situation in Roman Corinth was not dramatically different from that in modern Western society. Although the arguments may run differently, the acceptance of sexual

incontinence as "common" or "something to be expected" remains so widespread that objections to this "norm" sound prudish and backward. Faced with such a situation, Paul reminds the Corinthians of the importance of marital intimacy. Since sexual intimacy creates a unity between the partners that goes beyond mere physical pleasure (6:16), sexual intercourse and intimacy belong exclusively inside a marriage, between a wife and husband. Paul's emphatic use of "her/his own" must not be missed. Each man or woman must have sexual relations with his or her *own* spouse. Christians who are finding arguments—either emotional or rational—for promiscuity are missing the deepest issues related to sex, relationship, and spirituality. Sex should occur only between a husband and wife because it builds and expresses a bodily and spiritual unity that demonstrates God's intentions for his creation (Gen. 2:24) rather than violating it (1 Cor. 6:18b).

2. Rather than condemning sexual intimacy as sinful or a hindrance to true spirituality, as some Corinthians would have it, Paul sees it as a protector against sin. In fact, he considers it a spiritual responsibility for both the wife and the husband to make sure sexual intimacy remains vibrant. Sexual withdrawal or disinterest from either party invites temptation and opens the door for Satan to break

A husband and wife with their right hands clasped together is a motif seen on Roman funerary monuments. The joining of right hands, known in Latin as *dextrarum iunctio*, conveyed unity, loyalty, and fidelity. This first-century AD urn shows a couple holding hands in *dextrarum iunctio*.

the unity between spouses. Paul's stress on mutuality in this matter is both unusual and striking, but it exemplifies the character of the Christian marriage. Spouses should not consider themselves individuals who simply have decided to live together in the same place to share a bed and living space. Rather, they have become *one* and have ownership of each other to the point where decisions, even decisions about their own bodies, must be made together. As extensions of each other, their individual focus is to benefit the other and strengthen their unity. Sexual intimacy is at the very center of this experience. Paul's vehement repetition of the importance of mutuality makes it impossible to interpret these verses as giving one spouse rights against the will of the other. But these verses do demand that each spouse look to the needs of the other with a desire to guard against sexual temptation and to enhance their unity of body and spirit.

3. Paul's discussion in these verses deals with the question of celibacy. Although teachings that accentuate the spiritual value in remaining celibate for life seem less than common in modern society, Paul's comments remain important. Some in Corinth argued that sexual abstinence placed them on a higher spiritual plane. To that, Paul says no. But to the broader question of singleness versus marriage, Paul's response is neither affirmative nor negative. Singleness, which in Paul's mind means being celibate, is not for everyone. The natural human proclivity is to desire sexual relations. Celibacy is not something to be sought for spiritual benefit but something to be appreciated as a special spiritual gift. In terms of sexual relations, God gifts people in two ways:

some receive the gift of celibacy, others the gift of marriage ("one has this gift, another has that" [7:7b]). Each should rejoice in the gift he or she has received from God.

Illustrating the Text

Sexual expression is reserved for marriage between one man and one woman.

Human Metaphor: Fire is a wonderful gift that can enhance human existence immensely. Restricted to the proper locations, it heats our homes, makes our food safe to eat, destroys rubbish, and is a source of energy. But outside of its proper place, fire can completely destroy property, disfigure and wound, and utterly ruin on a massive scale. Marriage is to sex what a fireplace is to a fire; it is the only context in which the positive effects of God's gift may be enjoyed without lives being consumed or destroyed. Expressing sexuality outside of the institution for which God ordained it carries deep consequences in our relationship with the Lord and others. For more on this metaphor, see Proverbs 6:27–29 (cf. 1 Cor. 7:9).

The vibrancy of the Christian's marriage bed is intertwined with the marriage's health and each spouse's intimacy with Christ.

Human Metaphor: Ask what listeners would think of a Christian who says, "I love Jesus with all my heart—I just never spend time with him in worship or prayer, nor do I allow him to change me. We have an understanding." The reason this seems false and offensive is that the person would be claiming to live within a covenant yet failing to have any real loyalty or sense of responsibility. He or she would be treating the covenant as a one-sided contract, not an organic union of reciprocity and mutual concern. The parallel in marriage would be a person saying, "My spouse and I love each other deeply—we just never spend time with one another in wooing, sharing secrets, or making love with regularity. We have an understanding." This is false and offensive for the same reasons: persons are claiming to live within a covenant, yet they are failing to exhibit loyalty and faithfulness. Now crank the metaphor up one final notch: since the marriage covenant is given by God as a model of his relationship to the church, failure to be faithful in either of these covenants actually violates the other as well.

Celibacy is a faithful expression of sexuality for the unmarried who receive it as a gift from God.

Quote: Elisabeth Elliot. "The gift of virginity, given to everyone to offer back to God for His use, is a priceless and irreplaceable gift. It can be offered in the pure sacrifice of marriage, or it can be offered in the sacrifice of a life's celibacy."[14] This quote highlights the fact that the starting point for all Christian sexuality—male and female—is virginity and that the character of all Christian sexuality is the setting aside of one's rights and self-centeredness for the edification of others and the glory of God. Whether expressed by other-centered care and ministry to a spouse's needs within marriage or restrained in other-centered care and ministry to a hurting world, a believer's sexuality is a gift given by God to be stewarded in faithfulness according to God's plan, not our own agendas.

Marriage and Singleness

Big Idea *Singleness becomes a hindrance to a Christ follower when, instead of setting people free to focus on Christ, it imprisons the mind to a focus on satisfying personal desire. For this reason, a married Christian who cannot remain single for the rest of his or her life should not seek divorce.*

Understanding the Text

The Text in Context

Having answered the question generated by ascetics who claim that sexual abstinence within a marriage enhances spirituality, Paul now turns to the questions of singleness, marriage, and divorce. The passage naturally falls into two smaller sections: widowers and widows (7:8–9), and marriage and divorce between Christians (7:10–11). Paul's brief discussion of singleness in verses 8–9 sets the stage for a longer, more detailed, and inclusive exposition of his perspective in verses 25–40.

Historical and Cultural Background

The difficulty for modern readers of this text is to properly understand a historical context that radically differs from ours. To modern readers, Paul's advice to widows or widowers seems rather innocuous—especially, maybe, as the words "widow" and "widower" often suggest an older person. In the first-century Roman world, however, it was not uncommon to find teenage widows, as a variety of complications claimed young victims (cf. 1 Tim. 5:11–14).

Cohick's study on the Samaritan woman in John 4 sheds helpful light on the situation.

> [The Samaritan woman's] history of several husbands fits the pattern we find of women marrying in their mid to late teens, and becoming widows very early. They might marry three times before they reach their mid-twenties, as was the case with Herod's grand-daughter Berenice. Born about AD 28 to Agrippa I and Cypros, she had been married twice by the time she was 16 years old (Josephus, *Antiquities* 18.132).[1]

Berenice (Bernice) enters the biblical story in Acts 25:13, 23; 26:30, where she seems to be ruling with her brother Agrippa II. She was remarried later to King Polemo of Cilicia, who agreed to undergo circumcision to marry her. Her last relationship was with the Roman emperor Titus, whom she was forbidden to marry because of the anti-Jewish sentiment in Rome during that time.

Although the Samaritan woman has little in common with the wealthy and prominent Berenice, "both women were equally vulnerable to becoming widows."[2]

The pressure to remarry quickly was enormous. The Augustan law prohibited younger unmarried men and women (including the widowed and divorced) from receiving inheritances. "A widow was expected to remarry within a year, a divorcee within six months."[3] The law required the woman to produce at least three children to secure the husband's inheritance. Marriage was designed for the procreation of legitimate Roman children, as only they received citizenship.

The question of whether Paul was an unmarried bachelor or a widower is not possible to settle with certainty. Most of the church fathers claim Paul never married.[4] Diligent studies and extended periods of itinerant teaching caused some first-century rabbis to delay marriage until their late thirties. However, given the theological significance and social prominence of Genesis 1:28, which was promoted by rabbinical teaching as a command that described God's design for human multiplication through

Roman legislation concerning marriage and children was introduced by the emperor Augustus, who ruled from 27 BC to AD 14. Known as the *lex Julia de maritandis ordinibus*, it penalized Roman citizens for remaining unmarried. Shown here is a statue of Augustus (the head is from the first century BC).

- What is the relationship between singleness, ministry, and sexual passion?
- How should Christians understand marriage and divorce?
- Can Christians remarry after a divorce?

marriage, it seems quite likely that a zealous Jew like Paul (Rom. 11:1; Phil. 3:5; Acts 23:6), who enjoyed great recognition among the Sanhedrin leaders (Acts 8:1–3), would be married. Furthermore, according to Hillel, who was the grandfather of Gamaliel, who was the president of the Sanhedrin and Paul's Jerusalem teacher, a man must have at least one son and one daughter (*m. Yebam.* 6.6). Additionally, if Paul was an ordained rabbi, which seems probable in light of his commissioning to persecute the church on behalf of the Sanhedrin (Acts 9:2; 26:10), it would be highly unusual if he was not married at one time. Whether his wife died (7:39) or simply left him when he converted to join the Christ followers (7:15) remains unknown. Nothing hints he ever had any children.

Interpretive Insights

7:8 *It is good for them to stay unmarried, as I do.* Paul addresses the widowers and the widows with an encouragement to remain unmarried unless they find themselves unable or unwilling to

The Unmarried: Both Men and Women?

Paul's use of the masculine noun *agamois* ("to the unmarried") in 7:8 could be inclusive. Verse 11 seems to suggest he has a specific woman in mind when writing these words. If so, the masculine gender must be understood inclusively (similar to *adelphoi*) and he is addressing the unmarried in general (all not-yet and no-longer married; cf. 7:34). The reason for singling out the female widows would then be their special recognition in the early church (1 Tim. 5:3–16). If, however, Paul's stress on mutuality carries over to this verse, *agamois* refers strictly to men, so that his address in 7:8 is to widowers (*agamois*) and widows.

remain sexually abstinent. Paul limits his comments here to a terse statement that functions as a bridge to connect his discussion on abstinence (7:1–7) to his discussion on marriage and divorce (7:10–16). He has no Jesus saying to reference; but his own life proves sufficient as a touchpoint for his teaching: "I say" it is good to remain single. (Some translations elevate "good" to a comparative ["better"; e.g., NLT] or a superlative ["best"; e.g., NET]. Although this is grammatically possible, such an interpretation is mandated neither by the text nor by the context.) Paul's fuller and more inclusive exposition will follow in 7:25–40.

7:9 *better to marry than to burn with passion.* Context must guide our understanding of Paul's strong language here. He is hardly suggesting that widows or widowers either possess strength to subdue their sexual urges to live in celibacy or have passions burning so hot that unless they hurry up and remarry,

they will find themselves in the arms of prostitutes. Is Paul's use of *pyrousthai* ("to be aflame") referring to judgment rather than passion ("better to marry than to be in the fires of judgment or hell")?[5] Or is he deliberately playing on the connection between adultery/fornication and judgment by using this term (6:9–10)? The answer to these questions may be found in the word "self-control" (*enkrateuomai*). By "lack of self-control" (NIV: "if they cannot control themselves") Paul probably is referring not to an insatiable sex-craze but to an inability to concentrate on the service to Christ (cf. 9:25). Athletes exercise self-control and stay focused on their task (*enkrateia* is listed also as evidence of the Spirit's fruit [Gal. 5:23]). The meaning of the verse would then be something like this: "Those whose minds continue to be occupied by the desire to marry should marry. For it is better to marry than to be distracted by passion."

7:10–11 *To the married I give this command (not I, but the Lord).* Paul's correction of himself ("not I, but the Lord") does not set up a

Paul's instruction in 7:9 may be interpreted as saying, "Those whose minds continue to be occupied by the desire to marry should marry. For it is better to marry than to be distracted by passion." Painted on this Greek pottery piece called a *pyxis* is the part of the marriage ritual where the bride is taken to the house of her future husband.

contrast of authority, as if Paul in 7:8 simply states his opinion, something they can take or leave, while in 7:10 he delivers a prophetic statement from God. Rather, in 7:8 he has no direct Jesus saying to quote; in 7:10 he does (Matt. 5:32; 19:9; Luke 16:18). This also explains his rhetorical change from "I say" (7:8) to "I give this command" (7:10).

The distinction Paul makes between married believers in 7:10–11 and believers married to unbelievers in 7:15 could relate to his understanding of the sanctity of the Christ community and the challenges of a pluralistic setting. Jesus's saying in Matthew 5:32 applies to covenant believers, not to unbelievers. But why does Paul seem to soften his application of Jesus's saying regarding the woman—allowing her to divorce if she remains unmarried—with no concession to the man?

A wife must not separate from her husband. Paul speaks as a pastor dealing with a specific delicate situation that requires careful theological and relational guidance rather than theoretical theological exposition. His uncommon sequence, speaking about the wife first, and his use of the aorist passive infinitive (the wife "should not have separated" from her husband)[6] suggests that Paul speaks to a specific situation where the wife has already left her husband. The subsequent aorist subjunctive (7:11)—"if she is separated" (NIV: "if she does [separate]")—further alludes to such a scenario. Whether she left in pursuit of spiritual perfection through celibacy remains uncertain, but it seems possible in light of Paul's preceding discussion. In this specific situation, Paul requires that she either stay unmarried or reconcile with

her husband (notice how Paul uses two imperatives in this either/or statement). Whether she left because of her husband or for personal reasons proves less significant. Remaining unmarried keeps the door open for reconciliation with her husband, and the command of Christ is not broken (Mark 10:11–12).

The husband, for the same reason, must not seek a divorce. Paul's consistent use of *chōrizō* ("separate," "depart," "leave") about the wife's action and his shift to the stronger *aphiēmi* ("divorce") in the command to the man could hint that he is hoping the wife will come to her senses and return to her husband. For that to happen, it is important that the husband not legally formalize a divorce and make such reconciliation impossible (cf. Deut. 24:1–4).[7]

Teaching the Text

1. If singleness can be difficult to maneuver in today's world in general, it can at times be even more difficult in Christian circles. The strong emphasis on the Christian family in most evangelical churches gives the clear impression that singleness is undesirable and should be considered an unfortunate, temporary situation. Many Christian ministries to singles are designed to help singles connect with other singles of the opposite sex in a way that can lead to a successful marriage. Single-again ministries often focus on helping people get through the pain of a divorce or a loss of spouse in order to facilitate a new successful relationship. Put differently, the pressure on Christian singles to marry or remarry can be extraordinarily heavy.

To heed Paul's teaching in these verses, churches must begin to highlight the power of singleness for kingdom ministry. Churches using secular days like Mother's Day and Father's Day to promote great Christian teaching could consider including a "Single's Day" to help highlight Paul's teaching in this area. Paul's call to marriage and/or remarriage is rooted mostly (if not exclusively) in his awareness that sexual desire will handicap some Christians' ministry for Christ. Singles who do not struggle with this desire should, according to Paul, be encouraged to rejoice that God has gifted them to focus all their energy on serving Christ.

2. If Paul's refusal of remarriage after divorce between two Christians seems unrealistically uncompromising to the modern reader, it was only worse in Paul's day. Paul was well aware of the Roman law guiding the census and the pressure to remarry quickly. His command to remain unmarried must therefore be understood as a charge to reconcile. Those who call the one who reconciled the world unto himself Lord

As Paul writes from Ephesus to the Corinthian believers, he recognized that his desire to remain unmarried is a gift from God. But not everyone would have that gift. This painting of Paul is from a sixth-century AD fresco in the Grotto of Saint Paul in Ephesus.

should submit to one another and find reconciliation. Nothing less will evidence Christ's power and presence. That is the principle among Christians as taught by Christ. Paul's keen awareness of the specific situation in Corinth, however, and his obvious change of tone in these verses, from directives to pastoral guidance, gives this command a softer edge. As verses 8–9 and 12–15 show, special circumstances must be considered—not with indifference to the Lord's command but with grace.

Illustrating the Text

Christians should endorse singleness as an honorable and fruitful lifestyle for those gifted with celibacy.

Personal Stories: Devote a Sunday to celebrating biblical singleness. Invite one or two people known to be living in authentic, faithful singleness to share their testimony on video. Include shots of how that person uses his or her singleness as an opportunity to serve others. You might even include a few quotes from others who have experienced that person as a spiritual mother or father, or who have been mentored faithfully by the single person in accordance with Scriptures like 1 Timothy 5. Consider honoring people who have wisely stewarded the special freedom that comes from living in faithful singleness; perhaps you may choose to do so through a special prayer or time of recognition.

Reconciliation and restoration of a marriage is possible even after divorce and should be sought in lieu of new marriages.

Bible: Matthew 19:1–12. Matthew 19:1–12 may provide another window into this topic.

Personal Stories: If you have a couple within your congregation who have reached the precipice of divorce (or even been divorced) and then were brought back to a healthy marriage with one another, now is the time to have them speak. Have them share the ways in which, even after they had given up on the marriage and one another, God refused to give up and helped them reconnect with the bride or bridegroom of their youth.

Visual: Using two large vases, wrap one in a towel and smash it with a hammer so that it shatters into pieces. Hold up a bottle of super glue and ask if people think you could put it back together. Then break the other vase in a second towel. Ask them to consider what new obstacles you might face in repairing both vases, like pieces getting intermixed, lost, and so on. Ask what steps might be taken to ensure that two intact vases emerge from the repair, such as keeping the pieces separate or dealing with one at a time. Also, ask if the resulting repairs would be anything close to the original vases. Suggest that they think of each vase as a marriage broken by divorce. Picking up the pieces and remixing them in different combinations with other broken pieces from other marriages will never bring back the wholeness of the originals. However, if all the pieces are handed back over to God, he can do something no human being could ever do: fully restore the broken pieces to wholeness, just like raising dry bones back to life (Ezek. 37). While it is impossible for us, nothing is impossible for God; if he can raise Jesus from the dead, then the same power of that resurrection can raise the broken pieces of troubled marriages.

Marriage between Christians and Unbelievers

Big Idea *Marriage is ordained by God. Christians who are married should not seek divorce. When someone becomes a Christian after marriage, Christ's presence will work positively in the marriage in favor of the unbelieving spouse and the children. The believer, therefore, should not seek divorce for spiritual reasons.*

Understanding the Text

The Text in Context

Having given the briefest of comments on marriage and singleness among Christians, Paul moves his discussion to the question of divorce in a marriage between a Christian and a non-Christian. The sandwiched nature of these five short verses reveals how Paul sees a clear connection between these questions. His excursus in 7:17–24, on not changing one's social situation, functions as an illustrative theological grounding for his singleness, marriage, and divorce discussion, which concludes in a longer, more detailed, and more inclusive exposition on marriage and singleness in 7:25–40.

Interpretive Insights

7:12–13 *I say this (I, not the Lord).* Again, this is not Paul's way of hinting that what he says is pure opinion that the

Corinthians can take or leave. He is simply admitting he does not have a Jesus saying that deals with the marital relationship between a believer and a nonbeliever.

If any brother has a wife who is not a believer. No longer commenting on a particular person and circumstance, Paul switches back to the male first, then female, sequence. He now turns to the somewhat complicated, but probably common, situation ("To the rest I say . . .") where only one of the spouses has become a Christ follower. How should a Christian react in marriage toward the unbelieving spouse?[1] If Plutarch's *Advice to Bride and Groom* (*Mor.* 138B–146A) was generally heeded as the marital norm in Corinth, it highlights the complication in such situations.

A wife ought not to make friends of her own, but to enjoy her husband's friends in common with him. The gods are the first and most important friends. Wherefore it is becoming for a wife to worship and to know only the gods that her husband believes in, and to shut the front door tight upon all queer rituals and outlandish superstitions.[2]

Whether the wife was the one converting without the consent of her husband or the husband was unable to lead his wife to Christian faith after his own conversion, their religious disparity exposed a rift that placed the husband in a culturally awkward position. If, at the same time, members of the church considered such marriages spiritually corrupting, the stress on the marriage would have been almost intolerable, and divorce looked like the only solution. Paul focuses on the latter scenario, commenting that the Christian should not initiate the divorce. Ultimately, it is the believer who sanctifies the nonbeliever, not the nonbeliever who spiritually corrupts the believer.[3]

7:14 *For the unbelieving husband has been sanctified through his wife.* Flying in the face of Western individualism by suggesting that one person can be sanctified through a relationship with another, this verse has generated innumerable interpretations. The "Western" question posed runs something like, how can an unbelieving spouse become holy (sanctified) as an individual

Key Themes of 1 Corinthians 7:12–16

- Should a Christian divorce a non-Christian spouse?
- Should a Christian marry a non-Christian?
- What is the spiritual status of young children when only one spouse is Christian?

through a mere relationship with a believer? Translating *hagios* ("holy") in terms of separation rather than belonging,[4] and relating the saying to eternal salvation, many commentators search for an interpretation that explains Paul's saying as a reference to the significance of continuous exposure to the gospel. Some suggest sanctification results from behavior (staying in the marriage expresses God's will),[5] from daily hearing a Christian testimony (as spoken/lived by the spouse),[6] or from something similar.

This verse, however, is probably better understood in cultures with greater appreciation of community. Read in light of God's election of Israel, for example, where the recognition of Israel as God's holy people does not seem to be jeopardized even by the idol worship of some community members, the inclusion of the unbelieving spouse and children in the group of the sanctified becomes understandable. Paul's point in this verse is not to explain sanctification in the systematic-theological sense of that term but

Plutarch's advice that a wife should worship the gods of her husband would have been difficult for Christian wives to follow. Plutarch was a Greek philosopher (ca. AD 45–120). This marble bust has been identified as a philosopher, perhaps Plutarch (second to third century AD).

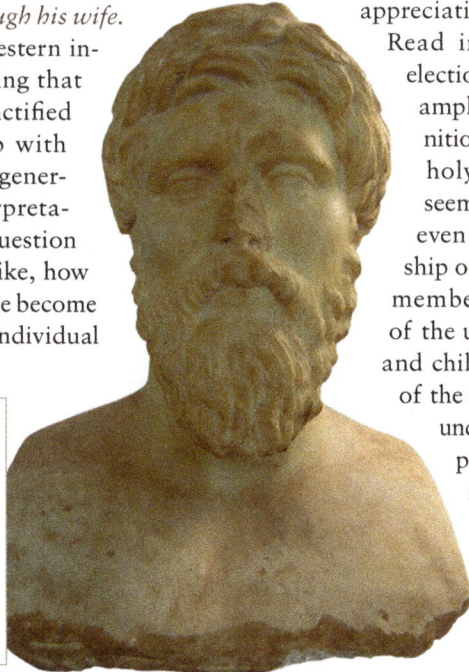

to give an argument against divorce. Since one of the spouses by faith has become a member of Christ's community, the whole family is covered by that blessing, and the believer should not seek a divorce. A believer must not marry an unbeliever; that would be a direct violation of God's will—as if the believer sought fellowship with a spirit different from God's Spirit (6:15–17). But if a spouse becomes a Christian after marriage, God's presence will bless the whole household (cf. Exod. 30:29; Lev. 6:18).

they are holy. Whether Paul hopes the influence of the Christian spouse will result in the conversion of the other spouse and the children is outside the language and discussion of this verse, although 7:16 indicates such rather directly. That Paul uses "unclean" (*akathartos*) as his antonym to "holy" (*hagios*) places his discussion in the realm of spiritual powers,[7] but not as a statement on eternal salvation. Christ's holy presence overpowers the realm of uncleanness, not vice versa.

7:15 *if the unbeliever leaves.*[8] Paul has no authority over the actions of the nonbeliever. He can tell the believer not to initiate the divorce, but if the nonbeliever decides to divorce, the believer is not required to resist the action.

The brother or the sister is not bound. Paul's word choice, "enslaved" (*douloō*; NIV: "bound"), could seem to indicate that he thought of a Christian's marriage to an unbeliever as bondage or a form of enslavement.[9] Although suggestions have been made that this imagery is found in Greco-Roman Cynic and Stoic literature, as well as in Jewish divorce legislation, Collins's semantic argument favoring mutual spousal "submission" (7:4) proves more helpful.[10] Christian spouses should be submissive to each other; when a nonbelieving spouse leaves, however, the Christian is free. "Paul does not say such a Christian is free to remarry," but the social situation in Corinth was "such that remarriage was a likely possibility."[11]

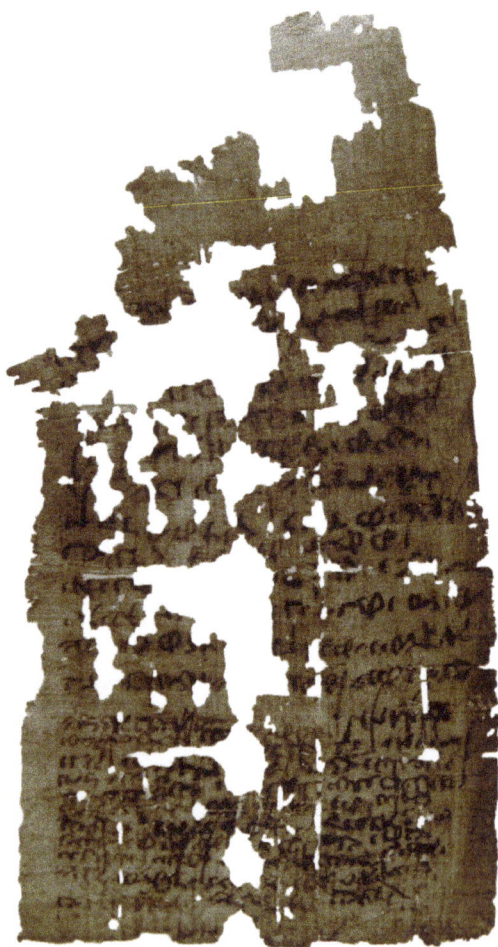

A Jewish bill of divorce, like the one shown here, would have contained the words "you are free," which would have allowed the wife to remarry (Aramaic papyrus discovered at Wadi Murabba'at, AD 72).

God has called us to live in peace. Some manuscripts read "you" instead of "us," and this may be the original reading. Early copyists may have changed it to "us" because the sentence reads like a summary statement. Paul's aim, however, is likely not to give a sweeping statement about a general Christian truth. Nor is he writing from a modern psychological perspective suggesting that it is better to get a divorce and gain peace. To the contrary, his use of the adversative "but" (*de*; not included in the NIV rendering) hints that the statement is yet another argument for the Christian spouse to remain in the marriage: if the Christian spouse wants to divorce, so be it, *but* . . . Put differently, the Christian spouse should recognize that if the marriage was harmonious before he or she became a Christian, God's call does not frustrate peace; it generates it.

7:16 *whether you will save your husband . . . your wife.* Again, strikingly, Paul's trust in the gospel's power remains undeterred and allows him yet another statement on mutuality. Corinthians who think their own spirituality is obstructed by their marriage to a nonbeliever should instead recognize that the attractiveness of Christ's power in their lives can result in the conversion of their spouse.

Theological Insights

The relational character of marriage reflects God, whose triune character makes him inherently relational. For the Christian to break the marriage bond for spiritual reasons therefore does not make sense. Rather, when someone who is already married becomes a believer, the marriage bond brings the whole family into the blessings of God's community.

Teaching the Text

1. Paul's guidance to the difficult situation that can arise when the conversion of one spouse creates disparate priorities in the home proves significant to modern Christians. His instruction is exegetical in that it pursues serious obedience toward Jesus's command rather than writing it off as no longer applicable. Wrestling with the tension between Jesus's marriage statement and the new reality (marriage between a believer and a nonbeliever), which Jesus did not address directly, Paul holds firm to Christ's command for the believer while recognizing the impossible situation an irreconcilable nonbeliever can create. Paul's desire is not to create a theological principle (divorce is always permissible in mixed marriages); rather, he aims to strongly urge the believer to recognize the power that Christ can have in a marriage and home when the Christ follower remains a strong witness to Christ's grace. Christ's presence through the believer should generate greater peace, not discord, in the marriage and the home as Christ's Spirit now motivates the believer. If, however, the unbeliever remains set on divorce, the believer does not sin by accepting such a decision.

2. Although Paul does not spell out that the believer is free to remarry another person if the unbeliever has "forced" the divorce, the contrast in language between 7:15b and 7:11 indicates this to be so. The freedom of the believing spouse in such a scenario ("the brother or sister is not bound" [7:15]) parallels the freedom to remarry when a spouse dies (7:39).

3. Paul's teaching on the blessing and spiritual covering a Christian brings to the

home where the spouse is an unbeliever can be difficult to understand for highly individualized Westerners. Paul's purpose in this text, however, is not to comment on the eternal salvation of the unbelieving spouse and the children but to give a directive word and pastoral encouragement to the Christian spouse in the relationship. As the believer remains faithful in his or her worship of, and devotion to, Christ, God's power will work through the believer and bring the blessing of his presence to the home. The focus of Paul's teaching remains on Spirit endowment of the Christian believer and the testimony to Christ's renewing presence that the believer will bring to the home situation. The spouse who now has become Christian has a unique opportunity to reveal Christ's grace to the unbelieving part of the household (cf. 7:20–24).

Paul directs the believing spouse not to divorce his or her unbelieving partner if the unbeliever desires to remain in the marriage relationship. This Roman funerary relief shows a married couple clasping hands (ca. 43 BC to AD 18).

4. The question of divorce, marriage, and singleness was as difficult an issue in the early Corinthian church as it is in modern societies today. Social pressures to be married made it difficult, if not suspect, to remain single. Marriages could be dissolved with no formal judicial action. Divorce and remarriage were common to the point of becoming a norm rather than an exception.[12] Into this situation, Paul speaks with theological clarity a word that both liberates and guides. Caring for the Christian home, he directs his audience toward mutual submission and reconciliation. Caring for the Christ follower who may need to be rescued from an intolerable situation in a mixed home, he dismisses the guilt of unavoidable divorce. Caring for the unmarried, he declares it "good"—not "acceptable" or "necessary"—but "good" to remain single. Paul is convinced that Christ's presence becomes evident through reconciliation and mutual submission. Put differently, the empowerment of Christ's Spirit will provide the grace needed to remain focused on Christlikeness in the given situation. Paul's aim is not to create a new "Christian law" that fits all imaginable scenarios but to give theological and pastoral guidance for how Christians can and must remain focused on imitating Christ in difficult domestic situations.

Illustrating the Text

A believer whose conversion creates a mixed-faith marriage should trust that Christ can bring conversion to the whole household.

Personal Stories: If you have a person in your congregation who was converted through the invitation or testimony of a believing spouse, he or she could be an excellent illustration of this topic. Use an interview format to draw out how he or she saw Christ in the other spouse and how that spouse's adherence to Paul's instructions worked. Invite him or her to share words of encouragement to any other believers struggling in mixed-faith marriages.

A believer in a mixed-faith marriage or home has an enormous privilege to evangelize humbly and authentically every day.

Visual: Bring a large box with you. Inform your listeners that the box is full of dark and shadows. Ask what they think will happen when you open the box in the lighted room: Will the darkness escape and snuff out the lights in the room, or will the light in the room spill into the box and eradicate the shadow? What if the situation were reversed and the room was pitch black and the box full of light? Suggest that in the same way that a box full of light can illuminate darkness, but a box full of darkness cannot snuff out the light, so a believer's faith and example have the ability to shine and impact the lives of others. Assure your listeners that Jesus's light shines in them and that, because it is based on his strength and righteousness, the darkness cannot overcome it.

Quote: Erma Bombeck. Humorist and author Bombeck says of her family, "We were a strange little band of characters trudging through life sharing diseases and toothpaste, coveting one another's desserts, hiding shampoo, borrowing money, locking each other out of our rooms, inflicting pain and kissing to heal it in the same instant, loving, laughing, defending, and trying to figure out the common thread that bound us all together."[13] Home is a place marked by close proximity, where people see you at your most unadorned, unspectacular, and human. If you are a false or superficial

Christian, your family will know it first. In this environment, only sincere and sustained transformation will convince people that Christ is at work in you. The upside of this truth is that if you remain authentic and gracious as you minister the gospel in this setting, your testimony is far more credible and effective as well.

God's teachings about divorce and remarriage balance hard words with mercy; ours should too.

History: Land mines have historically been one of the most difficult and deadly weapons troops have faced in times of combat, and undiscovered ones can do horrific damage to civilians even years after the war ends. There are several ways to deal with land mines. Some armies develop armored vehicles with mechanical flails to intentionally detonate the mines and clear a path for vehicles. Other armies focus on specially trained personnel searching for and digging up mines by hand at great personal risk. The issue of divorce and remarriage in Christian circles is like a minefield we all want to navigate without losing limbs. Some might take the minesweeper approach and simply plow a path through the issue and let the bodies fall where they will. Jesus is more the hand-digging type, and we should be too. We need to be willing to openly and honestly address explosive issues surrounding divorce and remarriage with the honesty that says, "This is not God's best" or "The church cannot endorse that choice," while displaying the compassion and tenderness that say, "I am willing to get down on my knees and dig in with prayer until God brings you the restoration and healing he desires."

Life's Circumstances and the Christian Testimony

Big Idea *Because the time until the return of Christ has been shortened, Christians must be careful to recognize how their present circumstances are useful avenues for the Christian testimony. Pursuit of change can steal the focus from undivided service to Christ.*

Understanding the Text

The Text in Context

Paul's pastoral discussion on marriage, divorce, and singleness moves to a climax in this section. Paul does not add more Christian rules to these concerns but places the issues in a grander theological framework, paralleling the discussion with the broader issues of human relationships and Christian faith. Given the proximity of the Lord's return, the eschatological reality of human experience, all Christian relationships should be guided by an overarching concern to please the Lord (7:29–31). Whether the relationship in question is ethnic (Jew/Greek), social (slave/free), or marital (married/single), Christians should let their eagerness to please God trump their anxieties about their worldly predicament. They can imitate their Lord regardless of their present circumstances. Paul's argument is not that the Corinthians should maintain the status quo but that they should realize how significant their confession of Christ

as Lord is for all earthly relationships and situations (cf. Gal. 3:28).

Interpretive Insights

7:17 *each person should live . . . just as God has called them.* Paul's somewhat redundant use of "each" (*hekastos*) reveals that his encouragement goes beyond a mere "just accept your situation" to center on God's unique calling on each person's life. The only rule that fits all, which Paul requires "in all the churches," is that Christ followers must focus on pleasing God; their present life situation is an avenue to live out this calling.

7:18–19 *He should not become uncircumcised.* Since the days preceding the Maccabean revolt (second century BC), some Jews had sought to remove their mark of circumcision to find greater acceptance in the Hellenistic world.[1] Whether some Corinthians may have used their Christian faith as a spiritual excuse to get an operation that helped them fit in while others sought to find spiritual advantage through being circumcised is somewhat irrelevant to Paul's rhetoric. His point is simply to say that Christ followers do not gain spiritual advantage or disadvantage from their religious or ethnic background. The only thing that matters is obeying God's commandments.

7:20 *Each person should remain in the situation they were in when God called them.* Context clearly requires that we translate *klēsis* ("calling"; NIV: "situation") as "life situation" (7:24, 26). Paul's aim is not to command Christians to consider their social, religious, or marital situation an unchangeable divine appointment but to help them consider their present life situation an avenue for Christian ministry. A specific life situation can change a person's service for God; it cannot hinder it.

7:21–23 *the one who was a slave . . . is the Lord's freed person.* In concentric circles, Paul expands his discussion from ethnic/religious issues (7:18–19) to social realities. Roughly one-third of the Roman population were slaves and another third freed slaves. Legally speaking, slaves were not "persons" and had no rights. Aristotle even calls a slave "a living tool."[2] Roman slavery, however, was not a uniform experience. Many slaves held significant positions in Roman households, and some were given opportunities to thrive through education and business endeavors.[3] Paul does not argue for the social status quo ("if you can gain your freedom, do so" [7:21]); he underscores that physical slavery cannot hinder full devotion to God. Relationship to Christ turns things upside down. Christ followers have been set free through their

purchase by Christ, while those who have physical freedom remain slaves of Christ.

7:24 *remain in the situation they were in when God called them.* The imperative *menetō* ("remain") is best understood as a hortatory plea: "let him or her remain." Paul's addition of the prepositional phrase "with God" (NIV: "as responsible to God") reemphasizes his point. The Corinthians, who are focused on upward mobility, should be more concerned with God's involvement in their present situation.

7:25–26 *Now about virgins: I have no command from the Lord.* By revisiting the issue of marriage, Paul completes his discussion on how Christian faith impacts social and interpersonal issues with a theological conclusion anchored in his anticipation of Christ's imminent return. His introductory "now concerning [NIV: 'about']" hints that he feels a question posed by the Corinthians needs further explication. His recognition that he does not have a command from the Lord is a mere disclosure statement; he does not have a specific Jesus saying to quote. The reference to his own opinion (*gnōmēn*) does not suggest that what he now says is spiritually unreliable or lacks authority. Rather, Paul specifies that a faithful (*pistos*) consideration of Jesus's

1 Corinthians 7:17–40

teaching will result in the exposition he now gives.[4]

Paul here adds a new category of people, the *parthenoi* ("virgins"). *Parthenos* can refer either to unmarried women of marriageable age or to young people, male or female, who have not yet engaged in sexual activity. Although a firm conclusion on which meaning Paul intended remains elusive, his inclusive *anthrōpos* in verse 26 ("person" rather than "man") and his male-directed advice in verse 27 suggest that he may have both genders in mind. At any rate, the "present crisis" (or "austere anxiety of the present time," *enestōsan anankēn*) should discourage both men and women from seeking to change their marital status. The "present crisis" possibly included the famine that hit Corinth in AD 51, which Paul could have considered a precursor to the new eschatological reality God would soon inaugurate (7:29). In light of this, Paul now introduces a slogan of his own (paralleling the Corinthian slogan quoted in 7:1): "It is good for a man [or 'person'] to remain as he is."

7:27–28 *you have not sinned . . . But those who marry will face many troubles.* It follows logically that those who are married should remain so, while those who are not should remain unmarried.

Paul considers this a good guideline, not a Christian mandate. If someone should choose to marry, it is not a sin. To remain unmarried is preferable simply because it spares a person from the worldly concerns that a marriage triggers. Being married in that context meant setting up a household, which might be difficult to sustain in the face of a severe famine.

7:29–31 *the time is short.* In light of Paul's earlier discussion (7:5), verse 29 should not be read as promoting sexual asceticism. Rather, as verses 30–31 show, Paul's rhetorical aim is to highlight the brevity of time and the impending appearance of a new eschatological reality (lit., "the time is shortened").[5] Verses 29–31 do not give prescriptive commands to specific behavior relating to spouses, personal emotions, possessions, and business. They speak of Christian focus giving a framework for behavior. With rhetorical finesse, these verses bring into relief that the new reality—that the present has no permanence and will pass away—must change the way Christians experience life. Therefore, "brothers and sisters" (*adelphoi*), Paul says, do not let your present situation become

Paul encouraged the Corinthian Christians to live differently in light of Christ's return. In 7:30 he tells "those who buy something" to live "as if it were not theirs to keep." In ancient Corinth, buying and selling would have occurred in shops adjacent to the forum in ancient Corinth. These are the remains of the northwest shops from the second century AD.

the arbiter of your experience and focus—the married shall be as the unmarried, the mourner shall rejoice, the rejoicing shall be as mourners, the rich as poor, those burdened by worldly worries as unburdened.[6]

7:32–34 *be free from concern . . . please the Lord.* Paul brings the focus back to the issue of marriage, simultaneously answering the Corinthians' question and using his answer as a case-in-point illustration for his larger perspective just outlined. His aim is to help them change their thinking so they become free from worldly anxieties[7] that keep them from recognizing God's direct involvement in their present circumstances and stifles their ability to please God (cf. 1 Tim. 5:5; Matt. 6:25; Luke 10:41). Paul's rhetorical play on "anxious" (NIV: "concerned") does not suggest that unmarried men somehow should have deeper anxieties about serving the Lord than married men. Rather, it is the privilege of the unmarried to focus on God without the responsibility of the family concerns belonging to the married. The same holds true of "pleasing" (*areskō*). Paul's paralleling of pleasing God and pleasing the wife does not suggest that he sees them as mutually exclusive or somewhat similar in quality. The distinction is one of unitary focus versus being pulled in several directions. There is nothing wrong with being married (7:28).[8]

Paul's reference to both unmarried women and virgins is not to make a sharp distinction between two groups but to be inclusive of all the unmarried—divorcees, widows, and the never married. The target of Paul's comments is those who are distracted in their service to God by their zealous focus on finding a spouse.

7:35 *for your own good . . . undivided devotion to the Lord.* As if to make sure no one takes his words as an expression of a Christian law, or for some reason considers his advice burdensome, Paul offers a strong motivation: "for your own good."[9] His concern is not that they remain unmarried but that they remain "undistracted" (*aperispastōs*; NIV: "undivided") in their devotion to Christ. That alone is proper behavior (*euschēmon*; cf. 1 Thess. 4:12) for a Christ follower.

7:36–38 *he who marries . . . does right, but he who does not . . . does better.* The difficulty posed by the lack of direct referents in verse 36 has created a debate among scholars and translators (see comments on possible translations in the endnote).[10] Paul's conclusion, however, is unmistakable. He does not side with the ascetics but speaks pastorally—neither those who are married nor those who are unmarried sin. Neither group can claim spiritual preeminence over the other. When he says the unmarried do "better," it reemphasizes that this is not a matter of right and wrong but a consideration of which situation best enables a person to give undistracted devotion to Christ. In Paul's own situation, remaining unmarried proves preferable in the pursuit of that goal.

7:39–40 *A woman is bound to her husband as long as he lives.* Paul's last word in this inclusive discussion on relationships concerns widows. The perfect tense of the verb "bound" (*deō*) explains that the commitment given in the past continues to have effect in the present—"as long as he lives" (cf. 7:27; Rom. 7:2). Divorce for the sake of remarriage is not an option for Paul. Although the parallel in Romans

7:2 suggests that this statement may be a simple reference to the Roman legal system, Paul seems here to allow for a theological reading of this forensic reality. What God has joined, humans should not separate (Matt. 19:6). Still, in light of 1 Corinthians 7:13–15, verse 39 cannot be understood as a one-size-fits-all rejection of remarriage for people whose former spouse remains alive.

but he must belong to the Lord. The qualification for remarriage after the spouse dies is that the new spouse is a part of the Christ community. Grammatically, "only in the Lord" (NIV: "but he must belong to the Lord") could refer to the widow's reflection of Christ's presence in her life. No matter whom she marries, she must act as a Christ follower, guided by her devotion to Christ. Context, however, as well as Paul's rather clear statement in 2 Corinthians 6:14, makes the former reading the most likely: Paul advises believing widows and widowers to remarry only a fellow believer.

Paul himself opted to remain unmarried and is convinced greater blessings will flow from that.[11] He is quick to remind the Corinthians that this is his opinion (*gnōmēn*)—not a flippant remark they can take or leave, but a thoughtful reflection from someone whose every word is bathed in prayer to seek spiritual guidance and wisdom from the Spirit of God.

Theological Insights

The most important life purpose for a Christian is to be faithful to Christ and his mission. When other life pursuits and desires take prominence, they can blur this purpose. The call for the Christian is to focus on God's kingdom and trust God to take care of life's needs.

Teaching the Text

1. Dissatisfaction with present circumstances is not a modern thing. Self-promoting Corinthians considered worldly success an important life goal, if not a principal life focus. But Paul says there is no such thing as being trapped in a certain circumstance. Any circumstance is suitable to bear witness to Christ and to share the gospel. In fact, Christians *should* consider their present circumstance a gift from God designed to enable a testimony to his power and grace in that particular situation. Present circumstances are opportunities that should be treasured, not hindrances to be dreaded (Phil. 1:12).

2. Directly related to this is the question of occupation. If a distinction is made between occupation (job) and vocation (calling), Paul encourages Christians to consider their occupation a vocation. Paul coaches those who seem eager to change their present circumstance to look beyond their personal desire for self-fulfillment and seek God's guidance to choose what benefits his kingdom.

3. "Keeping up with the Joneses" is a human desire that mature Christians should eschew. Paul's statement that slaves are free in Christ while those who have been set free remain slaves of Christ reminds Christ followers that their motivation for success comes from a different place than the non-Christian's. Paul's broader argument, which runs as an undercurrent throughout this letter, that God alone is the patron Christians should worry about pleasing, finds a strong application in these verses. Social recognition in the cultural marketplace matters not at all; faithfulness to God's opportunities to demonstrate his presence is what matters.

4. Regardless of the Bible's clear teaching that marriage is ordained by God, Paul does not shy away from extolling the benefits of singleness for the kingdom. When singleness is a gift from God, it can release huge measures of extra energy to serve Christ. Far from a hindrance for effective ministry, Paul considers singleness a preferable vantage point from which to serve. His point is not that Christians should seek singleness over marriage but that singles should realize their situation could strengthen their service in God's kingdom.

5. The undercurrent of this passage is that not all things related to Christian teaching are either/or. Paul's pastoral guidance reveals his sensitive concern for people's and families' individual situations. Guiding principles lifted from the teaching of Scripture can lead to different conclusions in different situations where people are equally faithful to God's calling and purpose.

Illustrating the Text

Ask not, "How will God get me out of this situation?" but "How will God use me while I am here?"

Bible: Elaborate on Paul's own use of time when imprisoned for the faith. Point out that while God did get Paul out of many jams, Paul did more ministry and church leadership in jail than most modern ministers do in a lifetime packed with technology, freedom, and resources. He wrote letters, sent messengers, converted jailers and government officials, and preached to fellow prisoners. He had learned to focus on finding and knowing God's will in his situation and experiencing God's provision for ministry in the most dire of circumstances.

Personal Stories: Share a story about a time of crisis (car wreck, medical scare, untenable job situation, financial disaster, scrape with death, etc.). Share some of the deals and appeals presented to God and how he didn't answer them exactly as expected or asked. Then, tell how God did answer by granting himself and an abiding sense of his presence and how he used that situation and its effects to birth a testimony that is able to bless others in unexpected ways.

Contrasting Concept: In a psychological phenomenon known as the Stockholm syndrome, hostages being abused and even tortured by captors develop feelings of empathy and sympathy with their captors. People have tried to explain this in many ways, but the bottom line is that these feelings are an irrational way in which the human psyche attempts to survive trauma by bonding with one's tormentor and mistaking the commonality of the traumatic situation for intimacy. The intimacy we develop with God in the midst of suffering is different, first and foremost because of the cross. When we see the way Jesus willingly and soberly laid down his life for us, we know that our God is not a despot who manipulates us by torture but a bridegroom who loves us enough to endure our scorn to be with us. This suffering, then, is an opportunity to practically experience the goodness and mercy of God and transform it into a rich platform for compelling testimony.

Consider Others Higher Than Yourself

Big Idea *Genuine knowledge of Christ causes a believer to consider how personal behavior affects the faith of fellow believers. Christian love and care for others must trump personal rights.*

Understanding the Text

The Text in Context

Paul now takes up the next question posed by the Corinthians in their letter (cf. 7:1).[1] Moving from the larger question of human relationships, with a special focus on marriage, divorce, and singleness, he now takes up another pertinent question that relates directly to the domestic situation of the Corinthian believers, which includes relatives, friends, and co-workers. What about the meat Christ followers were served at dinner parties? Were Christians allowed to eat whatever they could buy in the marketplace? (See the "Additional Insights" following this unit.)

This relief from the end of the fifth century BC shows a ram and bull as sacrificial offerings.

Interpretive Insights

8:1 *We know that "We all possess knowledge."* Still speaking as a pastor, Paul immediately steps away from the specific case-in-point issue to deal with the underlying social issues of pride, prominence, and personal rights. Rather than simply pontificating his opinion on the matter, he teaches the believers how to think "Christianly" by establishing a theological foundation on which to build his argument.

The "stronger" Christians claimed to have knowledge (*gnōsis* [8:1, 7, 10–11]). *Gnōsis* functioned as a Corinthian buzzword used to parade superiority. Paul's ingenious insertion of "all" into the pithy *gnōsis* claim (we *all* have knowledge) levels the playing field within the Christ community. Everyone knowing the teachings of Christ can claim *gnōsis*. The *gnōsis* of

Christ, however, is of a different quality. The *gnōsis* generally claimed by Corinthian elites aimed to destroy community—it puffs up.[2] The *gnōsis* of Christ, on the contrary, generates love and aims to build up the community.

8:2 *Those who think they know something do not yet know as they ought to know.* As if to unplug all attempts at pride and superiority, Paul reminds the Christ community that all present knowledge remains partial (13:12). Those who claim to already possess knowledge (as would later become a full-blown claim by the gnostics) must realize that such is "not yet" possible.[3] Wisdom comes from humility before God, who alone knows sufficiently (3:18; cf. Gal. 6:3). Christ alone possesses the full measure of knowledge (Col. 2:3); those who live to incarnate his teaching will gain true knowledge—partly now, fully when he appears.

8:3 *whoever loves God is known by God.* The connection between the imitation of Christ and knowledge comes to full light in Paul's pregnant statement on the true significance of *gnōsis*. In the tersest of statements, Paul switches from the active form of the verb ("they know" [8:2]) to the passive form ("is known" [8:3]), making relationship with God the direct origin of *gnōsis*. Even more powerfully, he connects this with the believers' incarnation of the Christian lifestyle.

Several old manuscripts lack the word "God" in the first part of the sentence. If this is the original reading, it makes Paul's statement even more powerful: "We do not yet know, but if we love (one another) [i.e., imitate Christ], we will be known by God." To the Christian, it is more important to be known by God than to parade personal

Key Themes of 1 Corinthians 8:1–13

- Christian behavior cannot be guided by simple "right" and "wrong" considerations.
- Christian knowledge originates in Christ's life and teaching and must be guided by that.
- Christian knowledge must inform and then transform preconversion habits.
- Christian thinking must overcome the lure of individualism and personal rights.

knowledge (cf. Gal. 4:9; 2 Tim. 2:19).[4] Love and knowledge should not be separated in Christian understanding.

8:4 *about eating food sacrificed to idols.* Having established the foundation for true knowledge, Paul returns to the question, Can Christ followers eat idol meat? Verse 4 reads almost like a "for the record" statement. Paul says, "Let me begin by the clear biblical assertion that idols are a figment of people's imagination; since there is only one God, idols do not exist in reality" (cf. Deut. 6:4; 32:39; Isa. 41:29; 44:6, 9–17; Jer. 10:3–11).

8:5 *so-called gods, whether in heaven or on earth.* Idols may not exist in reality, but idol worship does. Although idols are only "so-called gods," cultic worship of them was the daily experience of the people in Corinth. Participation by the general public in the cultic celebration of gods, be they powerful earthly rulers (*kyrioi*)[5] or imagined heavenly beings (*theoi*), gave the very setting of the Greco-Roman culture an idolatrous flavor.[6]

8:6 *yet for us there is but one God, the Father.* Paul likely quotes a confessional statement already known to the church, maybe a hymn sung when the Christ followers met to worship. Paul uses it as a Christian confession in this context for a double purpose. It places the Christian faith in a category that is incomparable to the general temple-worship scene in Corinth, and it reminds the "weak" believers that the so-called gods of the temples remain powerless. For Christian believers there is "but one God, the Father," and "one Lord, Jesus Christ, through whom all things came and through whom we live." Put differently, the way to fulfill God's purpose in creation is through Jesus Christ. The source of *gnōsis* is Christ, not *Sophia* ("Wisdom").[7] The *gnōsis* of Christ teaches the "strong" to consider the weak before themselves and sets the weak free to recognize Christ's power over man-made gods.

8:7 *But not everyone possesses this knowledge.* Paul reveals here that the "weak" are the new converts to Christ or those whose understanding has not yet been shaped by their relationship to Christ and Christian teaching. These have not fully let go of their former understanding and spiritual allegiances; they still consider meat an element of pagan worship. Therefore, when they see the "strong" eat meat, they conclude it is possible to worship Christ and idol gods at the same time. This leads them away from Christ and back into sin.

8:8 *we are no worse . . . and no better.* Eating or not eating meat does not prove anything in relation to God. The strong are not proving their Christian freedom by eating and do not gain special acceptance from God by proving they can eat idol meat without falling back into the thinking and behavior associated with idol meat. Idol meat is morally neutral. What is not morally neutral is the behavior of the strong.

8:9 *Be careful . . . not become a stumbling block to the weak.* Paul's characterization of certain Christ followers as "weak" may surprise modern sensitivities. He may, however, simply pick up the language used by the "strong" to describe those who have raised concern about their practice of eating idol meat. This is the first time Paul directly refers to a group as "the weak." In verse 7, he refers to those whose conscience is weak, but he does not label a group that way. The "strong" may have done so, as Paul's substantival adjective ("the weak ones") seems to indicate. It is worth noticing that Paul never labels a group or certain individuals as "the strong" or "the knowledgeable." His point is that if the knowledge they have in this area truly originates from Christ, it should lead them to consider how they can use this knowledge to

The exercise of a believer's rights to participate in pagan activities for social gain could be a stumbling block to other believers. One example of this may have been attendance at the imperial cult sacrifices offered as part of the Isthmian Games. This *kylix* (wine drinking cup) decoration shows a young boar being sacrificed (ca. 510–500 BC).

strengthen those who still struggle with their former way of life. Shifting to second-person plural, Paul speaks directly to those who consider themselves knowledgeable and warns, "Be careful. Your actions [lit., "your right"; *exousia*] can become a stumbling block for those you call weak."[8]

8:10 *For if someone with a weak conscience sees you . . . eating in an idol's temple.* Paul's sentence structure seems to set up a hypothetical scenario rather than refer to an actual event he has been told about. Dining rooms were common in pagan temples, but it is likely Paul here refers to the imperial cult (the official Roman religion of emperor worship), as Winter points out.[9] Sacrifices offered in the imperial cult were an essential part of the Isthmian Games (see "Sport and Tourism" in the introduction), and participation may have been significant for public prominence. Those using a theological argument ("God is one") to claim a personal right may in actuality confuse their own desire for prominence with genuine Christian knowledge. Paul sees right through that and now restates his earlier question in a most contrastive way. From warning them about bruising the weaker believers' walk with Christ, he now asks those who consider themselves knowledgeable if they by their actions are trying to encourage (lit., "build up" or "edify"; *oikodomeō*) the weak's return to paganism. In other words, "are you trying to educate the weak in the wrong direction?"[10]

8:11 *weak brother or sister, for whom Christ died, is destroyed.* The strong may look overbearingly, or with disdain, at the weak, but their own actions may express the gravest of sins. They may find themselves destroying what Christ died to rescue (Col. 1:13).[11] Paul's language could not be any stronger. Christian knowledge, which comes from Christ, works from a position of love in an effort to strengthen the faith of others. By contrast, the knowledge of those who consider themselves strong works from a position of personal rights and results in the destruction of the faith of others (Rom. 14:15). This reference to the very center of Christian faith, Christ's saving death (1 Cor. 15:3), highlights the severity of such indifference toward the faith of fellow Christ followers. They are not just in disagreements over minor matters; they are working actively to undo what Christ came to do.

8:12 *When you sin against them . . . you sin against Christ.* As if to make sure the strong do not miss his point, Paul puts it succinctly: to sin against a fellow Christ follower is to sin against Christ. The emphasis remains on causing them to stumble, not on offending sensibilities. Paul's concern is for the newer Christians whose faith might be shattered by the actions of the more mature Christians, not for the mature Christians whose sensitivities are offended by the behavior of the younger Christians.

8:13 *Therefore . . . so that I will not cause them to fall.* The Greek *dioper* expresses a strong logical connection with the preceding verse. To avoid sinning against Christ, Paul would "therefore" (*dioper*) not eat meat if there were a chance it could cause others to sin or could bring their faith down (*skandalizō*). Rather than condemning the strong and giving arguments to the weak, Paul shifts to the first-person singular. In effect he says, "My rights are worth nothing compared to the importance of strengthening the weak."

Theological Insights

Because imitation of Christ is the foremost purpose of the Christian life, personal rights hold second place compared to the importance of strengthening a fellow believer or bringing a clear testimony to an unbeliever.

Teaching the Text

1. Many serious Christians are focused on right and wrong. They want to do right. Life is often easier if we have a rule to follow and can distinguish between right and wrong. Paul's concern in this text is not that wrong can ever be right but that right sometimes can be wrong. Eating meat sacrificed to pagan gods is a case in point. Following the teaching of Christ (Matt. 15:11), Paul stresses that nothing is wrong with eating meat, regardless of its connection to pagan rituals. Meat in itself is good, and Christians have the right to eat it. However, Christians must follow an overarching theological principle that guides all singular issues. Does a given action reflect the love of Christ? Could the action negatively affect another believer's relationship to Christ? If so, a "right" action becomes wrong.

2. Christians are not individuals following a behavioral rule book; they are followers of Christ who, filled with his Spirit, aim to imitate him. Christians who are serious about their faith are often bombarded with information overload concerning God's will. Christian television personalities, websites, books, ministers, songwriters, and so on often parade a plethora of disparate teachings on true Christian living. "Knowledge" seems to abound. Paul's teaching in these verses proves helpful in such situations. The way to discern if a teaching is Christian in the true sense of the word is to measure it against the life and teaching of Jesus Christ. Does it focus on the rights and privileges of "me," or does it emphasize a true concern for the growth and spiritual strengthening of others? Common knowledge derives from a variety of sources; the knowledge Christ inspires flows from the awareness of his suffering and sacrifice on behalf of others.

3. Paul directs his pastoral concern in this chapter toward mature and immature Christians alike. He seems to mostly address the strong, but his encouragement for the weak to realize the truth of the "knowledgeable" remains throughout the text. His real aim is to help all Christians to recognize that the knowledge gained from Christ must *inform* and generate a desire to *transform* their preconversion habits. To become a Christian is not merely a matter of mental assent (information) but a call to follow Christ (transformation). Although habits formed over extended periods of time are hard to break, they must be transformed by Jesus's Spirit (Phil. 1:19–21). Spiritual *formation* often requires a significant *reformation* of old habits. Paul's balance in this text is to emphasize that both the weak and the strong are called to encourage such reformation among each other.

4. The lure of self-elevation always looms. In Western societies, where individualism reigns supreme and Christians often consider their faith a personal and private matter, it proves easy to conclude

that each person is solely responsible for his or her own faith. Paul faced a similar reality in a new and competitive Corinth, where the newly wealthy among people who did not historically belong to the "noble" families claimed rights and personal privileges. Parading privileges deemed necessary for social promotion became the norm. Paul rejects such individualism among Christians. He removes on christological grounds any argument suggesting that the weaker Christian "just has to deal with the confusion the lifestyle of the stronger Christian causes." Those belonging to Christ are first and foremost responsible to strengthen the faith of the community; personal and individual rights come second. In Paul's thinking, human rights do not equal personal rights for a Christian.

Illustrating the Text

Wrong will never be right, but without selfless love, right can become wrong.

Human Metaphor: Share several scenarios in which a person's right to do a thing becomes inadvisable because of love for another person who would be adversely affected. For example, a couple marries and discovers that one is severely allergic to the other's beloved pet. Or a father who enjoys growing a beard discovers that it petrifies an infant daughter for a season of her childhood. Or perhaps a person who is legally allowed to drink alcohol discovers that a dear friend is a recovering alcoholic. Suggest the various responses that a person may have the right to offer ("go see a doctor or sleep in the basement—I love this cat," "she's got to get over it—I'm not the only man in the world with a beard," or "I love a cold beer on a hot summer day—get over it"), and contrast them with a response governed by love that sets aside personal rights in order to serve and honor weaker brothers and sisters. (If your church uses grape juice during communion in order to protect "weaker" consciences regarding alcohol, point this out as an example of loving accommodation in the life of the congregation.)

Prior to heaven, we never graduate from humility and personal sacrifice.

Bible: John 13:12–17 and Philippians 2:1–11. If no servant is greater than his or her master, and if Jesus (the greatest, and our master) served and sacrificed his entire life on earth (poured himself out and became a curse for our sake), then we should not expect a different outcome in our lives. We must never seek to elevate ourselves over others, shirk our cross, or graduate to a status of nobility that exempts us from humility and personal sacrifice.

Church Government: Teach about what leadership means in your congregation and how those who lead and steward the congregation show servant leadership after the example of Christ. Point out that sometimes the things that most qualify someone for leadership in the business world, in the military, and so forth are not at all related to what qualifies someone for leadership in the body of Christ. If you have any documents that define leadership in your organization or explain your vetting process for finding leaders of biblical character, or even a class for leadership training, point people to those resources for further study.

Meat Sacrificed to Idols

The question in chapter 8 relates directly to the issues Paul deals with in chapter 10. In chapter 8 Paul seems rather easygoing, playing down meat's "participation" in pagan worship. The contrast to chapter 10, where Paul expresses deep frustration with the pagan practices of some, could not be any stronger. Some scholars even consider the difference between the two chapters so stark that they think the chapters originally belonged to two different letters from Paul. It is more likely, though, that Paul addresses two different groups of people in the church. The "stronger," who pride themselves in their "knowledge," claim that their Christian faith teaches them the existence of only "one God" and that they therefore have the right to eat anything. Idols have no real existence. Whether they participate in cultic meals at the pagan temples or serve meat from there in their homes has no impact on their Christian faith. These "strong" likely belong to the financially secure and politically prominent end of society. The other group, "the weak" (or cautious), is not convinced by these arguments, and they vocally express their worries (or criticisms) toward the stronger. Most of these likely belong to the poorer ranks of the society. They are not only weak in faith but inferior in status and influence.

Fee argues strongly that the issue in chapter 8 primarily deals with participation in the cultic meals served at pagan temples (8:10).[1] However, Paul's rather relaxed treatment of the idolatrous aspect in this chapter compared to his firm statements on the strong's consideration of the weak indicates that his main concern may be to eliminate social divisions within the Christ community and highlight how Christian values must transform common thinking about community responsibility.

Idol meat could be eaten in the courtyard of an idol's temple (8:10); it could be bought in the marketplace (10:25) and served at domestic dinner parties (10:27). Since not all the meat of an animal offered as sacrifice was burned, "leftovers" were sold at the market. Often idol meat (eidōlothytōn [8:4]) would be the only meat available. At other times, city temples supplied idol meat to citywide festivals, thereby making meat available to those who never had it otherwise.[2]

At times when meat that had not been used in idol worship was available alongside the idol meat, the different kinds may not have been easily distinguishable for customers at the butcher's counter. Corinthian Christians who tried to avoid idol meat were therefore faced with the difficulty of determining whether the meat they were purchasing had been part of a pagan sacrificial ritual.

Adding insult to injury, Isenberg hints, from a quote in *Vita Aesopi*, that sacrificial pig tongues were blended with other meats, maybe even as an "irrecoverable sly dig aimed at the early Christians."[3] If

Idol meat could be purchased in the Corinthian marketplace. This inscription was part of a Roman meat and fish market (27 BC–AD 14).

such a scenario subconsciously is a part of Paul's discussion, his pastoral discussion on meat includes a delicate treatment of Jew-Gentile fellowship issues as well. Paul needed to tread carefully in dealing with an issue that may have been both an ethnic and status issue.

Meat was expensive in the first century, if it could be found at all, and was not the daily food of most Corinthians. Enjoying meat in a private home was therefore a luxury enjoyed by the wealthy. That, of course, created a real dilemma of fellowship between members of the Christ community. Invitations to dinner parties where meat was served put the weak in a difficult predicament, and the temptation to experience the luxury of tasting meat likely caused genuine soul searching. The strong, however, had no qualms; it was a rather "normal" experience for them. Paul's pastoral response to the weak was: go ahead—eating meat will not violate your relationship to God. To the strong he said: do not claim your own rights, but instead make sure you do not frustrate the faith of the weaker believer.

Meat Sacrificed to Idols

Personal Rights and Christian Testimony

Big Idea *Personal rights must be put aside when they hinder an effective witness to unbelievers, or if they endanger the faith of immature believers. Even theological arguments that disclose certain behaviors as immaterial to the Christian faith become irrelevant in light of the greater assignment to imitate Christ.*

Understanding the Text

The Text in Context

The transition from chapter 8 seems quite abrupt. Is Paul taking a ninety-degree turn from a question about participation in Corinthian parties (eating meat) to his rights as an apostle to receive monetary compensation for his work as an evangelist? Probably not! The thread that binds the two sections together is personal rights (*exousia*; e.g., 8:9 and 9:4–6). Paul continues his discussion of rights by underscoring that he himself has every right to command and require just about anything from the Corinthians. He is an apostle, uniquely called by Christ, and he is the agent Christ has used for their salvation. If they want to speak of rights, he is their spiritual patron, and they are his spiritual clients (9:2; cf. Philem. 19b). They owe him!

Interpretive Insights

9:1 *Am I not free?* Picking up the claim of the "strong" from chapter 8, Paul states that if that is true of them, it is even more true of him (2 Cor. 11:23). In terms of social freedom (not being a slave, or a mere tool of a master), he belongs to no one; he is a Roman citizen (Acts 25:10–12, 21, 25; 26:32). In terms of spiritual freedom, he is a freedman in Christ, even one called to be an apostle. If the strong claim their rights on the basis of freedom, Paul has more reason to do so—yet he does not use his freedom for personal benefit (9:19).

Am I not an apostle? Some scholars have suggested this rhetorical question is Paul's defense against those who questioned his apostleship. However, if the Corinthians had questioned his apostleship, his following defense of special rights would have been wasted on his audience. It would seem strange if his major defense of his apostleship was the waiving of his rights as an apostle. It seems more likely that this reminder of his rights was met with full affirmation. The sting of his emphasis, then, was that although he had all kinds of rights, he gladly gave them all up for the sake of the gospel (9:23). His rhetorical question is simply another way of, once again, telling the Corinthians, "Imitate me" (4:16; 11:1).

Are you not the result of my work in the Lord? Paul is careful *not* to claim the Corinthians are *his* church or to suggest that he is the cause of their salvation. Rather, Corinth is God's field (3:9), and the existence of a Christ community in Corinth has resulted from Paul's faithfulness as God's field worker (3:6).

9:2 *Even though I may not be an apostle to others, surely I am to you!* "Others" likely refers to nonbelieving Corinthians. The statement is not defensive (as Gal. 1:6–7; 5:10; Rom. 3:8) and thus does not imply that a group inside the Corinthian church, or a Christ community in a different city, has rejected Paul's authority as an apostle. Rather, he says, "If nonbelievers do not recognize I am a messenger of Christ, certainly you do."[1]

Key Themes of 1 Corinthians 9:1–12

- One's own personal rights are insignificant.
- The Christian's concern should be for the community of faith.

you are the seal of my apostleship. A seal is a stamp that proves authenticity or genuineness. The Corinthians recognize Paul's rights as an apostle because their own existence as Christ followers demonstrates his apostleship (2 Cor. 3:3; 10:13–15).

9:3 *This is my defense.* In the Greek "this" (*hautē*) concludes the sentence rather than beginning it. Paul does not suggest that what he just said was a defense. To the contrary, what follows becomes his explanation or argument (*apologia*; NIV: "defense") against the "strong" when they question why he defends the "weak." Verses 1 and 2 function as a reminder that gives the basis for what he is about to argue in the following verses.

9:4–7 Paul's list of rights uses the case in point as the springboard for a larger discussion of the principle involved. The rhetorical questions in verses 4–5 can be answered only in the affirmative by those toward whom his argument is directed. Surely he has the right to participate in dinner parties and various meals (cf. 6:12).[2]

9:5 *the right to take a believing wife along with us.* Given Paul's previous discussion, this cannot refer to his own wife and must therefore be an example of how Paul would have the right to ask the church to supply the needs for both himself and a wife. "Believing wife" is literally "a sister wife"; although "sister" (*adelphē*) refers to a female believer, the reference cannot be to a female believer who traveled with Paul. As Collins points out, "In the Mediterranean world a woman who traveled with a man would enjoy his protection but if she were not his wife she would have been considered a prostitute."[3] Although Paul's rhetoric here is designed to highlight his rights, it also gives very early evidence of a pattern of Christian couples traveling together to spread the gospel.

as do the other apostles and the Lord's brothers and Cephas. "Other apostles" can refer to "the Twelve" (15:5), to Paul's co-workers (Phil. 2:25; Rom. 16:7), or to other unspecified evangelists (cf. 15:7; 2 Cor. 11:5; some are false apostles [2 Cor. 11:13]). Whom he specifically has in mind cannot be determined with certainty. The Lord's brother James and Cephas are singled out because they are recognized by the Corinthian believers. Peter's marriage is well known and mentioned in the Synoptic Gospels (Matt. 8:14–15; Mark 1:29–31; Luke 4:38–39).[4]

9:6 *Or is it only I and Barnabas.* The strained relationship that developed between Paul and Barnabas after the first missionary journey apparently had been healed (Acts 15:36–41). Although Paul did not bring Barnabas on his so-called second missionary journey, Barnabas must have been known among the Corinthians and recognized for approaching ministry and work in a way similar to Paul (1 Thess. 2:9). In a culture where landowners often belonged to the privileged societal class, Barnabas's willingness and need to work after (because?) he had given his land to the church would not have gone unnoticed (Acts 4:36–37). Paul, like a good rabbi, had learned a skill that sustained him while teaching (Acts 18:3).

9:7 *Who serves as a soldier . . . plants a vineyard . . . tends a flock and does not drink the milk?* To bring his point home, Paul utilizes three "that's obvious" illustrations posed as rhetorical questions with a given affirmative answer. Soldiers do not supply their own food while serving;[5] those planting a vineyard clearly eat of its fruit (Deut. 20:6); those shepherding a flock of sheep drink of the milk the sheep produce. The three images are all well known from the Hebrew biblical texts and underscore the basic and natural relationship between a worker and the work. Paul does not argue in favor of compensation for hire (as if a vinedresser got paid in grapes or a shepherd in buckets of milk) but brings home his point that as an apostle who has fought for the Corinthians, planted them as a vineyard in God's kingdom, and shepherded them as sheep in God's flock, he has certain evident rights.

9:8–12a *Do I say this merely on human authority?* Reiterating that he is not trying to simply make a rhetorical argument, as was so common among the sophist street-philosophers of Corinth, Paul points to the Torah to give foundation for his claim. Still *not* attempting to persuade doubting Corinthians of his rights, Paul uses texts from the Hebrew Bible (Deut. 25:4) to remind his audience that his rights are rooted in Scripture ("Doesn't the Law say the same thing?" [9:8]). Since the Corinthians agree, his later argument, that he willingly gives up rights that are obviously his, will strike with even stronger force.

Do not muzzle an ox while it is treading out the grain. The quote from Deuteronomy 25:4 sets the stage for Paul to give a typical rabbinical *qal wahomer* (from lesser to greater) argument.[6] Oxen, the lesser matter, are not the real concern of the text; rather, God's command gives direction to his people, the greater matter.[7] Paul neither attempts a wild-eyed allegorical exposition nor tries to pick a fight with animal lovers.[8] He simply applies a fully accepted method of interpretation to demonstrate his point.[9] When God gives guidelines for the threshing floor, it brings hope to those plowing, sowing, and threshing that they will share in the crop. Since Paul has plowed, sowed, and brought a harvest to God's threshing floor in Corinth, he has the divine right to benefit from it. In fact, if other apostles have come through Corinth and have rights in this harvest, Paul has more.

9:12b *we did not use this right.* In 7:21 Paul encouraged slaves to "take advantage" (*chraomai*; NIV: "do so") of an opportunity to become free. Here he refuses to "use" (*chraomai*) his own rights to do the same. He is a slave of Christ and has no desire to take advantage of an opportunity to be set free from that. Rather, he is willing to "put up with" or "endure"[10] the burden in order not to hinder or hold back the progress of the gospel (10:33). This, again, reminds the Corinthians of Paul's imitation of Christ (and consequently their need to imitate him [11:1]), who also gave up his rights for the sake of the gospel (2 Cor. 8:9; Phil. 2:7).

Theological Insights

In Christian thinking, God's community trumps individual rights. As is clear

Paul quotes from the Old Testament, "Do not muzzle an ox while it is treading out the grain" (9:9), to make his point about a laborer deserving compensation. This copy of an Egyptian wall painting shows oxen treading grain (tomb of Menna, Thebes, 1422–1411 BC).

throughout Scripture, the action of the individual impacts the whole (e.g., Josh. 7; cf. Josh. 6:25).

Teaching the Text

1. If one thing stands out in this chapter, it is the issue of personal rights of individual Christians. Paul's theological discussion of meat may seem rather irrelevant to most modern Christians; his point, however, remains as relevant as ever. A large variety of issues facing contemporary Christians raise the same theological question that faced the Corinthians. If, for example, participation in a certain setting arguably is harmless to a person's Christian confession of Jesus as Lord, does this automatically justify such participation? Paul's balance gives good direction: (1) He does not condemn those whose actions are being questioned. (2) He highlights the greater principle of forgoing personal rights in the effort to imitate Christ. Paul's concern is that the "strong" Christians do not cause the "weak" Christians to lose faith. He is not concerned that the strong Christians may feel offended by the weak Christians. To the strong he says, "Your rights are irrelevant—your greater commission is to imitate the Christ who gave up his rights in order to make salvation possible for others."

2. Paul's focus is the community of Christ followers. His emphasis on forgoing personal rights centers on every Christian's responsibility for the whole community of faith. In Paul's thinking, all questions of rights are communal. The task of Christ's community is to exemplify Christ. That is done by taking care of the weakest members. Stronger (and more mature)

One of the credentials Paul could have used to demand his rights was that he saw Jesus. Paul's dramatic encounter with Christ on the road to Damascus is depicted in this painting by Nicolas-Bernard Lepicie (1735–84).

Christians should see it as their task to strengthen the faith of weaker Christians. In effect, Paul dismantles Christian elitism and eliminates "worldly" distinctions. The "strong" were often the wealthy and well educated—the "weak" the poor and uneducated. Christ calls those in his community to rethink their relationship to each other and to realign their relationships to reflect his gospel. Paul's teaching on rights, then, speaks as much to issues of wealth and privilege, race and gender, as it does to narrower questions of behavior in specific issues (e.g., teetotalism). The Christian community must stand in radical contrast to the broader Corinthian community in its care for the weak.

Illustrating the Text

As a Christ follower, you have the right to remain silent . . . about your rights.

Television: We have all watched crime shows in which a person is read his or her Miranda rights; that is, he or she is "mirandized." If we were mirandizing a newly convicted and converted sinner in the ways of grace in God's kingdom, the script would be a little different: "Child, you have the right to remain silent from now on about your rights. You gave them all up when Christ bought you with his blood, and you forfeited any claim you thought you had on your person, your possessions, and your life. You are not your own, but belong body and soul, in life and in death, to him. If the Lord of the universe gave up all of his rights for a sinner like you, let's have no more quibbling from you about yours; you have already been given that which you had no right to expect in order to nullify the damnation you were fully entitled to receive."

Christian community is meant to be "one for all, and all for one."

Literature: *The Three Musketeers*, **by Alexandre Dumas.** In this swashbuckling adventure, three friends famously pledge to be "one for all, and all for one" in their fellowship. The idea behind this motto is that the full loyalty and strength of each individual is at the disposal of the others and that, conversely, the collective power of the fellowship is available to each individual member, such that battles and adversities affecting one member will be met with the resources and ingenuity of all. In the same way, Christian community is meant to be a situation where the individual's gifts benefit the whole body and vice versa.

Personal Stories: Interview a short-term-mission team about the group dynamics on their trip. Often, in a setting like this, a sense of community and commonality is established in a way not often experienced by people in Western culture. Ask members of the team to share stories about how the ups and downs of the trip brought them together and how they experienced a sense of commonality and "having each other's backs" in the work they did, the challenges they faced, and the kingdom impact they made.

Financial Support and Freedom to Preach the Gospel

Big Idea *One must be careful to avoid situations that can force limitations upon one's freedom to preach the gospel. One's own personal rights that would stand in the way of preaching the gospel must be disregarded.*

Understanding the Text

The Text in Context

Paul's rights extend to receiving financial help from the Corinthians. He could easily have claimed their monetary support, but he has abstained even from this benefit. For the sake of the gospel, he is more than willing to give up any rights for the greater purpose of leading new people into the Christ community and of strengthening the faith of those who are already there (9:22–23). After all, just as they are, he is ultimately responsible to God—of whom they are clients through Christ (9:24–27).

Interpretive Insights

9:13–14 *those who serve in the temple . . . In the same way, the Lord has commanded.* Almost as if he has just thought of

another argument, Paul adds two more examples to his list. First, he refers to the cultic practices of Corinth. The priests handling the sacred things (*ta hiera*), including the meat discussed in chapter 8, rightfully eat from the sacrifices and benefit from the offerings. Second, in an impressive display of rhetorical skill, Paul tops his list with a command of Jesus. The Corinthians who stubbornly hold on to their rights ought to consider Paul, who—beyond all the examples he has just given, including common Corinthian practices and scriptural

Those who served in the temple, like this woman who was a priestess at the temple of Artemis, received a portion of the sacrifices that were offered (Perge, Turkey, second century AD).

commands—even has instruction from Jesus himself about his rights; but he has given it all up (Matt. 10:10; Luke 10:7).[1]

9:15 *I have not used any of these rights.* Paul's point is not dissatisfaction, or a semi-concealed attempt to request assistance from the Corinthians. On the contrary, it is the very refusal of his rights that sets him free to preach the gospel.

I would rather die than allow anyone to deprive me of this boast. This somewhat-awkward-sounding phrase is rooted directly in the soil of patron-client relationships. Opening with a perfect-tense dismissal of his rights, Paul highlights the ongoing reality of the decision he made ("I am not writing this in the hope that you will do such things for me"; cf. 2 Cor. 11:9–10). The Corinthians boast of their rights; if Paul has any boast, it is in the disclaimer of his rights. Put differently, Paul's boast is a nonboast. In a society where the right relationships and associations determined social and financial progress, the ability to claim (boast about) rights was a double-edged sword, a privilege that came with strings. The rights that free and wealthier Corinthians could claim were secured by a patron (ultimately Caesar in Rome), who in turn could demand loyalty (see "Grace and Patronage" in the introduction). Paul owes nothing to anyone in Corinth. Since his only patron is Christ, he is bound only by his loyalty to Christ (1:31; 3:21; 2 Cor. 10:17).[2] That loyalty forces him to give up his personal rights when they potentially conceal Christ's significance.

9:16–18 *I cannot boast, since I am compelled to preach.* Paul's boast is a nonboast because he is without choice in the matter of his rights. His phraseology functions

simultaneously as an explanation for his refusal of their financial support and as an indictment of the Corinthians who have claimed freedom. Christ drove him (lit., "necessity is imposed upon me") to preach the gospel; something else drove them to claim their rights. Paul's "woe to me" may be his way of translating a Hebrew prophetic exclamation (e.g., Isa. 3:11; 5:11; 6:5; etc.),[3] but in the Corinthian situation it probably illustrates the severity of a servant's disloyalty toward a master. If Paul had been a free man, hired to preach the gospel, or if he had done so as a favor to a friend, he would have had a reward.[4] But, as it is, Paul's relationship to Christ is not one of equal status; rather, Paul is a household manager (*oikonomos*) entrusted with a task—a task normally given to a highly trusted slave (Luke 12:42–48).[5] Such a slave would have a high degree of freedom and trust from the master, but woe unto the slave if the task was not performed as charged and the trust was broken.[6]

What then is my reward? With extraordinary finesse, Paul draws his argument to a conclusion that exposes how the thinking of "strong" Corinthians is upside down from what it should be. It is exactly because Paul has given up his personal rights that he is free to make use of rights that benefit the gospel. That is his reward! Because he is preaching for free, without claiming his rights as the spiritual patron of the

Corinthian Christ followers, he has the right, and is set free, to preach the gospel to everyone.

9:19–23 *Though I am free and belong to no one, I have made myself a slave.* Paul summarizes the paradox of a Christ follower's lifestyle in yet another "imitate me" statement that gives content to his charge in 9:24. Verses 19–23 set the stage for his exhortation in verse 24, illustrating how his life exemplifies what theirs should be. Instead of focusing on their rights, they should "run in such a way as to get the prize" (9:24). The specific examples function as personal illustrations designed to highlight the goal. They are not designed to highlight Paul's achievements. He simply covers the fields of tension among the Corinthians—the areas that generated conflict between the "strong" who claimed rights and the "weak" whose faith was hurt or hindered because of those claims.

To the Jews I became like a Jew, to win the Jews. All the common English translations translate the Greek *Ioudaios* as "Jew." As a mere rhetorical contrast to Gentiles, such a translation seems natural. However, Paul obviously was a Jew, even a law-abiding one (Phil. 3:4–6). Emphasizing that he "became" a Jew to the Jews seems somewhat odd and suggests that Paul was less than a Jew to other groups. It is possible, therefore, that Paul refers to Judeans as an ethnic group distinguished from, for example, Galileans in their clothing and traditions.[7]

Traditionally, verses 20–21 are read as a simple contrast between Jews and Gentiles. On the surface it seems Paul argues in favor of a somewhat duplicitous approach to evangelism. When among Jews ("those under the law"), he keeps the law; when among Gentiles ("those not having the law"), he feels free to break the law. Part of the difficulty is Paul's wordplay in verse 21, which proves rather difficult to express in an English translation. He uses *anomos* four times, referring to those outside Jewish law, and *ennomos* ("under the law") once, referring to Christ's law. In regular Greek usage, the terms *anomos* and *ennomos* respectively mean "illegal" and "legal." Paul's parenthetical statement in 7:21 then highlights that his eagerness to be "legal" in relation to Christ's demands does not make him "illegal" in relation to God's. Paul does not argue in favor of duplicity (the end justifies the means), but he underscores how his personal rights and preferences must be put aside for the sake of evangelism (7:22).

I do all this for the sake of the gospel. Paul's motivation and purpose do not waver. He is driven by one vision and one love—that he may become a participant of the gospel. Verse 23b expresses his longing through a purpose statement (introduced by *hina*): "that I may share in its blessings," or "that I may become its participant" (lit., "co-sharer"). The reference is the gospel, not those he wins for it. To participate in the gospel means to participate in the life of Jesus, sharing in the suffering necessary to bring salvation to the weak and those outside God's community. This means bringing together the socially dependent and the socially superior, restoring love between alienated ethnic groups, and establishing a Christian community, where suffering for the sake of others finds direction and motivation from the death and resurrection of Jesus.

9:24–27 *Everyone who competes in the games . . . to get a crown.* A final motivational illustration puts Paul's point in the clearest light. Because the prominent Isthmian Games were celebrated biannually in Corinth, athletic illustrations function as explanations of "how things are." That an athlete competes to win a prize proves self-evident;[8] that Christians should focus on accomplishing their goal to become like Christ *should* prove just as self-evident. Paying the price by giving up all kinds of normal pleasures and rights, athletes compete for a prize that fades (a wreath made of pine or celery).[9] Christians should therefore be more than willing to give up their rights to receive a prize that never fades (imperishable, everlasting; 15:52; cf. 1 Tim. 1:17; 1 Pet. 1:4; 5:4; Rev. 4:10).

so that . . . I myself will not be disqualified.[10] This statement seems rather difficult to understand if approached from the perspective of Christian doctrines like the security of the believer. Paul's point, however, is not doctrinal in that sense. Rather, he stays within the illustration and speaks about the danger of not aiming to become Christlike—as an athlete who loses and therefore has trained in vain. The illustration still retains its soteriological force, though. The possibility looms that the faith of the weak vanishes. Just as an athlete cannot rest until the race is over, a Christian must work out his or her salvation with fear and trembling (Phil. 2:12). The Christian life is a process of being re-formed into the image of Christ. The active exercise of Christian life and faith keeps a person fit for the race and will result in a crown of victory that will be fully revealed at the second coming of Christ.

Teaching the Text

1. Paul's eagerness to underscore his independence of financial support from the Corinthian church must be understood from the background of their patron-client awareness. His emphasis on the rights of a laborer to receive support makes untenable any claim that gospel workers must work without financial support. Giving and receiving financial support creates a special relationship between the giver and the recipient. Negatively, this means that any support that comes with strings, or that puts the gospel worker in debt to certain individuals within the church,

"Everyone who competes in the games goes into strict training. They do it to get a crown that will not last" (9:25). This relief shows two contestants, each placing a crown on the head of a trainer and holding palm branches, which are symbols of victory (Athens, early third century AD).

must be refused. No messenger of Christ's gospel can afford to preach, or be seen as preaching, on behalf of anyone but Christ. Thus Paul has refused any support from Corinth. Positively, this means that when a church supports those teaching and sharing the gospel among them, a relationship is forged that makes the gospel workers and the church members participants in each other's lives and ministries. Thus Paul accepts support from the Philippians.

2. From the perspective of the church, Paul's teaching here points to the need for vigilance in ensuring that their financial support strengthens the kingdom of God. Positively, salaries and other financial support must come with encouragement for the beneficiaries to use the support in a way that honors Christ and expands his kingdom. Negatively, it is a reminder to the church or wealthy individuals in the church that they violate their trust from Christ if they try to use their financial support to "make" the beneficiaries minister only to their kind, in their way, or according to their interest.

3. The phrase "become all things to all people" (9:22) is easily misunderstood to mean that Paul suggests Christians should take a chameleon approach to behavior for the sake of evangelism. Actually, Paul's aim is directly contrary to this. The context is his willingness to give up personal rights, to not accept things that run contrary to the gospel or behave in a way that may devastate the faith of weaker Christians. Otherwise, Paul could simply have affirmed the "strong" Christians' rights to eat idol meat and argued on their behalf that they were merely trying to "become all things to all people." Paul's argument, however, runs the other way; he does not suggest a

willingness to compromise Christian convictions. We may summarize his statements like this: "To win the poor, I am willing to live like the poor; to win those with ethnic traditions different from mine, I am willing to change my preferences; to win those who have less freedom than I do, I am willing to give up my Christian freedom."

Illustrating the Text

The gospel transforms our identity and our values.

Business: The profit and loss statement, or P&L, is one of the key measures of a business's health. It summarizes income and expenses over a given period of time to provide a measure of success and financial well-being. Individuals likewise review bank statements to see how income lines up with expenses. And for both individuals and businesses, the effect on the balance sheet is a key deciding factor in evaluating actions. But in Philippians 4:7 Paul declares, "Whatever were gains to me I now consider loss," a fundamental reversal of values with regard to salvation that also permeates all of life. The gospel transforms our identity, from being self-focused to being Christ-focused. This same transformation occurs in the way we calculate value and purpose. We no longer live for ourselves but instead live to the Lord and for his purposes. In giving of our rights and our resources we discover and communicate that God's work is more important than our personal desires. Our motivation for giving is not personal benefit or earthly profit but kingdom benefit and gospel progress. Our personal benefit is a byproduct resulting from the gratitude that stems from our recognition that God has made us stewards of his household. We find our joy in how God has used us for his purposes.

We are called to set aside our rights and preferences to reach people who may be unlike ourselves.

Contrasting Concept: Worship wars and other battles over preferences in a church can turn this concept upside down. When the strong become offended by the spiritual needs of the weak, intolerance and inflexibility can carry the day. Rather than becoming all things to all people in order that by all means we might reach some, we become one thing to our people that by no means shall we be disturbed. The sincere worship of selfless servants acting as winsome ambassadors for the God who seeks and saves lost people is quickly endangered in this climate.

Biography: Father Damien. Father Damien was a Belgian Roman Catholic priest who took on a mission to an isolated colony of exiles on the island of Molokai, Hawaii, from 1873 to 1889. He was the first priest to volunteer to live and minister there among the 816 persons suffering from leprosy (also known as Hansen's disease), a choice that all knew could be a death sentence. He did not just minister as a priest; he dug graves, dressed wounds, built a church and coffins, and even researched the disease, inventing new surgeries and treatments to ease the suffering of the people. In explaining his actions to his brother via letter, he alluded to this passage of Scripture, saying, "I make myself a leper with the lepers to gain all to Jesus Christ." This was not only true

Paul writes, "To the Jews I became like a Jew, to win the Jews" (9:20). Although Paul forcefully made the point, illustrated by Titus (Gal. 2:3), that circumcision was not required for inclusion in the people of God, Paul had Timothy circumcised (Acts 16:3) to remove a possible barrier to effective ministry among the Jews. Timothy, like Paul, acted in service to the advance of the gospel, setting aside his freedom in order to overcome social barriers to evangelism. This stained-glass window depicting Timothy is originally from the church of Neuwiller in Alsace, France (AD 1160).

spiritually, but it was a prophetic statement as well. Damien contracted leprosy and began to suffer along with the people he came to serve. Leprosy took his life, and he died on Molokai in April 1889 at age forty-nine. He has been made a saint of the Roman Catholic Church and is known as a martyr of charity. His legacy shows the power of a willingness to sacrifice in order to reach others with the love of Christ and the power of his gospel.

1 Corinthians 9:13–27

Trust versus Self-Reliance

Big Idea *Christians who consider themselves mature must be careful not to confuse trust in God's grace with self-reliance. Rather than putting God's forgiveness to the test, they should focus on passing God's test, which will reveal that their primary and most trusted relationship is with him.*

Understanding the Text

The Text in Context

The key verse in this unit is verse 12: "So, if you think you are standing firm, be careful that you don't fall!" Using an example from the Hebrew Scriptures, Paul compares the self-confidence of the "strong" (chap. 9) to the attitude of the Israelites, who, in spite of having experienced God's mighty salvation through the sea, grumbled about their new situation. Instead of thanking God, they violated their covenant and put God to the test. Their example is a warning to the Christ followers who think themselves strong enough to participate in pagan feasts. Like the Israelites of old, they too might find themselves overcome with temptation. The God who gives freedom is also a jealous God who punishes all who participate in idol worship.

Interpretive Insights

10:1 *For I do not want you to be ignorant . . . that our ancestors.* The Greek connective *gar* ("therefore," "for this reason"; NIV: "for") identifies what follows as the explanation for why Paul keeps himself under control (9:27).

When Paul uses the Hebrew Scriptures' grand salvation narrative not only as the guiding framework for his personal narrative (chap. 9) but also as the "instructor" for Corinthian behavior, he intends to highlight the centrality of Israel's history for God's saving purposes. God's future does not disconnect from God's past. Those Moses led out of Egypt were the spiritual ancestors, not just of the Jews, but of the Corinthian Christ followers.

10:2 *baptized into Moses.* The experience of Moses became the experience of the people who through "baptism" were initiated into God's covenant with Moses (Exod. 19:5; 24:7–8; Deut. 5:2). Paul's typological use of the term "baptism" in this context can hardly be missed (cf. 10:6, 11). The Corinthians likewise entered into God's covenant through baptism. "In the cloud and in the sea" may indeed allude to both Jesus's initiatory baptism (under God's voice [cloud] and in the "sea") and their own experience of baptism in water and Spirit. Paul does not try to give a theology of baptism, but he gives an argument for allegiance to Christ and for the calling of the new covenant.

10:3–5 *ate the same spiritual food and drank the same spiritual drink*. Paul's typological parallel here goes directly to the Corinthian celebration of the Lord's Supper. Israel's experience of God's salvific care through food and drink finds a parallel in the Corinthians' experience of God's salvific care for them through their celebration of the Lord's Supper.[1] Paul's aim is not to correct an errant application of the "Christ meal"; he simply gives a typological argument that exposes the danger of forgetting God's jealousy in their reliance on God's grace. The God who revealed his grace by opening the sea also revealed his jealousy by leaving the Israelites' bodies "scattered in the wilderness" when they became idolaters (10:5).

Paul's comparison of the rock Moses struck in the desert to Christ has caused a flurry of discussions about Paul's hermeneutics. Paul's point, however, is not to give an allegorical, ahistorical interpretation of the wilderness rock. "Rock" was a well-known title for God.[2] Paul merely parallels Christ's presence among the Corinthians with God's providing presence in the wilderness.

The "spiritual drink" (10:4) that God provided to the Israelites in the wilderness was the water from the rock. This section of a sarcophagus lid from the fourth century AD shows Moses striking the rock and water coming forth.

- Christians must trust God rather than self for strength to remain faithful.
- Christians must not be presumptuous about God's love.
- Christians must realize the Bible's paradigmatic quality when describing how God interacts with his people.
- Christians must not reduce faith to a mere participation in religious rituals.

10:6 *Now these things occurred as examples*. The Greek word translated "example" is *typos*, which literally means a "mark" (or "trace") left by a blow or pressure.[3] It refers to an image or an impression. When applied to an event, it gives the event a formative characteristic. The event in the desert is not merely an example but a paradigmatic expression of how God works—it typifies something characteristic about God and people. The salvific event of the Hebrew Scriptures, the exodus–desert–promised land event, is thus a *typos* of the Christian experience of salvation in Christ. The historical specifics differ, but the character of God and the pattern of his actions do not. God expressed himself in these former events "so that" (*eis to*, expressing purpose or result; NIV: "to") Christians would not fall into the same.

setting our hearts on evil things. God was displeased with the people's cravings, as these revealed their dissatisfaction with God's provisions and their disregard for his zealous love.

10:7 *Do not be idolaters*. This is the first point in Paul's four-point list of evil cravings. The reference to the "strong" Corinthians is unmistakable. Participation in a banquet where idol meat was served brought with it the temptation to participate in other elements of the banquet.

got up to indulge in revelry. By quoting Exodus 32:6, Paul gives content to the temptations he has in mind. The most pronounced act of idolatry in the exodus wandering was the golden calf event at Sinai—an event where idolatry led to uninhibited drinking and sexual orgy. Paul's use of the Greek word *paizein* ("to play") on the backdrop of Exodus 32:1–6, therefore, does not suggest a mere lack of sincerity on the part of the Corinthians; it speaks to erotic dance and sexual immorality (10:8).[4] Paul's warning is not against the spiritual danger of the meat itself but against the temptation of its context.

10:8 *We should not commit sexual immorality*. Paul's choice of a first-person plural subjunctive ("Let us not . . . "; NIV: "We should not . . . ") rather than a second-person plural imperative brings a pastoral tone to the warning. He is not necessarily charging the Corinthians with sexual immorality but accentuating the danger of playing with fire—twenty-three thousand died in a single day because of idolatry (Num. 25:1–9).[5]

10:9 *We should not test Christ*. Paul presents his third point in the same pastoral tone as his second. Since the *typos* of Christ was the rock at Meribah, which exemplified God's undeserved blessing to a rebellious people (Exod. 17:6–7 to Num.

20:1–13), Paul's parallel flows naturally. When people refuse to recognize God's graciousness, God's judgment comes swiftly. Challenging God to prove his power after he so generously has revealed his saving grace is ill advised (Pss. 78:18–20; 95:8–9; Deut. 6:14–16).

killed by snakes. God sent poisonous snakes as punishment for the people's actions. This brought about another transformative moment of faith. As the people were bitten by the snakes, the only means of healing and salvation was to look to a bronze snake on a pole Moses had made on God's command (Num. 21:6–9; cf. John 3:14–16).[6]

10:10 *do not grumble*. On his fourth point, Paul returns to a direct command. Grumbling was the norm rather than the exception for Israel and a continuing cause for God's aggravation.[7] The sheer number of references to "grumbling" during the desert experience makes it difficult to determine Paul's direct point of reference in 10:10. Maybe Paul mentions Israel's grumbling because he has faced similar reaction from the "strong" as response to his stance against participation in the idol banquets.

There is no direct reference to "the destroying angel" in the context of grumbling in the biblical exodus account, but see Numbers 16:1–35.[8]

10:11 *happened to them as examples and were written down as warnings for us*. For the significance of "examples" (*typoi*), see comments on 10:6. Paul's then/now contrast stresses the significance of the Old Testament events as paradigmatic of God's interaction with his people (happened to

The incident in which the Israelites were "killed by snakes" (10:9) is found in Numbers 21:4–9. Because of their grumbling in the wilderness, God sent poisonous snakes, which killed many Israelites. When the Israelites confessed their sin, God instructed Moses to mount a bronze serpent on a pole. Anyone who was bitten and then looked at the bronze serpent would live. This bronze serpent was found in the inner chamber of the Midianite shrine at Timna.

them . . . written for us).[9] God's wrath and God's love are two sides of the same coin.

on whom the culmination of the ages has come. The geographical term "has come" (*katantaō*) speaks of destination ("arrive," "reach"). The destination point toward which all of time has moved is the event of Jesus Christ (Gal. 4:4; 1 Pet. 1:20). This event has now arrived and is the very event that called the Christ community in Corinth into being. The typological event Paul just referenced from Hebrew Scriptures is therefore particularly relevant for the church.

10:12 *So, if you think you are standing firm, be careful that you don't fall!* With proverbial precision, Paul summarizes his point in a most memorable and terse seven-word warning that in Greek includes no fewer than four verbal forms/moods and three verbal tenses.[10] Translating the grammatical points of Paul's expression into English would sound something like this: "As a result, the one who continues to think[11] that he/she is able to stand must remain watchful lest he/she may fall." Paul's point is not to sow a seed of uncertainty about faith but to warn against taking God's love for granted without considering his wrath. It is a warning against confusing self-reliance with trust in God.

10:13 *No temptation has overtaken you.* The Greek word *peirasmos* can mean "trial," "test," or "temptation." When the expected result is negative, translators prefer "temptation"; when a text expects a positive result, "test" proves preferable; "trial" hints at a period of struggle (cf. James 1:2, 14). In this text, there is no agreement among the English Bible translations. All three translations are possible.[12]

If Paul speaks to the weak (which would be a shift in emphasis), "temptation" could be a fitting translation. The weak could be tempted to participate in certain idol banquets for social prominence, financial security, or other reasons. If so, Paul recognizes the difficulty associated with declining an invitation to such an event and encourages them to recognize God's faithfulness (Deut. 7:9). If he speaks to the strong, however (which seems most likely), who consider participation in such banquets their right, the word "test" may best express the sense. If they abstain from participation in these idol banquets, they are heeding Paul's call to watch out that they do not fall. They will therefore pass the "test." God is faithful; his test is not intolerable—they will be able to endure it. The test reveals their willingness to follow Christ. They do not need to worry; God will provide a way out of the test (Gen. 22:1–19).

Theological Insights

From the earliest pages of Scripture, faith in God is described as a relational experience. It follows that Christian maturity expresses itself as eagerness to strengthen the relationship to God and as awareness of dependence on him—*not* as reliance on personal ability to accomplish God's purpose.

Teaching the Text

1. Paul's proverbial statement, "If you think you are standing firm, be careful that you don't fall!" (10:12), comes as both warning and encouragement. Self-reliance in faith can visit Christians with Pharisaic

force. Christians who consider themselves "strong," acquainted with God's Word and accustomed to life in Christ, face the constant temptation to forget the necessity of vigilant reliance upon God's strength to remain faithful. The cocksureness of Paul's own pre-Christian Pharisaic faith may well have informed this warning. Paul's point is not to create fear that God's grace will be less than sufficient; it is to encourage an unwavering awareness of the need to remain faithful.

2. We must not presume on God's love. The issue in the Corinthian context was participation in public events that were significant both for the social structure of the city and for the personal prominence of the individual. Participation in the imperial cult was an important opportunity for social interaction and networking. It may have been seen as a civic duty by Corinthians eager to display their loyalty to Rome. The early apologist Tertullian (AD 160–220) admits to participation in the banquets for the emperor's birthday out of civic duty but is quick to underscore how Christian participation should differ markedly from non-Christian participation.[13] The parallel to our modern situation seems direct. Human desire for personal prominence and the excitement of hobnobbing in socially important circles presents a variety of temptations to downplay the importance of one's relationship with God.

3. Paul's unapologetic typological use of key Old Testament texts to explain God's character more than hints that he did not perceive a disconnect between the precross and the postcross God. God's character was not changed by Christ but revealed in Christ. There is no discrepancy between the God of the exodus and the God of the new covenant in Paul's mind. The structure of Paul's argument in these verses leaves the not-so-subtle impression that Old Testament Scriptures remain authoritative for New Testament followers. They are not only informative for religious understanding but instructive for Christian living. Paul's vehement rejection of the saving quality of the Mosaic law does not equal a refutation of God's character as revealed through his actions prior to the cross. New Testament Christians are not free to take a few grand ideas, like love, grace, forgiveness, and Spirit, and reinterpret these apart from the greater story of God.

4. Paul's application of the word "baptism" to the crossing of the sea in the exodus account conjures up images of, and establishes typological parallels to, Christian baptism. Those crossing the sea were baptized *into* Moses. Because of this baptism they considered themselves partakers of God's covenant with Moses. They were now participants in God's purposes and recipients of God's blessings. Put differently, their "salvation," present and future, was secured through their baptism. Paul's aim

Paul looks back into Israel's history, saying in 10:2, "They were all baptized into Moses in the cloud and in the sea." A sixth-century AD fresco depicting the crossing of the sea was found in the Via Latina Catacombs.

is to expose and reject such a reduction of relationship to ritual. He could not make the parallel to the Corinthians' baptism any clearer. The "spiritual rock" the exodus generation drank from was Christ—yet their rebellion still caused their death. The lesson for the self-proclaimed strong Corinthians is that although they have been baptized into Christ, they should not risk their relationship in reliance on ritual. It is the distinctiveness of their relationship to Christ that safeguards them, not the claim of a religious ritual.

Illustrating the Text

Becoming stronger in God's grace requires remaining ever more dependent on it.

Contrasting Concept: Talk about the idea of using a crutch or cane to recover from an injury. (Bringing some crutches as props and trying them out or having a volunteer try them out could add to this illustration.) We use crutches to buttress our own strength and protect injured or weakened legs until they can bear weight again. This passage teaches that dependence on God's grace is the exact opposite of a crutch. It is not a prop that we use temporarily and then hope to discard when health is restored. Unending dependence on God's grace is itself precisely the state of health into which spiritual recovery leads us. Those who call God's grace a crutch misunderstand the full gravity of sin and the character of salvation: they imagine our default state to be spiritual health and see salvation as a prop to use on occasions when slips make us temporarily unstable. The truth is that our default state is irreparable rebellion

and crippling depravity brought about by independence from God, and salvation is his way of transforming us into people purified by undeserved but eternal intimacy with God and restoration of proper dependence on him.

Rituals remind us of relationship, but they can never replace it.

Christian Worship: The Lord's Supper is a good example of how a ritual (even a holy sacrament), as a reminder of relationship, has power to bless *only* when it coincides with the reality of that relationship. Regardless of the way in which we believe Jesus is present in his supper, the supper is ordained "in remembrance of" the relational Lord, who insists on intimate interaction with his people. We cannot be reminded of a relationship we have not yet experienced; thus, fellowship with Christ and his church is part and parcel with the sacrament. This is an opportunity to teach what your church believes about sacraments like communion and baptism, and the Sunday on which this illustration is given could be a great opportunity to celebrate the sacraments.

Human Experience: There are certain rituals we do to remember relationships and keep memories alive. For example, we place flowers on a grave, watch family movies of loved ones who are far away, or eat at a once-favorite restaurant to honor the memory of an old friendship. These rituals are helpful, but they do not make fitting substitutes for the relationships they are meant to commemorate. In the same way, participating in baptism or other religious rites without growing in real relationship to Jesus is an aberration from what those rites are meant to be.

1 Corinthians 10:1–13

Imitation and Role Modeling

Big Idea *Christ followers must aim to become imitators of Christ in all they do. Their testimony to their relationship to Christ trumps their Christian "rights" and leads to a rejection of contexts that hamper this testimony.*

Understanding the Text

The Text in Context

After a rather direct warning to the "strong" Christians in Corinth against self-assuredness and the pursuit of personal rights at the expense of the "weak," Paul now returns to his earlier differentiating argument about the relationship between idol meat and faith. The issue is a theological one. It is not that idol meat has evil powers but that its celebration evokes the jealousy of God and blurs the testimony of exclusive devotion to Christ. Covenantal loyalty is at stake! This section functions as a clarifying conclusion to the preceding and enables a smooth transition into another rights-versus-testimony issue Paul will discuss in the following section: worship and head coverings.

Interpretive Insights

10:14–15 *Therefore, my dear friends, flee from idolatry.* The inferential "therefore" coupled with Paul's endearing relational reminder "my dear friends" gives the opening command to flee idolatry a passionate, pastoral tone. Paul is not dealing with a minor issue but is touching on the core of the Christ community's covenantal understanding. The parallel structure of the command to "flee idolatry" with "flee from sexual immorality" in 6:18 brings a comprehensive quality to this text.

I speak to sensible people. What Paul says should be obvious, and he relies on their ability to recognize it. Calling them *phronimos* ("discerning," "thoughtful"; NIV: "sensible") is a simple request for them to use their common sense.

10:16–17 The defining covenantal meal of the Christ community is the Lord's Supper (11:23–26; Matt. 26:26–28; Mark 14:22–24; Luke 22:19–20). Paul's reference to this meal reminds his audience how unsuitable participation in an idol banquet is for those seated at Christ's table. Breaking the bread and drinking the cup express the community's participation (*koinōnia*, "mutual sharing") in the life and suffering of Christ. It is a celebration of the defeat of the demonic powers celebrated in idol banquets.

10:16 *the cup of thanksgiving for which we give thanks.* Paul's genitive ("of thanksgiving" or "of blessing") does not hint that the cup itself has divine power (a cup from which blessings flow); it simply points to the blessing/thanksgiving spoken over the cup and the bread (11:24–25) before the celebration of the Christ meal.[1] If Paul has in mind a specific cup, of the four used in the Jewish Passover seder, the reference here is likely the third cup, which represents redemption. In the Christ meal, the cup then represents the redemption achieved through the blood of Christ (replacing the lamb in Jewish tradition).[2]

10:17 *for we all share the one loaf.* Paul's repetition of "one" in verse 17 (one bread, one body, one bread)[3] not only accentuates the unity of the Christ community but also rejects any notion of individualization or separation into groups like strong and weak. The Greek *heis*/*hen* ("one") contrasts *polloi* ("many") and *pantes* ("all"; cf. 10:2–4)—an idea Paul will expound on in 12:12–26 (cf. Rom. 12:5).

10:19–22 *Do I mean then that food sacrificed to an idol is anything . . . ?* To make sure no one confuses the meat itself with the idolatrous banquets, Paul sets up a rhetorical question that enables him to make a finely tuned distinction between issues (10:23–31). The idol meat does not matter; the object of the sacrifice does. Paul's acquaintance with the sacrificial system in

- Believers should recognize their personal weaknesses.
- Fellowship should not be separated from worship.
- What is lawful should not be confused with what is helpful.
- The life of Christ should not be separated from the testimony about Christ.

Jerusalem and his Jewish conviction that the whole earth and everything in it belong to God (10:26; Ps. 24:1; cf. Pss. 50:12; 89:11) jettison any notion that the meat itself could be evil or demon possessed. The problem is the communal participation, which makes all celebrants partners (*koinōnoi*) with the demons, regardless of individual claims to the contrary.

arouse the Lord's jealousy. Paul picks up the imagery of jealousy from his Jewish tradition, where God's jealousy arises directly from the idolatrous practices of his people (Deut. 32:21; cf. Exod. 20:5; 34:14; Deut. 4:24; 5:9; Josh. 24:19; 1 Kings 14:22; Ps. 78:58–61; Ezek. 8:3–5).

Are we stronger than he? Paul exposes the absurdity of the "strong" risking God's jealous wrath. As a plethora of examples from God's dealings with his people amply show, the fire of God's jealousy is not something to play with or to test. When God removes his protective blessing from those who presume upon his grace, the consequences are devastating.

10:23–24 *"I have the right to do anything,"* *you say.* Paul opens his conclusive remarks on idol meat by requoting a well-known Corinthian slogan.[4] In

a fashion similar to 6:12 (see comments there), this allows him to contrast the elitist slogan of the Corinthians with slogans of his own that expose the christological flaws of their unqualified egotistical libertarianism. Rather than claiming their individual rights, the strong should ask whether their actions are advantageous and bring unity to the community of believers (the Greek verb *sympherō*, "is beneficial," can also mean "bring together"). Do these actions build community or destroy community? Paul's second contrastive slogan picks up the building metaphor (*oikodomeō*, "construct," "build up") he applied earlier (3:9; 8:1, 10) and will utilize repeatedly in chapter 14.[5] The Corinthians' focus on personal liberty skews the message of Christ, which concentrates on the needs of others (Matt. 22:37–40; cf. Rom. 14:7; 15:2; Gal.

Because everything belongs to the Lord, Paul tells the Corinthians they can eat anything purchased in the meat market. One suggested location for the meat market in Corinth is the North Market, built in the first century AD. Its excavated remains are shown here in the foreground.

6:2; Phil. 2:1–8): "No one should seek their own good, but the good of others" (10:24).

10:25–26 *Eat anything sold in the meat market.* After pointing to the error of the Corinthian libertarian argument, Paul now addresses the positive application of Christian freedom. Christians can eat meat from the marketplace "without raising questions of conscience." Neither the strong nor the weak need to have concern. The reference to "conscience" speaks to the origin of the meat—an issue of grave concern for Diaspora Jews.[6] Since everything belongs to the Lord, Paul argues (10:26), Christians do not have to inquire whether or not the meat came from a pagan temple.

10:27–30 *If an unbeliever invites you . . . eat.* Paul's concern remains on the Christian testimony. When Christ followers are invited to a private dinner in the home of an unbeliever, the question of the meat's origin is moot. They are not bound by Jewish food laws and are free to eat.

"This has been offered in sacrifice," then do not eat it. If the unbeliever accentuates the origin of the meat, eating it becomes

a matter of testimony to the exclusivity of Christ. The believer need not be confused, but the unbeliever apparently is (10:29). The fact that the meat's origin is mentioned signifies that the unbeliever considers eating it a matter of idol worship. The believer, then, must consider the conscience of the unbeliever, who otherwise would draw the wrong conclusions about Christ. The freedom of the believer becomes a stumbling block for the unbeliever.

why am I denounced because of something I thank God for? Paul's two rhetorical questions (10:29–30) are both in the first person, a somewhat common way of casting a question of universal significance.[7] Paul calls the believers to an awareness of their testimony: "Why should I set myself up to be judged [10:29] and blamed [10:30]?" Paul's aim is not to highlight the error of those judging and blaming but to underscore the necessity of the Christian testimony. The meaning of his questions would then be this: "If I dine with thanksgiving,[8] why should I make that an opportunity where people could condemn my faith [10:30] rather than finding it for themselves [10:33]?"

10:31–33 *do it all for the glory of God.* Paul's argument has come full circle. Those claiming personal rights must recognize that their personal freedom is subject to the rights of God, who is their patron. Believers remain clients of God, whom they are called to serve in faith (see "Grace and Patronage" in the introduction). Paul's use of God's glory (*doxa theou*) often stresses the salvific nature of God's presence (e.g., Rom. 3:23; 6:4; 8:18; 9:23; 2 Cor. 1:20; Eph. 1:17–18; cf. John 13:31–32; 17:4). Believers' actions must be directed by such focus on

God's saving purposes—in all they do—and toward "Jews, Greeks or the church of God" (everyone inside and outside the church). Paul's word *aproskopoi* (NIV: "do not cause anyone to stumble") speaks to a damaging of faith or a hindrance of the opportunity for faith (cf. Matt. 18:6; Rom. 14:20–21; 2 Cor. 2:2–4). This was the focus of Paul's life: seeking ways to benefit others (10:33). The reason for this behavior can be summarized in a simple purpose clause (introduced with *hina*): "so that they may be saved."

11:1 *Follow my example, as I follow the example of Christ.* This short verse concludes the preceding section rather than opening the following. The theme of imitation proves especially powerful when compared to the Corinthian love for sophist rhetoric. Sophists mastered the art of separation between word and deed (contrast to 4:16). Paul's biblical examples (10:1–12) patterned how *not* to live before God; Paul's own life exemplifies the pattern of a true Christ follower.[9] The Corinthians should imitate him because he imitates Christ. Put differently, they can look to him to see what the Christ hymn (Phil. 2:6–11) looks like when exemplified by a Christ follower in their setting. Paul's actions, summarized in 10:33, are caused by his imitation of Christ. The Corinthian believers should do the same.

Theological Insights

Because Christian faith is relational and expressed in real-life experiences, the key word for discipleship is "imitation." Rather than giving his followers a list of rules to memorize, Christ revealed a new set of priorities and a life pattern for his community to imitate.

Teaching the Text

1. The Corinthian elite, or the "strong," saw it as their civic and Christian right to participate in the city's celebrations. Paul is concerned about their disregard for the incongruity between worship of God and the idolatrous worship of pagan culture. The strong see themselves as able to handle direct participation without being led into an idolatrous participation. Modern Christians can easily miss Paul's point by thinking idolatry primarily is participation in a specific worship service for a pagan god—something rather uncommon in many modern secular settings. The reality of the Corinthian situation, however, makes 10:14 correspond more to modern Christians' desire to participate in a plethora of social, business, or political events that arguably can be harmless but that often call for a compromise of the Christ message. Enticement can be subtle—just as the beauty of a rose entices the beholder to grab onto it, only to discover an untold number of thorns.

2. Cutting straight to the point, Paul explains his warning through the use of the Greek word *koinōnia*. *Koinōnia* means fellowship in the sense of significant participation. People who have joined their financial fate in a common business venture are said to have *koinōnia*; people whose lives are joined in marriage have *koinōnia*—they have become one, so to speak. Paul's point in 10:16–21 is to warn against the idea that it is possible to worship God while having fellowship with another god. *Koinōnia* and worship go hand in hand. Fellowship with demons will lead to worship of demonic powers. This invariably will lead to a disfellowshiping of Christ (10:21). The antidote

Paul exhorts the Corinthian believers to "flee from idolatry" (10:14). Throughout its history, many temples were erected in ancient Corinth to honor different pagan deities. This inscribed architectural fragment is from building remains designated "Temple H," which may have been built for the worship of Heracles (second century AD).

against this, says Paul, is to capitalize on the *koinōnia*, or oneness, of the body of Christ (10:17), which leads to worship of the one true God.

3. The claim that something is legal does not make it right. Christians, Paul says, are guided by a more significant question: Is it helpful? Questions of legal permissibility are helpful only from the negative side. If it is illegal or impermissible, it should *not* be done; if it is legal or permissible, there is a chance it still should not be done. The scale to weigh this on is community edification. Does it contribute to or hinder the strengthening/edification of Christ's community? Paul's response to the claim of legality proves exceedingly instructive for Christian thinking. Rather than agreeing to a set of Christian laws to be applied indiscriminately, he places two statements before his audience that force them to think in terms of imitation: Does the aspiration to do a certain action arise from a desire to seek personal benefit? Or does it arise from a yearning to do good toward others (10:24)?

4. Making permissibility rather than helpfulness one's guide for Christian

behavior makes it possible to disconnect Christian doctrine from Christian living. Turning faith into a set of propositional statements to which Christians must claim mental assent has been a temptation since the days of Paul. Forensic readings of "grace" and "faith" enable an interpretation of community membership that proves foreign to the "body" language Paul uses to describe the Christian life. To Paul, the litmus test for being a Christian is not simply a matter of adherence to statements about salvation through Christ. Paul's issue in Corinth is that some claim a truth about their freedom (no law requires them to abstain from certain foods) while disregarding their responsibility to Christ's community. Paul's corrective is a call to imitate Christ. In fact, Paul's whole theological endeavor is to let Christ's life evidence Christ's teaching and to use that (rather than law) as the directive for Christian life and thinking. In a way similar to how Christ-rooted indicatives (Christ did this) function as the basis for Christian imperatives (therefore do this!), Christian teaching must not be disconnected from Christian living. Paul's statement about imitation reverberates back through everything he has said.

Illustrating the Text

Idolatry and moral compromise are often hidden in culturally accepted activities.

Contrasting Concept: Throughout church history, and around the world today, many martyrs have given their lives rather than deny their faith in Christ. This bravery has had a profound influence on the church. If it came to that point in our own lives—deny Christ or die—many of us would probably also be brave and stand firm. But how do we fare when the seemingly minor, everyday denials come up? We deny him thousands of times in the little things—the white lie told, the salacious rumor savored, the objectionable material not objected to, the kind word we thought too troublesome to utter to a person too difficult to approach. All of these things are everyday opportunities for martyrdom in which we fail to die to ourselves and live to Christ. It is the little things that get us.

Be discerning about the causes, people, and projects in which you invest yourself.

Popular Sayings: We often hear people refer to "guilt by association." The idea that we can be perceived as participating in other people's crimes simply by associating with them is a reality of the human heart. We are called to share Christ with all people, no matter what their station in life and no matter what marks may be against them—they are no different from us in terms of our common need for grace. And sharing the gospel is often best done in relationship with others. At the same time, we need to discern the difference between love and approval, for God will hold us to account for keeping silent (e.g., Ezek. 3:17–21; Rom. 14:22). The difference between association that ministers grace-filled conviction to others and association that brings guilt on us is our mission and behavior within the association. In other words, if we are there to get along and be liked, we will likely approve of (either actively or passively) things for which our consciences will condemn us. If we are there to lovingly warn and bear witness to the gospel, our presence can lead to salvation and blessing.

1 Corinthians 10:14–11:1

Worship and Proper Attire

Big Idea *The form of the Christian worship service must express the nature of Christ, and the behavior of the worshipers must exemplify his character and humility.*

Understanding the Text

The Text in Context

After a strong call to Christians to avoid participation in pagan banquets, which ultimately were worship services, Paul now turns to the Christian worship service itself. Since the behavior at pagan worship services so clearly was an abomination to God, how should Christians reconsider their practices when approaching the Triune God? Chapter 11 deals with two major issues regarding this question. Verses 2–16 tackle the question of hair and head coverings for men and wives, and verses 17–34 tackle the question of social status and equal participation in the community's fellowship meal, the Lord's Supper.

Historical and Cultural Background

The issue of hair and veiling is sufficiently foreign to most modern readers that this section often receives little serious consideration among regular Bible readers apart from being used as a proof text in gender debates. Paul's point, however, is a deeply serious one that goes beyond the modern gender debate to deal with troublesome questions related to worship in a home setting.

1. Head coverings for men (11:4, 7). The fact that Paul begins his discussion by commenting on the veiling of men rather than of women hints from the outset that this paragraph is not primarily about women and gender roles but about Christian versus pagan worship. Augustus, in a great propaganda campaign designed to promote himself as the imperial head even of religious affairs, erected statues throughout the empire that portrayed him with his toga pulled over his head (see the image of Augustus). His posture showed him as the sacrificant presiding over a Roman ritual in pagan worship events.[1] Pulling the toga over one's head indicated a leading role in pagan rites; it was not the common posture of every participant. Because this became the image of the emperor, the social elite followed suit. When now the Christian elite took this same posture when they prophesied in the Christian gathering, it automatically created division along the lines of pagan worship. If, furthermore, covering the head with a toga became the accepted posture fitting for prophetic utterance, Christian gatherings would look like pagan worship events.

2. *Head coverings for wives (11:5–6).* The Greek word for "wife" is *gynē*—a word used also for "woman." A "girl" (*pais*) became a *gynē* at age fourteen and was usually married shortly after that. The central moment (or feature) in the Roman marriage ceremony was the veiling of the bride. The veil was a woman's social indicator to show she was married. When Paul speaks about the veil in this context, therefore, he speaks about wives, not women in general.

Much was changing in fast-paced Roman colonies like Corinth, and it created a new reality for women. In the traditional Roman setting, the norm for the Roman wife was sexual modesty. The norm for her husband ran the opposite direction, however. He was expected to provide casual sexual companions (usually slaves) for dinner guests (see the sidebar "Food and Sex" in the unit on 6:12–20). With things changing, upwardly mobile "foreign" women and freedwomen now saw an opportunity in providing these sexual pleasures among the elite men— behavior that was obviously intolerable for Roman matrons.[2] Since these "new" women were unmarried, they were unveiled.[3] Yet they were not slaves. When a man, therefore, was seen in public accompanied by an unveiled woman, it signaled she was not his wife but a banquet woman.[4]

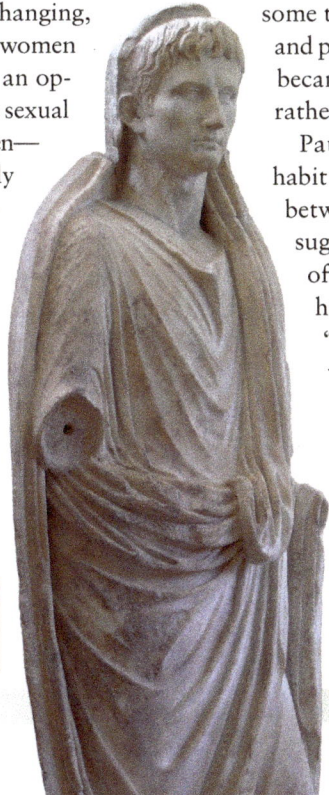
Statue of Augustus using his toga to cover his head (first century AD)

Key Themes of 1 Corinthians 11:2–16

- The form of a worship service can "paganize" Christian worship services.
- The way people dress can impact Christian worship services.
- Spousal relationships can impact Christian worship services.

Part of the difficulty surrounding the question of the veil in 1 Corinthians derives from the location of the Christian gathering, which happened in the home of the congregation's patron. A wife was not expected to wear a veil in her own house; neither were friends once they entered the house. By not wearing a veil in the house, a woman could parade her wealth. Those who took it off were obviously friends of the patron's family; those who did not were evidently not at the same social rank. This created division in the church. When some took the veil off while praying and prophesying, the act of worship became an occasion for segregation rather than unification.

Paul's strong reaction to this habit reveals the parallels he draws between it and pagan worship. His suggestion that when a wife takes off her veil she might as well cut her hair off (11:6) is a rather "unveiled" way of calling such women adulterous. Cutting off the hair was a punishment designed for public humiliation of adulterous wives. In Paul's mind, a Christian wife who unveils herself in a public setting makes it appear that she is one of the high-class "new Roman women." In effect, her actions parade a rejection of the Christian teaching on marriage.[5]

3. *The man is the head of his wife (11:3)*. Paul's opening line about headship relates directly to the issue of veiling in this context.[6] This is about worship and exclusive relationships, not about authority as such.[7] Paul's theological argument runs something like this: God is the head of Christ because Christ bears the mark of exclusive relationship to God. Christ is the head of the Christian man for the same reason, and the husband likewise for his wife. A Christian man should *not* cover his head; when he does, he looks like a pagan and covers his sign of relationship to Christ (11:7). A woman *should* cover her head; the veil is *her* sign of exclusive relationship to her husband. Taking off her veil suggests that her relationship to her husband is less than exclusive—the exact same thing that happens to a man's relationship to Christ when he puts a veil on.

Interpretive Insights

11:2 *I praise you for remembering me in everything and for holding to the traditions*. The best way of understanding this praise, which seems overly lavish in light of the preceding, is as an argumentative platform for what follows: "Since you remember everything I taught[8] and keep the traditions that I handed to you, I want you to know . . ." The "traditions" likely refers to the stories about and teachings of Jesus (cf. 11:23–26; 15:1–7).

11:3 *I want you to realize*. In line with Paul's usual indicative/imperative pattern, he draws theological and behavioral conclusions from the Jesus story: "Based on the traditions, which you do keep, it follows

that Christ is the head . . ." (see the "Historical and Cultural Background" section above).

11:4–7 Contrary to verse 3, Paul's use of "head" in verses 4–7 is not metaphorical but refers to the husbands' and the wives' physical heads. Again, the context is Christian worship and the communicative power of forms and symbols—specifically the communicative power of the use or nonuse of the veil. The ease with which Paul switches from the metaphorical to the physiological use of *kephalē* ("head") between verses 3 and 4–7 only strengthens the rhetorical force of his argument. This is true even if Paul intends, as some argue, for his second use of "head" in verses 4 and 5, respectively, to have metaphorical meaning—"a man who covers his physical head disgraces Christ, his metaphorical head."

11:6 *she might as well have her hair cut off*. The suggestion by some that Paul may have had a Nazirite vow in mind is intriguing but unlikely.[9] His point would then be that if a woman takes off her veil in worship, it had better be due to a specific vow to a period of extraordinary devotion to God. Paul's focus in this context, however, is on the disgrace it brings for a woman to have her hair shaved, not on special vows.

11:7 *since he is the image and glory of God; but woman is the glory of man*. Genesis 1:26–27 speaks of humankind as created in God's image and likeness. Paul changes "likeness" to "glory" and, in line with Genesis 2, makes a distinction between man and woman. The word "glory" does not appear in the creation narrative, but its use here may come from Psalm 8:5 ("you . . . crowned them with glory and honor"). Paul's aim is not to give an exposition of the creation narrative but to use it typologically to express his point about worship. A man's purpose is to bring honor and glory to God;[10] he does that by not wearing a veil. The wife does the same to her husband by wearing the veil.

11:8–12 *For man did not come from woman, but woman from man.* The NIV's "man" and "woman" would be better translated "husband" and "wife" (see the "Historical and Cultural Background" section above). Paul's relational point clarifies his reasoning surrounding the proper attire for worship. Moving from a simple "to be" verb in verse 8 ("is"; NIV: "come") to a causation statement in verse 9 ("the husband was not created because of his wife"; NIV: "neither was man created for woman") allows him to qualify his statement about the necessity of a wife's veil. As Adam was created for exclusive devotion to God, Eve similarly was created for exclusive devotion to her husband, Adam. Christian husbands and wives are not independent of each other (11:11–12).

because of the angels. The word translated "angels" (*angeloi*) can also mean "messengers" and could perhaps refer to messengers from other cities visiting the Corinthian church (cf. Luke 9:52). If so, Paul does not want the Corinthians to send a message of religious pluralism to visitors. Paul likely has heavenly beings in mind, however. From the perspective of worship and testimony, Paul's reference to angels may reflect the same thinking that is behind Peter's statement about angels longing to know the gospel (1 Pet. 1:12). Such positive participation of angels in worship fits well with Jesus's own statement about angels

rejoicing when sinners repent (Luke 15:7, 10; cf. Heb. 1:6; 12:22–23).

11:13–16 *Judge for yourselves . . . the very nature of things . . . we have no other practice.* Paul counts on three appeals to remove any remaining doubt about his teaching: common sense (11:13), nature (11:14–15), and Christian custom (11:16). The common-sense appeal speaks to propriety: "Judge for yourselves: Is it proper . . . ?" (11:13). Paul must have been able to count on general agreement on this matter in Roman society. The nature appeal to long and short hair likewise follows Corinthian commonsense conclusions and probably refers to Roman expressions of homosexuality (Rom. 1:26–27). Paul does not attempt an argument about hair length from a biological or philosophical perspective. Rather,

In the culture of ancient Corinth, long hair on men was considered a disgrace. This statue of a long-haired captive from Phrygia once decorated the North Basilica in ancient Corinth (late second to early third century AD).

long hair for men was considered effeminate and an expression of homosexuality, as can be seen from Corinthian statues dating to that period. The Christian-custom appeal is aimed at those challenging Paul's argument, letting them and others in the congregation know that they are opposing not only Paul but also a practice common to all God's assemblies.

Theological Insights

The Triune God is both the subject and the object of Christian worship. For worship to be Christian, worshipers must focus on revealing the God who has made himself known through Christ. Anything that stands in the way of that points to idolatry.

In ancient Roman society, wives would wear a veil to indicate their married status. This carved head of Livia, wife of Augustus, shows that the veil covered the hair, not the face (20 BC).

Teaching the Text

1. The problem of form versus content in a worship service is not a new one. Paul can take for granted that the Corinthians know the life and message of Christ. They claim the traditions he delivered (11:2). Yet when they meet to worship, the service takes the form of a pagan worship service. When the men who actively participate in the worship service employ the very form used by the pagan priests (pulling the toga over their heads) to express their devotion, this "sign language" (semiotics) becomes the communicated message (semantics). Rather than highlighting the distinctive unifying and self-emptying message of the cross, the Corinthian service has become an event that extols the pagan message of division and self-glorification. Although this likely was unintended and only subconsciously motivated, Paul's exposure of the connection between form and content reveals how easily Christ's message can be distorted.

2. Using clothing to exhibit social distinction is nothing new. Paul's chastising of men who pray with their head covered speaks directly to the correlation between dress code and worship. Beyond the direct relation this has to pagan worship, Paul also addresses this out of a concern that the distinctions that are declared null and void in the Christ community divide the church at the very point of worship. The same is true with women, when they take off their veil. Since only wealthy friends of the patron had that privilege, doing so would create divisions within the body of Christ and lead the focus away from Christ to the ones who are able to "unveil." Paul's point is obviously not that the veil itself has religious value but that dressing in such a way takes the focus away from Christ. Those who claim the right to not wear a veil without being wealthy matrons (wives of patrons) are exposed as promiscuous and scantily (scandalously) dressed. They too violate the message of Christ.

3. Paul's point about spousal relationship and worship goes to the heart of the Christian faith. His teaching that the wife's lack of a veil communicates a lack of sexual fidelity to the husband relates directly to

a breakdown in the Corinthian believers' understanding of true worship. Paul knows well how the Hebrew Scriptures use the imagery of spousal infidelity to describe Israel's idolatry toward God. When spouses, who belong to one another (11:11), do not see how a rift in their relationship affects their worship of God, they have missed how their relationship is exemplified in the relationship between Christ and God (11:3). As Paul sees it, a violation of marital fidelity is a violation against the very being of God, whom Christians worship as perfect community between Father, Son, and Spirit. Paul's elevation of the wife ("nor is man independent of woman" [11:11]) is surprising in the Corinthian context, but the reverse statement speaks volumes to the centrality of spousal unity for genuine worship.

Illustrating the Text

It is wrong to use outward appearances to establish a pecking order in church.

Personal Stories: Share about a time when you were judged or misjudged based on clothing or other kinds of outward appearances. Tell about the situation and the cultural traditions and assumptions behind it. Explain how you felt and how this situation affects the way you feel about appearances and clothing. Compare or contrast that with the truth taught in this passage.

Visual: Dress drastically differently from how you usually do. If you are a robe wearer, wear blue jeans and a T-shirt or motorcycle jacket; if you are a suit-and-tie type, try coming in a mechanic's uniform or running suit. If you usually dress down, wear a suit, or borrow clerical robes or a Roman collar. The point is to make a (tasteful and appropriate) radical departure in dress and invite people to consider their reactions. Is it harder for them to listen to you when you dress differently? How does it affect their perception of you? Why? What might outsiders not familiar with church think of the new clothes—would they feel more or less welcomed if you dressed that way all the time? Point out that in the early church era (and still today), many preachers are bivocational. Even Paul probably preached dressed as a tentmaker, a prisoner, and a castaway. If the outward appearance of the messenger limits the listener's ability to hear the Word (or your confidence in delivering it), perhaps outward appearances are as much a stumbling block in your church as they were at Corinth.

Behavior in church that undermines or dishonors God-given roles and order in the home is inappropriate (and vice versa).

Everyday Wisdom: This teaching is a great opportunity to impart some practical, everyday wisdom to your listeners: any person who is seeking to divide you from loving, God-ordained authority in your life does *not* have your best interests at heart. This includes seducers who bad-mouth one spouse to another, false teachers seeking to separate sheep from faithful shepherds by subtly questioning their competency, dates who want to separate teens from their parents' morality by insisting they are out of touch, teachers or professors who encourage students to rebel against their parents' worldview and beliefs, and so on.

Worship and Humility

Big Idea *Christian worship must happen in an atmosphere of humility and self-giving. Self-promoting pride desecrates Christ and brings devastation to his community.*

Understanding the Text

The Text in Context

The danger of an amalgamation between pagan and Christian worship loomed in the Corinthian setting. After pointing out how clothing (veiling) blurred what should have been a clear distinction between pagan and Christian worship practices (11:2–16), Paul now turns to the issue of the Lord's Supper itself. The very rooms in homes that used to host pagan worship in the setting of a private dinner were now the space for Christian worship, including the Christian meal called the Lord's Supper (see the "Additional Insights" following this unit). A mere change of liturgy, prayers, and readings is insufficient—Christian worship requires a form that expresses the content of Christ's gospel.

Interpretive Insight

11:17 *In the following directives I have no praise for you.* Striking a sterner tone, Paul contrasts his commendation in 11:2 with the opposite statement here. Whereas the issue of clothing in worship settings needs correction to avoid confusion with

paganism and to avoid sending a message about communal and marital relationships that does not portray Christ, turning the Lord's Supper into a traditional private dining experience is a direct violation, if not an outright desecration, of the Christ meal. They have transformed the meal that is supposed to exemplify Christ's self-giving sacrifice into an event designed for divisive self-glorification. As Paul sees it, their gatherings "do more harm than good."

11:18 *when you come together as a church, there are divisions among you.* Although the same word is used as in 1:10, the divisions (*schismata*) referenced here are not between patrons but within the individual house groups. A Christian patron would gather with friends of his (or her) own rank in the *triclinium* while slaves and clients would gather in the *atrium*.[1] Here they would eat standing or, at best, seated tightly together while the patron and prominent friends were reclining within view in the adjacent room. Beyond being socioeconomically motivated, these divisions probably followed ethnic/racial lines as well. Roman slaves, generally speaking, were "spoils of war." A certain hierarchy existed even among the slaves, as Romans often preferred barbarian tribes for protection and military efforts, Greeks for education and cultural development, and tribes of other descents for more menial tasks. When, therefore, Paul tells Philemon to receive Onesimus as a brother, even as Philemon would Paul himself (Philem. 16–17), it is a drastic alteration of the common order, underscoring the radical nature of Christ's transformative call. The removal of the divisions (*schismata*) goes to the heart of this issue of equality in the Christ community (Gal. 3:28).

to some extent I believe it. This somewhat difficult statement does not suggest that Paul considers this might be a rumor. Rather, it is an expression of outrage, like saying, "This is unbelievable—I can't believe you are doing this."[2]

11:19–21a *there have to be differences among you to show which of you have God's approval.* On the surface it seems as if Paul speaks in favor of division. Most of the English translations indeed seem to promote such a reading.[3] This then refers to the eschatological revelation of who among the Corinthians were genuine Christians. Given the context, however, it seems highly unlikely that Paul suddenly switches to a soteriological statement. Rather, Paul, with a hint of sarcasm, expresses concern about social distinctions that destroy the very meaning of the Christ meal and the unity of the Christ community. The Greek *hoi dokimoi* (lit., "the approved"), then, refers to the wealthy who considered themselves the approved (or significant) Christians in distinction from the "riffraff" group (usually called *hoi polloi*) that met in the *atrium*.[4] A few verses later, then, with a brilliant wordplay, Paul indicts the elite.

- Socioeconomic divisions between Christians violate the message of Christ.
- Well-to-do Christians must look out for less fortunate members of the church body.
- The celebration of the Lord's Supper must be an expression of Christ's self-giving love.
- The Lord's Supper calls Christians to examine the relationship between their faith claims and their patterns of behavior toward fellow church members.

Rather than considering themselves *dokimoi* ("approved"), they should *dokimazetō* ("examine") themselves before they participate in the Lord's Supper (11:28).

11:21b-22 *humiliating those who have nothing.* The idea that these verses suggest the wealthy went ahead and ate the available food before the poor were able to come probably roots in a translation of the Greek word *ekdechesthe* (11:33) as "wait for." However, as Winter has shown, the better translation of *ekdechesthe* is "receive."[5] (The NIV uses the ambiguous phrase "eat together.") Paul's point is not that food had run out but that the rich were humiliating the poor (11:22) by eating the superior food in the *triclinium* with the poor watching from the *atrium*. Verse 33 then resolves the problem expressed in 11:18: "When you gather to eat, you should all eat together" (or "show hospitality to one another"). The format for the supper needed to change. If a small group of the elite enjoyed their dinner in the *triclinium*, the poor would have to be there for the ceremonial breaking of the bread before the dinner—then wait while the elite ate—in order to participate in the "cup of blessing" at the dinner's conclusion (11:25). As Paul puts it, "one person remains hungry and another gets drunk" (11:21).

11:23 *For I received from the Lord what I also passed on to you.* Following his usual pattern, Paul grounds his argument in the Jesus tradition. The opening "for" (*gar*) gives reason; what follows explains why the divisions at the Lord's Supper celebration are intolerable. The formulation "I received . . . I also passed on" follows the rabbinical pattern for authoritative explanation of entrusted tradition.

11:24 *This is my body.* Paul's subtle change of the word order recorded in the Gospel narratives ("this is my body")[6] to (literally) "this of mine is the body" hints that his point is not to quote a liturgical saying but to use Jesus's words as a corrective to the errant ways of the Corinthian behavior. The demonstrative pronoun "this" (*touto*) is a neuter and cannot well refer to bread as such, which is a masculine word in Greek.[7] Rather, it refers to the self-sacrificing event of Jesus—an event so outwardly dishonored by the Corinthian elite's behavior. They have taken the event Christ himself designed as a constant reminder of his self-sacrifice ("do this in remembrance of me") and turned it into an event for self-glorification.

11:25–26 *new covenant in my blood.* This points to Jesus's self-sacrifice and power to reconcile (cf. Col. 1:20; Eph. 2:13–18). The new covenant is a covenant of self-sacrifice established in Jesus's blood. If

Exodus 24:7–8 was recited as part of the ritual surrounding the cup of blessing (see comments on 10:16), which is likely, Paul's use of the tradition would have hit with full force as a stern corrective to the Corinthians' behavior. They were blaspheming the very covenant of Jesus and acting as if he were not their *kyrios* (patron) and they were not his *douloi* (slaves or clients). Such behavior completely contradicts the meal Christ designed to be his community's repeated proclamation of their covenant with him until he comes.

11:27 *whoever eats . . . in an unworthy manner will be guilty.* Contrary to what often seems suggested in modern Western churches, Paul does not design this verse as a call to quiet reflection upon the worthiness of one's personal relationship with Christ while the music is softly playing. Paul's point is that those who so blatantly desecrate the Lord's table through the behavior just outlined stand guilty[8] of dishonoring their covenant with Christ—they act in *spite* of Christ's blood and thereby call God's judgment against themselves (11:29). They treat the Lord's Supper like a pagan event—in effect becoming idolaters and not worshipers of Christ.

Treating the Lord's Supper like a pagan event was a problem for the Corinthian church. This sarcophagus lid fragment shows a banquet scene with loaves of bread (from the Cemetery of Via Anapo, Rome, AD 280–300).

11:28 *Everyone ought to examine themselves.* Instead of considering themselves "approved" (*dokimoi* [11:19]), they should "examine themselves" (*dokimazetō . . . heauton*). The Greek *houtōs* ("thus") speaks to the manner in which they should come. If they approached the Lord's Supper with humility, they would all join for a common meal without distinctions (11:19). The self-examination is the test that reveals whether their behavior and lifestyle reflect Christ's (cf. Mark 14:17–21).

11:29 *without discerning the body of Christ.* Lack of concern for the body brings judgment. It is uncertain whether Paul has the church or the elements of the Lord's Supper in mind with this phrase. It is possible he deliberately plays on the dual application of the expression. Those who lack concern for the church (Christ's body [10:16]), which they show by the way they break the bread and drink the cup (the representation of Christ's body [11:27]), will face judgment.

11:30 *weak and sick . . . fallen asleep.* Paul's direct linking of weakness, illness, and death to a manipulation of the Lord's Supper seems crass to most modern readers. However, his aim is not to create a measuring tool for the individual Corinthian to conclude backward that those who were weak and ill, or who died, had desecrated the Lord's Supper, while those who were in good health had not. Nothing in the text indicates that Paul refers to the elite as being the ones who are sick and dying. Paul speaks corporately; this is God's judgment on the community as such. He *may* refer simply to specific illnesses (and deaths) stemming from poverty issues such as hunger and malnutrition—issues

that could, and should, have been avoided in Christ's body (the church).[9] Because they were not, the church experienced the same judgment as the surrounding community. The Christ community had become as weak as the community around them and was no longer expressing the presence of Christ (Matt. 11:4–5; Luke 7:22).

11:31-32 *we would not come under such judgment.* Paul's emphasis, "If we were more discerning with regard to ourselves, we would not come under such judgment," relates his comment in 11:28–29 directly to his audience's experience of divine judgment.[10] What they experienced now was avoidable. Thankfully, God's temporary judgments are meant to function as instruments of discipline. Their purpose is to bring about a change in the community that rescues it from the ultimate condemnation that will come to the world (cf. Heb. 12:7).

11:33-34 *you should all eat together . . . eat something at home.* Paul's point may be not merely to give mundane practical advice but to say that the purpose of the community's gathering is to proclaim the gospel (the Lord's death) and not to satisfy one's own desire. They could do the latter at home. Paul's focus is the community and their Christlikeness. Those who have come merely for personal interest should stay home.

Theological Insights

Because worship must reveal Christ in order to be Christian, worshipers must worship with the attitude that characterized Christ (Phil. 2:3–5). Divisions in the Christ community—whether socioeconomic, ethnic, or other—hinder God-honoring worship.

Teaching the Text

1. Erasing socioeconomic distinctions in the church community has not become easier since Paul wrote these verses. The form may have changed, and the outrageous expressions described by Paul may have become subdued. Still, Paul's call to a community life in which everyone comes to the Lord's table as a servant of the One who invited them and called them to give their lives for others remains pertinent. Contrary to the patrons who used their dinner invitations to show favoritism, Christ shows no favoritism in the invitation to sit around his table (cf. Luke 22:25–27; 7:36–39, 44–46; James 2:3). The very act of considering the socioeconomic realities and the divisions of the present world as valid in the Christ community shows a blatant disregard for Christ's invitation. Among Christians, the first shall be the last and the least shall be the greatest. Service, not socioeconomic realities, determines the order at Christ's table (Matt. 25:34–45).

2. It follows from Paul's teaching that he considers it an abomination that some in the Christ community go hungry while others live a gluttonous lifestyle. Paul's word about eating and drinking without consideration of the body speaks directly to the responsibility of the privileged for the nonprivileged. As followers of Christ, the privileged could not turn their responsibility into a mere theoretical principle and reduce it to a handout of their leftovers. Paul's call goes to the core of what it means to be community—when one member suffers, every member suffers. When, therefore, Paul speaks about some who are ill

and weak, even some who have died, he does not need to specify who they are or which group they belong to (the haves or the have-nots). The suffering that occurs in the community affects everyone. If it does not, they are not a true Christ community. When God has blessed one with means to help another, it is to empower the community. What God has given to the one is for the common good of the community (12:7; cf. Luke 12:48; John 6:11).

3. Paul's emphasis on eating at home before the Lord's Supper does not suggest that he desires to turn the meal into a mere liturgy disconnected from the dining experience. Rather, the community celebration of fellowship and worship, experienced daily during the evening meal, needed to reveal the presence of Christ and not look like a pagan feast. The sharing Paul calls for is the communal articulation of the caring of Christ. To examine oneself in light of Christ's sacrifice means to request God's wisdom for how one can express such self-giving. Put differently, to commemorate the

Unlike the wealthy Corinthian believers who relegated those not of their class to the *atrium* of the house, Christ invites all to sit at his table. Shown here is the *atrium* area of a restored third-century AD Roman house on the Greek island of Cos.

Christ event through a common meal, even if it is a mere liturgical event, is a call to revisit the Christ follower's call to self-sacrifice. Only in this way will Christians come to "proclaim the Lord's death until he comes" (11:26).

4. Frequently celebrating the Lord's Supper (Acts 2:46–47) functions as a powerful reminder and highlighting of the Christian faith's content. Through the breaking of the bread and the pouring of the wine, Christ reminds his followers how to live their lives mimicking his self-giving. Paul does not allow his audience to reduce the meal to an expression of gratitude for Christ's sacrifice on their behalf only; he calls them to imitate Christ's sacrificial lifestyle. When Jesus reinterpreted the Passover meal, he moved the meal's emphasis from a celebration of what God had done to a celebration of what God was doing. The focus, then, is not on the unleavened bread but on the Christ event expressed through the community's sharing of the one bread. Examining the significance of one's faith claims for a Christian transformation of behavior is the only table manner (11:27) worthy of Christ's invitation.

Illustrating the Text

The church and sacraments are meant to be status neutral.

Contrasting Concept: Show or describe a clip from a reality television show that involves celebrity contestants surviving or competing together or with "ordinary people" (e.g., *Undercover Boss, The Apprentice, Survivor*). The best clip will be one in which status or fame give no advantage (e.g., starting a fire, answering trivia, or navigating obstacles). Invite listeners to think about the appeal of seeing famous or powerful people robbed of their advantage and forced to compete outside their area of privilege or comfort. The type of status-free zone this passage describes for the Lord's table is not the same thing people feel when watching celebrity reality shows. It is neither a favoritism toward the powerful and renowned nor a delight in their being humbled. In light of God's grace we all have the same status: forgiven and accepted sons and daughters, adopted by means of the undeserved shedding of Jesus's blood on our behalf. As we look around at one another, we ought to see what Christ sees: the absolute dereliction we all experience under the law and the absolute acceptance we all experience in the gospel.

Communion without compassion and charity is an unbiblical abomination.

Hymn: "They'll Know We Are Christians by Our Love." This old standby is a convicting picture of the love that ought to mark Christian fellowship. Many listeners may have opinions on the song itself, but challenge them to think over the lyrics. Would a neutral observer be able to see the love of Christ in the way your church celebrates communion, or would it seem like a cold ritual? Would they see the oneness of communion lived out in the lobby, at congregational meetings, and throughout the week in a way that would be undeniably Christian in character?

Roman Homes and Households

A typical wealthy Roman home had two clearly distinct dining areas—the *triclinium* and the *atrium*. The *triclinium* was the private dining area for the patron, a lavishly decorated room designed for a small group of friends and business associates. It usually seated nine to twelve people reclining for dinner. Three (*tri*) couches (*klinē*), or rows of couches, were placed in a horseshoe-type fashion with tables in the middle. The rest of the household (slaves, servants, children, etc.) ate in the *atrium*. The *atrium* was a large open-air room (courtyard) in the middle of the house designed, among other things, to collect rainwater.[1] It gave access to most other rooms in the house and would be directly connected to the *triclinium*. The *atrium* traditionally held thirty to forty people for a stand-up dinner. Those gathered in the *atrium* would receive cheaper food and, if any, the leftovers from the *triclinium*. The whole dining experience would highlight the distinctions in social rank between those eating.

The normal Corinthian household did not look much like a modern Western "nuclear family"—at least not in the traditional sense of mom, dad, and the kids. To the contrary, the home was not necessarily the family's place of privacy or place to withdraw from the hustle of public interaction. Rather, the family's business (the store) was a room in the house. "Home schooling" was the norm of the day, unless people were wealthy enough to send their children (or one of them) to school for training in rhetoric,

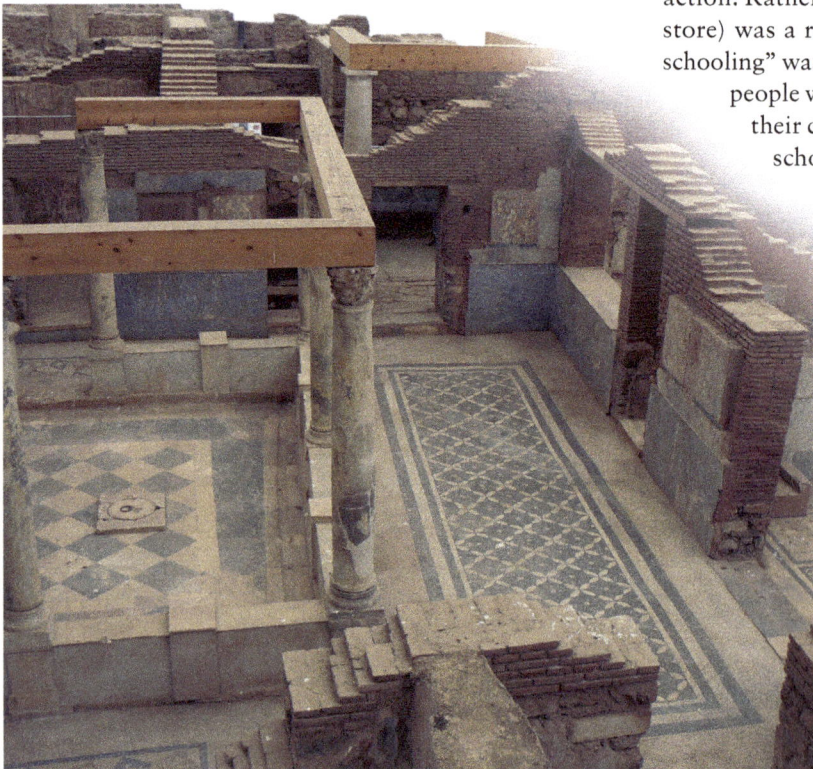

A typical Roman house would be constructed around an *atrium*, which would give entrance to other rooms used for sleeping, working, and formal dining (the *triclinium*). Shown here is the interior of one of the terrace houses excavated at Ephesus, which was occupied and renovated between the first century BC and the seventh century AD. The columns reveal the location of the *atrium*. Entrances to several rooms can also be observed.

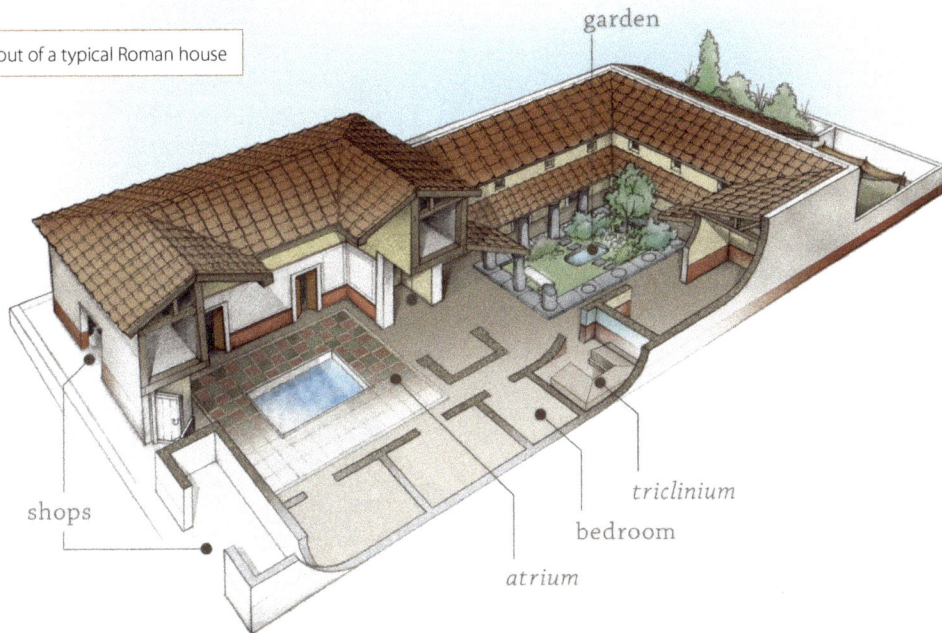

The layout of a typical Roman house

garden

shops

triclinium

bedroom

atrium

and so forth. Helpers/slaves were part of the family structure and lived in the house, as opposed to special slave quarters (even medium-income families had five or six slaves). In the case of a patron's home, a flow of clients would come daily for food, help, approval, signatures, and so on. Extended families without wealth of their own would likewise be part of the home. As all the common Roman household codes, including Paul's (Eph. 5:21–6:9; Col. 3:18–4:1) show, the home was a place of interaction between a number of different groups—husbands and wives, parents

and children, masters and slaves—not a place of escape and family intimacy.

It is into such a situation, where the spousal relationship had become a mere part of the business of the home, that Paul speaks this word of liberation and pastoral guidance (see, for example, 1 Cor. 7). Gospel informed, Paul's directives run contrary to the ordinary customs in Roman Corinth, where a phrase like "a husband does not have authority over his own body but yields it to his wife" (7:4) would sound odd—if not completely off.

Unity and Community (Part 1)

Big Idea *God empowers his people by his Spirit for the common good of his community, not as a personal favor to the individual. When individuals use their God-granted power for personal gain, they act like pagans attempting to manipulate their idol god.*

Understanding the Text

The Text in Context

Moving to the next question posed by the Corinthians (see 7:1, 25; 8:1), Paul continues his discussion on worship and ecclesiology. Distinguishing the Christian assembly from the pagan proves exceedingly significant not only for the various expressions of socioeconomic relations (chap. 11) but for speech patterns and the experiences of the Spirit's gifting and empowerment as well. Christ's call to communal responsibility includes a clear awareness of how God's communal character impacts his Spirit's endowments. Just as God blesses some in the community with material wealth for the community's benefit, he also pours out his Spirit "for the common good" (12:7) in other areas. Verses 1–3 speak directly to a situation where the Corinthians appropriate pagan practices in the name of Christ; verses 4–6

present the broader trinitarian theological basis both for the discussion of the particular gifts that follows (vv. 7–11) and for the whole section on spiritual empowerment (chaps. 12–14).

Historical and Cultural Background

Winter's insightful comments on religious curses prove helpful for unlocking the meaning of 12:1–3.[1] The ancient world was well acquainted with the practice of cursing an opponent in the name of a patron god. Tablets have afforded us rich evidence of this from the arenas of sports, love, politics, and business. Some tombstones

An example of cursing was found on this sixth-century AD tombstone inscription that ends, "Whoever violates this tomb shall suffer the fate of Judas."

included curse formulas designed to ward off potential grave robbers. One Christian tombstone, for example, calls for the "curse of Annas and Caiaphas" to come upon anyone trying to open the grave.[2] A Coptic Christian text even utilizes a countercurse formula, calling on the God of heaven and earth to avenge a curse in the name of the beloved Savior and to bring down those who brought the curse and abandon them to demons.[3]

Interpretive Insights

12:1 *Now about the gifts of the Spirit.* In terms of grammar, the genitive plural *pneumatikōn* (NIV: "gifts of the Spirit") can be either neuter or masculine. If masculine, Paul's following discussion would concentrate on those who consider themselves spiritual ("the spiritual ones"; cf. 3:1). If neuter, Paul's discussion focuses on the things that pertain to the Spirit, such as the gifts. The general emphasis on the Spirit's manifestation throughout chapters 12–14 seems to favor the latter of these readings. However, Paul may be deliberately ambiguous in his phrasing, wanting to make a general reference to all issues pertaining to the Spirit (people and gifts). The better English translation of the phrase may be "concerning the questions related to the realm of the Spirit."

I do not want you to be uninformed. The irony seems thick. Paul addresses those who think they possess knowledge (*gnōsis*; cf. 8:1–4) with a statement that exposes their lack of knowledge (*agnoein*).[4] The point is not that what follows is something he forgot to tell them about (as the word "uninformed" seems to suggest); rather, their behavior proves that they do

Key Themes of 1 Corinthians 12:1–6

- To use Jesus's name to curse rather than bless is a rejection of his lordship.
- The triune character of God forms the basis for Christian unity in diversity.

not have *gnōsis* in this area as they claim to have. Instead of learning from Christ, they have allowed their pagan *gnōsis* to inform their spiritual understanding. As a result, they act as if they have not been informed—embarrassingly parading their lack of *gnōsis*.

12:2 *when you were pagans.* Paul's stress is on the religious and idolatrous background of the Corinthians, not on their ethnicity. "Pagan" is therefore a proper translation of *ethnē* in this context. Paul does not suggest that the Corinthians no longer are ethnic Gentiles; rather, he highlights that they no longer follow their former gods. Paul reasons along the lines of the Old Testament covenantal statement in Deuteronomy 11. You either "love the LORD your God and . . . serve him with all your heart and with all your soul" (Deut. 11:13), or you are "enticed to turn away and worship other gods and bow down to them" (11:16).

mute idols. That idols are mute is a common Old Testament prophetic theme (e.g., Isa. 46:6–7; Jer. 10:5; Hab. 2:18–19; Pss. 115:5; 135:15–16). Mute idols stand in contrast to the God who does not keep silent (Ps. 50:3).

12:3 *no one who is speaking by the Spirit of God says, "Jesus be cursed."*[5] The difficulty that the lack of a verb in Greek creates has resulted in a flurry of attempts to explain Paul's double noun phrase "cursed Jesus" (*anathema Iēsous*).[6]

If Jesus is the object of the curse ("may a curse be placed on Jesus"), as most English translations prefer (see the NIV), only one option seems viable. Since it proves next to impossible to imagine one of the Christ followers standing up in a Christian worship service and declaring a curse on Jesus, Paul must simply have thought of this statement as parallel to what he just said about the pagan experience. The idea of the verse then is something like this: pagans follow mute idols, and Jews curse Jesus; Christians, in contrast, call Jesus Lord. The first two are pre-Christian experiences. The Christian experience of calling Jesus Lord is a gift from God's Holy Spirit (12:13).[7] Cullmann considers both statements confessions. The confession "Jesus be cursed" would be required under the threat of persecution (cf. Matt. 10:17–20) with the demand to instead shout, "Caesar is Lord." Only those whom the Spirit had empowered would withstand such pressure and give the confession "Jesus is Lord."[8] Those without this empowerment and confession do not belong to Christ (Rom. 8:9).

It is far from certain, however, that Jesus is the object of the curse. If the Corinthian believers time and again tried to find

The pagan idols formerly worshiped by the Corinthians could not speak, but God uses the Holy Spirit to speak through believers as they declare that Jesus is Lord. Shown here is an idol of the god Pan from the early second century AD.

room for their pagan (or cultural) practices within the Christ community (see chap. 11), it is quite likely they also tried to continue their pagan practice of cursing their opponents. The "Christian" change from their pagan days was that they now cursed in the name of Jesus, who had more power than any of their former gods (cf. 1 Pet. 3:19). Jesus, then, may be not the object of the curse but the subject, the power they call on to cause the curse ("Jesus grant a curse!"). If this pagan practice indeed is the reference of Paul's phrase, which seems likely, it connects directly to the corrective tone of chapter 11. Paul's aim, then, is to say: "You cannot use Jesus's name in curse formulas as the pagans use their gods to bring curse on others." Reformulated, the sense of Paul's statement is this: "No one speaking in the Spirit asks Jesus to bring a curse on others" (or "uses Jesus's name to curse"). Quite to the contrary, those who speak by the Holy Spirit call Jesus Lord (*Kyrios Iēsous*). To call Jesus *Kyrios* ("Patron" or "Lord") is to accept suffering, not cause it.[9] Since such acceptance of suffering runs contrary to the common sense of cultural and pagan practice, it can be done only through the enabling power of the Holy Spirit. Those who use Jesus's name in formulas of cursing rather than blessing are not guided by Christ's Spirit. The confession "Jesus is Lord" requires willingness to love in return for hate and to bless in return for curse (Luke 6:28; Matt. 5:44; Rom. 12:14).

12:4–6 *same Spirit . . . same Lord . . . same God.* Paul's theological argument for the oneness of the many rests in the triune character of God. The three statements—highlighting diversity and unity relating to Spirit, Lord, and God, respectively—are rhetorical parallels. Paul does not suggest a sharp distinction between gifts (*charismata*) given by the Spirit, services (*diakoniai*) rendered to the Lord, and empowerments (*energēmata*) activated by God. Rather, his point is that the Corinthians should realize they are all clients of the same patron, who reveals himself as Spirit, Lord, and God.[10]

Describing God as the gift giver, the patron benefactor, places every client in the same debt of gratitude and calls for their unqualified praise and glorification of the one who has lavished such gifts on them. For the well-to-do in the church, it reminds them of their standing as clients. For the poor, it is a reminder that they belong among the privileged who receive recognition and gifts from their patron. In a patronage-driven society like Corinth, Paul's argument functionally works to denounce the social divisions that exist outside the church as shameful inside the Christian community.[11] Although the "same Spirit" grants them different gifts (7:7), they have all equally been empowered by the "same God," to serve the "same Lord." The patron's (God's) purpose, therefore, is for all his gifts to work together in order for them to benefit everyone in his community (12:7; cf. 14:14, 26; Eph. 4:12). The Spirit, in other words, operates in direct contrast to the Corinthian perception alluded to in 6:12 and 10:23.[12] The patron grants enabling gifts to his clients in order to empower his community to accomplish his purpose.

Theological Insights

Being filled with God's Spirit transforms a person and enables him or her to call Jesus Lord. To call Jesus Lord means to accept, even strive for, a life that resembles Jesus's by loving one's enemies and responding to curses with blessings (Luke 6:27–30; Matt. 10:24–25; John 15:20; cf. 1 Pet. 3:9).

Teaching the Text

1. Paul's opening statement about not being ignorant about the issues of the Spirit results in an application that highlights the meaning of Jesus's lordship. In line with the Corinthians' pagan, or cultural, background, they have tried to use Jesus's name as a magical tool for personal benefit. Being aware of Jesus's power and concluding that he has to be on their side, they have tried to use him in their fight against their enemies. In effect, they have attempted to make him do their will instead of being willing to submit to his. Paul considers this a complete lack of knowledge about the function and works of the Holy Spirit. First, using Jesus's name in a curse formula—whatever that may look like—turns Christian faith into pure paganism. God grants his Spirit and his power for the purpose of reconciliation and restoration. The Spirit will cause people to pray for their enemies, not curse them (Luke 6:27–28). Second, the confession the Spirit generates is the lordship of Jesus. To call Jesus Lord, or to consider him patron, means to consider oneself a client, or follower. A client, or follower, aligns her or his life with the patron's and lives as the patron's representative. A follower of Jesus, therefore, lives a life of self-sacrifice and accepts the suffering that comes from that, in radical contrast to those who try to bring devastation on those who oppose them (Matt. 20:24–25).

2. In Corinth, as in contemporary societies, personal pride could turn diversity into disunity and self-glorification. In the struggle for prominence and recognition, it seems easy to think that when I am different—when I have qualities, wealth, pedigree, education, or ethnicity that others do not—I must be superior to them. In the Corinthian church, this line of thinking found further fodder from the spiritual realm. The church turned the diversity of gifts granted by God's Spirit into an opportunity for pride rather than an enablement to serve. This, Paul says, is a violation of God's intention in the highest degree. Not only does it violate God's intentions; it violates his very nature. The unity of the three persons in the Godhead militates against even the notion that diversity can give grounds for preeminence. All spiritual gifts, different as they are, are generously given without merit by the same Spirit. Their purpose is unification, not divisiveness—a divine enablement to build up the common unity (community) of believers. God grants every believer gifts to use for the good of others (12:7; cf. Matt. 25:14–30).

Illustrating the Text

The gifts of the Spirit are God's power at work in us, unlocking our potential to serve others.

Contrasting Concept: The *Star Wars* franchise has been one of the most popular families of films in the history of cinema. One prominent feature of the films is the Jedi religion, which teaches a Zen-like balance with the force, an omnipresent energy field flowing between living things. Jedi knights are skilled in sensing and wielding the force

Ancient Corinth was a pagan city. It is not surprising that the deeply rooted pagan practices of its citizens would influence the behavior of the infant church. Lead curse tablets were among the artifacts discovered during excavations at the sanctuaries to Demeter and Persephone located at the northern base of the Acrocorinth (shown here), showing that it was customary to ask deities to curse one's adversaries.

to achieve feats that range from telekinesis to mind control and anticipating the future. However, the gifts of the Spirit are nothing like the Jedi's use of the force in *Star Wars*. Rather than flowing between created things, the Spirit proceeds from the Father and the Son. Rather than being wielded and manipulated by skilled initiates for their own missions and quests, the Spirit blows where he will, unpredictably, for the purpose and glory of the Father, using humble humans for the Great Commission. Rather than being available to only a few, the Spirit pours out his gifts on all believers without favoritism, equipping each to support the mission of the body of Christ.

Bible: **Acts 8:9–25.** Simon was a pagan magician who made his livelihood by conjuring signs of power. In this passage in Acts, Simon sees the amazing works that are being done by the Holy Spirit through the ministry of Philip, one of the early church's deacons. When he sees that the Holy Spirit is given to believers at the laying on of Peter's and John's hands, he offers them money in an effort to buy the authority to grant the Spirit's power to others at the laying on of his own hands. He is soundly rebuffed by Peter for his wickedness. In the same way, we often seek ways to earn the Spirit's gifts and presence in our lives as if the Spirit were mere magic that we could concoct with good works or proper prayers. The Spirit refuses to be bought with money, good works, or manipulation. He gives his gifts freely to humble servants whose only agenda is being useful and ready in the Lord's plans.

The Spirit gifts us differently so we will be interdependent, not to reveal a hierarchy of status and power.

Visual: Bring in equipment from a sport or hobby you enjoy and about which you are knowledgeable. The key is that there should be at least two components to the equipment that work interdependently. For example, you may choose a rod and reel, a bat and ball, a golf club and golf ball, a bow and arrow, a climbing rope and harness, a mixing bowl and spoon, and so on. Display the two components and remark about how differently they are designed and made. Suggest (playfully) that there might be some out there who believe that rods are more important than reels, since the manufacturer made them farther reaching than reels, or reels than rods because they make great clicking noises and carry line. Others might believe bats are more remarkable than balls because they have more mass, or balls than bats because they use more complex materials, and so forth. Then explain that such talk is foolishness—reels are made for rods and rods for reels so that together they can catch fish! Baseball cannot be played with all baseballs and no bats, and a climbing harness without rope is rather pointless for climbing. In other words, some things are simply designed differently in order to function interdependently; to elevate one above the other is ridiculous. It is the same in the Spirit's design and wisdom regarding the gifts he pours out.

1 Corinthians 12:1–6

Unity and Community (Part 2)

Big Idea *Paul calls the church to recognize the communal nature of God's spiritual endowment. As a generous patron, the Triune God gifts each of his clients with power to serve others in eager pursuit of a Spirit-willed unity.*

Understanding the Text

The Text in Context

Christian unity comes not as a mere command to do what is right; it flows from the very character of God himself. The issue is not uniformity (there are varieties of gifts, services, and activities) but an experience of oneness as they all serve the same Triune God (Spirit, Lord, God [12:4–6]). With this trinitarian statement as the sounding board, Paul now highlights how all gifts are manifestations of the same Spirit, designed to equip Christ's body, the church (12:12–31). God has designed each gift, whatever function and expression it may have, for the common good (12:7). The Christ community's patron (God) gives his gifts not to show favoritism among his clients but to equip his clients to serve his kingdom. Because of the diversity of his gifts, they can together accomplish his call and purpose.

Interpretive Insights

12:7 *to each one.* Paul's following use of the body metaphor (12:12–26) underscores his use of "each" (*hekastos*) in this verse. He intends to say that each individual Christian has received at least one particular gift designed to strengthen Christ's community. In typical Hebrew fashion, Paul applies a theological passive ("is given," *didotai*) to underscore the gifts' origin.[1]

manifestation of the Spirit. That Paul avoids making a distinction between the Spirit's "manifestation" (*phanerōsis*) and spiritual gifts (12:9) more than suggests that he understands the spiritual endowments as vehicles to publicly reveal God's presence. The genitive phrase "manifestation of the Spirit" is, then, likely objective (the gifting demonstrates [publicly] the Spirit's presence) rather than subjective (the Spirit displays the gifts).

for the common good. The Greek participle *sympheron* (lit., "bringing together") speaks to advantage or helpfulness—that which benefits.

12:8–11 The variety of ways in which the Holy Spirit reveals his presence cannot be limited to a list of specific gifts.[2] In this list Paul uses the word "gift" only in connection with healing. This does not mean that this sample list is coincidental. Rather, Paul addresses the issues that prove especially divisive to the Corinthian community. To classify these nine areas of the Spirit's manifestation is next to impossible, as the array of disparate attempts by commentators shows.[3] Also, Paul's choice to use "gift" only in connection with healing may be nothing other than a desire to vary his language.

His list of "to another" (*allō*) is interrupted twice by another word with synonymous meaning (*heterō*).[4] If Paul deliberately intends to divide his list this way, his purpose likely is to single out the two issues of pride that trouble the church the most—their elevation of wisdom and knowledge (12:8) and their use of glossolalia ("tongue speaking" [12:10c]). The five other expressions of the Spirit (connected by *allō*) then constitute a list of commonly recognized manifestations of divine power (12:9–10b).

12:8 *message of wisdom . . . message of knowledge.* Although Paul separates wisdom (*logos sophias*) and knowledge (*logos gnōseōs*), it is not likely he intends to make a sharp distinction. Rather, he opens the list by highlighting that the content of "Christian" wisdom and knowledge comes from God's Spirit. Because of this, it unifies and is not divisive like the kind of wisdom/knowledge the Corinthian society

The Spirit gives gifts of healing. Healing powers were sought by the pagan community from the god Asclepius, whose statue is shown here (third to fourth century AD).

Key Themes of 1 Corinthians 12:7–11

- The diversity of the Spirit's endowment provides the basis for communal maturity.
- Christian wisdom and knowledge flow from God's presence and encourage unity.
- God's Spirit empowers his people to evidence his kingdom presence.

generally considered attractive. That God's Spirit grants wisdom, knowledge, and recognition of God's will is well known from the Old Testament (Exod. 35:31; Isa. 11:2; Dan. 1:4; 5:11–12; see also Ps. 111:10; Prov. 9:10).[5] In line with this, Paul likely considers the gift of wisdom and knowledge to be God's empowerment to guide others in the ways of Christ's self-sacrificing love (1:23–24; 6:5–6).

12:9–10a *faith . . . gifts of healing . . . miraculous powers.* Paul's reference to "faith" here is distinct from the saving faith known by all Christians. It points to a special faith that enables a believer to trust God to do things for which the gifted person cannot claim a promise from Scripture or a reality grounded in the structure of the gospel itself (13:2; Matt. 17:20; 21:21; cf. Isa. 40:4; 49:11).[6] Related to extraordinary faith are "gifts of healing" and "miraculous powers" (or "activities of powers"). That both "gifts" and "activities" are plural suggests that Paul does not think of these as permanent gifts belonging to certain people. These, rather, are gifts given to whoever is serving in any of a variety of ministry situations where that particular gift is needed to evidence the power of God's kingdom (Matt. 11:4–5; contrast Acts

14:9–10; 19:11; 28:8 with Phil. 2:27; 2 Tim. 4:20; 1 Cor. 11:30; Gal. 4:13).[7] The "miraculous powers" clearly include healings but are not limited to these. They stand in contrast to the activities of God's adversary (2 Thess. 2:9).

12:10b *prophecy.* Paul's understanding of *prophēteia* ties directly to the Old Testament. Prophecy is a message from God to his people. The new covenant promise that the Spirit will come upon all flesh potentially makes all Christians prophets (Jer. 31:33–34; Ezek. 36:26–27; Joel 2:28–29; Acts 2:17). What is less clear is how the prophecy is delivered—speaking in tongues, in regular language, or both. Paul feels no need to spell this out, but 14:3–4 suggests the mode of prophecy is intelligible language. Nothing in the text itself, however, suggests that Paul equates prophecy with something comparable to a modern-day prepared sermon, although it may certainly include elements of such.[8] Rather, the hints he gives allude to a spontaneous empowerment from the Spirit that allows the gift's recipients to speak words that reveal God's presence and guidance in a specific situation (14:3, 24–25, 30–31, 37).

distinguishing between spirits. The struggle to distinguish between genuine and false prophets is well known from the Old Testament (e.g., Deut. 13:1–3; 1 Kings 22:21–22; Jer. 27:9; Ezek. 13:3). Paul refers not to a special ability to evaluate whether a prophecy is true but to whether the one speaking is empowered by the Holy Spirit or another spirit. The plural "spirits" recognizes that spirits other than God's can generate displays of power that can lead believers (including the "prophets" themselves) to draw errant conclusions about

The gift of prophecy was given to Peter as the Holy Spirit empowered him to address the crowd at Pentecost. This fresco (1425) by Masolino da Panicale from the Brancacci Chapel in Santa Maria del Carmine in Florence illustrates the scene.

the true authority behind a "prophetic" message (Matt. 24:24; 1 Thess. 5:20–21; 1 Tim. 4:1; 1 John 4:1). God gives the gift of spiritual discernment to protect his people (2 Cor. 11:1; Gal. 1:6) and build his church in the likeness of Christ (1 Cor. 6:11; 14:12; 2 Cor. 3:3; Phil. 2:1–11).

different kinds of tongues . . . interpretation of tongues. The extraordinary interest in tongues among believers then and now (pro or con) is likely rooted in a sense that it evidences the Spirit (14:12). Being able to speak in a language that does not communicate with other humans while apparently communicating with God carries with it a sense of manifestation of divine presence (14:2).[9] To Paul, however, since God gives his gifts for the benefit of the community (12:7), tongue speaking lacks the very quality of divine presence it claims unless God grants another (*allos*) person the gift of interpretation (14:19). The word for "interpretation" (*hermēneia*) can mean either "translation" or "interpretation." It is doubtful that Paul is making as sharp a distinction between these as we do today. His point is to remind the Corinthians that when God's Spirit gifts a person to speak in tongues, the same Spirit will gift another person to make it intelligible to the church, for the purpose of edification.

12:11 *just as he determines*. Concluding this brief outline, Paul reiterates that whatever enablement or power any have received, it has been granted by their benefactor/patron, God's Spirit, and according to his will, not theirs. Spiritual endowment, in other words, gives no reason for pride and is not given for personal benefit.

Theological Insights

Spiritual gifts are communal and not given for mere personal benefit. God grants the gifts of his Spirit in order to enable the Christ community to manifest Christ and to continue *his* ministry of revealing the presence of God's kingdom (Mark 1:15).

Teaching the Text

1. As becomes evident from Paul's body metaphor in the following section (12:12–27), gifts receive their purpose and power from their connection to the other gifts granted to the body. For gifts to become effective demonstrations of the Spirit's presence, evidence that the kingdom has come, they must be understood as instruments designed to enable the client (the

Spiritual Gifts

According to Paul, divine gifts are indispensable to the Christian life, which without them would fail to bear witness to its supernatural origin. The two terms he uses for these gifts—*pneumatika* ("gifts of the Spirit") and *charismata* ("gifts of grace")—identify them as gifts bestowed freely and sovereignly by God through his Spirit. They are gifts, not earned qualities, and they belong to those whom the Spirit has filled (2:12), while being withheld from those who are ignorant of the Spirit (2:14). These grace gifts, though they do not differ in nature (12:4–11), vary in function (12:12–26; Rom. 12:4–8; Eph. 4:11–13) and importance (1 Cor. 12:28–31). Paul gives three lists of *charismata* (Rom. 12:6–8; 1 Cor. 12:4–11, 28–30; Eph. 4:7, 11). Since the content of each of these lists so clearly fits a specific literary (and historical) context, they are not meant to be exhaustive but to function as examples of how the Spirit manifests himself in Christ's community (1 Cor. 12:7).[a]

[a] For a fuller general statement on spiritual gifts, see my article "Spiritual Gifts," in *BIBD*, 1572–74.

Christ follower) to accomplish the patron's purpose. Put differently, Christ endows his household with manifestations of the Spirit to empower his community to represent him. This gives direct purpose to the lives of individual clients (Christians) as their particular gift (or gifts) helps fulfill the purpose Christ has for his community. When individuals understand their specific gift as an expression of the patron's (Christ's) preference for them over others, they are using their spiritual gift to manifest themselves rather than Christ. They are bringing glory to themselves rather than to their Lord.

2. In the short sample listing of gifts in 12:4–10, Paul highlights wisdom and knowledge. Various groups of "street philosophers" used *sophia* ("wisdom") and *gnōsis* ("knowledge") as catchphrases to extol their own superiority and brilliance. Their ability to give a message that revealed *sophia* or *gnōsis* distinguished them from

the masses, who were characterized by ignorance (*agnōsis*). As a contrast, the wisdom and knowledge revealed through God's Spirit promoted humility, not pride. The wisdom granted by the Holy Spirit gave people a deeper knowledge of God by revealing how the character of Christ impacted their specific situations. In line with Old Testament understanding of wisdom and knowledge, Paul's litmus test for whether messages of wisdom and knowledge originate from the Holy Spirit is their quality as guides for believers to know God's will as true followers of Christ. In this way, the gifts of wisdom and knowledge connect with the gift of prophecy. Like prophecy, these can derive from a spirit foreign to God's Spirit. When they do, they separate believers by giving prominence to the speaker. When, in contrast, they come from the Holy Spirit, they unify believers by revealing what effect Christ's lordship has for their particular circumstance (Matt. 15:24; Luke 14:26; John 14:15).

3. The supernatural quality and Spirit dependency of the gifts Paul lists leave little doubt that he considers these demonstrations of God's kingdom. Beyond their unifying quality as expressions of a generous patron's care for his clients, they are empowerments for the believers to push back on the consequences of the fall (Gen. 3). They reveal the presence of the coming new age (Mark 1:15; Matt. 12:28). In a very real sense, they demonstrate what Jesus pointed to when John the Baptist's disciples came and asked Jesus if he was the one to come.

Jesus replied by pointing to the restoring power of God's kingdom presence (Matt. 11:2–5; Luke 7:20–22). Each of the gifts mentioned here is a kingdom announcement (*phanerōsis* [12:7]). Wisdom, knowledge, and prophecy make known the will of God, which sin hides. Faith, healings, and empowerments counter the physical effects of life outside God's presence. If Paul considers tongues angelic languages of sorts, direct communication with God is now given a new avenue. In short, the Spirit has empowered the Christ community to experience God's kingdom as they live in the fulfillment of the prophetic promise.[10]

Illustrating the Text

The gifts of the Spirit are meant for service, not for our self-glorification.

Personal Stories: Tell about a time you were trusted by someone to buy or deliver a gift for a third party but ended up coveting the gift. Maybe your parents gave you money to buy Christmas presents for a sibling, or an organization trusted you to

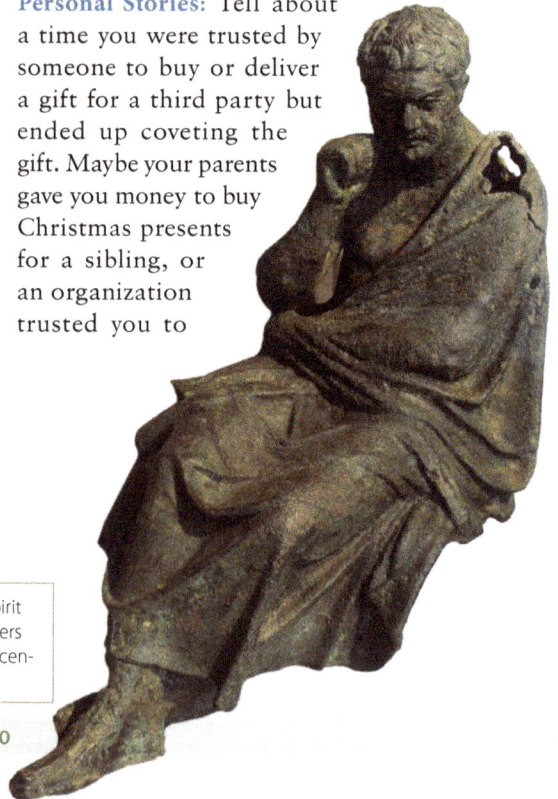

The messages of wisdom and knowledge given by the Spirit differed from the rhetoric of the contemporary philosophers of Greece and Rome. This bronze statuette from the third century BC shows a typical philosopher's pose.

spend a gift budget on a peer. In any case, you shopped with your own preferences in mind, bought something you would have wanted, and then felt distressed to see it go to the originally intended recipient. In the same way, we often ask for spiritual gifts that would be of benefit to us in increasing our sense of worth, solving our problems, or gaining the respect of others. If we do receive such gifts, we often feel tempted to use them for our own agendas and to better our own lives. Rarely do we eagerly desire the greater gifts and ask for them based on the needs we see around us. Rarely do we seek gifts that deepen our ability to serve, suffer, and be humbled so that others might be elevated. Rarely do we delight to see God's gifts to us poured out to the point of depletion, trusting that he will give more tomorrow if we leave it all on the field today. What might happen if we focused more on staying connected to the Giver and delighting to reflect his giving nature, rather than obsessing with the gifts themselves?

Television: **The Simpsons.** In an early episode of this animated series (Season 1, Episode 9, "Life on the Fast Lane") the main character, Homer, buys his wife (a nonbowler) a custom bowling ball as a last-minute birthday present. Worse, she realizes he has had his own name engraved on it, assuming that she will decline the gift and he will get to enjoy it. She sees through his ruse and accuses him of simply buying a gift for himself and pretending to offer it to her in an effort to look generous.

Sometimes believers approach spiritual gifts this way, developing abilities they feel will make them happy and later trying to pass them off as spiritual gifts for the benefit of others. Instead, we must humbly and authentically remain open to the gifts and calling Jesus has for us in each situation and pour it all out for others.

The gifts of the Spirit authenticate the gospel by doing things people could do only when reconciled to God.

Science: In the field of forensics, investigators are ever more dependent on biometric and biological clues. DNA and fingerprints leave behind calling cards that distinctly identify each individual from a sea of over seven billion faces. A person can claim to have had no involvement in a crime, but if his or her DNA is found at the crime scene, or a fingerprint is spotted on a piece of evidence, there can be no doubt that that person was in some way present or involved. In the same way, the gifts of the Spirit are like God's fingerprints in a congregation or movement. They are his way of authenticating his involvement. These gifts differ from abilities in that they create lasting fruit that can be achieved only supernaturally. A human can give a good talk, but only the Spirit can use that talk to bring conviction that leads to conversion. When the Spirit does this, we can look back and say that it was a gift of preaching being exercised, not just savvy oratory. Why? Because God's fingerprints were left behind, leaving a mark unlike any a human can create.

Many Parts, One Body

Big Idea *In a fashion parallel to the physical body, which God created with a plurality of parts with different functions, God grants a multiplicity of spiritual gifts in order for the Christ community to function as the incarnate body of Christ.*

Understanding the Text

The Text in Context

After giving a theological basis for unity in diversity, Paul now turns to a most memorable explication that stands out in a special way in the Corinthian situation. The multiplicity of spiritual gifts is designed to enable Christ's members to function as parts of Christ's body. Paul's thought flows naturally through this section. A physical body has many parts (12:12–14); these parts are all different (12:15–20), yet they all depend on each other (12:21–26); the same is true in Christ's body (12:27–30). (See the "Additional Insights" following this unit for background on Paul's body metaphor.)

Just as the physical body has many parts that depend on each other, so it is with the members of Christ's body, the church. All are different but need each other to function properly. Shown here are terracotta votive legs, feet, and hands from the Sanctuary of Asclepius at Corinth (fourth century BC).

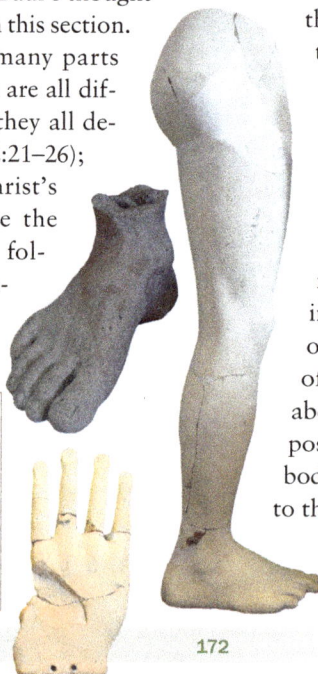

Interpretive Insights

12:12 *has many parts.* The watered-down notion of "members" (*melē*; NIV: "parts"), as carried by clubs, websites, various organizations, and even some churches, is a far cry from Paul's thinking in this context. Paul thinks of the interdependence of individual "members" in the Christ community in parallel fashion to the interdependence of body parts in the human body.

so it is with Christ. Paul's transitional sentence, switching his language from Spirit to body, keeps the readers' focus on God. His language moves from Spirit to Christ, not to church. To Paul, the church is not simply an organization finding its unity in a common challenge or charge; it is a living representation of the incarnate Christ. Paul talks about union, not just common purpose or similar persuasion. Individual body parts have life only in connection to the rest of the body.

12:13 *all baptized by one Spirit so as to form one body.*

The primary significance of 12:13 is to establish 12:14–30 as expositional of the reality of the Spirit-inaugurated new covenant (Jer. 31:33–34; Ezek. 36:26–27; Joel 2:28–29).[1] The unity believers have with Christ and each other is guaranteed by the Spirit, who has made them "one body." Furthermore, given the parallelism of 12:13 with 6:15–16, where the allusions to Genesis 2:24 are unmistakable, the quality of this union almost carries a sense of corpo-reality in Paul's thinking. Analogous to a husband, who joins his wife and becomes one flesh with her, believers, who are joined by the Spirit, become one body—Christ's body (cf. Eph. 5:28–30).

12:14–20 *the body is not made up of one part but of many.* Contrary to a surface reading of this text, and what certainly would be attractive in a (post)modern setting, Paul does not argue that the differences between the various body parts mean that church members who have received diverse gifts should be free to do whatever they feel their gifting enables or "allows" them to do.[2] The purpose of each body part is to function in accord with the others. If or when the parts do not, they cease to be one body. A limb must fulfill its assigned purpose in the body or it will itself cease to be a limb and consequently leave the rest of the body impaired.

Paul's concern centers on those who feel insignificant in gifting and status. By letting the body parts speak in the fashion of fables ("if the foot should say . . ."), Paul addresses the community's divisions head-on. Preferring hands over feet (12:15), eyes over ears (12:16), or even ears over nose (12:17) would be absurd. The very notion of ranking particular body parts in terms

of significance proves farcical. The Corinthians should realize the preposterous nature of suggesting that God's gifting of some members carries higher significance than his gifting of others (12:18).[3] Just as a healthy body needs different parts, the Spirit gifts everyone differently to fully equip Christ's body (12:19–20).

12:21–26 *the head cannot say.* Paul's surprising introduction of "head" (12:21) as a simple parallel to other appendages and organs proves his point. Even if some should claim to be head of the body, they do not have priority over the feet.[4] In Christ's body, over which Christ alone is head (cf. Eph. 1:22; 4:15; 5:23; Col. 1:18; 2:10, 19), the weaker parts are indispensable.

God has put the body together, giving greater honor to the parts that lacked it. With rhetorical prowess, Paul pushes his metaphor to drive home his point in a way that stands out unforgettably in an honor-shame society. The body parts we think are "less honorable" (*atimos*), the sexual organs, are treated with special modesty (*timē*; NIV: "honor"). The point seems impossible to miss. The slaves and the poor, those considered *atimoi* ("dishonorable") outside Christ's community, Christ considers honored in his community.[5] In fact, to topple any division among believers (12:25), God gives "abundant honor" (*perissoteran timēn*; NIV: "greater honor") to those who are without status (*hysteroumenō*; NIV: "the parts that lacked it"). The Corinthian Christians should do the same and care equally for everyone (12:25).[6]

If one part suffers. The unity of the body means that when one part of the body suffers, the whole body suffers and every part hurts, and when one part of the body is honored, the whole body is honored and every part rejoices. When this is not the case, the body has ceased to be a body and has become a collection of disjointed parts.[7]

12:27–30 Paul turns from the more abstract discussion to a direct discourse, opening with an emphatic "Now *you*[8] are the body of Christ, and each one of you is a part of it" (cf. Rom. 12:5). The following list of gifted officers (apostles, prophets, teachers) and specific ministry gifts (miracles, gifts of healing, helping, guidance, different kinds of tongues) is separated by numerators that point to either levels of authority or the temporal order in which these gifts have been given to the church (cf. Eph. 4:11). All of the gifts are listed as plural. Paul moves without hesitation from the more permanent "office gifts" to the more ad hoc "ministry gifts." Apparently, not much distinction needs to be made between them at this point other than to highlight the first

"And God has placed in the church first of all apostles" (12:28). This ivory plaque, called *The Mission of the Apostles*, is from Constantinople (tenth century AD).

three, which all relate directly to the teaching of the gospel message.

12:28 *first of all apostles.* Beyond referencing the Twelve (e.g., Gal. 1:17), Paul specifically uses the title "apostle" only of himself, his fellow Jews Andronicus and Junia (Rom. 16:7), and James the Lord's brother (Gal. 1:19). In 1 Thessalonians 2:7 he seems to also include Timothy and Silvanus, and in 2 Corinthians 11:13 he relates that his opponents claim to be apostles. Luke names Barnabas as an apostle alongside Paul (Acts 14:4, 14). Although the term itself means "one who is sent," Paul, along with the New Testament in general, presents this office as belonging to a limited group of people who enjoyed a special calling connected to the founding of the church in the first century.[9] That Paul does not consider apostleship a matter of superior status is clear from the other titles he gives himself: servant, worker, assistant, steward. All these terms relate to a low status.

second prophets, third teachers. Paul deals with this in a fuller fashion in chapter 14 (see also comments above on 12:10b). Thiselton's note that teachers provided the instruction that inspired the prophets' pastoral message provides helpful insight into the connection between the two offices.[10]

A primary function of the teachers was to protect the church's foundational teaching by explaining how God by the Spirit revealed himself through Christ. This included "communicative explanation, interpretation of texts, establishment of creeds, exposition of meaning and application."[11] Paul himself had the role of a teacher (14:6; 1 Tim. 2:7; 2 Tim. 1:1).

then gifts of healing, of helping. Listing "helping" in the same breath as the gift of healing reveals the breadth of Paul's thinking and his unwillingness to separate spirituality from ministry. Beyond the general ability to support others in need, Paul likely refers to the role of the patron as the benefactor of the weak.[12]

guidance. The Greek word *kybernēseis*, sometimes translated as "administration" or "leadership," points to those who are given directive roles.[13] The English word "administration" tends to yield a different sense from what Paul expresses here.

tongues. Tongues were a particular problem in Corinth as they divided rather than unified, not only because some tried to parade their spiritual superiority by using this gift in high-profile settings but also due to the linguistic divisions unintelligible language created in the community (14:9–12).[14]

Theological Insights

The church is called the body of Christ. More than a nomenclature, this image carries the reality of its content. In a body, all parts are important; when one is missing, the body is handicapped. Furthermore, no part can exist separate from the body. If a finger is severed from the body, the body is handicapped, but the finger dies.

Teaching the Text

1. The tension between unity and diversity is not a new one. In Paul's thinking, however, this tension is overcome through clarity of purpose. Paul argues that diversity can thrive in community and even strengthen its unity. Diversity becomes a threat to unity only when individual believers confuse God's purpose with their own desire for prominence and recognition. Members of the Christ community must revisit what it means to live as the incarnate body of Christ. As in the physical body, no part is dispensable; everyone is significant. Any notion that a believer can be disconnected from active participation in the body is foreign to Paul. Limbs that are cut off from the body die, and the body is handicapped and less efficient when parts are missing. God's purpose in granting his gifts—diverse as they are—is to enable and empower every individual Christ community to exemplify Christ's ministry on earth. The challenge for the recipients of the gifts, all believers, is to recognize their functions as "body parts" and how God has designed their particular gifts to strengthen other parts in order for the body to accomplish its God-given purpose.

2. Realizing that the church is a charismatic community means recognizing that without the empowerment of God's Spirit, "Christ's body" is reduced to an organization of the like-minded. Learning to depend on the Spirit's endowment of gifts can indeed be a tough lesson for many modern churches that have grown used to relying on attractive facilities, strong programs, natural talents of a few members, and ministers' rational power to persuade spiritual seekers. Paul's emphasis on the

importance of spiritual gifting stands in sharp contrast to such thinking. While he does not necessarily attempt to distinguish gifts of the Spirit from gifts of nature, he highlights the necessity of the church's constant dependence on the Spirit's evident endowment of every church member. The ease with which Paul speaks of gifts of healing and powers to perform miracles as nothing more than variant expressions of the same Spirit who also gives capacities to help and lead clearly suggests an awareness of extraordinary divine presence. Paul's whole argument in this section rests on the unquestioned reality of God's bestowal of gifts. Individuals could possibly boast of natural talents as personal abilities, but they have nothing to boast about when their enablements are undeserved gifts from God's Spirit (4:7).

3. The thrust of Paul's argument is the communal nature of God's gifting. Every gift is placed (*etheto* [12:28]) by God according to his purpose. Just as God gives different functions to eyes and ears on the physical body, he also gives different spiritual gifts to different parts of Christ's body. Stressing that God is the gift giver not only highlights the unifying purpose of diverse gifts; it also describes their sufficiency as God's provision for his community. To claim that God's gifting of a church is less than sufficient, or that some necessary gifts are missing, is to overlook a significant conclusion from Paul's argument in this paragraph. According to Paul, churches that think they need more, or different, gifts from what the Spirit has given them must consider whether they are using their gifts according to God's purpose or attempting to become a community that

"If the whole body were an eye, where would the sense of hearing be? If the whole body were an ear, where would the sense of smell be? But in fact God has placed the parts in the body, every one of them, just as he wanted them to be" (12:17–18). Shown here are terra-cotta votive eye and ears from the Sanctuary of Asclepius at Corinth (fourth century BC).

is different from what God intends them to become.

4. Paul's emphasis on Christ (12:12) throughout this section functions as a practical theological measuring stick for the community experience of the believers. Since they are Christ's community, the gifts are designed to enable the church to continue Christ's revelatory and incarnational ministry. Put differently, the church is not free to write its own agenda, and when it does, it ceases to be Christ's body. The measuring stick is whether the life of the community produces a clear confession to Jesus's lordship (12:3). From this perspective, Paul's discussion in chapters 10 and 11, about the lack of significant transformation in thinking and lifestyle among believers, finds its conclusion here. The way to discern genuine spirituality is to ask how it empowers Christ's body to reveal its incarnational quality. Diverse as the Spirit's gifting is, every gift granted by the Spirit functions as a part of Christ's body and must therefore be revelatory of

Christ's lordship. Paul's body language in chapter 12 brings a corrective word to those who disconnect their faith statements from their lives (see chaps. 10 and 11). Gifts granted by the Spirit empower *Christ's* body and therefore cause their recipients to demonstrate *Christ's* lordship.

Illustrating the Text

Followers of the Triune God are able to express a sustainable unity made up of diversity.

Personal Stories: Invite two outwardly diverse parishioners to be interviewed in front of your listeners. One might be older and the other younger, one might be a soldier and the other an activist, one might be a hunter and the other an artist. In any case, they ought to know and have a genuine love for each other. Ask a few warm-up questions that highlight differences, elaborating on hobbies, demographics, careers, childhood experiences, musical tastes, and so forth. In this first half, you are not likely to get any similar answers. It should be pretty funny. Then, switch topics to issues of faith. Ask them to describe the most important relationship in their lives (Christ). Ask them to talk about where they will spend eternity and the meaning of life in a nutshell. Ask them their most fervent hope for their friends who do not know Jesus. Finally, ask them if there is anything in the world they would be willing to die for. In this second half, you should be hearing nuanced but very similar answers. Ask your listeners if they know of any other place in the world where two people who are so different would love one another and agree on the essentials. Only those adopted into the Triune God's family can boast such radical unity in diversity!

Spiritual gifts make sense and have purpose only in community.

Popular Sayings: Remind listeners of the old question "If a tree falls in the forest and there is nobody there to hear it, does it make a sound?" (You may also want to offer up some of the humorous variants, like "If a man speaks in a forest and no woman is around to hear him, is he still wrong?") Then point out that the saying is adaptable to spiritual gifts: "If a believer exercises a spiritual gift in a vacuum and there is no one there to be edified, is the 'gift' either spiritual or exercised?"

Visual: Bring two long, double-dutch jump ropes. Assert that you have some incredible jump rope skills and are going to do some sweet double-dutch moves, then try to work the ropes by yourself. If you are good at physical comedy, this could be pretty involved. Try to twirl the two ropes from one end, then run over and try to catch up on the other end. Then run to the middle and try to jump. If you have young kids in the congregation who know how to jump rope, you could rehearse ahead of time and have them come up and offer to help. They can take over the other two roles in the process and you could commence to jump a few turns. Then, explain that no matter how gifted someone might be, the person's spiritual gifts make sense only in community and partnership with others. (This would also work with other team stunts, like building a human pyramid, doing the limbo while trying to hold the bar for yourself, playing both sides of a table tennis or foosball match, etc.)

1 Corinthians 12:12–30

Paul's Body Metaphor

To most modern Christians, Paul's body metaphor is a unique way of explaining the church as the body of Christ. In the ancient world, however, comparing the human body to the society and community structures was rather commonplace. The ancient fable by the Egyptian Aesop (*The Belly and the Members*) gives a helpful example of this. Aesop tells the story of a belly having issues with the feet about who was more important. The feet argue that they carry the belly around, the belly that it gives nourishment and strength to the feet. When Aesop's fable became known in Greece, it changed from a fable to an allegory with didactic purpose.[1] The story was applied to soldiers (feet) and the general (belly). Stories like these were usually designed to give an argument for societal unity and order by giving an illustrative explanation of the necessity for the subordinate classes to accept their place in society as the natural order of things.[2] For example, Paul's contemporary Seneca writes:

> What if the hand should desire to harm the feet, or the eyes the hands? As all the members of the body are in harmony one with another because it is to the advantage of the whole that the individual members be unharmed, so mankind should spare the individual man, because all are born for a life of fellowship, and society can be kept unharmed only by mutual protection and love of its parts.[3]

Paul uses the same metaphor but turns it on its head. In Christ's body there is no hierarchy—no division between superior and inferior. In fact, the way God put together the body, he gave "greater honor to the parts that lacked it" (12:24). It is the "parts of the body that seem to be weaker" that are indispensable (12:22). God did this to secure that every part would "have equal concern for each other" (12:25).

The finds of the terra-cotta models of various body parts, now exhibited in the Museum of Ancient Corinth, give further evidence to the significance of Paul's description. Connected to the temple of Asclepius (the god of healing), these terra-cotta models of afflicted body parts show, if nothing else, a keen awareness of the significance individual parts have for the well-being of the whole body.

The illustrative force of 12:12–30 seems obvious, but it would be a mistake to reduce Paul's body metaphor to a mere illustration. Verse 12's conclusion, that the many parts of the one body explain Christ rather than the church, hints that Paul thinks in ontological terms. His body metaphor does not *only* illumine the interdependence of the individual church members; it explains the relationship between Christ and his church. Put differently, Paul's point is not to illustrate how the church functions as an organization but to show that the church is the means through which the incarnate Christ reveals himself on earth.[4] The gifts of the Spirit, then, are given not for the members' sake as such but to enable Christ's continued work on earth. As Hicks comments:

> There is thus a close similarity between the Christian and Stoic points of view in this period. The difference lies in the fact that in Paul's view it is in Christ that social and national barriers are cast down whereas the Stoics ground their attitude in the belief that men are all human beings by nature and thus related to one another. Their view is founded not on a God in whom all are equal but on kinship through one's very humanity.[5]

Leftovers from such use of body language are still found in modern vernacular. They are, for example, used with reference to social hierarchy in expressions like "head of state" or "he is just a foot soldier."

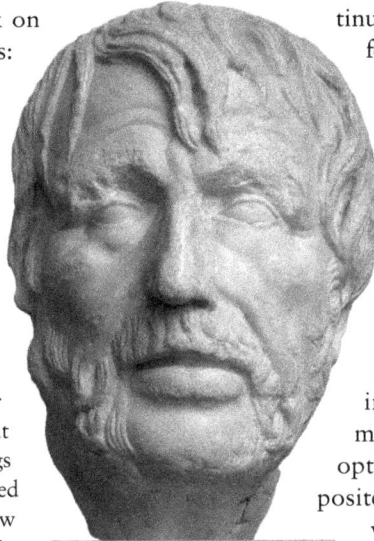

Paul's use of a body metaphor as he describes the relationship that should exist between church members was not unique. Seneca also used this metaphor to suggest why members of society should be in harmony with each other. This second-century AD sculpture may portray Seneca.

Societal structures consist of a variety of "bodies." Similarly, the heart continues to work as a metaphor for ideas in expressions like "the heart of the matter" and for emotions, as in "he is all heart." When a discussion culminates, it is "coming to a head." The hand shows up in terms like "handicapped" and "handsome." "Handicapped," of course, refers to a body in which a limb or part is missing or does not function optimally. "Handsome," oppositely, points to perfection—where all elements work together beautifully. Even in our modern tech-driven society, Aesop's fable continues to inform our metaphors, language, and conceptualization. Because of this, Paul's Christ-focused use of the body metaphor remains an important reminder of how Christ's body differs from worldly bodies.

The Priority of Love

Big Idea *Unless Christ's loving character becomes evident in the use and application of any and all of the Spirit's gifts, their practice becomes worthless for God's kingdom and mere demonstration of Christian immaturity.*

Understanding the Text

The Text in Context

Although God grants his gifts as an act of grace and not on the basis of merit, there is a dynamic relationship between the effectiveness of the gift and the life of the Christian.[1] Paul treats this connection between spiritual gifts and the quality of the believer's life most directly in this chapter. The abrupt insertion of this outburst on love in the midst of his discussion of spiritual gifts (chaps. 12 and 14) signals the intrinsic relatedness of life and gifting in Paul's mind. Moreover, the unrelenting emphasis that the Christian is nothing (13:2) and gains nothing (13:3) without love exhibits how in Paul's reasoning spiritual gifts require godliness for true effectiveness.

Interpretive Insights

12:31 *I will show you the most excellent way.* This transitional sentence functions almost like a reset button that lets Paul start over. The Corinthians thought of the more numinous gifts as the highest experience of spirituality and divine presence, but Paul will now show them the "most excellent" (*hyperbolē*) way. Spiritual gifts are significant (on *charismata*, see the discussion on 1:7 and the endnote there), and the Corinthians should be zealous (*zēloō*) to experience the greatest gifts—a topic Paul will revisit in chapter 14. But something is greater than any and all of the gifts, something that is not itself a spiritual gift given to just some in the body; rather, it is the foundation, a "way of life"[2] that should give guidance to the expression of all the gifts: love.

13:1–3 Seven parallel examples solidify Paul's point. With rhetorical force, Paul sets up a hypothetical scenario (subjunctive mood) in which he makes himself the case in point—"If I should . . ."

13:1 *tongues of men or of angels.* Any speech (tongues or regular human language) becomes mere sound waves without love. "Loud brass," or "resounding gong," contrasts with the sound of a beautiful musical instrument and refers to bronze jars used in theaters as resonators—a form of ancient sound amplification. They were loud, lifeless noise machines.[3] Paul designs his language to conjure up crass and distasteful images in the minds of his audience.

13:2 *gift of prophecy and can fathom all mysteries . . . faith that can move mountains.* Paul moves from the least of the gifts to the greatest. In spite of receiving even the greatest of the Spirit's gifts (the ability to hear God's voice, understand his revelations,[4] communicate his truths, and evidence a level of faith that evokes God's power), a believer would be nothing (*outhen*) without love. Paul does not say the person's gifts become less helpful or beneficial without love; he nullifies the very quality of such a believer.

13:3 *give all I possess to the poor.* Paul's surprising inclusion of an act of extreme benevolence[5] drives home his point. Even acts that look like expressions of love can be done for self-promotion and self-glorification. Paul's subtle change of verbs, from "I *am* nothing" to "I myself *benefit* nothing," reveals his careful nuancing of language. Giving one's possessions away is not worthless (see comments on 11:21b–22 and 11:30; cf. Matt. 25:55; Mark 10:21; Luke 14:13; 18:28–30; 19:8–9); it is just of no spiritual benefit unless it is done on the basis of love.

give over my body to hardship that I may boast.[6] Those who would sell not only their things but even themselves into slavery, to give everything to the needy, benefit nothing if they do it for the sake of boasting. Even Paul, who has given up everything

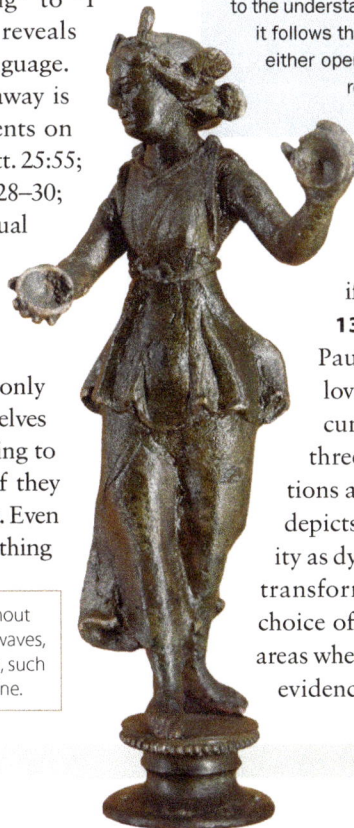

Key Themes of 1 Corinthians 12:31–13:13

- Christian spirituality must be rooted in Christ's character.
- The Spirit gives gifts to evidence Christ's loving presence.
- The actions love inspires are focused on helping others see Christ.
- Spiritual gifts evidence God's presence and point to God's future.

Guidance for Exercising Gifts

By abruptly inserting an excursus on love between chapters 12 and 14, Paul makes the same point he repeats in Rom. 12:6, speaking about the "measure" with which God bestows *charismata* ("gifts") to each individual. That Rom. 12:6 occurs in the midst of an exhortation on godliness likewise suggests that Paul understood *charismata* to have dynamic qualities. The Spirit grants "in proportion." Moreover, when Paul begins his exhortation on the use of gifts by stating that prophecy must be done "in proportion" to the prophet's faith, he is asserting that it must result from the prophet's relationship to God. Since this is the opening statement that gives guidance to the understanding of the subsequent gift list (Rom. 12:7–8), it follows that in Paul's mind the believer's faith and "walk" either open the door or set the limitations for a kingdom-revealing use of spiritual gifts.

and surrendered his life for the Corinthians' sake (9:17–24), benefits nothing if he has no love.

13:4–7 Most dramatically, Paul expresses the qualities of love with a series of verbs.[7] Accumulating fifteen verbs in just three verses to describe the actions and nonactions of love, Paul depicts Christ followers' spirituality as dynamically active and visibly transformative. Negatively, Paul's choice of verbs reflects precisely the areas where Corinthian actions do not evidence *agapē*. Positively, they are verbs describing the generosity of God, their patron (e.g., Matt. 18:26).

13:4 *Love is patient*. The more excellent way (12:31) is one in which Christ followers wait patiently (Rom. 2:4; 9:22). Actively being patient is a mark of the Spirit's presence (Gal. 5:22), evidence of holy living (Eph. 4:2; Col. 1:11; 3:12; 1 Thess. 5:14), and something the Corinthians could learn by imitating Paul (2 Cor. 6:6; 1 Tim. 1:16; 2 Tim. 3:10).

love is kind. Doing acts of kindness, or mercy, exemplifies God's character (Rom. 2:4; 11:22; Eph. 2:7) and presence (Eph. 4:32)—something Christians should imitate (Col. 3:12).[8]

It does not envy. According to Paul, being enraged by envy, behaving like a braggart, and being inflated by self-praise are marks of the flesh, not the Spirit (3:3). It comes from a pursuit of worldly things rather than the things of the Spirit. Contrary to the popularity of such behavior, encouraged by the sophists (see "Rhetoric and Truth in Corinth" in the introduction), a proper understanding of Christ, who willingly emptied himself of his divine privileges (Phil. 2:3–8), should cause Christians to rejoice when status, honor, and blessings are poured on others.

13:5 *It does not dishonor others . . . keeps no record of wrongs*. Continuing this list of contrasts between Christ-inspired and sophist-inspired behavior, Paul extends his description of actions *not* caused by love. Love does not "dishonor others"—a term that may include reference to sexually lewd behavior (7:36; cf. 5:1–2). It "is not self-seeking" (pursuing advantages, benefits, or rights [10:24, 33]) and "is not easily angered" (as even the Israelites were [10:10]). The passive *paroxynetai* speaks to a sharpened sense of touchiness, of allowing oneself to become irritated without substantial cause.[9] Love "keeps no record of wrongs"; it rejects the very notion of retribution.[10]

13:6 *Love does not delight in evil but rejoices with the truth*. That Paul uses forensic terminology suggests that love's transforming power reaches even to legal matters (see comments on 6:1–4). Misery and injustices done toward others cannot be a source of joy, even if those others are opponents. To sophists, combatant patrons, and others, winning a case superseded the pursuit of truth (cf. 5:8; Rom. 1:18, 25; 2 Cor. 13:8; Gal. 4:16; Phil. 4:8). Levels of wealth usually determined the outcome of a case, often at the expense of justice.[11] Sophists especially excelled in smear campaigns designed to dishonor their opponents and bring them misfortune. In contrast, those transformed by Christ's love trust God for their personal well-being; they find no gratification in the misfortune of others.

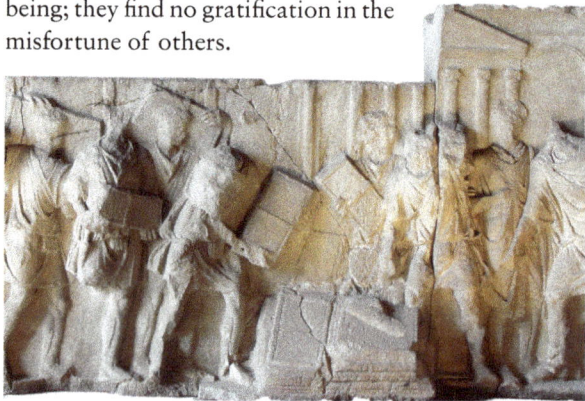

Love "keeps no record of wrongs" (13:5) and gives no thought to retribution. In this second-century AD frieze found in the Roman Forum, tax records are being placed on a pile to be burned. If wrongs were like these debts, according to Paul, love would not have kept records in the first place.

13:7 *It always protects, always trusts, always hopes, always perseveres.* In almost dialectic fashion, Paul switches from what love does *not* inspire or create to what it *does*. To express the limitless character of love's actions, Paul redundantly repeats *panta* ("all things"; NIV: "always") in front of each verb. Positively, love "protects" without limits. The verb *stegō* is rare, but its noun *stegē* means "roof" (Matt. 8:8; Mark 2:4). The verbal idea relates to covering and protection (as a roof covers and protects a house).[12] Included in this lies the idea of endurance, a willingness to "put up with," as the one who loves places a protective cover over the missteps of others (1 Pet. 4:8) and is prepared to accept the pain this causes to oneself (1 Cor. 9:12). That love "always trusts" expands this idea further. The point is not gullibility but a constant readiness to trust, and renew trust, because hope remains unquenchable, or without limits. Love, therefore, always "perseveres" (*hypomenō* [Matt. 24:13; Rom. 12:12; 2 Tim. 2:10; Heb. 12:1–3; James 1:12]).

13:8–12 Spiritual gifts are manifestations of God's presence, evidence that the kingdom of God has come (Mark 1:15; Luke 7:22). They are demonstrations of the "already" in the already/not-fully tension of God's kingdom. When the perfect comes (13:10) and Christ fills all in all (15:28; Eph. 1:23), when every knee bows and every tongue confesses Christ as Lord (Phil. 2:10–11), the gifts of the Spirit will cease.

13:8 *prophecies, they will cease.* Because these gifts have temporal purpose, their use will come to an end, or be exhausted (*katargēthēsontai*; NIV: "cease"). As a contrast, love will never end, or collapse

(*piptei*; NIV: "fails"). Gifts are means (or vehicles) God uses to show his presence and love until his people shall see him face-to-face (13:12; cf. Rev. 22:4); love is the very essence and expression of God's presence and therefore will never end.[13]

When the perfect comes, in other words, the imperfections sin brings to love will vanish, and the purity of the relationship God intended from the beginning will be fully restored (John 17:23; Col. 3:14–15; 1 John 4:17–19; Rev. 21:3–4; cf. Isa. 65:19–25). At that time gifts will cease to have purpose and will be abolished, along with all God's adversaries (1:28; 2:6; 15:24, 26; 2 Thess. 2:8; 2 Tim. 1:10; cf. 1 Cor. 6:13; Luke 13:7).

tongues, they will be stilled. That Paul chooses a different verb for the "ceasing" of tongues is due to the word "tongues" being the object. It has no substantial consequence for meaning. Tongues will be made quiet (*pausontai*; NIV, "will be stilled"). There will be no need for them when believers in their resurrection bodies (15:44) meet God face-to-face (13:12; Rev 22:3–4).

13:10–11 *when completeness comes.* When the fullness of maturity (*teleion*) comes, the empowerments the Corinthians presently claim as demonstrations of maturity will prove to be mere expressions of immaturity, even child's play (*ta tou nēpiou* [13:11; cf. Eph. 4:13–14]). The evidence of genuine maturity, therefore, is not a particular spiritual gift but love. Gifts cease while love continues.

13:13 *now these three remain.* Although debates have flourished around whether "now" (*nyni*) should be understood as temporal or logical, and whether the Greek *menei* ("continues" or "remains") is future or present tense, Paul's point seems to focus on the distinction between what passes away and what continues. Again, love expresses God's presence; gifts are temporary vehicles of grace.

faith, hope and love. The sudden introduction of faith and hope implies that Paul's aim is not to make a theological statement about the eternal nature of faith, hope, and love. Rather, the triad is shorthand for the fullness of the Christian life (e.g., 1 Thess. 1:3; 5:8; Gal. 5:5–6; Col. 1:4–5). Still, even among these three, love is the greatest. Because love expresses God's eternal nature, it is everlasting. Faith and hope are foundational elements of Christian experience, but they will not continue into eternity (2 Cor. 5:7; Rom. 8:24).[14]

Theological Insights

God willed to reveal himself to his creation as love (John 3:16). For spiritual gifts to function according to God's purpose, their use must reveal the character of the God who gives them. Without love, spiritual gifts will obscure what they were given to reveal.

Teaching the Text

1. Christian spirituality refuses reduction to a mere personal experience of the divine. Inspired by love, its focus is to reveal Christ. It points outward rather than inward. The aim of a Christian spirituality is to shout from the rooftop what was revealed in the prayer chamber (Matt. 10:27). Paul's argument is that a Christ follower must demonstrate Christ's character. Christian spirituality is not about feeling good but about willingness to participate in the sufferings of Christ. In Paul's mind, the connection between faith, hope, love, and suffering is immediate. "We also glory in our sufferings . . . because God's love has been poured out into our hearts through the Holy Spirit" (Rom. 5:3, 5).

2. The Spirit gifts believers in order to empower the Christ community to exemplify Christ. Since gifts are expressions of power, their misuse can produce the opposite of their intended result. This happens when they bring glory to the person receiving the gift(s) rather than to the giver of the gift(s). Paul's point here is that all gifts, whether spectacular or more ordinary, must become embedded articulations of Christ's love rather than illustrations of personal devotion. Paul calls love the more excellent (lit., "hyper-propelling") way exactly because it safeguards against such selfishness. When love drives the use of spiritual gifts, they become expressions of Christ's presence and thereby strengthen Christ's body. When selfishness drives the use of gifts, they reveal the presence of the gifted and thereby come to obscure rather than amplify God's voice.

3. Because gifts are provisions for the present time given to enable the continuation of Christ's ministry, their significance is found only as they bear witness to Christ. Paul illustrates this by highlighting an exceedingly selfless act—giving everything one owns to the poor. Even that can be done for the selfish reason of parading one's devotion. As testimonies to Christ, however, selfless gifts help lead both believers and nonbelievers to a deeper understanding of the nature of Christ and his transforming power. Love transforms

speech into revelatory events of blessing and instruction. Love converts knowledge and wisdom from points of pride to instruments for counsel and guidance. Love relocates mountain-moving faith from the avenue of display to the path of empathy and help. Love even transports giving from the realm of self-gratification to the place of suffering and participation.

4. Paul's contrast between the temporal nature of the gifts and the eternal nature of love leads him to give an array of unforgettable images that all contain a promise of something greater to come. What we have now is partial, but the partial will be replaced by the perfect. The grandest expressions of God's power and presence are mere examples of what will become the norm. Just as the childish ways of the young are put aside when they are recognized as immature, gifts also bear witness to a greater time to come. Likewise, the promise of a dim mirror is the clarity of twenty-twenty vision. What the dim mirror vaguely reveals must exist and will later come to be seen with full clarity—face-to-face. Then, as Paul exclaims, "I shall know fully, even as I am fully known [by God]" (12:12).

Illustrating the Text

Spirituality is not about feeling good; it is about willingness to participate in Christ's sufferings.

Drama: Come up with an advertisement for a strange new product: suffering. The ad should make a poignant and/or humorous illustration of the fact that nobody goes around shopping for suffering, and anyone trying to sell it can do so only by promising benefits on the other side of the suffering that allegedly outweigh it. Explain that almost every product advertised in our world promises some sort of pleasure or relief from suffering—no one advertises suffering for its own sake. Nevertheless, Scripture tells us repeatedly that there is joy in sharing in Christ's sufferings. Christianity is not a feel-good experience that promises only happiness. Rather, our faith is a "be-close" and "persevere-together" experience that promises to give us Jesus, who is more satisfying than we could ever imagine.

"For now we see only a reflection as in a mirror" (13:12; Roman mirrors, Hierapolis, Turkey, first century BC to fourth century AD).

Spiritual gifts have an expiration date; love does not.

Visual: Display a variety of consumer products that have expiration dates and consider what might happen to the product after the expiration date. Have one or two products with no printed expiration date—maybe a rock or stapler. Suggest that even these have an invisible expiration date. For, when Christ returns and heaven and earth are made new, even the elements will be tested by fire. Consider whether human beings have an expiration date. What about missions and outreach? Suggest that the passage emphasizes one thing that will remain throughout eternity: love. We need to be careful to invest the bulk of our focus in what will last.

Spiritual Gifts and Spiritual Growth

Big Idea *Although the Spirit's gifts do not grant status to their recipients, the gifts that benefit and build up Christ's community are of greater significance and value than those used only for the personal benefit of the individual.*

Understanding the Text

The Text in Context

Paul now returns to his discussion of spiritual gifts begun in chapter 12. To fully appreciate chapter 14, however, chapter 13 cannot be dismissed as a digression or a simple aside. Although 14:1–25 seems to focus primarily on tongue speaking and the perils thereof, Paul's real point is the character of Christian worship. In this way, chapter 14 connects directly to the extended exposition beginning in chapter 10 and guided by chapter 13. For Paul, love encapsulates the ethics of the life in the Spirit: it fulfills the law (Rom. 13:8, 10). Spiritual gifts gain their usefulness in the church from the Christlikeness of their recipients. In Paul's mind, this is not an either/or proposition but an expression of the dynamic more-or-less quality of a Christ follower's commitment to the *kyrios* (patron).

The problem with tongues was not God's gift but the believers' use of the gift. They used it as a platform for pride and considered it a sign of spiritual superiority. Such an understanding militates directly against God's intention for any of his gifts. Paul's aim is not to damn one of God's gifts but to help the church refocus and recognize its communal calling. For this purpose, prophecy is the greater gift; tongue speaking has become a hindrance.

First Corinthians 14:1–19 divides rather naturally into three sections. Verses 1–5 describe the communal character of the gifts and their relation to the character of their recipients. Verses 6–12 illustrate the shortcomings of tongues. Verses 13–19 clarify the proper use of tongues.

Interpretive Insights

14:1 *Follow the way of love and eagerly desire gifts of the Spirit.* Although these two imperative statements function to make a logical connection back to chapter 12 while transitioning from chapter 13, Paul's change of *charismata* ("grace gifts") in 12:31 to *pneumatika* ("spirit gifts"; cf. 12:1) in 14:1 suggests he has more in mind than a simple restatement.[1] Equating 12:31 and 14:1 has led some teachers and commentators to conclude that the "greater gifts" in 12:31 refer to "prophecy" in 14:1. This, however, is not Paul's intention. Rather, introducing a discussion on tongues and prophecy, he creates a direct link between the desire for gifts and the pursuit of love. Without love, gifts lose their effectiveness as Christ-empowered tools of the Spirit. Since the imperative verbs are unequal in force ("pursue" [NIV: "follow the way"] and "desire"), the two statements are not parallel, as if Paul simply advocated two good things for them to do. Rather, the eager desire for gifts is embedded in the pursuit of love.

especially prophecy. Paul's elevation of prophecy over tongues in this section does not imply he thinks prophecy is superior because it is above manipulation and does not need to be evaluated for its authenticity as revelatory of Christ (14:29; 12:10; cf. 11:4). Rather, the subjunctive mood of the plural verb (*prophēteuēte*) indicates his desire that every part of Christ's body would know God's word and voice and use it to encourage the whole body (14:3). "Prophecy" refers to a revelatory message in which the Spirit inspires the speaker to pastorally apply the Jesus story to a given situation (encouragement or correction) or an expositional word in which the speaker interprets biblical texts for the edification of the community.[2]

Key Themes of 1 Corinthians 14:1–19

- Christ followers must eagerly desire spiritual gifts in their quest to give evidence of Christ's love.
- Building Christ's community takes precedence over personal desires and preferences.
- The edification of both heart and mind is necessary; neither can be without the other.
- The purpose of the Spirit's gifts includes reaching "outsiders" with the blessings of God's salvation.

14:2–5 *does not speak to people but to God.* The trouble with tongues is their divisive quality. Their aim is the individual, not the community. As such, tongue speaking is the antithesis of prophecy. By contrasting the gifts' purposes in this way, Paul is able to affirm tongue speaking as a God-directed gift while exposing its lack of value for public worship.

The problem, then, is not the gift of tongues but the setting of its exercise. Since no one understands the speaker, there is no message and no one is built up.[3] Paul's objective is not to belittle the gift but to correct those who use it to promote themselves in the community. Paul does not deny the spiritual benefit tongues may have for personal devotion (14:4), and from that perspective he wishes that all had the gift (14:5). Yet the Spirit grants gifts primarily to strengthen Christ's body. People exercising the gift of prophecy are therefore of greater (*meizōn* [14:5]) significance for the body.[4] For tongues to be usable as a communal gift, the Spirit must also give the ability to translate the tongue into intelligible language (14:13).

The finesse of Paul's rhetoric allows him to simultaneously dismiss the claims of those who considered themselves spiritually superior because of their tongue speaking and to promote a keen awareness of the importance of the Spirit's gifts for Christ's body (cf. 1 Thess. 5:19; Eph. 4:29–30).

14:6 *if I come to you and speak in tongues, what good will I be . . . ?* To prove his point with even greater clarity, Paul recasts the situation, introducing a hypothetical scenario that reminds the Corinthians how they themselves came to faith. When they first heard Paul speak in Corinth, of course, he spoke intelligibly, and it resulted in their salvation. Shrewdly, Paul counterposes tongues with *gnōsis* ("knowledge"). Both are points of Corinthian pride; unintelligible tongues, however, render *gnōsis* mute. The new element in this list is "teaching" (NIV: "word of instruction"). It likely refers to the explanation of the Jesus tradition, the description of the core of Christian faith and how it relates to God's promises in Scripture (cf. 11:23–26).[5]

14:7–11 *pipe or harp . . . trumpet . . . all sorts of languages.* A musical, a military, and a linguistic analogy bring home Paul's point. If someone plays an instrument, who can recognize what is played without distinct notes? In other words, without distinct notes, beautiful instruments, like harps and flutes, turn into noisemakers (cf. Rev. 5:8; 14:2; 15:2). Similarly, soldiers going to battle depend on the distinctive clarity of the trumpet for various commands (cf. 1 Thess. 4:16). Likewise, speech must be intelligible to have effect. Even languages that are intelligible in foreign places, and commonly spoken among such peoples, remain obscure to those who do not understand.

14:12 *Since you are eager for gifts of the Spirit.* The plural *pneumatōn* refers to the plurality of gifts, not to a plurality of spirits. This verse connects to 12:1 and clarifies that the "greater gifts" of 12:31 are those that build up the church.

14:13 *For this reason . . . pray that they may interpret.* Paul concludes his statements with an inferential conjunction (*dio*) that implies the self-evident character of what follows. He does not suggest that the gift of interpretation necessarily belongs to someone other than the tongue speaker. If anything, he advises that a tongue speaker who does not have that gift must remain silent.

14:14–15 *my spirit prays, but my mind is unfruitful.* Paul returns to the first person and speaks out of personal experience. Deciphering how tongue speaking works to

"How will anyone know what tune is being played unless there is a distinction in the notes?" (14:7). Musicians play a harp and pipe (flute) in this sarcophagus relief (fourth century BC).

build up the individual, he makes a distinction between his spirit and his mind (not between the divine and the human). Singing and praying in tongues may encourage his spirit (his soul or his inner being),[6] but his mind does not benefit. Although encouragement of one's spirit is important, it does not offer anything to share with others except the emotion. Paul recognizes the necessary balance between heart and mind and confesses his own practice of singing and praying in tongues outside public settings.

14:16–17 *praising God . . . say "Amen" to your thanksgiving.* In the public setting, the only way an outsider can know whether a speaker is blessing or cursing is if the outsider understands what is said. Paul's switch of terms, from prayer (14:13–15) to blessing/praising and thanksgiving (14:16), conjures up images of the cup of blessing in the Lord's Supper (10:16). Moreover, the phraseology alludes directly to pagan practices of cursing and blessing (see comments on 12:3). How can someone who is ignorant of Christ (*idiōtēs*; NIV: "inquirer") join the thanksgiving if he or she remains unsure whether blessings or curses are spoken? The blessing, in other words, does not benefit the outsider (14:17). "Amen" is the affirmative conclusion to doxologies (Neh. 8:5–6; Rom. 1:25; 11:36; Gal. 1:5; Rev. 1:6).

14:18–19 *rather speak five intelligible words . . . than ten thousand words in a tongue.* Paul's conclusion that five intelligible words are better than a countless number (*myrios*; NIV: "ten thousand") of words in tongues repeats his emphasis that the importance of edifying Christ's body outweighs any amount of personal religious experience. Still, Paul is careful to not dismiss personal experience (14:18).

Teaching the Text

1. Paul's connection between the pursuit of love and the eager desire for spiritual gifts informs his audience's understanding of the significance spiritual gifts have as divine enablements for love. Far from something similar to a testing of psychological profiles among church members, designed to reveal hidden desires and talents, Paul encourages each member to strive for gifts that build the faith of others. Love, for Paul, at least in this context, is to look away from personal desire and focus on strengthening the life and faith of others. Gifts, both spectacular and ordinary, serve this purpose. Since they are given by God's Spirit, they reveal Christ's character. The eager desire for gifts, then, is not a side issue for the especially devoted but the Spirit's empowerment of Christ's body, without which they cannot reveal Christ's love. Put differently, believers who are pursuing love seek the Spirit's gifts to be able to evidence Christ's transforming presence. Gifts enable believers to do for others what they otherwise could (or would) not have done.

2. Paul's issue with tongue speaking in the church runs parallel to his issue with misappropriated knowledge (8:1). Because both of these prioritize personal benefit, they fail to evidence the self-giving love that flows from the character of Christ. From this perspective, tongues are a mere case in point for Paul. From another perspective, however, Paul highlights something even more sinister about the Corinthians' use of tongues. Paul sees tongues as positive expressions of personal devotion. Yet when used in a public setting as bragging points, they become expressions of self-glorification and are therefore both

destructive for the church and a violation of Christ-empowered love (cf. Luke 18:9–14). Unlike the knowledge that blatantly claimed its rights (8:1–13), misused tongues falsely gave the appearance of submission (cf. Luke 11:42). Paul's point is that personal desires, even personal desires for a specific approach to worship and devotion, must be subordinated in the public setting. The needs of the body always take precedence over the desires of the individual. The pursuit of love generates a desire to look away from self and to serve others.

3. Paul seems to go out of his way to make sure the Corinthians do not misunderstand his teaching and conclude that gifts (tongues) designed to encourage the heart are unimportant to the individual. Repeated affirmations of tongues as speech directed toward God, as speech flowing directly from a person's own spirit, and as a practice in which he himself is highly active accentuate the care Paul takes to make sure he does not quench the Spirit's work in the individual. Although private devotion is of little use in the church, it is essential in personal worship and prayer. Paul's point is not that everyone should speak in tongues in private (he rejects that directly in 12:30); rather, the point in 14:15 is that God inspires both mind and heart. Neither can live and give evidence of Christ without the other. Experiencing God's presence in private devotion often provides strength and gifting for service in Christ's

body. Paul's repeated return to first-person singular, even if he has shaped it as a rhetorical subjunctive, more than hints that he himself finds this to be the case.

4. In the concluding argument for why public worship and/or Christian gathering must be intelligible, Paul introduces the need of those who are not yet members of the Christ community. Making sure the gospel is presented with clarity is more than an afterthought for Paul.[7] The gifts are given for the conviction of "outsiders." As Paul will spell out in the following verses, churches are charged with the call to present a convicting message about Christ to those who are ignorant of him (14:24–25). The presentation of the gospel must enable the non-Christian to recognize God's blessing in Christ (14:16). The building of Christ's body that the Spirit enables, therefore, includes those who have not yet become a "body part." The pursuit of love includes the earnest desire for spiritual gifts that communicate the gospel clearly. Churches whose language has become unintelligible for outsiders must rethink whether their corporate devotion has become private and therefore no longer builds Christ's body.

It was important for the unity and growth of the church that those speaking would use words that all could understand and so receive instruction. Paul likens this to the need for clear trumpet signals to be given so that soldiers know what to do in battle. The long, straight trumpet being played by the Greek soldier decorating this piece of Greek pottery is known as the *salpinx* (late sixth to early fifth century BC).

Illustrating the Text

To love well, seek spiritual gifts; to use spiritual gifts well, seek love.

Human Experience: There are other scenarios in life where two things interconnect in a seemingly circular way. For example, if you want to be good at waiting, you need to grow in patience; if you need to grow in patience, you need to practice it by waiting. Or, if you want to interact compassionately with others, you need to be more selfless; if you want to be more selfless, try interacting compassionately with others. There are a handful of these types of "learning circles" in life, and they are all based on providentially paired tensions that the Lord has instituted and designed to deepen our character. They work because each outcome is fueled by the other process. In this way, Jesus has created a constructive tension between spiritual gifts and love; love fuels and motivates our use of spiritual gifts, and spiritual gifts equip and enable our practice of love.

Spiritual gifts convict unbelievers and empower the church's evangelism.

Object Lesson: Bring some children's toy tools and some real building materials. (For example, a rubber saw and a real two-by-four, or a plastic hammer and a real nail or two. The bigger the tools, the better. The toys should not be loved by an actual child; they will likely be damaged.) Show people the building materials and explain the task (cutting the board, hammering in a nail), and ask if they believe the tools you brought will suffice. Then proceed to try. You will probably end up with a punctured plastic hammer, a crumbling rubber saw, a twisted plastic screwdriver, and so on. Point out that the problem is that you are using the wrong kind of tool for the job. The same problem would have occurred if you had used woodworking tools on sheet metal, ratchet sets as hammers, and so forth. Explain that the real work of evangelism is completely out of our control. Conversion starts with conviction, and conviction is a mysterious inner work of the Holy Spirit. We have no tool that can break through the stony heart of unbelief. The Holy Spirit, however, does. When we minister in our spiritual giftedness, we are allowing the Spirit to give us the right tools for the job and to use us in the right way at the right time to break through.

Contrasting Concept: Show a short video clip of a magician doing a trick, the more dramatic the better. Point out that what makes the trick gripping is the fact that what we see seems beyond the natural abilities of humans and appears to be supernatural. Magicians claim to be the ones exercising this supernatural power for their own fame and glory, but we call it a "trick" or an "illusion." The difference with manifestations and gifts of the Spirit is that the persons involved point to God as the one exercising supernatural power for his well-deserved fame and glory. Believers call these moments "manifestations," "signs," "gifts," and "fruit"—all terms that point to God, not humans.

The Focus of Christian Worship

Big Idea *Christian worship gatherings must be conducted in an orderly fashion to avoid confusion and to ensure that the character of Christ is clearly portrayed throughout the service. Individuals desiring to share their gifts must submit to the greater purpose of portraying Christ.*

Understanding the Text

The Text in Context

Having dealt generally with the matter of tongue speaking (the exercise of private devotion) in a public gathering, Paul now turns to the more specific subject of how several of the questions he addressed in the previous sections relate to a public worship gathering. Since a primary objective of a Christian worship service is to honor Christ, Christ followers must make sure their gathering bears witness to the character and self-giving love of Christ. Pulling together his broader discussions on worship beginning in chapter 8, Paul now gives practical advice on how to accomplish the necessary order at church gatherings. His broader argument is that outsiders and unbelievers will come under conviction *only* if Christ is revealed. Christ is not revealed, however, if all clamor to parade themselves rather than to submit themselves. Anyone empowered by God's Spirit will recognize that this is the will/command of the *kyrios* ("Lord," or "Patron" [14:37]).

Interpretive Insights

14:20 *stop thinking like children.* By applying a present tense imperative, Paul instructs the Corinthians to stop doing what they presently are doing. It is time for them to give up their childish way of thinking (13:11; cf. 3:1–2).[1] When it comes to evil, however, they should move the other way and become like infants (*nēpiazete*). Paul distinguishes between children and infants to underscore that in matters of evil they should be as those who have no reflective, deliberative capacity at all. When it comes to their thoughts and deliberations, however, they should be mature (cf. 2:6).[2]

14:21–22 *In the Law it is written.* As his quote from Isaiah 28:11–12 shows, Paul uses "Law" as a general reference to the Old Testament rather than to the Pentateuch (cf. Rom. 3:19; John 10:34). In Isaiah's context, these verses speak judgment to Israel's leadership, who showed their "unbelief" by refusing to listen to God's advice. Consequently, God sent his judgment by way of the Assyrians ("foreign . . . tongues"). Through a slight rhetorical change in wording, Paul is able to use the quote to explain the function of unintelligible tongues in a congregational context. Parallel to the situation in Isaiah, God uses unintelligible tongues to speak judgment to unbelieving Jews. When Paul calls tongues a "sign" for unbelievers, therefore, he makes his present situation analogous to the situation in Isaiah's context. God uses foreign tongues to speak to unbelievers, and intelligible prophecy to speak to believers. In Paul's argument, tongues are God's negative sign to expose unbelievers' alienation from God (they do not understand God), while prophecy is God's positive sign[3] to reveal his gracious forgiveness and restoration offered to those who believe.[4]

14:23–25 *if the whole church comes together.* Paul refers to the "whole church" only here and in Romans 16:23. Whether his hypothetical example alludes to an actual or imagined occurrence when all house groups on occasion meet simultaneously in an extraordinarily large home is not certain and is somewhat insignificant for his argument. His aim is to depict the horror of a situation that would both violate the diversity of God's gifting and disaffect outsiders and nonbelieving Jews—a situation where church "visitors" hear unintelligible babble instead of a convicting word about Christ. The contrast could not be

starker. The visitors will either conclude that Christ followers are mad (*mainomai* [14:23] may be a reference to drunkenness as experienced in pagan cults) or be convicted of their sins (secrets of their hearts) and conclude, "God is among you," and as a result begin to worship God.

14:26 *Everything must be done so that the church may be built up.* Highlighting the diversity of God's gifting, Paul now summarizes the previous section ("What then shall we say?") and sets the stage for a concluding exhortation on the need for order in the worship gathering ("When you come together . . . everything must be done . . ."). The whole section from verse 26 to verse 40 is framed by the same statement put in two different ways: "Everything must be done so that the church may be built up"

In Corinth, God could use "other tongues" to speak to unbelievers (14:21), just like he used the lips of the Assyrians to speak to unbelieving Israelites in Isaiah's day (Isa. 28:11–12). Shown here is the Assyrian siege of Lachish, which occurred in 700–692 BC.

(14:26), and "everything should be done in a fitting and orderly way" (14:40). Paul's list of worship elements is not intended to be exhaustive or to indicate that each of these particular elements must be present in every worship service. It connects well to Luke's list in Acts 2:42–47 (teaching, fellowship, Lord's Supper, prayer, miracles, sharing of finances, praising God, and evangelism).[5]

14:27–33a *For God is not a God of disorder but of peace.* Paul's precise guidelines for gifts' use in the assembly are all instructed by verse 33a. To secure that community experience supersedes private devotion and that the presentation of Christ outshines the "presenters," Paul stresses the limitation of those displaying their gifts. Tongue speakers must pray in silence unless God grants an interpretation. When he does, only two, possibly three, can speak and must do so one by one. Prophets likewise are limited to two or three speakers, each of whom must recognize that God has given other members power to evaluate the truth of their speech (14:29). Paul's description of prophecy is not one of ecstasy; prophets can control whether or not to speak. Therefore, they can submit to order and yield the floor at will when God gives a new revelation to another person.

14:33b–35 *Women should remain silent in the churches.* Rounding up his discussion on worship, Paul reaches back to his earlier discussion in chapter 11 on the behavior of women and wives in the Christian assembly. How does this issue relate to the question of "order"? If verse 34 relates to 29, a wife should not participate in the public evaluation of a prophecy and risk speaking out against her husband. Another possibility is that women treated prophets like oracles and used the worship services to inquire about personal issues such as "When will I get married?" and "Will my child be healthy?" For a fuller discussion of these options, see the "Additional Insights" following this unit.

14:36 *Or are you the only people it has reached?* Whom does Paul rebuke in this verse? The masculine adjective "only ones" (*monous*) implies a broader group than the women addressed in the verses above. Collins suggests that Paul addresses males in the church who tried to limit the speech of women.[6] More likely, Paul addresses the congregation as a whole (NIV: "only people"). Apparently, they had come to conclude that their own prophetic word sufficed as (or even replaced) God's word (14:36a),[7] acting as if they were the only believers it had reached (14:36b). By this they had placed themselves outside the fellowship of Christian churches (14:33b; cf. 1:2b), putting in doubt the very spirituality in which they claimed to excel (14:37–38). They proved to be ignorant in the things of the Spirit (12:1).

14:37–38 *what I am writing to you is the Lord's command.* These verses answer the objection Paul anticipates from his rhetorical question in verse 36. His tone is firm, using the word "command" (*entolē*), a word he otherwise avoided except for Colossians 4:10. Confusing God's word with personal agendas and removing the focus from Christ in a Christian worship service is no minor matter. The warning recalls Jesus's words in Matthew 7:22–23.

14:39–40 *be eager to prophesy . . . in a fitting and orderly way.* In a final concluding remark, Paul reiterates the primacy of prophecy over tongues and reminds objectors that both are gifts from God's Spirit designed to empower the church as Christ's body (14:1). The key to safeguarding against self-indulgence is order, although order without passion fails to build up Christ's body (1 Thess. 5:19–21; Eph. 4:30). In the words of Garland, "The Spirit of ardor is also the Spirit of order."[8]

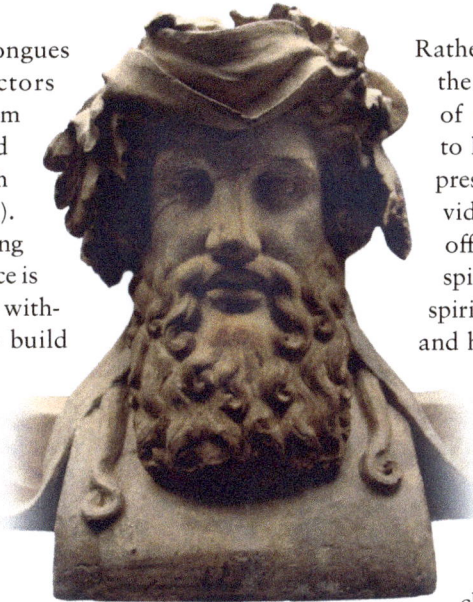

Teaching the Text

1. Paul's emphasis on order has very little to do with what modern churches traditionally think of as liturgy. His aim is not to structure the Corinthian services in a specific way but to bring order to a situation that has become chaotic (14:26). There is little doubt that the earliest Christian worship services to some extent took the form of a Spirit-infused synagogue gathering. The emphasis on the Scriptures, the story, and the tradition, transformed as these were by the Christ event, is clear enough throughout the New Testament. However, the Spirit's extraordinary gifting and enablement brought a vibrancy of divine presence that proved a challenge to the Corinthian psyche. The struggle of Corinthian worship gatherings was not dullness but rowdiness.

Paul's concluding remark about the Corinthian church's worship practices was that "everything should be done in a fitting and orderly way" (14:40). Christian worship should bear no similarity to the frenzied, chaotic pagan worship associated with pagan gods like Dionysus (Greek) or Bacchus (Roman). This bust from Rome depicts the god Bacchus (AD 50–100).

Rather than submitting to the overarching purpose of the worship service, to honor and reveal the presence of Christ, individuals sought to show off their own personal spirituality. Personal and spiritual pride before God and humans confused the portrayal of God's Son. The church no longer functioned as the body of Christ but acted like a gathering of competing individuals who all claimed a special relationship with Christ.

2. Paul's call for order is not a call for solemnity. The care with which he treats even troublesome elements in worship, like tongues, discloses his own humility, even trepidation, before God's Spirit. He rebukes the Corinthian gatherings not for their passion but for their misguided application of the Spirit's endowments. As he emphasizes in all his churches, it is a serious matter if worship services no longer testify to the Spirit's presence (1 Thess. 5:19). "Order" must not eliminate spontaneous demonstrations of the Spirit; rather, it must guide these lest they become expressions that grieve or insult the Spirit (Eph. 4:30). Paul's teaching aims to keep a balance between order and passion. Order without passion lacks the quality that confirms the presence of God's

life-giving Spirit; passion without order lacks the quality that confirms the power of God's *Christ-revealing* Spirit.

3. In line with the synagogues, the Corinthian worship services were events designed to teach and educate the members (and visitors) about God's kingdom work and the transformation of thinking and action the Christ event produces (cf. Luke 4:16–21). Far from being unquestionable monologues, the exposition of Scripture and the spiritual guidance provided by the Christian prophets were interactive events. On the one side, prophets were not talk-show hosts who were free to spout personal opinion. Their message could not be "their own" but had to stand the scrutiny of evaluation by a comparison to the message of Christ.[9] On the other side, prophets were charged with the responsibility to further explain the ramifications of their expositions. Their speech would be followed by a question-and-answer session, so to speak. The "building up" of the believer was not a matter of mere inspiration but a matter of transformation of mind and action (Rom. 12:1–2). The evaluative measure of the prophets was whether their message produced a change in lives and thinking. Did it empower the listeners to substantiate their faithfulness to Christ? The evaluative measure for listeners was whether their questions aimed at the same. The purpose of the prophetic event was not esoteric disputation (cf. 1 Tim. 4:6–7) but the building up of the church.

4. Paul's worship discussion on order is about unity. His body metaphor, the church as Christ's body, relates directly to the

The worship services of the early church may have been structured much like the services that occurred in the synagogues. Both included teaching as an important component. Since the local synagogue was usually Paul's first stop on his missionary journeys and many of the early believers were converted Jews, this is not surprising. This inscription, which says "synagogue of the Hebrews," was found at Corinth, evidence for a Jewish presence in the city (late Roman, ca. AD 250–450).

practice of worship. All the "body parts" that are participating in a given service do so as members of Christ's body. Christian worship is, in other words, a body experience where the function of each member is to bring about a unified expression of Christ. When Paul warns against the misuse of tongues and silences the questioning of the wives (and/or the personal inquiries of the women whose focus remains on their own issues), it is to secure a Christ-revealing worship service for outsiders. A significant point of the Christ gathering is the revelation and communication of Christ to outsiders who come to "see" the God of the Christians. In this light, the worship wars of the Corinthian church did not differ in essence or result from those of modern churches. Various members of the Corinthian church clamored for their own preferences, and in the process they devastated the unity of the body and blurred the revelation of Christ as Savior. Paul's corrective guidance is for the church to make sure the message of Christ remains undiluted and undisturbed and to do so in a way that allows outsiders to "see Christ."

Illustrating the Text

If the form of our worship tramples others, we undermine its servant-hearted, loving content.

Music: Paint a picture for your listeners of an orchestra giving a command performance for the king. He sits alone in the audience, enjoying the music. Meanwhile, as all the different instruments play their parts and rhythms, the cumulative effect is beautiful order and harmony that surpass what any one player could accomplish. Then, a single player gets an idea in his head. Perhaps he wants to be noticed, or he wants the king to hear him above all others. Maybe he wants the other players to respect his overlooked abilities, or he wants to feel fully free and unshackled in his playing. Whatever the reason, he goes off the page and begins to dance around wildly, knocking over others' music stands, playing different rhythms, and making a horrendous noise. Soon the entire orchestra is distracted and out of time, and all the other players are highly annoyed. The director breaks his baton and stomps off, and other musicians try to complete the tune on their own recognizance. Meanwhile, and without anyone seeing, the king has slipped out the back door and gone home. (Consider having the worship team or choir help you to act this out as a drama or object lesson; one member could go rogue unexpectedly and you could build your illustration from there.)

Prophecy is evaluated by the fruit it produces in the lives of its hearers.

Popular Sayings: Perhaps you have heard the old saying "The proof is in the pudding." That is actually a shortened and corrupted version of an older and longer phrase: "The proof of the pudding is in the eating." It simply means that you can say what you want about a pudding recipe, but the real test for a dessert is what happens when it hits your tongue and slides down your throat. Prophecy is measured in much the same way. An utterance can be flashy or dire, unpretentious or cryptic, popular or despised; the real, biblical test for a word of prophecy is the fruit it produces in its hearers. If it leads to faith, obedience, holiness, love, and hope, then it is very likely to have been from God.

"Worship wars" is an oxymoron; if it comes to war, we have ceased to worship.

Christian Worship: This would be a great time to explain your congregation's chosen worship style and the way it fits with your stated mission and theology. Teach people the differences between having personal preferences in worship and appointing themselves the official arbiters of what is "good" or "bad" worship. Explain how your church's commitment to unity in worship is expressed in terms of compromise, sensitivity to various groups and their needs, and a spirit of love and concern for discipleship.

Quote: Dwight L. Moody. "I have never yet known the Spirit of God to work where the Lord's people were divided." If this is true, then claiming to join in adoration of Christ while simultaneously spurring one another on to conflict and division is both theologically impossible and spiritually destructive.

Women, Worship, and Prophecy

As shown in chapter 11, a unique difficulty presented itself when the church met in a patron's home. Was the home's matriarch to behave as she would in her home (as a decision-making mother and host) or as she would in a public gathering outside her home (appropriately attired, evidencing her relationship to her husband)? In chapter 11, Paul's concern was that wives behaved as wives and not as "new Roman women" (see the "Historical and Cultural Background" section in the unit on 11:2–16); here his concern is how this relates to speech. The Christian gathering is a public event. Different rules are at play. Just as misuse of tongues would hinder, or confuse, the revelation of Christ to those who were outsiders, women's behavior likewise impacted what outsiders saw and heard when they visited the assemblies of the Christ communities.

Paul's concern in this context is clearly *not* that women in general cannot speak in churches. That would directly contradict his statement in 11:5. One of two scenarios seems possible for the situation Paul addresses.

Having just stressed that prophecy should be evaluated (14:29), Paul relates this principle to a practical situation facing the churches. A wife should not publicly challenge a prophecy given in the assembly worshiping Christ (14:34). Instead, she should seek clarification from her husband in private (14:35). The image Paul's description conjures up is one in which family debates remove focus from the prophetic message and turn the "weighing" of the prophecy into a cross-examination designed to question the prophet's faithfulness as a Christ follower. Put differently, in an honor-driven society, when a wife speaks shamefully to her husband, people (outsiders) will draw the conclusion that the wife's relationship to her husband is less than exclusive (see the

One explanation for Paul's comment that "women should remain silent in the churches" (14:34) is that women in the church at Corinth may have been treating those with the gift of prophecy like pagan oracles. Shown here are the remains of the temple of Apollo at Delphi, where the famous oracles of Delphi were received, interpreted, and proclaimed.

"Historical and Cultural Background" section in the unit on 11:2–16). Parading her independence from her husband in this way would violate the honor of the *paterfamilias* and violate the message of Christ. Consequently, the church would not be built up, and outsiders (unbelievers) would not be convicted of their sin. Like uninterpreted tongues, this kind of questioning may be appropriate in private, but it is destructive for public worship in the assembly of Christ. As mentioned in the historical background comments on 11:2–16, the confusion likely arose because the public worship occurred in the private home, and two sets of "appropriate behavior" seemed to collide. Appropriate "private behavior" sent the wrong message in a public setting.

Whether Paul sees a connection between this kind of Corinthian "dishonor" of a prophet in his home and Jesus's saying that a prophet is not without honor except "in his own home" (Matt. 13:57 // Mark 6:4; cf. Luke 4:24; John 4:44) is obviously impossible to determine with any kind of certainty. But it does not seem completely unreasonable to suggest. If so, Paul might also have made the connection to the follow-up statement that Jesus "did not do many miracles there" (Matt. 13:58; cf. Mark 6:5).

Witherington outlines another plausible scenario.[1] Prophecy was a common phenomenon in the Hellenistic world, something the Corinthians (along with the ancient world in general) were well acquainted with. The common pattern was for people to bring questions of personal interest before a supposed prophet, who then would respond with a prophecy.[2] The most famous of these was the oracle at Delphi. The women Paul addressed, then, were women who treated Christian prophets as if they were pagan oracles. In the time set aside for questions, they would bombard the prophets with personal questions about marriage, pregnancy, children, and so on, expecting a prophecy (oracle) in reply to their questions. They were, in other words, confusing pagan practice and Christian worship. On this background, Paul's corrective words are designed to clarify that Christian prophets prophesy not in response to questions but in response to the Spirit's prompting.

Dunn suggests the background for Paul's comment was that these women disturbed the process of prophetic evaluation and Paul's words about silence were designed to address this issue head on.[3]

As in verse 21, Paul's reference to the "law" (14:34) is broad and does not result in a quote from a specific verse in the Pentateuch. Some commentators suggest that Paul may allude to Numbers 12:1–15, where God punishes Miriam for questioning Moses's authority as a prophet. It is also possible that Paul simply gives a general reference to the creation narrative (cf. 11:8; Gen. 2:18–24).

Resurrection and History

Big Idea *The veracity of bodily resurrection is not up for debate. Christ's resurrection is the climactic point of salvation history—the moment when God most decisively altered the course of history—as announced beforehand in the Scriptures and attested to by faithful eyewitnesses.*

Understanding the Text

The Text in Context

Chapter 15 functions both as a crescendo of this letter and as the high-water mark of Paul's theological exposition. It provides the theological key that reveals Paul's mind to his audience and explains the structure of his ethics. For Paul, everything he has said in this letter hinges on the historical reality of Christ's bodily resurrection from the dead. Christ's resurrection stands as the climactic point, *without which* his suffering and death have no significance, and *because of which* God's restorative grace toward his creation is now revealed. Because of Christ's resurrection, Christ's followers have hope for eternal life in God's presence—a life that has already begun and has proved its power in Christ's community. Believers who have become parts of Christ's body and recipients of his Spirit have assurance that they will be raised from the dead with Christ. Christ, who relates to his body as its head, also relates to his followers as the firstfruits of those who are raised from dead (15:23).

Chapter 15 divides into three sections. In verses 1–11, Paul argues for the fact of bodily resurrection, making the case that Christ's resurrection was observed over a period of time, in a variety of settings, by a variety of trustworthy people and groups. Verses 12–34 highlight how Christ's death-conquering resurrection functions as the firstfruits of the Christian experience. Bodily resurrection is not merely a historical event in the life of Jesus; it is the cornerstone of the Christian faith and has significant ethical consequences. In verses 35–58, Paul describes how bodily resurrection is possible and how the resurrected body relates to the present body.

Interpretive Insights

15:1–2 *Otherwise, you have believed in vain.* Through a string of relative clauses and prepositional phrases rhetorically shaped as a punch line,[1] Paul succinctly sets the stage for saying that resurrection is foundational to the gospel and essential for the Corinthians' salvation. The force of this opening is to underscore that if they reject the reality of resurrection, their faith is of no use (*eikē*, "useless," "without cause or purpose"; cf. Gal. 4:11; see also 1 Cor. 15:14). Rejecting resurrection equals rejecting Paul's gospel, through which they have been saved (cf. Rom. 1:16). His praise for their willingness to hold firm (*katechō*) in 11:2 is here replaced by a first-class condition—"By this gospel you are saved, if you hold firmly." The first-class condition shows Paul is not raising doubt about their faithfulness but expects them to hold firm to the substance of what he has taught.[2]

15:3–4 *what I received I passed on to you.* Paul introduces a most succinct summary of his gospel, using an introductory formula that parallels his Lord's Supper account (11:23). What he preaches aligns directly with the accounts of Jesus's first disciples—Paul has delivered what he received. His first and foremost[3] message to Corinth was that Jesus died for our sins, was buried, was raised on the third day according to the Scriptures, and was seen after the resurrection. Paul's purpose in repeating "according to the Scriptures" likely is to stress that the Christ event (death, burial, resurrection) happened according to God's

Key Themes of 1 Corinthians 15:1–11

- Christian faith stands or falls with the historical veracity of the bodily resurrection of Jesus Christ.
- Christians anchor their faith in the testimony of eyewitnesses to the resurrection.

The Resurrection and the Church

The restoration of God's kingdom and the repealing of the consequences of the fall (Gen. 3) have become the experience and promise of the Christ community. Christ's resurrection guarantees that what is already operating among those who belong to Christ will come to its completion. Paul's argument has come full circle. The church's hope in the resurrection is also its call to full unity in the present. Without resurrection, sin and death have not been conquered and Christ's followers remain slaves to the ways of Corinth. Put differently, resurrection is the indicative that gives theological foundation to Paul's imperative that believers must overcome their cliques, divisions, and self-serving behavior. To deny the resurrection is to deny the church's reason for existence. If the point of eternal division (death) has not been overcome, the church is for this life only (15:32) and no lasting community is being built. As it is, however, the provisions of the church's patron, the eternal God, are everlasting. He has removed even the sting of death.

"Christ died for our sins according to the Scriptures, . . . he was buried, . . . he was raised on the third day according to the Scriptures" (15:3–4). The Church of the Holy Sepulchre was built to mark the site of the crucifixion and burial of Jesus.

plan (cf. Gal. 1:4). If Paul has Old Testament texts in mind regarding the third day, he may, in midrashic fashion,[4] be thinking broadly of God's deliverance of his people on the third day (Hosea 6:2; Gen. 42:18; Exod. 19:16; Josh. 2:22; Ezra 8:32; Jon. 1:17; cf. Matt. 12:40). The "third day" refers to the day after tomorrow (Luke 13:32). Christ was raised on the third day, not three days after his death.

Paul's shift from aorist tense (when speaking about Jesus's death) to perfect tense (when speaking about the resurrection) is not without significance. Aorist is the default tense that simply gives reference to what has happened; the perfect tense highlights that an event has lingering consequences for the present. The Corinthians' present experience of Christ is caused and empowered by the resurrection.

15:5–7 *he appeared to Cephas, and then to the Twelve.* First in the list of postresurrection appearances is Cephas. Paul follows his common pattern of using Peter's Aramaic name (1:12; 3:22; 9:5; Gal. 1:18; 2:9, 11, 14). This appearance is recorded in Luke 24:34. "The Twelve" is a technical term referring to the inner group of Jesus's disciples and does not reflect on Judas's absence (or replacement). This could be the appearance in Luke 24:36–43.

more than five hundred . . . James . . . all the apostles. Neither Acts nor the Gospels record a postresurrection event that includes five hundred believers. Paul could be referring to a broader group at the Great Commission event (Matt. 28:16–20). The point Paul makes here is that many of those who saw Jesus are still alive and can verify his account. Acts also remains silent on an appearance to James, although James's

significance in the early church is well attested (Acts 15:13; 21:18; Gal. 1:19; 2:9, 12), which seems to necessitate a resurrection appearance (cf. Acts 12:17). "All the apostles" is a broad term that includes the Twelve, James, and others (Gal. 1:19).

15:8–9 *last of all he appeared to me also, as to one abnormally born.* Paul's inclusion of himself does not suggest that he needed to defend his apostleship to the Corinthians, but it affords him an opportunity to stress the gracious character of God's call and its effect on his own life (15:10). Paul calls himself a "miscarried child" (*ektrōma*; NIV: "abnormally born"), a term that refers to a premature birth or miscarriage, where the child, if surviving, could be severely handicapped.[5] God's grace alone has made Paul worth more than a dead corpse (cf. Num. 12:12; Job 3:16; Eccles. 6:3). Paul's unworthiness as an apostle is displayed by his life before his encounter with the resurrected Christ: he "persecuted the church of God."[6]

15:10–11 *his grace to me was not without effect.* Contrary to some of the Corinthians, what drives Paul is not a sense of self-worth or a need for self-promotion but a deep awareness of God's gracious call. Grace does not demand specific action; it evokes love that in turn motivates action. In line with the ideals of patron-client relationships (see the introduction, especially "Grace and Patronage"), Paul accentuates that the grace his patron has shown him "was not without effect," or was not "empty/in vain" (*kenē*; cf. 15:58; 2 Cor. 6:1; 1 Thess. 2:1; 3:5). Rather, as a good client, he works harder than the others. This comparison is not a bragging point but a result of his indebtedness (Luke 12:48b).

Paul emphasizes the historical bodily resurrection of Jesus by recounting the people that saw the risen Lord, including Peter, the Twelve, James, and over five hundred others. Carved on this capital from the twelfth century AD is the scene from John 20:24–29, where Jesus appears to Thomas, one of the Twelve, and shows him the wounds in his hands and side.

Most likely, his comparison refers to his sufferings for Christ as more severe than commonly experienced by Christ followers (2 Cor. 11:23–29; cf. Rom. 15:18–19). Verse 11 summarizes the section and connects back to 15:1–2.

Theological Insights

God created humans to enjoy eternal fellowship with him. The fall (Gen. 3) violated and disabled the fulfillment of this purpose. The promise of the resurrection is that God will restore what was destroyed at the fall. Christ's resurrection, as witnessed by his followers, is the Christian's evidence of this promise.

Teaching the Text

1. The veracity of the gospel hinges on the historical bodily resurrection of Jesus. Paul's use of Jesus's postresurrection appearances as the launching pad for his theological argument is designed as a reminder of what his audience should know. Paul's introductory formula, "What I received I passed on to you as of first importance" (15:3), suggests he is quoting or summarizing a confessional statement they will recognize as determinative for their faith. His aim is not to engage in a historical debate about the trustworthiness of the testimony of the people he mentions. All Christ followers should acknowledge the credibility of those witnesses without question. Rather, Paul is showing in the strongest way that the issue of resurrection is foundational and indispensable to the Christian faith. To reject the resurrection is to refuse the gospel itself. Christ's resurrection launched the Christian faith, and if some should question Paul's testimony about his encounter with the risen Christ, other firsthand witnesses, the so-called pillars of the faith (Gal. 2:9; cf. 1 Cor. 1:12; 3:22; 9:5), are still there to tell about it (15:6). To reject the resurrection as a historically verifiable event is to move Christian faith from the realm of history to the realm of mythology. Those who do so are rejecting God's historical action for humankind and reducing Christian faith to a matter of private devotion.

2. By launching his theological argument from the platform of an eyewitness account that he himself is part of (15:8) and

by paralleling it with the promise of Scripture (15:4), Paul immediately places those who deny the resurrection as opponents of the Christian faith. They are arguing not against Paul's interpretations but against God's historical actions through Christ. The gospel tradition, what they have "received" as the content of the Christian faith, rests in its totality on the eyewitness accounts of the very people Paul names. Rejecting the eyewitness accounts of the resurrection therefore equals rejecting the gospel itself. Far beyond disagreeing with (or not grasping) a specific application of the Christ story to their lifestyle (cf. Paul's discussion of the "strong," who should have considered the faith of the "weak" [chap. 8]), those who deny the resurrection are rejecting both God's promises from Holy Scripture and the persons God caused to become eyewitnesses to his Son's resurrection. It is an out-and-out rejection of every source of their faith—indeed, a rejection of God himself. Moreover, since they claim to belong to the Christ community, they are denying what they themselves believed (15:11). By doing so, they have rendered useless (*eikē*, "without cause or purpose" [15:2]) the faith they used to have.

Illustrating the Text

Doctrinal primacy—believing first things first—is central to the Christian life.

Anecdote/Object Lesson: (Either tell this story or turn it into an actual object lesson with your listeners.) A professor stood

in front of a college class with a large, transparent container. First, he filled it with large rocks. He then asked his class, "Is the container full?" They all said, "Yes." Then the professor pulled out a container of smaller pebbles and poured them in. They slid into the spaces and fit between all the larger rocks. He asked again, "Now is the container full?" Most said, "Yes," but a few hesitated. Then he pulled out a container of sand, then one of water. As he added each, he asked if the container was full yet, and got fewer and fewer yeses. After he poured in the water, he finally asked, "So, if this container is your life, what does this lesson mean?" A student spoke up and said, "There's always room for more in your life." The professor said, "No—it means that if you don't put the big rocks in first, they'll never fit; if you do get the big rocks in first, the rest will sort out fine." In the same way, Christians must identify the "big rock" doctrines that define our faith and lay our theological foundations there first. If we do that, everything else will sort out. If we focus on disputable matters first, we may never establish our moorings in the basics of the gospel, and then we may find ourselves hopelessly adrift.

To reject the resurrection is to refuse the gospel and to render our faith useless.

Church History: The resurrection had a profound impact on the early church: it transformed the disciples as individuals, it caused a primarily Jewish fellowship to shift worship from Sabbath to Sunday, and so on. If the resurrection were just a myth or a figurative term, would the apostles have been martyred for it? Would it have changed the faith of so many faithful Jews? The bodily resurrection of Christ was the theological lightning rod of the early church. Without it, Paul says, Christianity is a useless and foolish faith.

Quote: *The Reason for God: Belief in an Age of Skepticism*, by Timothy Keller. "If Jesus rose from the dead, then you have to accept all he said; if he didn't rise from the dead, then why worry about any of what he said? The issue on which everything hangs is not whether or not you like his teaching but whether or not he rose from the dead."[7] In other words, the resurrection is a first-importance issue.

1 Corinthians 15:1–11

Resurrection and Christian Living

Big Idea *The resurrection is the foundation of the Christian faith; without it, faith cannot stand and Christian living has no motivation. It is the announcement that God has reversed the curse of the fall. Death no longer has any sting.*

Understanding the Text

The Text in Context

After solidly grounding the resurrection in the soil of history, Paul moves on to establish its theological significance. His theological argument moves through three stages. He begins by a theological restatement of his Scripture/eyewitness argument (15:12–18). From here he draws a direct connection between the resurrection of Christ and the resurrection of his followers (15:19–28) before concluding that this has significant ethical implications (15:29–34).

Interpretive Insights

15:12 *But if it is preached . . . how can some of you say . . . ?* Those rejecting the resurrection do not simply oppose Paul; they deny the cornerstone of the Christian message. They have responded to the preaching of Christ but not exchanged some of the basic tenets of their culturally guided belief structure. Most Greeks believed that at death the soul was released from the body and the "good" soul would soar back to the realm of God (or the gods).[1] To them, human beings consisted of two parts, one eternal and of divine origin, the other mortal and made of matter. To Paul, such an understanding militates against the Christian message, which envisions neither the existence of a disembodied soul nor an eternal soul with no need of recreation. Rather, the promise of Christ's resurrection is that God, in a re-creating act, will raise those who belong to Christ's community with a new body and a new soul fit for a postfallen world. Those who deny the resurrection, then, deny God's power to repeal sin's all-encompassing effect. They claim eternal separation; Paul proclaims eternal unification. Christ's resurrection has guaranteed an everlasting restoration of his community in God's presence, not an eternal separation of body and soul.

15:13–15 *If there is no resurrection . . . we are then found to be false witnesses.* Sharpening his rhetoric even further through two if/then statements, Paul depicts the denial of resurrection as both a rejection of the Christian faith and a claim that makes him a false witness to God.[2] Paul leaves no room for compromise; the deniers' claim goes to the center of the faith and must be refuted in the strongest way (cf. Gal. 1:6–9). Paul's use of the passive voice throughout this whole passage does not suggest Paul thinks of resurrection as something that happens automatically without the need for God's direct intervention (as if his view is a mere variant of the Corinthians' view). That it is God who actively raised Christ and who actively will raise believers becomes unquestionably clear from verse 15. Eternal life is not an inherent quality of human life (15:53; cf. 1 Tim. 6:16).

15:16–19 *if Christ has not been raised, your faith is futile.* Refuting the resurrection includes nullifying Christ's work on the cross. Believers' faith is empty and meaningless (15:14, 17), and their sins continue to define their life and identity. Both the living and the dead are affected by the resurrection. If resurrection does not occur, the living remain in sin (15:17) with no hope of ever experiencing anything different (15:19). The Christians who have already died "are lost"; that is, they have simply faced destruction (*apollymi*). Sin and death have won (15:54–56); believers who are hoping for what does not exist are "to be pitied," more pathetic than anyone else (*eleeinos*).[3]

15:20–22 *in Christ all will be made alive.* Having underscored the consequences of his opponents' argument, Paul now turns to the magnitude of Christ's resurrection by emphasizing its cosmic significance. Resurrection is not the escape of the individual from the sphere of sin and death but the central piece of God's redemptive and restorative work for all his creation. What was destroyed in Adam is restored in Christ. Adam brought death; Christ brings life. Adam caused alienation between God and his creation (cf. Rom. 5:12); Christ makes restoration between God and creation possible. More than just a hope for individual believers, resurrection is the reality that awaits Christ's community. The Christ community will be raised and become the community of God's restored kingdom

"And if Christ has not been raised, your faith is futile; you are still in your sins" (15:17). The Garden Tomb is a site near the Damascus Gate of the Old City of Jerusalem that many believe to be the garden and sepulcher of Joseph of Arimathea. Whether it is authentic or not is up for debate, but the site itself creates a reverent and meaningful atmosphere for visitors to reflect on Jesus's death, burial, and resurrection. When visitors turn around to exit the tomb, they see a sign reminding them, "He is not here, for he is risen."

(15:28; cf. 1 Thess. 4:16). Paul not only purports to counter the Corinthians' argument but aims to establish resurrection as the central feature in God's ultimate purpose for his creation—a purpose in which those who are "in Christ" play a central role.[4]

15:23–28 *But each in turn: Christ, the firstfruits.* Paul's language of firstfruits enables him to draw a direct relational connection between Christ and believers. The Greek term *tagma* ("in order" or "in turn") is used of an ordered group of soldiers. It conjures up an image of Christ as leading the way for those who follow him—just as the firstfruits tell harvesters that more will soon follow.

In 15:32 Paul says, "If I fought wild beasts in Ephesus with no more than human hopes, what have I gained?" This relief shows gladiators fighting wild animals.

Christ has led the way for believers, who will be raised at Christ's *parousia* ("appearing," "coming" [15:23]) when God establishes his kingdom in full (15:24, 28c).

Then the end will come. The "then" (*eita*) is not temporal, suggesting an interval between the resurrection of believers and the coming of "the end," but conclusive: "that's the time of the end." The flow of Paul's thought is logical. The powers and authorities that have opposed God since the fall of Adam, of which death is the most significant, will "be destroyed" (*katargeitai* [15:26]); they will cease to have any power.[5] Since resurrection overcomes the principal hostile power, death, it follows that all hostile powers will suffer the same fate. When death has lost its power, life will have full meaning, and God will fill "all in all" (15:28; cf. 8:6; Rom. 11:36; Col. 1:16).[6] Paul's strong allusions to apocalyptic end-time scenarios and his direct application of Psalm 110:1 to Christ[7] further accentuate the centrality of resurrection for God's final purposes.

15:29 *what will those do who are baptized for the dead?* The discussions on this difficult verse center primarily on the phrase "baptized for the dead."[8] Although baptism for the dead is not dealt with in any other New Testament text, Paul mentions it here without expressing particular concern. Furthermore, Paul does not speak directly to specific people (using a second-person plural) but employs a rare third-person plural (they/people). What, then, did Paul have in mind? Most likely, the Greek *hyper* ("for") does not mean "on behalf of" but means "for the sake of." Paul refers, then, not to a practice of vicarious baptism but to a practice where some were baptized because of a promise given to a dying loved one—so they could "meet again." Since those being baptized were believers, Paul did not need to give a theological correction of mystical misconceptions concerning baptism. The custom simply allowed him to refer to the issue as a general practice, and it functioned well as an argument for the obvious necessity of the resurrection. Paul's point is that the mere suggestion that baptism enables loved ones to meet up again after death demands a belief in resurrection.

15:30–32 *why do we endanger ourselves every hour?* Paul continues his argument by adding new questions that affirm the foolishness of rejecting resurrection. What would be the sense of exposing oneself to danger and risk of death if there were no hope beyond death? To make sure the Corinthians are aware that Paul has done just that, he mentions his brush with death in Ephesus (Acts 19:1–20:1; 2 Cor. 1:8–10; cf. 2 Cor. 4:10; 11:23–27). All that would be for nothing if death could steal his life.

15:33 *Bad company corrupts good character.* Using a quote from an old play (Menander, *Thais*) that had become as common then as Shakespeare's "to be or not to be" is today, Paul warns the Corinthians about deceiving themselves into thinking that the content of their faith can be disconnected from their lifestyle (3:18; 6:9). Hanging out with the wrong crowd (*homiliai kakai*, "bad social associations"; NIV: "bad company") likely for Paul refers to those in the church who see no difficulty in combining Corinthian values with membership in Christ's community. Or he may be warning against allowing such a pattern among members.

15:34 *Come back to your senses as you ought, and stop sinning.* As the punch line for his argument against those who deny resurrection, Paul calls for them to come back to their senses, using a term related to drunkenness. As drunkards come back to their senses after a binge, those who reject resurrection should sober up and realize how foolish their talk is and how destructive it has proven to be for their testimony as Christ followers. Those who are "ignorant of God" have adopted a lifestyle of sin that should be stopped (6:12–14; cf. Rom. 1:18–32; 1 Thess. 4:5; 2 Pet. 3:3–4). Paul's argument connects directly to Jesus's conversation with the Sadducees when Jesus concluded that their rejection of the resurrection was because they did not know "the Scriptures or the power of God" (Mark 12:24).

I say this to your shame. As already noted in the comments on 4:14 and 6:5, the word "shame" cuts to the bone of the Corinthian believers' identity as Christ followers. In an honor-shame society, being shamed equals being declared unworthy. It is not a mere slap on the hand, saying, "shame on you"; it speaks to their legitimacy as followers of Christ (cf. 2 Thess. 3:6, 14–15; 1 Tim. 5:20).

Theological Insights

Sin's most climactic result, death, will not have the last word. The Christ community's experience of intimate fellowship with God and one another will not come to an end with death. Rather, resurrection ensures that God will complete their present experience and restore them to full and eternal fellowship with him and with one another.

Teaching the Text

1. One major theological argument that Paul makes in relation to the resurrection is that it proves the eternal quality of Christ's community. As Christ's body, believers have

been filled with God's Spirit in order to live in a new community that evidences God's presence (chaps. 12–14). That this experience goes beyond a mere temporal enablement, designed to benefit believers through life's struggles, is proven by Christ's resurrection. Because Christ rose as the firstfruits of his community, his community will be raised as well. The powerful transformation of relationships called for and empowered by Christ in the present represents the everlasting reality of the age to come. Contrary to the common Corinthian claim that death causes eternal separation between body and spirit, Paul proclaims eternal unification of body and spirit. It is not about the survival of the soul but about the resurrection of the whole person. Death does not bring an end to Christ's community. Rather, in Christ death has lost its power. God will raise to new life the believers who have died.

2. As in the modern church, the challenge in the Corinthian church was to recognize the transformation Christ brings to members' traditional understanding of reality. Paul's rejection of the Corinthian conception that the spirit is eternal whereas the body is mortal goes to the root of this issue. A major point of 1 Corinthians 15 is that belief shapes behavior. Paul's warning in verses 33–34 reveals the depth to which he considers the influx of non-Christian ideas into the Christ community a problem. Unwillingness to reject the common tenets of the Corinthian "folk religion" led some members to reject *the* central point of the Christian faith—the resurrection. As a result, the church members' lifestyle remained unchanged, and they continued in the sinful ways of their preconversion lives.

3. Paul highlights the connection between thinking and lifestyle by underscoring how his emphasis on resurrection motivates his behavior. He has endured beating and mistreatment because he knows it is not wasted (cf. 15:58). Because death's power is temporal, death will come to an end, while he will be raised to reap the benefits of his commitment to Christ's body. Paul's awareness of the resurrection not only impacts his perspective on the present; it motivates him to live the Christian life under all circumstances. Paul argues that *if* the spirit is inherently immortal and the body temporal, the purpose of spiritual power is to benefit temporal existence by giving the greatest amount of pleasure in the present: "Let us eat and drink, for tomorrow we die" (15:32). Such a conception, however, is contrary to the life of Christ, who came not for personal pleasure but for self-sacrifice. What motivates Christian living is not the conviction that the soul will survive death but the awareness that following Christ through a life of self-sacrifice will result in the resurrection of both body and soul (15:58; cf. Rom. 6:5; 8:17; Phil. 3:10–11). Christians are raised with a new

Paul warns in 15:33, "Do not be misled: 'Bad company corrupts good character.'" This saying is ascribed to the Greek playwright Menander (ca. 342–ca. 292 BC), whose bust is shown here (fourth century AD).

body to live in God's restored order when he makes all things new and will come to dwell among his people (cf. Rev. 21:3–4).

4. Paul's focus on resurrection—in contrast to the teaching on the survival of the soul—gives new hope to the sick, the dying, and the mourning. Since death does not mean the end of the body, life's temporal end no longer proclaims the end of bodily existence or the eternal separation of loved ones. Those who are sick will not get rid of their bodies; their bodies will be resurrected to a state without the scars caused by sin and death. Those who are dying know that when resurrection comes, they will be raised with a body that will never die. Those who are mourning no longer have to fear the eternal separation from the ones they love or to think they will eternally be impersonal, disembodied spirits. Their loved ones who belong to Christ's community will be raised as full persons, body and soul. They will all live together forever when God restores his creation to himself (15:53–54; cf. 1 Thess. 4:16–18).

Illustrating the Text

The Christian hope is a bodily resurrection, of which Christ is the firstfruits—not a disembodied state of an immortal soul.

Art: Present several examples of art that purports to depict heaven. Ask your listeners to reflect or comment on the type of state being pictured. Point out that a lot of our ideas about heaven are not biblical, or are misinterpretations of apocalyptic imagery in books like Revelation. Invite them to form their ideas of heaven on the Bible, not on human imagination.[9]

The resurrection of the body argues against reckless living; this world is not the end of the story.

Contrasting Concept: Some may have seen bumper stickers with the quote "Drive it like it's stolen." Many people treat their bodies and lives as if this were their personal motto. Humans can be tempted to treat their bodies as if they are disposable vehicles for short-term pleasure, or possibly as if they are ruined and disappointing vessels to be escaped. Rather, this passage teaches that the body matters to God, and he has a plan to restore and transform it at the last day!

The resurrection of the body also means the complete reunion of the body of Christ.

Human Experience: High school class reunions are usually awkward or bizarre, as we all get together to see "whatever became of old so-and-so" and ask, "Can you believe how much we've all changed?" Our reunion with the body of Christ in heaven will be so much more than this. We will certainly discover what became of each precious brother and sister in the plans God had for them, and we will celebrate how much we have been changed by his grace. However, we will not be looking back to glory days long gone but rather beginning the eternal era of peace and fellowship won for us by Christ. More than that, we will be reuniting with millennia of faithful classmates whose names and stories have inspired us in our own walk. We will know them and our Lord face-to-face and celebrate the unending "best years of our lives."

Resurrection and Transformation (Part 1)

Big Idea *Death does not have the power to hold believers in the grave. God will raise them from the dead with a new body restored and fitted for a new reality in God's eternal kingdom.*

Understanding the Text

The Text in Context

As if to make sure no one will misunderstand and confuse his emphasis on the bodily resurrection with a notion that somehow the flesh that decays in the grave will be reinvigorated (cf. *2 Bar.* 49.2; 50.2), Paul concludes his discussion on resurrection with a climactic statement on the nature of the resurrected body. Different from the body that belongs to the age of decay and death, the new body will be fit for the new age in God's presence, where death and decay no longer exist.

Paul sets the stage for his discussion with a question about the nature of the resurrection body (15:35). His answer falls into three sections, concluded by a short concluding "so what" statement (15:58). First, in what reads like an exclamation of frustration ("how foolish!"), Paul profiles the whole discussion as caused by ignorance. His objectors should realize that God always creates bodies that are fit for their purpose (15:36–41). Two lines of conclusive

statements follow, the first mostly explanatory (15:42–49), the second mostly declaratory (15:50–57). By way of explanation, he concludes that what he has just said about the body's fitness for its present situation applies directly to the resurrection body, which will be fit to live in God's presence (15:42–49).

Interpretive Insights

15:35 *How are the dead raised?* The question of the natural body's relationship to the resurrection body was an issue that related to both Greek and Jewish sentiments (cf. Mark 12:23; *2 Bar.* 48–52).

15:36–38 *When you sow, you do not plant the body that will be, but just a seed.* Building on his argument that God grants bodies fit for their purpose, Paul draws an analogy from the well-known link between seed and plant to the relationship between natural and resurrected body. This allows Paul to stress continuity without rejecting transformation. And it affords him an illustration of how God turns death into a seedbed for new life. The analogy proves brilliantly helpful for Paul's argument. The seed must die before new life can come from it. Still, what comes up from the ground relates directly to what was put down. Yet there is no direct comparison between a seed and the plant it produces. The plant has a different "body" than the seed. One cannot by a mere look at a seed envision what the plant will look like. The seed changes completely. From the other side, however, one who looks at the plant can see the seed. Likewise, Christians may not know exactly what their resurrection body will be like, but when they are raised, there will be no doubt about its connection to their present bodies. The present matters to the future (6:13).

God gives it a body as he has determined.[1] Different bodies result from God's specifying will for his creation (Gen. 1:11–12), which will be restored from its fall through God's re-creating act of resurrection. God is not reembodying disembodied souls; he re-creates each Christ follower with a new heavenly body without breaking the tie to the natural body (2 Cor. 3:18; Phil. 3:21; cf. John 20:25–27). What was destroyed by the first Adam is restored by the second Adam (15:22, 45–49; cf. Rom. 5:12–17).

15:39–41 *Not all flesh is the same.* Expanding his argument to include the full creation narrative in reverse order, Paul moves from people

- Resurrection brings radical change but does not eliminate continuity with the present.
- Resurrection does not align with cultural conceptions but proclaims a word of redemption.

Baruch and the Resurrection Body

Chapters 48–52 of the *Apocalypse of Baruch* (or *2 Baruch*; a Jewish apocalyptic letter written shortly after AD 70) place Baruch in prayer before God, who reveals the fate of the faithful: "They shall behold the world which is now invisible to them" (51.8 [*APOT* 2:509]). Baruch's question and God's response are succinctly stated in 49.2 and 50.2 (*APOT* 2:508). Baruch asks, "In what shape will those live who live in Thy day? Or how will the splendor of those who are after that time continue?" God answers, "For the earth shall then assuredly restore the dead. . . . It shall make no change in their form, but as it has received, so it shall restore them. And as I delivered them unto it, so also shall it raise them." Baruch's question follows Paul's (15:35), but his answer that the raised bodies will experience "no change" is the exact opposite of Paul's announcement that "all will be changed" (cf. 15:51–52).

to animals (Gen. 1:24–26) to the whole universe. Paul's switch from body (*sōma*) to flesh (*sarx*) does not suggest a change in his perspective from a transformation of the whole being to a mere change of the external (or material) parts of that being. His usual preference

Just as God has designed the seed to "die" in the ground and a new plant to emerge, he will transform the physical bodies of believers at the resurrection. Egyptian theology used agricultural analogies as well. In this scene from the coffin of Nespawershepi, seedlings sprout from the mummified body of Osiris, as a sign of resurrection and new life (tenth century BC, Egypt).

1 Corinthians 15:35–49

for the Greek word *kreas*, when speaking about animal meat (8:13; Rom. 14:21; cf. *T. Jud.* 15.4; *Pss. Sol.* 8.12), indicates rather that he uses *sarx* here as a Greek translation of the Hebrew *basar*—the common Old Testament word for humans as creatures. He changes his vocabulary simply to allow for his contrasts between various bodies.

There are also heavenly bodies and there are earthly bodies. Concluding the discussion by considering heavenly bodies in contrast to earthly bodies brilliantly allows an analogy for understanding the difference between the preresurrection and postresurrection bodies of believers. Beyond differences of "form," observable in the earthly realm, God will grant distinct splendor (*doxa*, "brightness," "radiance," "glory") to different bodies in his own heavenly realm.[2] Highlighting this contrast between the two realms enables a full exposition of the differences between heavenly and earthly bodies. Beyond a change in form, *doxa* will change! The dishonorable character of the earthly body is transformed and given a glory (*doxa*) fit for God's realm (15:43; cf. Dan. 12:2–3; Matt. 13:43; 2 Cor. 3:18).[3]

15:42–44 *So will it be with the resurrection of the dead.* "So" (*houtōs*) transitions everything Paul has said into an explanation of the resurrection body. Paul gives four parallel statements to delineate the difference between the earthly body and the heavenly body.

sown is perishable . . . raised imperishable. Paul's first contrastive pair speaks to the end of decay—biological breakdown. The body that is put in the ground is *phthora* ("corruptible," "decomposing"; NIV: "perishable"); what is raised is *aphtharsia* ("not subject to decay," "imperishable"). Aging, ailments, and the struggles of flesh and blood will become unknown.

sown in dishonor . . . raised in glory. The second pair takes up the issue of honor and shame. What is sown in *atimia* ("dishonor" or "shame") will be raised in *doxa* ("high reputation," "fame," "glory," "honor"). The issue of honor and shame was of major importance to ancient Greco-Roman societies (cf. comments on 4:14; 6:5; 15:34). Contrasting *atimia* ("dishonor") with *doxa* rather than *timia* ("honor") allows Paul to connect the honor of the resurrected body with the high status of God. Since *doxa* is the Septuagint's[4] preferred word to translate the Hebrew *kabod*, it fits the honor assigned to the resurrected body, which shall live in God's presence (cf. Isa.

The resurrected body is raised imperishable, is raised in glory, is raised in power, and is raised a spiritual body (15:42–44). This stained-glass window from the Sainte-Chapelle, Paris (ca. AD 1200), portrays the resurrection of the dead.

6:1–4; 40:4–5; 60:1–3). The shame that can befall even the "honorable" in this age is removed in the resurrection. Moreover, the "shamed" Christ followers (the poor and the slaves) will be raised to high reputation. Their very status and splendor will be changed (cf. Rom. 6:4–5; Col. 1:27).

sown in weakness . . . raised in power. The third contrast speaks to the transformation of the believers' present state of humiliation. *Astheneia* ("weakness") is used of debilitating physical illness, moral weakness, and general helplessness. Expanding on his first contrast, Paul here includes the weakness of the human condition in general. The power of restoration, which believers have already witnessed in part through the gifts of the Spirit, will be made perfect in the resurrection (Rom. 1:4; 6:5).

sown a natural body . . . raised a spiritual body. The fourth contrast summarizes. What is sown a "natural" (*psychikon*) body shall be raised a "spiritual" (*pneumatikon*) body.[5] The present body shall be changed into a body fit for its new reality in God's restored order. Paul's aim is not to contrast body and spirit, or to say that "body" is transformed into spirit. Rather, he explains that the resurrected body will have none of the weaknesses of the natural body and therefore be fit for God's eternal kingdom (Rom. 8:21–23).

15:45–49 *"Adam became a living being"; the last Adam, a life-giving spirit.* To counter any gnostic (or Platonic) notion that the spirit (or soul) is first and the bodily experience is a mere interim state the spirit (or soul) goes through before being released again to its spiritual state, Paul reaches back to his Adam-Christ analogy to clarify (15:22). Quoting Genesis 2:7, Paul describes Adam as a "living being" (or "soul," *psychēn*). Then, to highlight both sequence and difference, Paul renames Christ the "last Adam" and describes him as a "life-giving spirit." The first Adam received natural life as a gift for the body; the last Adam grants the body life from the Spirit. Existence in the natural (*psychikon*) body therefore comes first; the Spirit-empowered body follows the natural and is initiated at the resurrection. Both stages are embodied. Paul understands eschatology in temporal terms (before and after) rather than in dualistic terms (spirit and matter).

The first man was of the dust . . . ; the second man is of heaven. Although verse 47 gives more than a subtle hint to the special birth of Christ, Paul's intention is not to suggest that Christ's birth was God-willed while Adam's was something less than God-willed. Nor does "man from heaven" propose that Christ is less than fully human. Rather, Paul's rhetoric of contrasts enables him to link Genesis's description of Adam's creation to the natural (Adam relates to dirt/dust [Gen. 2:7; 3:19; cf. Job 10:9; Eccles. 3:20]). In contrast, Christ's Spirit-induced conception announced the coming of God's new age of the Spirit (cf. Ezek. 36:26–28; Joel 2:28–29; Jer. 31:33; Isa. 42). It follows, Paul argues, that believers, who presently carry the image of dust from the first Adam, will be changed into the image of the last Adam when they are raised. Christ, the man from heaven, is the firstfruits of those who are raised to live in God's new reality. God will through Christ restore his creation to its original order (cf. Gen. 1:26; 2 Cor. 4:4; Col. 1:15).

Theological Insights

Since the fall placed creation in the intolerable situation of perishable mortality, all of creation must be transformed to be fit for the full presence of God. The promise of resurrection is also a promise of the garden experience of Genesis 1–2. God will restore his creation back to himself, as intended from the beginning.

Teaching the Text

1. Paul's teaching on resurrection must be seen in light of his opposition to the generally accepted idea in Corinth that at the point of death, body and soul/spirit will separate. His extended discussion on how God at the resurrection re-creates the body to make it fit for its new reality in God's presence underscores his eagerness to connect believers' present experience in the "body" with their future experience in the "body." Resurrection does not bring an end to what God is doing in the present but brings it to its fulfillment. Since the present body is characterized by death, it must be radically changed, but the body that will be raised to immortality relates directly to the present body. Just as a wheat seed brings up a wheat plant and an acorn gives life to an oak, the resurrection body of a believer relates directly to her or his present body. Just as the oak tree bears witness to an acorn, the resurrected body will bear witness to the present body. Although one by a mere look at an acorn cannot envision the grandeur of an oak tree, one looking at an oak tree will not think it came from a wheat germ. Christ followers may not know what their resurrection bodies will be like, but these bodies will give testimony to life in the present. Life now matters to life in the future.

2. Paul's allegiance to biblical anthropology makes his teaching on resurrection directly countercultural. Rather than simply following the common notion that death came only to the body and caused the soul/spirit (the "real" person) to ascend to heaven, Paul elaborates the point of bodily life on both sides of death. To Paul, death is not an event for promotion to glory. Death is the enemy! Christian hope speaks to redemption and re-creation of God's world and God's people, not to an escape from present realities. The promise of resurrection does not disconnect the coming age from the present. Death, pain, and suffering remain real and continue to be God's gruesome enemies, until the day when God through Christ redeems his creation unto

Sin ensured Adam's and therefore mankind's mortality. Paul argues that believers who presently carry the image of dust from the first Adam will be changed into the image of the last Adam when they are raised. The temptation and fall of Adam and Eve are depicted on this statue pedestal (AD 1210–20) at the Cathedral of Notre Dame, Paris.

himself and raises believers to live in his glory-filled presence. The ancient pagan, as well as the modern, notion that at the point of individual death souls fly away one by one to a disembodied spiritual state, joyfully aware of their disconnectedness from the pains of the earth, proves utterly foreign to Paul. Christians do not long to be set free from God's creation; they long to be raised to a new reality where death has lost its power and God's power and presence fill all in all.

Illustrating the Text

Resurrection does not destroy the body but rather transforms and quickens it.

Nature: A seed is an image often used in the Bible to illustrate salvation. Seeds bear the DNA code for new life, but they fall to the ground, shrivel, and are buried. Then, in secrecy and mystery, water and nutrients under the ground combine with energy from the sun to bring about a re-action. The latent, life-giving DNA code hidden in the dead seed begins organizing life out of death and decay. Slowly a sprout develops, and at the appointed time a new plant springs forth. In the same way, passages like Isaiah 6:13; Matthew 13:3–23; John 12:24; 1 Corinthians 15:37–39; 1 Peter 1:23; and 1 John 3:9 show us that the spiritual DNA contained in the gospel is planted in the ground with the shriveled husk of a saint's body, and there in secrecy and mystery the seed is nourished by water and the Word and warmed by the radiant love of the Sun of Righteousness. At the appointed time, the gospel organizes decay and death back into vibrant, undying life.

Death is the enemy of God's purposes for us and must be killed by Jesus's resurrection.

Bible: **Revelation 20:13–15.** Revelation clearly shows (in agreement with 1 Cor. 15:54–57) that death is our enemy and that Jesus intends to defeat it forever. Death is not a natural part of life—it destroys what God gave and must be eradicated. This is why the bodily resurrection is so essential—death is not simply a passage from one state (embodied spirit) to another (disembodied spirit) but rather a tempo-rary interruption of the life God wills for all humanity.

Object Lesson: Build a basic tower (use nursery blocks or cardboard boxes) and explain that you are its creator, and that your will for these blocks is that they be a tower that stands firm and tall forever. Then, ask for a volunteer "villain" to rep-resent sin/death/hell. Invite this "enemy" to spoil the tower (knock it down). Now ask your listeners, "Is what just happened a natural part of the tower's created nature or an attack that interrupts its creator's will? For the creator's will to be restored, what needs to happen?" Hopefully, they will say you need to rebuild the tower. Some may even say you need to bind your "enemy" first. (Have some rope and a chair handy, if you want.) In the same way, God has infused eternal life into each believer by his gospel, and promised to bind Satan and grant resurrection on the last day.

Resurrection and Transformation (Part 2)

Big Idea *The transformation of believers at the time of resurrection will be swift and comprehensive. The believers' participation in Christ's victory over evil and death invigorates their discipleship in the present.*

Understanding the Text

The Text in Context

After explaining the character of the resurrection body by utilizing a series of "transformation parallels" from nature and the planetary world, Paul now concludes his pregnant treatment of the resurrection in a first-person declarative statement pointed directly at the Corinthians (15:50–51). The transformation of the body, from perishable to imperishable, will happen instantaneously at the moment when all believers are raised. At that moment, sin and death will have lost all power, and believers will be changed—fit to live in God's new reality (15:52–57). Ending this discourse on a high note, Paul draws together the whole chapter (if not the whole letter) in a major "so what" statement (15:58). Since what is now perishable will be transformed and made imperishable, there should be plenty of motivation to remain faithful to Christ in the present. There will be no destructive discontinuity between the experience of Christ in the present and in the future.

Interpretive Insights

15:50–53 *I declare to you, brothers and sisters.* Bringing his discourse on resurrection to a crescendo, Paul strikes a personal and relational tone (*adelphoi* ["brothers and sisters"] is used broadly to refer to everyone in the church). Paul has already made his argument and can now draw declarative conclusions and focus on the suddenness with which the resurrection will cause a complete change.

flesh and blood cannot inherit the kingdom of God. Everyone (*pantes*) shall be changed—dead or alive (15:51). Such total transformation is necessary because "flesh and blood" (*sarx kai haima* [15:50]), the quality of the body in its fallen nature, cannot inherit the kingdom of God, where decay and death do not exist. Paul uses "flesh and blood" in the traditional Hebraic sense as a figure of speech that refers to

"For the trumpet will sound, the dead will be raised imperishable, and we will be changed" (15:52). In the Roman world trumpets were used to proclaim important events. In this relief a trumpet announces the triumphal return to Rome in AD 176 of the victorious emperor, Marcus Aurelius.

I tell you a mystery. The Greek *mystērion* refers to that which remained hidden, or unknowable, until God revealed it (something formerly unknown).[3] What God revealed was not the sequence of the *parousia* events but the necessity, suddenness, and fullness of the transformation at the *parousia*.[4] It shall happen while some are still alive and in a "split second" (*atomos*—the smallest amount of time; NIV: "in a flash").[5] Paul's imagery for suddenness is "the blink of an eye" (or "the brevity of a quick glance"; NIV: "the twinkling of an eye"). His imagery for announcement follows the common Old Testament tradition of connecting the arrival of God's presence with the trumpet (cf. Exod. 19:16–17; Lev. 23:24; 25:9; Num. 10:10; Josh. 6:20; 2 Chron. 15:14; Pss. 47:5; 150:3; Joel 2:1; Zech. 9:14; Isa. 18:3; 27:13; Matt. 24:31; Rev. 1:10; 4:1). The transforming moment happens at God's own time and is announced by the sound of a trumpet.

must clothe itself with. The clothing imagery of verse 53 further reflects the described change. As shown above, Paul does not suggest a reembodiment of disembodied souls; rather, he uses language of appropriate attire to connect to Jewish imagery of transformation from mortality to immortality (*1 En.* 62.15b–16; *2 En.* 22:8–10).[6] As if to make sure no one could misunderstand, Paul accentuates the full transformation of the present situation by a fourfold repetition of the demonstrative pronoun

human beings in their present fallen situation (Matt. 16:17; Gal. 1:16; Eph. 6:12; Heb. 2:14) as opposed to a reference to a separable physical (nonsoul) part of the human being, the body. The phrase is commonly used by Old Testament texts to express family relationship/lineage.[1] The idea of inheriting (*klēronomeō* [15:50]) God's promised gifts is a well-known biblical concept (often connected with the promised land).[2] Because fallen human beings cannot inherit the kingdom of God, believers shall be "raised" and "changed" (15:52).

(touto) in verses 53–54 (*this* perishable, *this* mortal, *this* perishable, *this* mortal; translated as "the" in the NIV). The very person (or nature/reality) that is now perishable will be changed and made imperishable.

15:54–57 *Death has been swallowed up in victory.* Bringing lyrical force to the crescendo of his discourse, Paul connects two poetical prophetic sections that both announce death's coming end (Isa. 25:8; Hosea 13:14). Although Paul's quote does not align very precisely to the wording of the Septuagint, it is close enough to leave little doubt that these were the passages in his mind. The Isaiah passage comes from a section announcing God's salvation to all nations or people groups (*panta ta ethnē*, "all nations" [Isa. 25:7 LXX]).

> On this mountain the LORD Almighty will prepare a feast of rich food for all peoples, a banquet of aged wine—the best of meats and the finest of wines. On this mountain he will destroy the shroud that enfolds all peoples, the sheet that covers all nations; he will swallow up death forever. The Sovereign LORD will wipe away the tears from all faces; he will remove his people's disgrace from all the earth. The LORD has spoken. (Isa. 25:6–8)

The Hosea quote comes from a judgment passage where Israel faces the punishment of elimination and death unless God rescues them from the power of Sheol ("the grave").

In 15:56 Paul says, "The sting of death is sin, and the power of sin is the law." The scenes of Adam and Eve's fall and Moses receiving the law are carved next to each other on this sarcophagus lid from fourth-century AD Rome.

> I will deliver this people from the power of the grave; I will redeem them from death. Where, O death, are your plagues? Where, O grave, is your destruction? "I will have no compassion, even though he thrives among his brothers." (Hosea 13:14–15a)

Paul combines these two quotes and changes the Hosea text from "death, where is your *dikē* ['judgment']" to "death, where is your *nikos* ['victory']." Resurrection, then, is the event where believers are rescued from the power of death. Although death may sting like a scorpion,[7] it has been "swallowed up" (15:54); death has become prey for immortality (2 Cor. 5:4; cf. 1 Pet. 5:8).

The connection between death, sin, and the law is a well-known theme in Paul. Sin is aroused by the law and results in death (Rom. 6:21; 7:5); death is the wage of sin (6:16, 23). Paul's point in verses 56–57 is to stress that since the sting of death has been removed, sin has lost its power to remove believers from God's presence. The resurrection that awaits gives evidence that Christ followers have died to the power of sin and been made alive to the presence of God (Rom. 6:11, 14; Gal. 3:21). The victory has already been won (cf. 1 John 5:4; Rev. 1:18), condemnation has been removed (Rom. 8:1), and new life from God's Spirit has broken through (2 Cor. 3:6).

15:58 *Therefore . . . Let nothing move you.* The inferential conjunction "therefore" (*hōste*) draws Paul's discussion to a conclusion that places Christ's resurrection as the central theological motivation for Christian life and worship. Since believers will be raised, their present struggles as faithful clients in the Christ community are not in vain (15:10, 14 and 3:8; 4:12; cf. Heb. 6:10). They have cause for standing firm in their faith (cf. Col. 1:23; 1 Pet. 5:9), being unwavering (*ametakinētos*;[8] NIV: "let nothing move you") in their commitment, and consistently overflowing in their work for Christ (cf. 2 Cor. 6:4–10; 1 Thess. 1:3).

Theological Insights

Christian discipleship is not empowered by a new set of rules to follow or commandments to obey. Rather, the believer's continuous motivation to imitate Christ is his or her ongoing participation in Christ's victory over evil. Resurrection guarantees that this victory will be ultimate.

Teaching the Text

1. Paul's teaching on resurrection connects directly to his already/not-fully description of Christian experience. Resurrection will bring to fullness what Christ followers now

Steadfastness

The issue of steadfastness under pressure was a well-known theme in the early church. The ongoing challenges from a variety of well-established teachings and attractions in the pagan world that surrounded the new Christian movement made a constant encouragement to stay faithful to the gospel a continuing necessity. Strengthening the Colossian church, Paul states this encouragement positively (Col. 1:21–23). Defending the Galatian church against the attacks from certain Jewish teachers, Paul argues for the importance of steadfastness using strongly negative language (Gal. 1:6–9).

The necessity of the ongoing encouragement to stay faithful to the gospel continues after the close of the New Testament. Writing at the beginning of the second century, Ignatius says to Polycarp:

> Do not let those who appear to be trustworthy yet who teach strange doctrines baffle you. Stand firm, like an anvil being struck with a hammer. It is the mark of a great athlete to be bruised, yet still conquer. But especially we must, for God's sake, patiently put up with all things, that he may also put up with us.[a]

[a] Holmes, *Apostolic Fathers*, 197.

experience in part. Paul's emphasis that death has already lost its ultimate sting and been swallowed up by victory speaks to the "already" of Christian experience. Paul clearly does not suggest that Christians no longer can sin or that they will not experience death; his point is that the present experience of the Spirit's enabling power has given a foretaste of what it will be like when the powers of sin and death are completely broken. Christian hope ties directly to this. As the outpouring of God's Spirit on his people provides direct evidence of God's presence, believers can know that the fullness of that presence will come (Rom. 8:11). Since this fullness of God's presence leaves no room for the perishable and the mortal, it must mean that death and sin have already lost their power. Christ followers, therefore, are no

1 Corinthians 15:50–58

Resurrection is the event in which believers are rescued from the power of death. This resurrection scene is from a fresco at the Voroneț Monastery, Romania (sixteenth century AD).

longer slaves to sin (Rom. 6:11). Although sin and death still show their heads, believers are neither helpless in the present (Rom. 8:12–14) nor hopeless for the future (1 Thess. 4:13).

2. As Paul himself concludes (15:58), it follows from the above that Christian ethics finds its strongest motivation in the resurrection. Contrary to those who might consider eternal life a final "reward" for remaining faithful, Paul speaks of resurrection as the motivator for faithfulness to Christ. Christian hope must not be disconnected from Christian living. Put differently, eschatology, Christology, and ethics cannot be separated. The resurrection is not an attachment to Christian living that brings everything to a nice conclusion after a hard life on earth. To the contrary, it is an integral part of Christian living in the present. Because the present bodies will be transformed rather than destroyed, resurrection becomes the nerve center for Christlike living in the present. Just as Christ's resurrection guarantees his community's resurrection, it also calls it to conform to the life that preceded his resurrection. As 6:14 makes clear, on the basis of the bodily resurrection it makes sense for Paul to say, "The body, however, is not meant for sexual immorality but for the Lord, and the Lord for the body" (6:13b). Based on the resurrection hope, then, Christ's community finds motivation and strength to live Christ's life regardless of its countercultural and often unpopular stance. Without such grounding in the resurrection, Christ's community will lose its power to live Christ's life and, as Paul says, become the most pitiable of all (15:19).

Illustrating the Text

Resurrection is an "already, but not fully" reality of which the Spirit gives us a pledge and foretaste.

Human Metaphor: Resurrection is a lot like marriage. Marriage is a state into which one enters in a day, and yet it lasts over a lifetime. On their wedding day, a couple pledges to be one flesh until death parts them. In that moment, they are just as legally bound as they will be on their fiftieth wedding anniversary; in God's eyes they are one flesh in every way. On the other hand, knowing what this new reality means and having any idea how to live into it fully are still a long way off. That part takes a lifetime to figure out and unpack. In the same way, the moment a person receives the gospel by faith, he or she is declared perfectly righteous in Christ Jesus, eternally accepted as his son or daughter by adoption through faith in Christ, and given the gift of resurrection. On the other hand, living into this takes a lifetime, and an eternity after that. The individual believer begins to experience the Holy Spirit as a pledge and down payment on the fullness of eternal life, but does not receive the Spirit fully until the last day and ever thereafter.

Contrasting Concept: In contrast to resurrection, earthly pleasure is an "all now, but never again" reality. We pursue what seems to be a great reward here on earth, but immediately after we receive it, its ability to please us is diminished, and we hunger for even more. The more we taste, the less it satisfies, and the process ends in deadness of our senses now and death to our spirit forever. The deadness in our senses (see Eph. 4:17–19) that comes now is the down payment and foretaste of more death to come. How different is the gift of God from the wages of sin!

Resurrection is the everyday substance of the Christian life, both now and forever.

Human Experience: In marriage, love is not something that should be expressed only at occasional milestones. It is not a wave of emotion that gets us through a wedding, a few birthdays and anniversaries, and a funeral. Love is not a thing that ought to bookend the marriage covenant—it is simply what married people promise to do every day in a thousand different ways. In other words, love is not a moment or season that starts a marriage; it is the fabric that marriage is made of in the first place. In the same way, resurrection is not a momentary milestone that kicks off eternity; it is the fabric of which our faith is made.

Collection and Travel Plans

Big Idea *Because the Christ communities in Corinth serve a Lord whose household stretches around the world, their local communities are members of a global community. With this come special relationships, privileges, and responsibilities for "brothers and sisters" who serve the same Lord (or Patron).*

Understanding the Text

The Text in Context

Paul has concluded his major discussions and is now rounding out his letter with a series of remarks on issues that just need a brief comment. Before his final remarks and greetings in 16:12–24, Paul underscores the global nature of the Christ community by including an instruction on how to prepare a collection for the poverty-stricken church in Jerusalem (16:1–4), as well as a detailed explanation of his travel plans before he comes to visit Corinth (16:5–11). Individual Christians and Christian communities are bound together by their common commitment to the same patron, Christ.

Interpretive Insights

16:1 *Now about the collection.* Paul's opening suggests he is either responding to a request about some details regarding the management of the collection (cf. 7:1, 25; 8:1; 12:1; 16:12) or alerting them to a matter that he has talked about earlier and that he still considers urgent. At any rate, the peculiarity of Paul using the Greek word *logeia* to name the collection (a word he uses no other place) may be due, as Garland mentions, to its play on *eulogia* ("blessing"; cf. 2 Cor. 9:5 [NIV: "generous gift"]).[1] The guidelines he gives are the same as those he gave to the churches in Galatia. They are an expression of his agreement with Jerusalem that churches everywhere should take care of the poor (Gal. 2:10).

16:2 *On the first day of every week.* This is one of the earliest references to Sunday as the day of worship. The Christian community moved its worship to Sunday to celebrate Christ's resurrection (John 20:1; Matt. 28:1; Mark 16:2; Luke 24:1; Acts 20:7), and Sunday quickly came to be interpreted as "the Lord's day" (Rev. 1:10).

each one of you should set aside . . . in keeping with your income. That Paul connects the collection to the first day of the week implies that he has a public collection in mind. He does not simply envision that each family puts funds aside at home to have them ready when Paul comes. They could have done that on any day of the week. Giving and sharing are part and parcel of participation in Christ's community and obvious expressions of worship rendered to their self-giving patron.

Paul's switch from an aorist in verse 1 to a present imperative in verse 2 speaks to his conviction that the setting aside must be an ongoing process, something that belongs to each Sunday.[2] The emphasis on "each one" makes the gift a community gift rather than a donation from a few Corinthian patrons. By this, each member will "store up" (*thēsaurizōn*; NIV: "saving it up") his or her share of an appropriate gift. The verb *thēsaurizō* evokes Jesus's words from Matthew 6:19–21 and Luke 12:21 and may signal that Paul associates the treasure they lay aside on Sunday with the treasure they lay up in heaven by doing so. They are not requested to give a set amount or percentage, as if it were a "temple tax" (Matt. 17:24–27), but to give "in keeping with [their] income."[3]

16:3 *I will give letters of introduction to the men you approve.* Already in 4:19 Paul has mentioned his plans to return to Corinth, a visit they seem to be expecting before they receive this letter. To make sure no one could charge him with misappropriation of the collected funds, he asks the Corinthians to approve messengers from their midst to bring the money to Jerusalem. Also, this allows for a face-to-face meeting between the communities to strengthen their unity in Christ.

The "letters" Paul will write on their behalf are letters of introduction and commendation to the church leaders in Jerusalem. Paul gives a similar commendation of Timothy in verses 10–11 (cf. 2 Cor. 3:1–3; 8:16–24; Acts 15:23–29; for an extended letter of commendation, see Rom. 16). If the Corinthians instead considered it appropriate for Paul to go with them, the Corinthian delegation would arrive in Jerusalem as his company, and they would not need a letter; he could commend them in person.

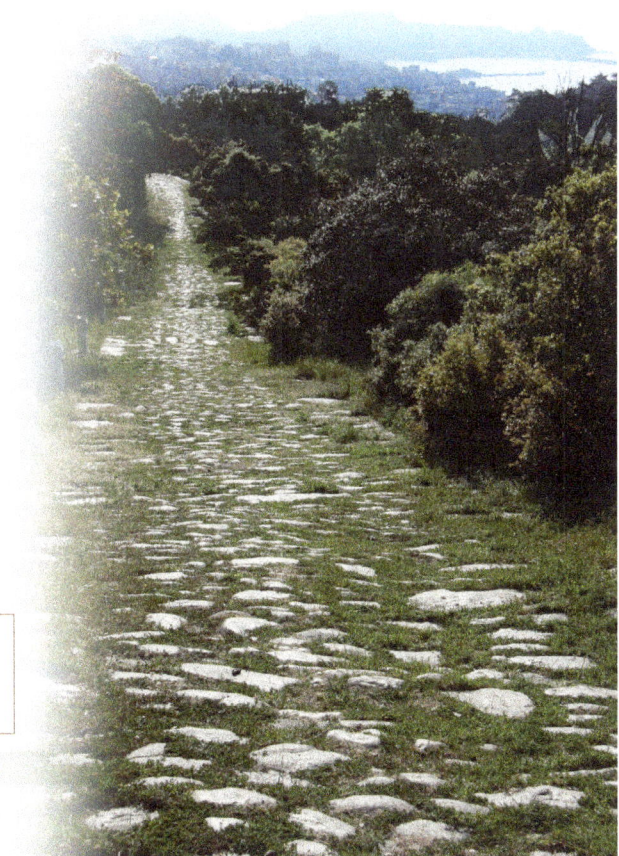

Travel along the Via Egnatia would have been part of Paul's itinerary as he journeyed to Corinth from Ephesus via Macedonia. A section of this major east-west Roman road is shown here.

send them with your gift. Paul chooses to name the "gift" a *charis* (an expression of grace) to stress its character as a reflection of the grace they themselves have received from the Lord. Their gift does not make them patrons of the Jerusalem church; it allows them to share the grace they have received. What they have and what the Jerusalem church receives is a gift from the same patron, Christ (cf. Phil. 4:10, 18b–19).

16:5–9 *After I go through Macedonia, I will come to you.* Traveling was cumbersome in the ancient world. Getting from Ephesus to Corinth was no simple matter and could not be done safely at all times of the year. Paul would most likely travel north along the coast from Ephesus to Troas, where he would cross to Neapolis in Macedonia. From there he probably would go west on the Via Egnatia through Thessalonica all the way to the province of Illyricum on the Adriatic Sea (cf. Rom. 15:19), before he turned south toward Athens and finally Corinth (see the map on p. 11). Paul's mention of Macedonia implies that he did not intend to sail directly from Ephesus to Corinth, although that would have been possible.[4]

even spend the winter, so that you can help me on my journey. Paul's outline of his travel plans reveals his effective use of time. Wanting to spend extended time with the church in Corinth,[5] he arranges to optimize the opportune travel time (late spring and summer) to visit a number of churches in Macedonia before arriving in Corinth in time for the winter, when travel was impossible or significantly hazardous.[6] This would give him time to further address the issues dealt with in the letter and to work out the travel plans for getting the collection to Jerusalem. Traveling was no easy matter,

and Paul would need the Corinthian Christians' help. The Greek *propempsēte* means "you may assist in sending me" (NIV: "you can help me on my journey") and generally refers to travel provisions like food, money, and travel companions (Acts 15:3; 2 Cor. 1:16; Titus 3:13; 3 John 6).

a great door for effective work has opened to me. Paul uses "open door" as an idiom for opportunity (2 Cor. 2:12; Col. 4:3). His use of the perfect tense ("door has been opened") brings a sense of permanence to the door's openness (God has opened a door and left it open).[7] An open door, however, does not mean he is outside personal danger or that the gospel can be spread without fierce opposition (cf. 15:32; 2 Cor. 1:8; Acts 19). Paul never concludes that hostility and opposition equal a closed door (e.g., Phil. 1:12–14, 28; 1 Thess. 2:2; 2 Tim. 3:12; cf. John 15:20), although danger from opponents sometimes could force him to leave a place (Acts 13:50–51; 14:5–6, 19–20; 17:5–10, 13–14).

16:10–11 *No one, then, should treat him with contempt.* Paul has already referred to Timothy's visit (4:17) and adds this recommendation to highlight that Timothy "is carrying on the work of the Lord." Whatever caused Paul to think that some in Corinth would speak negatively about (*exouthenēsē*, "disdain," "scorn"; NIV: "treat him with contempt"[8]) Timothy, he makes sure such disparagement is offset by his commendation. When Timothy speaks, he speaks with Paul's blessing. Rather than trying to intimidate Timothy, they should make sure he can work among them without fear (*aphobōs* [16:10]).

Send him on his way in peace . . . with the brothers. Paul desires to hear a good word from Timothy about the Corinthians, and he asks them to send him back "in peace." This expression follows the traditional Jewish pattern of departure greeting (Exod. 4:18; 1 Sam. 20:42; 2 Kings 5:19; Acts 15:33; 16:36; James 2:16) but could also include a subtle hint that such would be possible only if Timothy experienced peace while in Corinth. "Brothers" likely refers to Timothy's traveling partners. It was too dangerous to travel alone.

Theological Insights

Being a member of the body of Christ is not just a local experience but a global participation in God's kingdom purposes. Christians who move or travel should therefore, naturally, join the local body of believers, as their family of brothers and sisters, wherever they go.

> Travelers such as Paul and Timothy would have entered the ancient city of Corinth on the Lechaion Road, the main thoroughfare that led into the city.

Teaching the Text

1. One of the major charges against Israel by the Old Testament prophets was that they did not take care of the poor. The early Christians, who understood themselves as the end-time community promised by God's prophets, recognized the importance of this charge and vowed to show concern for the poor (Acts 2:44–45; 4:33b–34a). Giving to the poor became a natural expression of Christian devotion to God (Acts 9:36; 10:2, 4, 31; 24:23; 27:3; cf. Luke 4:18; 6:20; 7:22; 14:33). Since God provides for his people, Christian giving is participation in God's redemptive purpose. In Christ's community there is no distinction between givers and receivers. All members of Christ's body are receivers of God's redemptive grace, and all are therefore bound to make sure no one goes without the experience of God's provisions. Paul's address to the Corinthians on this issue follows this very line of thinking.

The poor in Jerusalem are members of the same community as the Corinthians, and the provisions Christ has given his community must benefit everyone in it. The issue, therefore, is not merely (or even primarily) one of monetary aid; it is a matter of worship. Monetary collections must be part and parcel of Christian worship services exactly because they express allegiance to the Lord, who gave himself to others. In a fashion similar to the way the Corinthian believers must express their unity with each other through sharing (11:18–22), Christ's communities around the world are called upon to look out for each other.

2. Contrary to what seems like a natural conclusion in a modern Western setting, Paul concludes that in spite of fierce opposition and danger to him and his message, God has opened a great door for effective gospel preaching. Put differently, personal pain and suffering, outspoken rejection and ridicule, do not determine whether a place is ripe to receive the message of Christ. Although Paul describes the situation in Ephesus in this particular passage, his inclusion of this line more than hints that those in Corinth who may come to experience suffering and rejection if they remain faithful to the gospel should not conclude that their faithfulness is wasted or ineffective. In fact, Paul repeatedly uses his experience in Ephesus as an encouraging reminder that suffering can be God's means of revealing his power (2 Cor. 1:8–11)—a tool to strengthen faith and prove its authenticity (Phil. 1:14). Heavy hostility and opposition can indeed result in open doors that would otherwise have been closed (Phil. 1:12–13; 1 Thess. 2:2). Moreover, a Christian life without any kind of persecution

may actually be suspect and lacking the very quality of Christlikeness (2 Tim. 3:12; cf. John 15:20). Christian hope generates boldness (2 Cor. 3:12).

Illustrating the Text

Giving and providing for others are integral to Christlikeness.

Hymn: "Good King Wenceslas." This old Christmas carol describes the virtue and charity of Saint Wenceslas I, Duke of Bohemia (ca. 907–ca. 929). It describes his generosity to a starving peasant in his realm and his desire to share what he had for others' provision. He is said to have gone about barefoot in the snow, accompanied by only one chamberlain, to visit churches and give alms generously to widows, orphans, those in prison, and those afflicted by every difficulty. It is said that he did this so often that he was considered both a nobleman and the father of all the wretched. Even though Wenceslas was not actually a king in life, the Holy Roman Emperor Otto I posthumously conferred on him the regal dignity and title due to a king. The text of the Christmas hymn describes the blessing of caring for the poor and needy this way: "Therefore Christian men be sure / Wealth or rank possessing / Ye who now will bless the poor / Shall yourselves find blessing." The story of Wenceslas is a great illustration of the way selfless generosity brings renown in God's kingdom because of genuine Christlikeness.

Suffering and ridicule often mean the moment is spiritually ripe.

Sports: In body building, resistance and temporary soreness are signs that you

replace the damaged ones and better prepare for the next time you ask so much of it. In the same way, if you wish to grow as a disciple of Christ, you must face resistance, suffering, and ridicule, as Jesus did. These experiences perfected and revealed his character and nature and allowed him a deeper fellowship with us in our need. When you face resistance, you will experience doses of death. This death will be replaced by more new life and growth, and the Lord will use it to prepare you for greater use in the future.

Quote: H. G. Wells. "The path of least resistance is the path of the loser." When it comes to following Christ, this is definitely the truth, since "wide is the gate and broad is the road that leads to destruction, and many enter through it. But small is the gate and narrow the road that leads to life, and only a few find it" (Matt. 7:13–14).

Bible: Matthew 5:10–12. This passage confirms that we are doing things right when we face resistance on account of Christ, and it offers great comfort and affirmation to those currently suffering for righteousness.

are doing your workout correctly. If you never faced weight resistance, your muscles would never grow. However, if your goal is building muscle, you engage in a process of lifting progressively heavier weights over more numerous repetitions. Each workout actually builds up toxic amounts of lactic acid and kills a certain number of muscle cells, causing soreness and discomfort afterward. The body then responds by building a greater number of new muscle cells to

1 Corinthians 16:1–11

Last Encouragement and Final Greeting

Big Idea *When strong, Christ-devoted Christians visit or join a fellowship, churches must receive these with love and submit to their ministry. As the strong believers come to encourage others' faith, they themselves should receive encouragement and be strengthened.*

Understanding the Text

The Text in Context

Albeit concise, Paul's concluding chapter functions as weighty pastoral guidance on practical community matters. He ends his letter by speaking to the relationship between individual communities, between a community and its itinerant leaders, between individual members within a specific community, and between individual communities and the Christian community at large. He uses his final few lines to give a last word of encouragement for the Corinthians to stay the course and remain strong in the faith (16:12–18) and concludes this encouragement

with greetings (16:19–20) designed to highlight the unity of call and purpose between all Christians who love the Lord (16:22–24).

Interpretive Insights

16:12 *Now about our brother Apollos.* Since Paul's introduction follows the pattern he uses throughout this letter when referring back to specific questions from Corinth, his commendation of Apollos likely comes as a response to a question about him. Some have suggested that the form of Paul's commendation indicates a

As Paul concludes his letter, he encourages the believers to "stand firm." Paul knew they were living in a pagan community where their Christian faith would be challenged as they interacted with other citizens. Many Corinthians would have enjoyed regularly discussing new religious, political, and philosophical ideas in the Corinthian forum, shown here.

hesitancy to endorse Apollos. Paul, however, considers Apollos a long-term coworker in God's kingdom and speaks of him in the warmest of terms, calling him "our brother."[1]

Paul assures the Corinthians that he has encouraged Apollos repeatedly to visit Corinth; but for reasons not revealed, Apollos had not yet found the opportunity. It could be that Apollos's unwillingness to visit was due to a poor reception from the Corinthians during an earlier visit (cf. 1:12; 3:4–6, 22; 4:6).[2] It is also possible that Apollos had been without opportunity to make a trip because it was costly, time consuming, and dangerous.

16:13–14 *Be on your guard; stand firm . . . be courageous; be strong.* Before Paul gives his letter of recommendation concerning the group of Christ followers that meets in Stephanas's house, he interjects four imperatives in verse 13 followed by a fifth in verse 14 that clarifies the manner in which these four qualities should be emboldened in the church. These imperatives function as words of encouragement to strengthen the church in the absence of strong teachers like Apollos, Timothy, and Paul himself. "Be on your guard" (*grēgoreite*) and "stand firm" (*stēkete*) encourage watchfulness toward philosophies that undermine Christian life and faith. They point back to everything he has said in the letter and what the believers know about the gospel of Christ from his teaching. "Be courageous," or "manly" (*andrizesthe*), and "be strong" (*krataiousthe*) add further emphasis rather than further content. These are not special words for the men of the church but broad encouragements not to capitulate when pressured to allow for thinking and conduct that

Key Themes of 1 Corinthians 16:12–24

- Letters of recommendation both reflect and secure unity among believers.
- Being called as a disciple of Jesus leaves no room for "interim" periods.

weakens the faith. Those who belong to Christ's community must be courageous and strong when painful consequences result from being true clients of Christ. As with everything else, love must always reign supreme (16:14; cf. 13:1–13; 16:22, 24).

16:15–18 *the household of Stephanas were first converts.* Paul's commendation of Stephanas's group reads like a statement of love to the whole Corinthian community. Stephanas and the two members from his household in Corinth, who are with Paul in Ephesus, bring encouragement to Paul. Calling them "firstfruits" (*aparchē*) places them in a special category among the Corinthians. Paul has already used this word repeatedly about the relationship between Christ's resurrection and the resurrection of all believers. In Jewish thought, the firstfruits of a harvest belong to God (Lev. 23:9–11, 15–17; Deut. 26:1–11). They are an announcement that a greater harvest is yet to come. The other Corinthian house churches therefore relate in a special way to the community in Stephanas's house (1:16; cf. Rom. 16:5).

they have devoted themselves to the service . . . submit to such people. Highlighting that the firstfruits are devoted to Christ's community gives more than a subtle hint that their pattern of "service of the Lord's people" should be the common pattern. In the absence of Paul's presence, therefore, the various Corinthian house groups would do well to follow their lead (submit to them). Rather than using an imperative, Paul places his call to submission (*hypotassesthe*) in a purpose clause. When the firstfruits are faithful servants, the purpose of the following fruit is already determined—they are to be like their firstfruits. Paul could therefore rest peacefully; Stephanas brought him relief from his worries (cf. Philem. 7). The difficult reports he received from Chloe's house do not exemplify everyone. Rather than looking to the troublesome communities for guidance, Paul charges that all Corinthians must give recognition to the community in Stephanas's house. Their example is worth following. Instead of demanding honor as "patrons" of all the other Christ communities, they imitate Christ as true servants. They are worthy of recognition, not as firstfruits, but as servants.

16:19–20 *The churches in the province of Asia send you greetings.* Paul's broad greeting from "churches in the province of Asia"[3] serves as a reminder to the Corinthians that *their* Christ communities are not God's central focus. Rather, they are part of a large family of Christ communities that span the "civilized" world (cf. Rom. 16:5). Whatever cliques they may have and whatever prominence some of their local patrons may portray, it all seems rather insignificant when compared to their true *kyrios*, Christ, who has communities of faithful clients everywhere (1:2; 4:4; 7:17; 11:16; 14:33, 36). Put differently, the true patron to whom their loyalty should be latched (see "Grace and Patronage" in the introduction) is Christ.

Aquila and Priscilla. This couple was well known to the Corinthians.[4] Beyond having lived in Corinth and serving the church, they were the very couple who instructed Apollos more precisely about the Christian faith and sent him to Corinth (Acts 18:24–19:1). The continued travel between the three major cities where they had established business (Rome, Corinth, Ephesus) could suggest they were running an international business—leaving their business in the hands of clients during their periods of absence.[5] At any rate, their home in Ephesus was large enough to be a gathering place for a Christ community. Those who functioned as leaders in Corinth, Christ now used as leaders in Ephesus; Corinth was simply one part of a greater movement of God.

Greet one another with a holy kiss. The greetings come not just from those the Corinthians know but from "all the brothers and sisters here" (in Ephesus; cf., e.g., 1:2; Phil. 4:21; Titus 3:15).[6] They all belong to the same patron and thus are all connected as if in the same family. By adding the adjective "holy" to the customary "kiss" greeting, he gives it a distinct relational quality with roots in common relationship to God (see the sidebar "Holiness and Sanctification" in the unit on 1:1–3). Whatever the specific form, or whether Paul by use of this term refers to an element in the Lord's Supper celebration, seems less significant. By sending this greeting from Ephesus, he once again underscores the common unity of all believers in Christ. Because they all belong to Christ, they can greet one another with a *holy* kiss.

16:21–24 *write this greeting in my own hand.* Writing a letter, especially one as lengthy as Paul's letters, was no small task and was usually done by a professional scribe. Paul likewise made use of a scribe to write his letters.[7] When Paul adds his signature and a short note written by himself, it assures his audience of the authenticity of the letter; but, more important, it gives the whole letter a personal touch and shows heartfelt affection for the audience (cf. Gal. 6:11; Col. 4:18; 2 Thess. 3:17; Philem. 19). What Paul has stated throughout the letter comes to them not as a cold philosophical discourse but as an expression of his genuine concern for their spiritual welfare.

let that person be cursed! Paul's curse follows his covenantal understanding. Curses fall on those who do not love the Lord, while blessings come to those who do (Deut. 28; cf. Jude 14–15). The undercurrent of Paul's thought is that love for the Lord creates obedience, which in turn brings blessings (2:9; 8:3). Loyal and faithful clients could expect blessing from a good patron, whereas those who lacked such loyalty would be cursed.

the grace of the Lord Jesus. Paul concludes his letter with his most common concluding benediction. He uses it in every letter. It includes the source "of the Lord Jesus," the wish "grace," and the recipients "with you." The verb is not expressed but understood (English translations supply a form of "to be," usually in the mood of a wish: "*may* grace . . . *be* with you").[8]

My love to all of you in Christ Jesus. From beginning to end, Paul assures the Corinthians of his unwavering love (cf. 4:14; 10:14; 13:1–13; 15:58), not just to some of them, but to all those who are "in Christ Jesus"—that is, all who call Jesus *Kyrios* and therefore are a part of Christ's community.

Teaching the Text

1. Letters of commendation were common in the ancient world, but Paul's use of this convention does not spring from nepotistic ambitions. The breadth and diversity of the people Paul commends (from wealthy individuals and highly esteemed orators to runaway slaves) evidence Paul's focus on building the church as a genuine community of Christ. Strong commendations serve two purposes. On the one hand, Paul's commendations highlight the unity of the Christian faith across individual communities, ethnic groups, and geographical distance. The message of Christ that is preached in both word and deed remains the same in essence wherever a particular Christian is called to serve. Commendations, therefore, speak to an individual's faithful walk with Christ and allegiance to the gospel. They are not lists of specific

Paul writes these final greetings in his own hand. This would have contrasted with the bulk of the letter, which was most likely written by a scribe. Shown here are some common writing implements from the Hellenistic period, including styli for wax tablets and inkpots for pen and papyrus or parchment.

1 Corinthians 16:12–24

giftedness designed to extol an individual for his or her own benefit. Paul recommends for the benefit of God's kingdom. On the other hand, Paul's commendations serve as guards against self-promoting individuals and those who promote a different gospel. Whether Paul speaks directly against such individuals (e.g., Rom. 16:17–18; Gal. 1:7–9) or simply questions their integrity as true messengers (e.g., 2 Cor. 11:5–6), his aim is to protect the church from people whose purposes are self-serving rather than Christ promoting (Phil. 3:18–19). Recommendations thus serve a very significant purpose in building the church, and Paul's examples should not just be read as interesting historical information. They give guidance to a significant element in the continuous growth of the church as new generations are introduced and as believers continue to hold up models of Christian commitment that faithfully promote Christ (4:16; Phil. 3:17; 1 Thess. 1:6–7; 2 Thess. 3:9; Heb. 6:12).

2. Paul's mention of Aquila and Priscilla leaves the Corinthians with a powerful example of faithfulness. The Corinthians knew the couple as serving patrons when they lived in Corinth and knew they had come to Corinth from a position of Christian leadership in Rome. When now the Corinthians are reminded of the couple's continued faithfulness in the Ephesian church, this functions as a model for what it means to remain vigilant in Christ's community. Not only do Aquila and Priscilla serve as an example that Christ's body is unified across ethnic groups, borders, and continents; they demonstrate how faithful Christians stay engaged at all times. Given the travel this couple did between the cities of their business, it would have been rather understandable if they had

Aquila and Priscilla and the members of their house church sent greetings to the believers in Corinth from Ephesus. Shown here is one of the main thoroughfares in ancient Ephesus, known as Curetes Street.

remained aloof and become only loosely involved in the local groups of Christian believers. The temptation to consider each place temporary, however, was overcome by the keen awareness of their position as disciples (clients) of their Lord (patron), Christ. Since Christ had appointed them for service in his household, they were not free to put that on hold while traveling or while waiting for the next place in their lives. Since Christ's household spanned the world, they served in the capacity he had given them wherever they were.

Illustrating the Text

Christian communities are sustained over generations by a continuity of Christlike leaders.

Bible: **2 Timothy 2:2.** Paul's instructions to Timothy in 2 Timothy 2:2 (which echo Exod. 18:21) clearly indicate that a process of discipling, vetting, entrusting, and releasing new leaders is the right pattern for passing on leadership and authority in Christ's church. We also see a picture of this in Paul's farewell to the Ephesian elders in Acts 20:13–38.

Christian faith is a call for all seasons of life; early retirement from our labor is never an option.

Quote: **Oliver Wendell Holmes.** Holmes once said, "Men do not quit playing because they grow old; they grow old because they quit playing." The same is true of believers when it comes to their calling and vocation: elderly Christians do not retreat from their mission and purpose in the kingdom because they are tired and depressed; they become tired and depressed when they retreat from their mission and purpose in the kingdom.

Bible: **Joshua 14:6–12.** Caleb, son of Jephunneh, gives a great example of courage and passion in old age. His speech in Joshua 14 shows the way God's promise can invigorate a lifetime of service, and the way the Lord's strength can enable great feats regardless of age or health, so long as there is courage and faith in one's heart. (Other great examples are Simeon and Anna in Luke 2:22–40.)

Notes

Introduction to 1 Corinthians

1. Contra Malina and Pilch, *Social-Science Commentary*, 3, whose otherwise very helpful comments reflect a disconnect between Paul's letters and the present-day situation of the modern church.

2. Witherington, *Conflict and Community*, 12.

3. For a more detailed discussion of patronage, see deSilva, *Honor*, 95–156.

4. Notice, for example, the reference in Sir. 30:6 (NRSV): "He has left behind him an avenger against his enemies, and one to repay the kindness of his friends."

5. Cf. Seneca, *Ben.* 2.18.5 (LCL).

6. Notice again Seneca's remark (*Ben.* 2.18.8; 2.19.2 [LCL]):

> It makes no difference what the gift is if it is not given willingly to one who accepts willingly; though you have saved my life, you are not for that reason my saviour. Poison at times serves as a remedy, but it is not for that reason counted as a wholesome medicine. . . . For, since that which I am forced to receive is not a benefit, that also which puts me under obligation to someone against my will is not a benefit. You ought to give me first the right to choose for myself, then the benefit.

7. E.g., building of temples, theaters, roads, and so on. Cf. Josephus, *J.W.* 1.21.

8. Aristotle, *Rhet.* 2.7.2 (LCL). For a fuller discussion of Aristotle's *Rhetoric*, see Kennedy, *Aristotle*.

9. Seneca, *Ben.* 1.3.2–5 (LCL).

10. Seneca, *Ben.* 7.32 (LCL); cf. 1.10.5. Notice also the admonitions in Pss. 103:2; 116:12.

11. Seneca, *Ben.* 3.14.2 (LCL): "Consider again and again to whom you are giving: you will have no recourse to law, no claim to restitution . . . look only to the good faith of the recipient."

12. Hock's description of Paul as working beside slaves from before daylight in rough workshop conditions devoid of any social status is probably exaggerated (*Social Context*, 67). There is little doubt that Paul as a good Pharisee considered working with his own hands an honorable task, but he is likely to have used hired help for the more menial tasks of his trade (like the actual sewing). If not, he would have been a simple employee of Priscilla and Aquila, which is not likely (Acts 18:2–3; 1 Cor. 16:19).

13. See the discussion in Hall, *Unity of the Corinthian Correspondence*, 76–77. See also Meeks, *First Urban Christians*, 66.

14. A typical *triclinium* would hold about twelve people for formal dining, while the remaining thirty to forty would fill the *atrium*.

15. Most people were raised to know whether they "belonged" in the *triclinium* or the *atrium* and were not likely to question this normal way of doing things.

16. The closest modern parallel may be segregation found in twentieth-century American Bible Belt churches. Here, too, the accepted social patterns of the society—races living segregated in different parts of town—led to segregated churches and division among Christians.

17. Both socioeconomic and racial/ethnic issues may have caused some of the divisions. See, for example, Paul's exhortation to avoid distinctions between Jews and Greeks, slaves and free (12:13)—and his deliberate mentioning of leaders of various backgrounds (e.g., Jews like Aquila, Priscilla, and Crispus; Romans like Fortunatus, Gaius, and Achaicus; and the use of Peter's Aramaic name, Cephas).

18. Winter, *Philo and Paul among the Sophists*.

19. Winter, *Philo and Paul among the Sophists*, 4.

20. Quintilian, *Inst.* 2.2.12 (LCL [Butler]).

21. Quintilian, *Inst.* 2.11.9–10 (LCL [Butler]).

22. See Pogoloff's discussion on rhetoric and antifoundationalism in *Logos and Sophia*, 26–35.

23. Moores, *Wrestling with Rationality in Paul*, 133–34.

24. The Gallio inscription is the strongest piece of data we have for any specific dating of events in Paul's life. That is, we determine the time for much of Paul's life and ministry by adding or subtracting years from AD 51–52.

25. Several of the modern Bible translations have put these in quotation marks (see, e.g., 6:12–13; 7:1; 8:1).

1 Corinthians 1:1–3

1. See Richards, *Paul and First-Century Letter Writing*.

2. Contra Fee, *First Epistle*, 28–29.

3. For more on *shaliah*, see Barrett, "*Shaliah* and Apostle."

4. Outside Paul's letters, the inclusion of a co-sender in a letter opening is exceedingly rare in Greek letters. See Richards, *Secretary in the Letters of Paul*, 47n138.

5. Thiselton, *First Epistle*, 69.

6. Os Guinness, *Prophetic Untimeliness* (Grand Rapids: Baker Books, 2003), 91–92.

7. Brian Moore, *The Color of Blood* (New York: Dutton, 1987), 107.

1 Corinthians 1:4–9

1. The whole section is filled with passive verbs, indicating that although the Corinthians are the subject, they are not the actors. God is!

2. Paul's repeated use of "in Christ" should be understood as a local dative—a Greek grammatical construction that references the "place" (realm or sphere) where Christ is proclaimed and obeyed as Lord.

3. Notice Paul's exaggerated repetition of Christ's name in the first ten verses of this letter. No individual in Corinth should be confused about who their true patron is. Cf. comments by John Chrysostom, *Hom. 1 Cor.* 2.7.

4. Cf. 2 Cor. 1:12; 2 Thess. 1:10; 1 Tim. 2:6; 2 Tim. 1:8.

5. The word *charismata* (lit., "grace gifts"; NIV: "gifts") is a neuter plural noun. *Charis* ("grace") moors this word to God as the graceful giver and underscores the unmerited quality of these gifts (Rom. 5:15; 6:23). With 1 Pet. 4:10 as the only exception, the word *charismata* is exclusive to Paul and functions mostly as a technical term for the distribution of specific service gifts by the Holy Spirit to each believer. As Paul highlights in 12:7, their purpose is to build up the church.

6. YHWH is the revelatory name God gave himself in Exod. 3:14 and is usually translated "I AM WHO I AM" or simply "I AM." English translations generally indicate the Hebrew text's use of YHWH by the capitalized "LORD."

7. Valerie Grove, "I Appreciate Your Gift More Than I Can Say," *The Times Online*, December 27, 2007, http://www.thetimes.co.uk/tto/life/article1854809.ece.

8. A. W. Tozer, *Renewed Day by Day: A Daily Devotional*, ed. G. B. Smith (Camp Hill, PA: Christian Publications, 1980), July 11.

9. Kristopher H. Kowal, "Something of the Gospel in Van Gogh," *Modern Age* 33.3 (Fall 1990): 259, 266.

1 Corinthians 1:10–17

1. A *propositio* is the major thesis statement of a deliberative discourse. See, e.g., Witherington, *Conflict and Community*, 94.

2. Bjerkelund, *Parakalō*, 74, 109–10.

3. Most likely Paul does not attempt to outargue the formal rhetoricians using their own medicine; he is simply making a strong appeal to those who have been called by the gospel. Scholars of rhetoric make a distinction between illocutionary speech and perlocutionary speech. The purpose of Corinthian rhetoric was mostly perlocutionary—aiming to persuade and transform the audience's thinking through various rhetorical devices designed to have a psychological effect.

4. The genitive formulation "those from Chloe" can refer to slaves (workers/business associates) related to the household of Chloe. If she is not a Christian herself, a likely scenario could be that her slaves (or business associates) traveled between Ephesus and Corinth. They would then have been church members in Ephesus who noticed the Corinthian struggles when they worshiped with the Corinthian church during business visits.

5. The Greek word *adelphoi*, though masculine, generally may refer to both genders. Only when a group was exclusively female was the feminine *adelphai* used.

6. See Thiselton, "Supposed Power of Words."

7. The Greek word *hina* introduces purpose. Context always determines its precise translation: "that," "in order that," "for the purpose of," and so forth. At times, it may even be left untranslated. What follows *hina* is in the subjunctive mood—an anticipated and encouraged (but at the present a "not quite there yet") reality. In this context it means "you should all agree" (you should, but apparently you do not yet).

8. It is quite likely that some ethnic/racial tension persisted in the church. Paul's use of the Aramaic name Cephas instead of Peter, as well as his use of *marana tha* in 16:22, could give hints of this.

9. Beyond his use of *hekastos* ("everyone"; NIV: "one"), notice the redundant repetition of *egō* ("I").

10. John Chrysostom suggests the latter (*Hom. 1 Cor.* 3), commenting on verse 12:

> For if it were not right for them to call themselves by the name of Paul, and of Apollos, and of Cephas, much less of any others. . . . By way of hyperbole then, seeking to withdraw them from their disease, he sets down these names. Besides, he makes his argument less severe, not mentioning by name the rude dividers of the Church, but concealing them, as behind a sort of masks, with the names of the Apostles. (*NPNF*[1] 12:11)

11. For an argument in favor of Peter visiting Corinth, see Barrett, "Cephas and Corinth."

12. Cf. Clarke, *Secular and Christian Leadership*, 92–93.

13. As both popular and academic commentators at times claim.

14. See George, *Theology of the Reformers*, 53.

15. Flannery O'Connor, "Revelation," in *The Complete Stories of Flannery O'Connor* (New York: Farrar, Straus and Giroux, 1975), 490–91.

16. Os Guinness, *Prophetic Untimeliness* (Grand Rapids: Baker Books, 2003), 15.

1 Corinthians 1:18–31

1. The direct linguistic connection in Greek between gospel and evangelism can easily be lost in English. The Greek verb *euangelizō* ("I evangelize") is in its noun form translated "gospel" in English rather than as "evangel." "Gospelize" would in English make a similar direct connection between noun and verb.

2. The contrast between the two messages (or "words") stands out clearly in Greek—the "word of the cross" (*logos staurou*) in verse 18 reveals the emptiness of the "word of wisdom" (*sophia logou*) in verse 17 (NIV: "wisdom and eloquence").

3. The use of the present tense further underscores that this is an ongoing process. They are in the process of destroying themselves.

4. Again, the present tense points to process. They are headed in the opposite direction. The force of the passive

here is clearly theological. The unmentioned agent, the one doing the saving, is God.

5. Paul quotes freely from the OT (LXX) throughout his letters. It forms the basis for his ethics and functions as Scripture for the early churches. Isaiah 29:14 is the first in a long series of OT quotes used in this letter.

6. Hengel (*Pre-Christian Paul*, 42) suggests that Paul describes the error of his pre-Christian life as a Pharisee. If so, the three correspond to the Hebrew sage, scribe, and commentator (in Hebrew, *hakam*, *soper*, and *doresh*, respectively).

7. The Greek *gar* ("for") gives reason for, or further explanation of, what was just said.

8. See Barbour, "Wisdom and the Cross," 63.

9. Caesar claimed status as *kyrios*, "lord," or savior, because he was the one who guaranteed the Romans peace and prosperity and thereby gave his subjects the opportunity to live flourishing lives.

10. Paul's reference to "Greeks" is not exclusive. Corinth was outspokenly Roman (not Greek) at the time of Paul. "Greeks" functions as a synonym for non-Jews, or Gentiles. If there is any significance to Paul's word choice, it may be that the Greeks exemplified the search for wisdom.

11. Notice that Paul introduces a third social divider. So far, he has mentioned only the two honors that could be acquired in the socially mobile Corinth (wisdom and power). To this list he now adds the honor that was inherited (noble birth).

12. See comments on 1:4.

13. Chuck Swindoll, *Come before Winter and Share My Hope* (Grand Rapids: Zondervan, 1988), 83.

1 Corinthians 2:1–16

1. See Epictetus, *Disc.* 3.19.1.

2. Beyond Paul's lack of eloquent wisdom, his appearance fell short of the usual expectations for effective wisdom promoters. Epictetus (*Disc.* 3.22.86–88; quoted in Hubbard, "2 Corinthians," 241) explains the importance of a strong appearance for philosophers: "Such a man needs also to have a certain kind of body: for if a consumptive comes forward, thin and pale, his testimony no longer carries the same weight. . . . 'Look,' he says, 'both I and my body are witnesses to the truth of my contention.'" Although we obviously need to be careful not to project our own modern conventions of attractiveness onto ancient descriptions of physical appearance, the depiction of Paul in the *Acts of Paul and Thecla* as small, bald, bowlegged, unibrowed, and hook-nosed seems unimpressive. Moreover, his health struggles worked against his effectiveness as well (2 Cor. 10:10; cf. Gal. 4:13–14). As Epictetus describes, a philosopher who "excites pity is regarded as a beggar; everyone turns away from him, everyone takes offence at him" (*Disc.* 3.22.89).

3. A decision on which reading is original is difficult. See Metzger, *Textual Commentary*, 480.

4. Aristotle, *Rhet.* 1.1.11 (Freese [LCL] translates *pistis* with "proof" here). For further discussion, see Kinneavy, *Greek Rhetorical Origins*, chap. 2.

5. In Greek, the perfect tense expresses completed action with ongoing consequences.

6. Following his usual pattern, Paul brings his point to an argumentative crescendo through an OT quote. Verse 9, however, although introduced as an OT quote ("as it is written"), seems to be his own summary of some Isaiah texts (e.g., 52:15; 64:4) and possibly Ps. 31:19–20.

7. *Pneumatikois* (masculine, "to the spiritual ones") *pneumatika* (neuter, "spiritual things").

8. Paul's word for interpreting, *synkrinō*, is used in the Greek translation of the OT (the LXX) for interpretation of dreams (e.g., Gen. 40:8, 16, 22)—without such interpretation, no one could understand (cf. Dan. 5:7–8).

9. T. S. Eliot, "Religion and Literature," in *Religion and Modern Literature: Essays in Theory and Criticism*, ed. G. B. Tennyson and Edward E. Erickson Jr. (Grand Rapids: Eerdmans, 1975), 21, 28–29.

10. Helmut Thielicke, *A Little Exercise for Young Theologians* (Grand Rapids: Eerdmans, 1962), 33.

11. Dorothy L. Sayers to John Shirley, December 28, 1939, cited by Laura K. Simmons, *Creed without Chaos* (Grand Rapids: Baker Academic, 2005), 130–31.

1 Corinthians 3:1–15

1. Cf. Aristotle, *Rhet.* 3.2.10; Seneca, *Mor. Ep.* 59.6; 78.16.

2. See Winter, *After Paul*, chap. 2.

3. Notice how this theme comes up throughout this letter. Here Paul calls them infants; in 13:11, in the midst of his discussion of spiritual gifts, he explains how he himself has moved from childish ways to mature ways; in 14:20, as the letter approaches its conclusion, he encourages the Corinthians to move away from childish ways of thinking. Cf. Heb. 5:12–13.

4. See the historical survey by Thiselton, *First Epistle*, 276–86.

5. A slight distinction exists between *sarkinos* (3:1) and *sarkikos* (3:3). *Sarkinos* refers to humans being "of flesh" and therefore not divine; *sarkikos* refers to humans behaving "fleshly," with an emphasis on their rebellious character.

6. Dio Chrysostom, *Disc.* 9.8.

7. D. B. Martin, *Corinthian Body*, 102. Later copyists tried to change the pronoun to masculine.

8. The striking nature of the singular noun "building," or "house," should not be lost on us as modern church members. Paul refuses to consider the various house groups a series of individual churches. There is no room for individualism in Paul's language. Together, not individually, they are God's building, God's temple (3:16).

9. Shanor, "Paul as Master Builder."

10. Cf. Mal. 3:1–3; 4:1; 2 Thess. 1:8; 2 Pet. 3:10; *Sib. Or.* 4.170–75.

11. The passive form of *zēmioō* means "to be punished." Workers delivering an unsatisfactory product would be slapped with a penalty fee.

1 Corinthians 3:16–4:5

1. When used of the temple in Jerusalem, *naos* referred exclusively to the building consisting of the Holy Place and the Holy of Holies.

2. "In your midst" is literally "in you [pl.]."

3. His inclusive plural, here pointing specifically to himself, Apollos, and Cephas, makes the statement general in nature—inclusive of each and every Christian leader.

4. Paul calls Timothy faithful/trustworthy in 4:17 and calls himself this in 7:25.

5. The literal translation of what most English translations translate "any human court" is "any human day." We sometimes use a similar expression, "having your day in court." In this context, Paul uses the expression as a comparison. To him, the day to be concerned about is not the "human day" but the "Lord's Day" (3:13; cf. 4:5).

6. Although *kyrios* ("Lord") is a common Pauline title for Jesus, its use here (as opposed to "Christ") fits his argument perfectly. Only when the true Lord (or patron) returns to the house can the manager of his estate be properly judged or praised. Receiving honor or praise, as opposed to being shamed, was coveted in the ancient world with a passion similar to how material things are coveted in the modern world. See deSilva, *Honor*, 24–27.

7. Theissen, *Psychological Aspects*, 66.

8. A. W. Tozer, *Of God and Men* (Harrisburg, PA: Christian Publications, 1960), 12–13.

9. Brother Lawrence, *The Practice of the Presence of God* (Old Tappan, NJ: Revell, 1969), 14.

1 Corinthians 4:6–13

1. See, for example, Thiselton, *1 Corinthians*, 349.

2. Garland, *1 Corinthians*, 136.

3. "Instead of a 'vanity wall' with plaques marking personal accomplishments such as we might see in our society, the first-century Mediterranean would feature masks, busts, and memorials of ancestors who made them to be who they were" (Malina and Pilch, *Social-Science Commentary*, 76).

4. Both verse 6 and verse 8 address the church as a whole (plural "you").

5. Paul gives this verse full rhetorical force, using asyndeton to separate three ultraterse exclamations. An asyndeton is a lack of the usual and expected connection between statements (and, but, etc.). The rhetorical effect is that each statement seems launched as a separate, fast-paced bullet. The Beatitudes (Matt. 5:4–11) use asyndeton as well. A desire to have full English sentences has made the rhetorical use of asyndeton less visible in some translations.

6. Since the text originally did not have punctuation, these terse sentences could be questions. "Have you already become . . . ?" However, the present context and structure favor reading these as statements rather than questions.

7. Epictetus (*Disc.* 3.22.63) refers to wise men as kings.

8. Dio Chrysostom (*Disc.* 3.10 [LCL]) calls a king one to whom "all things are permissible." Suetonius quotes Caesar Caligula as saying, "I have the right to do anything to anybody" (*Cal.* 29.1 [LCL]).

9. Philo, *Virt.* 174 (Yonge, *Works*, 657). Philo, a Hellenistic Jewish philosopher who aimed to harmonize Judaism and Greek philosophy, was one of the most significant and influential Jewish writers in antiquity. He died just a few years before Paul wrote 1 Corinthians.

10. For a helpful study on Greco-Roman lists of hardship, see Hodgson, "Paul the Apostle."

11. Although the text literally says "naked" (cf. Rom. 8:35; 2 Cor. 11:27), this is somewhat common language for those dressed in rags (Seneca, *Ben.* 5.13.3).

12. Literally "roughed up" or "mistreated"—physically and verbally (cf. Mark 14:65).

13. Jenkins, *New Faces of Christianity*.

14. Os Guinness, "Sounding Out the Idols of Church Growth," in Os Guinness and John Seel, *No God but God: Breaking with the Idols of Our Age* (Chicago: Moody, 1992), 159–60.

1 Corinthians 4:14–21

1. There is probably no reference in Paul's mind to the Western introspective notion of "feeling ashamed" (e.g., NRSV [cf. ESV]: "I am not writing this to make you ashamed"). This is not a psychological statement designed to make them feel better after he fussed at them.

2. E.g., *b. Qidd.* 22a.

3. E.g., *b. Sanh.* 19b.

4. Notice Paul's language—literally, "I have begotten you through the gospel." He has brought them to life through the gospel.

5. Although the role of the pedagogue changed, the differentiation between *paidagōgos* ("tutor") and *didaskalos* ("teacher") remained at the time of Paul. When Paul in Gal. 3:24–25 talks about the purpose and function of the law, he calls it the pedagogue that guarded until Christ came.

6. Cf. Castelli, *Imitating Paul*, 95–111, who sees this as a clever rhetorical device—simultaneously gaining sympathy through self-effacement and claiming his rights and authority as a father.

7. The phraseology could be a hint that Timothy was the letter carrier. It was common practice to use a so-called epistolary aorist, where the letter writer puts himself in the position of his audience, for whom the described event would be past tense. In light of 16:10 ("when Timothy comes . . ."), however, it is not likely that Timothy was the letter carrier. Acts 19:22 may refer to an earlier stop Timothy made on his way to Corinth.

8. The phrase "kingdom of God" is rare in Paul (4:20; 6:9, 10; 15:24, 50; Rom. 14:17; Gal. 5:21; Col. 1:13; 4:11; Eph. 5:5; 1 Thess. 1:5; 2 Tim. 4:18). With its clear reference to OT texts and metaphors, "kingdom of God" would have been readily understood in Hebraic circles, but not as much among Gentiles. This likely is the reason Paul uses Jesus's central phrase ("the kingdom of God has come near") so rarely. Paul's preferred phrase "righteousness of God" has almost the same function and frequency as "kingdom of God" in the Gospels.

9. As Garland points out (*1 Corinthians*, 149), "The 'rod' was an image of severe discipline and symbolized both Jewish (2 Sam. 7:14; Prov. 10:13; 13:24; 22:15; 23:13–14; 29:15, 17; Sir. 30:12) and Greek education." Cf. Philo, who calls the rod a "symbol of education" (Philo, *Post.* 28 [97] [Yonge, *Works*, 141]).

10. Thomas à Kempis, *Imitation of Christ*, 124.

1 Corinthians 5:1-13

1. Unnamed here, but it is not unlikely that the present report came from those referenced (1:11; 16:17). It apparently was not something the church itself brought up as a question in its own letter to Paul (7:1).

2. The sense of the Greek *holōs* (NIV: "actually") is here to remove any question about its truth—it is actually a generally known fact. An amplified translation could read something like, "It is actually reported, and there is no doubt that it is true, that . . . " (BDAG, 704).

3. About one hundred years before Paul's encounter in Corinth, Cicero (*Clu.* 6) described with the greatest disgust the marriage between a mother-in-law and a son-in-law, considering it unspeakably vile and "unheard of in all experience save for this single instance!" (LCL).

4. Given 7:12, it is possible that the father was a Christian, but not likely. Plutarch (a generation younger than Paul) describes it as "becoming of a wife to worship and know only the gods that her husband believes in" (Plutarch, *Advice* 19 [*Mor.* 140D] [LCL]).

5. Cf. Winter, *After Paul*, 53.

6. As the NIV translation, "I am with you in spirit," seems to suggest.

7. See also Fee's comment on 5:4, where he rightly rejects the notion that Paul considers his presence merely fictive (*First Epistle*, 204n39).

8. Whether Paul envisions "satanic" attacks on the man's physical body, expressing God's judgment on him, remains uncertain. Such, however, would not be outside Christian thinking (Luke 13:11; 2 Cor. 12:7; cf. Job 2:5–6).

9. Mitton, "New Wine in Old Wine Skins."

10. A number of European breads are still made this way. I personally eat some every day.

11. "Leaven" by itself is not a loaded term. It is used both negatively (Mark 8:15) and positively (Matt. 13:33).

12. For more on this vice list, see Kistemaker, *First Epistle to the Corinthians*, 169.

13. In contrast, Paul considers attenders non-Christian outsiders, or at best potential believers (14:16, 23–24), and does not imagine Christians who think of themselves as unrelated to the life and witness of a specific Christian community.

Additional Insights, pages 70-71

1. I am indebted to Bruce Winter for much of this discussion (*After Paul*, 44–57).

2. Cf. Gill, "Erastus the Aedile," 293–301.

3. Justinian, *Dig.* 48.39.7 (Mommsen and Krueger, *Digest of Justinian*, 4:814).

4. Justinian, *Dig.* 48.40.5 (Mommsen and Krueger, *Digest of Justinian*, 4:815).

5. See Kaster, "Shame of the Romans."

1 Corinthians 6:1-6

1. Thiselton, *First Epistle*, 421.

2. Although no real impartiality was available, Paul still considered the criminal system an arbiter of justice (Rom. 13:1–7). For more on fairness and the Roman judicial system, see "Additional Insights: Corinthian Law," preceding this unit.

3. See Winter, *After Paul*, 60.

4. NLT translates the sense well: "How dare you file a lawsuit . . . "

5. The English word "audacity" captures the outrage of this verse as a fitting translation of *tolma*: "Does someone actually have the audacity to . . . "

6. As Winter points out (*After Paul*, 62–63), more or less everyone in the Roman Empire, including the emperor himself, recognized the lack of justice found in these local courts.

7. For more on the term "holy," see the sidebar "Holiness and Sanctification" in the unit on 1:1–3.

8. The traditional rabbinical hermeneutical principle applied by Jesus is called *qal wahomer*. See further Longenecker, *Biblical Exegesis*.

9. Cf. 15:24; 2 Cor. 11:15. Arguing against the idea that "angels" should refer to unfaithful priests (cf. Rev. 2:1–3:22), John Chrysostom affirms, "[Paul's] speech is about demons. . . . For when the very incorporeal powers shall be found inferior to us who are clothed with flesh, they shall suffer heavier punishment" (*Hom. 1 Cor.* 16.5 [NPNF[1] 12:91–92]).

10. BDAG, 352.

11. The perfect tense expresses a completed action with ongoing results: "You have always despised them and you still do." In other words, nothing should have changed in the church's perception.

12. As jurors took sides—forced by bribes, social networks, financial pressures, patron-client relationships, and so on—so would church members. The church's oneness in Christ that had crossed social, financial, and racial/ethnic lines would be destroyed.

13. The party that lost was required to pay damages and major penalties.

14. For more detail, see Buckland, *Text-Book of Roman Law*, 121–27.

15. Keep in mind that the term *adelphos* ("brother") often is gender neutral. Masculine is used broadly when speaking to or about a mixed-gender group the same manner we today, telling a story, may say "a doctor, he . . ." Most people realize that the doctor could be a woman and that the one speaking is just making a general statement.

16. Kaster, "Shame of the Romans," 16. Kaster illustrates this value system further from Cicero's use of *audacia* ("boldness"): "The many passages where Cicero, for instance, attacks his opponents' shamelessness, *impudentia*, readily convey the impression that *audacia* was *impudentia*'s even nastier twin, and unambiguously evil: over and over and over again *audacia* is denounced as the raw expression of individual will trampling on the communal sense."

1 Corinthians 6:7-11

1. Conzelmann, *1 Corinthians*, 105.

2. Beasley-Murray, "Baptism," *NIDNTT* 1:153.

3. Church history reveals a litany of approaches to sanctification that prove to be little more than efforts toward personal betterment. The same holds true for much of the contemporary discipleship material.

4. The metaphor of the marriage is helpful here. Because I am married, I belong to my wife. From this exclusive relationship it follows that I do not belong to any other woman. As a married man, however, I am defined by my belonging to my wife, not primarily as one separated from others—although that is the unquestionable result.

5. A reduction of Paul's understanding of "righteousness" to a mere forensic declaration from God to his people, as has become rather common in some theological circles, misses the point of Paul's emphasis.

1 Corinthians 6:12–20

1. "'Virtue-lovers,'... mostly found among the non-privileged, were looked down upon with disgust as insignificant people of no means without the position and drive to indulge in life's pleasures. The elite considered such people filthy, sickly, and reduced to skeletons—in training for dying (*epitēdeuei apothnēskein*)" (Winter, *After Paul*, 79).

2. One generation younger than Paul, Epictetus (*Disc.* 4.1.1 [LCL]) says: "He is free who lives as he wills, who is subject neither to compulsion, nor hindrance, nor force, whose choices are unhampered, whose desires attain their end, whose aversions do not fall into what they would avoid.... Who wishes to live deceived, impetuous, unjust, unrestrained, peevish, abject?—No one. "

3. This is the sixth time Paul uses this phrase (see also 3:16; 5:6; 6:2, 3, 9).

4. Collins suggests that Paul considered this a mutilation of Christ's body (*First Corinthians*, 247).

5. Paul's word choice to express the "joining" with a prostitute (*kollaō*) alludes to Deut. 10:20, where the requirements of the relationship between God and his people are restated as "to him you shall cling, and by his name you shall swear" (LEB). Outside this context, the only other place Paul uses this term is in Rom. 12:9.

6. For a careful analysis, see Murphy-O'Connor, "Corinthian Slogans."

7. Numerous attempts have been made to distinguish qualitatively between sexual sins (against the body) and other sins. As most of these arguments go, only sexual sins relate exclusively to the body. Although other sins certainly can be harmful to the body (e.g., drugs, alcohol, self-mutilation, suicide), it is not possible to "become one flesh" with drugs, alcohol, and so on. Creating qualitative differences between sins proves inherently difficult and significantly coincidental. Furthermore, Paul does not seem to attempt a qualitative distinction between "bodily sins" and other sins but underscores the spiritual problem in not considering sins against one's own body.

8. As a matter of grammar, it is possible that Paul refers to a Christian house group (or the wealthier part thereof—those gathering in the *triclinium*) who claimed the right to hold on to their pre-Christian, well-established, and accepted (if not expected) cultural patterns for dining banquets.

9. See "Grace and Patronage" in the introduction.

1 Corinthians 7:1–7

1. Gaius, *Inst.* 1.113 (Scott, *Civil Law*, 1:97).

2. Witherington, *Conflict and Community*, 177, quoting A. C. Wire.

3. Bradley, *Discovering the Roman Family*, 6–8.

4. See Witherington, *Conflict and Community*, 171. In the Roman Empire, women and men had the same rights to divorce, at least in theory.

5. "Have sexual relations with" is literally "to touch" (*haptesthai*).

6. See, for example, Conzelmann, *1 Corinthians*, 115, who sees this as a reflection of such discussion.

7. Because of Paul's zeal as a Jew, rabbi, and possible Sanhedrin member, some scholars argue that Paul himself was married (cf. 9:5). For more on this question, see the "Historical and Cultural Background" section in the unit on 7:8–11.

8. See, for example, Collins, *First Corinthians*, 253–54.

9. Paul here follows his understanding from Judaism. The *Testament of Levi*, a significant rabbinical document from the first century BC, says, "Beware of the spirit of fornication; for this shall continue and shall by thy seed pollute the holy place. Take, therefore, to thyself a wife without blemish or pollution, while yet thou art young" (*T. Levi* 9.9–10 [*APOT* 2:310]).

10. The suggestion that a group of women in the church saw a command to sexual abstinence as a way to avoid marriage to older wealthy men has no support in the text (see, e.g., Wire, *Corinthian Women Prophets*, 75); neither does Margaret MacDonald's suggestion that these were the pneumatic women Paul also confronted in chapter 11, who "believed they transcended sexual differentiation" and therefore "removed their veil" during worship ("Women Holy in Body and Spirit," 166–67).

11. Although Paul's thinking follows Jewish teaching, his emphasis on mutuality clearly goes beyond the teaching of his rabbinical past: "For there is a season for a man to embrace his wife, and a season to abstain therefrom for his prayer" (*T. Naph.* 8.8 [*APOT* 2:339]).

12. The Greek *hina* introduces a purpose/result statement and could be translated "the purpose for this is" or "the result will be." The broad lines of Paul's argument run something like this: "Don't deprive each other [imperative], so that [*hina*] you may not be tempted." The purpose (or result) of the command is to avoid temptation.

13. Collins (*First Corinthians*, 260) notes: "Paul knows of no command of the Lord (cf. 7:10, 12) that would warrant even limited sexual abstinence. At most his Jewish tradition allows him to tolerate marital sexual abstinence under stated conditions."

14. E. Elliot, "Virginity," *Elisabeth Elliot Newsletter* (March/April 1990): 2 (available online at http://elisabethelliot.blogspot.com/2012/05/1990-marchapril-issue-part-3_30.html).

1 Corinthians 7:8–11

1. Cohick, "Marriage, Divorce, and Discipleship," 28.

2. Cohick, "Marriage, Divorce, and Discipleship," 29.

3. Rousselle, "Body Politics in Ancient Rome," 316.

4. Brown, Fitzmyer, and Murphy (*Jerome Biblical Commentary*, 263) consider the idea that Paul was a widower

postconversion but argue that Paul's inclusion of the word *menō* ("remain") "implies that Paul had never married."

5. Barré, "To Marry or to Burn."

6. As opposed to a present middle infinitive—the wife "should not separate" from her husband—as many modern translations choose in order to make the English reading smoother and harmonize it with 7:13. The difficulty of the aorist passive infinitive is reflected also in a number of older manuscripts, where the copyists apparently faced the same struggle.

7. Murphy-O'Connor lists an example from the Shepherd of Hermas (Herm. *Mand*. 4.4.1–11) where a husband is told not to remarry because it would make complete forgiveness of his wife impossible: "Therefore for the sake of repentance, a husband ought not to (re)marry" ("Divorced Woman," 35n15, citing Quesnell, "'Made Themselves Eunuchs,'" 350–51).

1 Corinthians 7:12–16

1. That Paul's reference here is to marriages where one spouse becomes a Christian after the marriage is clear from 7:39, where widows are allowed to remarry "only in the Lord" (NRSV), and from 2 Cor. 6:14–15, where Paul forbids Christians to marry non-Christians.

2. Plutarch, *Advice* 19 (*Mor.* 140D; LCL).

3. Garland (*1 Corinthians*, 285) suggests it might be Paul's previous letter (5:9–13) that made the Corinthian Christians conclude that "they could not allow a pagan to have power over their bodies (7:4), which belonged to Christ."

4. See the sidebar "Holiness and Sanctification" in the unit on 1:1–3.

5. For example, Murphy-O'Connor, "Works without Faith." About the children, he further says, "their behavior makes them *hagia*" because "children assimilate the behavior pattern of their parents" (53).

6. Fee, for example, understands it as a matter of influence and uses Rom. 11:16 (if part of the dough is holy, the whole batch is holy) as an explanatory parallel (*First Epistle*, 300–301).

7. In Paul's mind "unclean" likely relates directly to the parallel OT issue of idolatry and spiritual defilement by other gods. See also the sidebar "Holiness and Sanctification" in the unit on 1:1–3.

8. Paul's use of the middle voice (*chōrizetai*) emphasizes that the decision to leave is made by the unbeliever.

9. A good number of translations treat Paul's use of "enslaved" (*douloō*) as if it were a mere synonym of "bound" (*deō*), suggesting that Paul simply is trying to convey that the believer in such cases no longer is bound by his divorce prohibition. Nothing in the text seems to indicate such, though. Since *deō* is the more common word to use in the marriage context, *douloō* is Paul's deliberate choice. He aims to say something different.

10. Collins, *First Corinthians*, 271–72.

11. Collins, *First Corinthians*, 271–72.

12. The modern situation, where over a lifetime people have a number of spouses, or live-in partners if marriage is avoided, proves somewhat parallel to Paul's context.

13. Erma Bombeck, *Family: The Ties That Bind . . . and Gag* (New York: McGraw-Hill, 1987), 9.

1 Corinthians 7:17–40

1. Participation in athletic training, for example, would reveal a person's circumcision, since athletes competed in the nude. Corinthian gymnasia were common, as the city hosted the Isthmian Games (see "Sport and Tourism" in the introduction). To remove the circumcision required an operation to restore the foreskin. Celsus, *Med.* 7.25, explains the specifics of the medical procedure.

2. Aristotle, *Eth. nic.* 8.11; *Pol.* 1.1254b.

3. The experience of Joseph at Potiphar's house (Gen. 39) gives a better point of comparison than American slavery in the antebellum south. On "responsible" masters, see Seneca, *Dial.* 5; *Anger* 3.29. See further Weidemann, *Greek and Roman Slavery*; on buying slaves, including children, see chap. 6; on cruelty, chap. 9.

4. His use of *nomizō* in verse 26 likewise does not suggest an uncertain "I think"; it introduces the content of his *gnōmēn* ("understanding," "mind-set") in verse 25.

5. Paul says not "short" but "shortened," leaving the length of the period undefined.

6. Paul likely uses the phrase "those making use of the world" (*chrōmenoi ton kosmon*; NIV: "those who use the things of the world") in 7:31 in the broadest, most inclusive sense, much like we would use "worldly success" today—businesspeople doing well, slaves gaining freedom, and so on. Paul does not argue against worldly success; he reminds the Christians that such should not steal their focus and confuse their true aim, to please the Lord (7:32).

7. *Amerimnos* is freedom from anxious concern or worry. Paul does not suggest his audience become carefree or unconcerned in the flippant sense of that term. Notice the freedom with which Paul uses "anxiety" (NIV: "concern") when writing to the Philippians. On the one hand, he tells the church that Timothy is genuinely anxious for their welfare (Phil. 2:20); on the other, he encourages them not to be anxious about anything (4:6).

8. Paul's reference to the unmarried being able to concern themselves with holiness in "body" and "spirit" does not relate to sexual relations between spouses and does not hint at a dualistic anthropology. The expression simply refers to the whole person. Generally speaking, Paul's "body/soul/spirit" language may translate best into English using the fishing idiom "hook, line, and sinker"—the whole thing.

9. His use of the intensive *autōn* leaves the statement without any doubt; Paul says this not for his sake but for their sake only.

10. Verse 36 is notoriously difficult to translate. Consider these different versions:

"If anyone thinks that he is not behaving properly toward his fiancée, if his passions are strong . . ." (NRSV).

"But if any man thinks he is behaving improperly toward his virgin, if she is past the flower of youth, and thus it must be . . ." (NKJV).

"But if any man thinks that he is acting unbecomingly toward his virgin daughter, if she is past her youth . . ." (NASB).

What kind of relationship does Paul refer to? Does Paul deal with father-daughter issues? Does "anyone" refer to the father of the virgin/daughter who is concerned she is getting too old for marriage? Does he refer to "spiritual marriages" where two who have vowed celibacy but live together are overcome with sexual desire? Is the reference an engaged couple for whom sexual abstinence has become a problem? Does Paul think of a slave owner who is looking out for his virgin slave by giving her permission to marry? It proves impossible to arrive at any conclusion with indisputable certainty. Many, if not most, modern commentators hold that the relationship Paul refers to is the engaged couple who face strong sexual passions.

11. The comparative form of the adjective *makarios* may well be translated "happier." It is likely, though, that Paul has divine favor in mind—thus, "blessing" is preferable. The unmarried will find undivided devotion to Christ easier and from that come to experience "greater blessing."

1 Corinthians 8:1-13

1. For other usages of the formula "now about," see 7:25; 12:1; 16:1, 12.

2. Or it makes a person haughty. The picturesque word literally means to blow up or inflate—as with a pair of bellows. Today, an air-mattress pump might conjure up a similar image.

3. Paul may here refer to people who claim the spiritual gift of knowledge (12:8) and therefore cannot be opposed spiritually.

4. Some very significant ancient manuscripts even lack the last prepositional phrase, "by him." If that is the original reading, Paul's statement would be: those who love (one another) have recognized true *gnōsis*.

5. Paul may directly refer here to the imperial cult (emperor worship). Corinth found enormous pride and great political advantage through such expression of loyalty toward Rome. See further Winter, *After Paul*, 269–75.

6. These idols were not God, but the reality and influence of their temples and shrines could not be dismissed. The struggle of living in a culture filled with idol worship was faced by the rabbis as well (*b. 'Abod. Zar.* 54b).

7. Hellenistic Judaism affirmed God as the source of all things and argued that *sophia* ("wisdom") was the instrument by which God created (Wis. 8:1, 6). See Horsley, "Gnosis in Corinth."

8. A picturesque English expression that captures the Greek noun *proskomma* ("stumbling block") could be "a faith bruiser" (a cause of stumbling that leaves a bruise).

9. Winter, *After Paul*, 269–86.

10. Paul's phraseology here shows that his main concern is not those who simply get offended, or maybe jealous, by the action of other Christians who are doing what the former find wrong. Paul's true concern is for those who are new in the faith and whose limited Christian understanding makes them draw the wrong conclusions from what they see their more knowledgeable fellow Christians do.

11. *Apollymi* ("destroy") has eschatological significance—the "weak" who are led astray by the action of the "strong" will come to face final and eternal destruction rather than salvation.

Additional Insights, pages 120-21

1. Fee, *First Epistle*, 358–62.
2. Blasi, *Early Christianity as a Social Movement*, 61–62.
3. Isenberg, "Sale of Sacrificial Meat," 272.

1 Corinthians 9:1-12

1. Even if Paul also implies that he may not be an apostle to other Christ communities existing in places he has not been, his statement here does not express doubt about his universal position as a Christ-appointed apostle. If he has other churches in mind with this statement, his emphasis here is the positive—"I led you to faith in Christ even if there are other churches out there that I did not affect."

2. "Eat and drink" functions as an idiom for a meal—and here most likely the meals that the "strong" have claimed their right to participate in. The larger context does not seem to suggest, as some commentators claim, that Paul speaks about his right to eat on the church's dime.

3. Collins, *First Corinthians*, 336. Some later manuscripts, possibly to avoid any confusion about Paul's marital status, drop "sister" and make *gynaika* (translated either "wife" or "woman") plural (*gynaikas*). The statement would then speak to female co-workers (plural) rather than a wife. Some church fathers, like Tertullian, follow this reading.

4. Clement of Alexandria (AD 150–215) relates an anecdote about the relationship between Peter and his wife when she was martyred: "They say, accordingly, that the blessed Peter, on seeing his wife led to death, rejoiced on account of her call and conveyance home, and called very encouragingly and comfortingly, addressing her by name, 'Remember thou the Lord.' Such was the marriage of the blessed and their perfect disposition towards those dearest to them" (*ANF* 2:541).

5. The Greek *opsōnion* ("expense") here refers not to monetary compensation but to food rations. The emphatic "his own" bears this out. Paul's point is not that a soldier earns his hire and should be sufficiently compensated but that, while he serves, those he serves take care of his needs.

6. Jesus uses the same line of argument in the Sermon on the Mount (Matt. 6:26–30 // Luke 12:24–28). For more on rabbinical exegesis, see, for example, Longenecker, *Biblical Exegesis*.

7. Paul's inclusion of *pantōs* ("certainly" or "without a doubt"; NIV: "surely") in verse 10 removes any discussion. God's concern is not the oxen but the people.

8. God's care for animals is well attested in Scripture (e.g., Pss. 104:14, 21; 147:9). When employing animals for work, humans must treat them with care (e.g., Prov. 12:10; 27:23).

9. Oxen were allowed to eat as much as they wanted while they were pulling the heavy threshing sledge. If a farmer muzzled his ox (or, more likely, a rented ox) to keep it from stopping to eat, he might face public scourging in the synagogue (Str-B 3:382). For a discussion of the various interpretations of Deut. 25:4 and its application to this verse, see Verbruggen, "Of Muzzles and Oxen."

10. Lit., "to conceal," "to pass over in silence." The noun (*stegē*) means "roof" (cf. Mark 2:4; Matt. 8:8). See comments on 13:7.

1 Corinthians 9:13-27

1. Although, generally speaking, Paul's direct references to the Jesus tradition are comparatively few, a reference like this is a good example of how well acquainted Paul was with the story and teachings of Jesus.

2. It is no coincidence that Paul, after accepting help from friends in Philippi, goes out of his way to emphasize that this is a gift from God and that he now owes God, not the Philippians (Phil. 4:14–20). Paul accepted the gift for the benefit of the Philippians, not the other way around (4:17). Indeed, the God Paul serves will supply them more than they have given him (4:19).

3. This is Paul's only use of this expression.

4. The Greek *hekōn* (NIV: "voluntarily") speaks to free will or unforced action. Paul uses the term negatively in Rom. 8:20.

5. The story of Potiphar and Joseph in Gen. 39 illustrates this well. See also Josephus, *Ant*. 12.199–200. See further the comments on 4:1 and 4:2.

6. Notice the remark of Paul's contemporary Seneca: "The man who does something under orders is not unhappy; he is unhappy who does something against his will" (*Mor. Ep.* 61.3 [LCL]).

7. See, for example, Esler, "Jesus and the Reduction of Intergroup Conflict," and other works by Esler.

8. The Greek term *athlētēs* often referred to a professional athlete, in contrast to an amateur (*idiōtēs*). Though the term isn't explicitly used here, it is the former that Paul has in mind, an athlete whose serious efforts are all-consuming. The prize could be either a monetary sum or a tax reduction.

9. Laurels or olives were used in the Olympian and Pythian Games.

10. Collins (*First Corinthians*, 362) suggests the emphasis of *adokimos* is on "failure to qualify" or losing in the testing process. Cf. Rom. 1:28; 2 Cor. 13:5–7. Paul uses the related verb without negation (*dokimazō*) in 1 Thess. 2:4 to speak about himself as being qualified (NIV: "approved") to be entrusted with the gospel.

1 Corinthians 10:1–13

1. See Exod. 16; 17:1–7; Num. 20:2–13; Pss. 78:15–16, 23–29; 105:41; Wis. 11:4.

2. E.g., Gen. 49:24; Deut. 32:3–4, 15, 18, 30–31; 2 Sam. 22:47; Pss. 19:14; 78:35; 89:26; Isa. 30:29; 44:8; Hab. 1:12.

3. BDAG, 1019.

4. The Greek word *paizein* has a huge semantic field, ranging from innocent child's play (the Greek word for "child" is *pais* or *paidion*) to religious and erotic dance. Cf. *TDNT* 5:758.

5. The connection between idolatry and sexual immorality was commonly accepted and expressed in Jewish literature. See, e.g., Wis. 14:12; *T. Reub.* 4.6; Philo, *Moses* 1.55.302; cf. Rom. 1:26; 1 Thess. 4:3–5.

6. The symbol of a snake around a pole remains the symbol of healing used by pharmacies.

7. E.g., Exod. 14:11–12; 15:24; 16:2–3, 8; 17:3; Num. 11:1; 14:2–4; 16:11, 41; Deut. 1:27; 9:28; Josh. 9:18; Ps. 106:25.

8. For an angel of destruction, or the destroyer, see Exod. 12:23; 2 Sam. 24:16; 1 Chron. 21:15. Notice also Wis. 18:20–25's interpretation of Num. 16:41–50.

9. The Greek noun *nouthesia* (NIV: "warning") can mean either instruction (information for the mind) or admonition/warning (parental correction for the purpose of behavioral

transformation). See also Eph. 6:4; Titus 3:10; cf. 1 Cor. 4:14; Rom. 15:14; Col. 1:28; 3:16.

10. A present participle, a perfect infinitive, a present imperative, and an aorist subjunctive.

11. Conzelmann's term "cocksureness" captures well the contextual idea of this participle (*1 Corinthians*, 168).

12. E.g., NRSV: "testing"; ESV: "temptation"; NET: "trial."

13. "Why do we keep the votive days and high rejoicings in honor of the Cæsars with chastity, sobriety, and virtue? . . . Because we do not celebrate along with you the holidays of the Cæsars in a manner forbidden alike by modesty, decency, and purity" (Tertullian, *Apol.* 35 [*ANF* 3:44]).

1 Corinthians 10:14–11:1

1. This corresponds directly to the Jewish Passover meal, where the following prayers were spoken over the cup and bread, respectively: "Blessed be Thou, Lord God, King of the Universe, who created the fruit of the vine" and "Blessed be Thou, who brings forth bread from the earth" (cf. *m. Ber.* 6.1).

2. In short, the four cups represent the following, based on God's promises in Exod. 6:6–7: (1) sanctification (I will take you out of captivity); (2) deliverance (I will deliver you from slavery); (3) redemption (I will redeem you with my power); and (4) restoration (I will restore you as my people).

3. The NIV translates the same Greek word (*artos*) as "bread" in 10:16 and "loaf" in 10:17.

4. The NIV adds, "you say," to indicate this is a slogan. See also 6:12.

5. For more on *oikodomeō*, see *EDNT* 2:495–98.

6. The meat market in Corinth, the *makellon*, sold meat from the sacrificial offerings supplied by the temples alongside meat without this origin. To enable Diaspora Jews to shop at the *makellon*, the city made special concessions and required "that those who take care of the provisions for the city, shall take care that such sorts of food as they [the Jews] esteem fit for their eating may be imported into the city" (Josephus, *Ant.* 14.261 [Whiston, *New Complete Works*, 474]). For further discussion, see Winter, *After Paul*, 287–301. On the origin of *makellon* itself, see Gill, "Meat-Market at Corinth."

7. BDF, 281.

8. The Greek word is *charis* ("grace"; NIV: "thankfulness"), likely referring to a prayer of thanksgiving offered in silence at the table of an unbeliever. Verse 26 quotes Ps. 24:1, which gives a biblical basis for thanksgiving at meal times.

9. For a helpful and practical study of imitation, see Copan, *Saint Paul as Spiritual Director*.

1 Corinthians 11:2–16

1. For more on this imagery, see Gill, "Importance of Roman Portraiture."

2. Fantham et al., "'New Woman.'"

3. The veil worn by Roman wives was not a full face covering but a covering of the hair (fully or partly; see the image of the statue of Livia in this unit for one example). Expensive headbands holding the veils were used to parade

wealth. A modern wedding tiara, or a fashionable hat, could be thought of as a remnant of this.

4. See Plutarch, *Advice 7* (*Mor.* 139B).

5. Cf. Plutarch (*Mor.* 230C, 267A), who assumes that no respectable woman would be without a form of head covering in public.

6. For a fuller discussion on veiling as presented here, see Winter, *After Paul*, chap. 6.

7. The common suggestion that "head" (*kephalē*) means "supremacy" or "authority over" does not fit the context here well. Among other issues, it forces a theory of subordination on Paul's trinitarian understanding that seems unwarranted from other Pauline texts (e.g., Rom. 9:5; Phil. 2:6). Murphy-O'Connor's suggestion that "head" means "source" proves less than persuasive as well ("Sex and Logic in 1 Corinthians 11:2–16").

8. Lit., "everything of me." The genitive is a genitive of content and speaks to Paul's teaching.

9. Josephus gives an example of a female taking such a vow (*J.W.* 2.15 [313]). Cf. Acts 18:18; 21:23–24.

10. The close connection in Jewish exegesis between image and glory is well attested. The idea overflows to the fifth commandment (honor your father and your mother). The idea of honor here refers to children's responsibility to secure the continuation and good reputation of the family lineage ("that you may live long in the land" [Exod. 20:12]). The sense of Paul's statement in this verse, therefore, is this: A man must not cover his head; he should bring honor to God. A wife should bring honor to her husband.

1 Corinthians 11:17–34

1. See the "Additional Insights" section that follows this unit and "Self-Made Corinthians" in the introduction for comments on dining patterns in homes of Roman patrons.

2. Cf. Witherington, *Conflict and Community*, 247. Winter's argument (*After Paul*, 159–63) that the meaning of Paul's statement is "I believe a certain report" ultimately results in the same rhetorical conclusion. Paul believes a report that sounds, and should have been, unbelievable.

3. With this reading the meaning refers to the eschatological verdict of who among the Corinthians were genuine Christians and who were not. Given the context, however, it seems unlikely that Paul suddenly switches to a soteriological statement.

4. Cf. Garland, *1 Corinthians*, 539.

5. Winter, *After Paul*, 151–52.

6. Matt. 26:26; Mark 14:22; Luke 22:19.

7. Since the antecedent of the demonstrative pronoun is not the bread, it follows that the word "is" (*estin*) does not speak to mystical qualities of the bread but should be translated "stands for," "pictures," or "represents." Cf. Engberg-Pedersen, "Proclaiming the Lord's Death," 117.

8. The Greek term *enochos* means "guilty of," "held responsible for," or "answerable to."

9. On the Corinthian grain shortage, see Winter, "Secular and Christian Responses."

10. For Paul's communal understanding of judgment and blessing, notice his change to first-person plural ("we") in this section.

Additional Insights, pages 158–59

1. The rainwater was gathered in a pool (*impluvium*) in the center of the *atrium*.

1 Corinthians 12:1–6

1. Winter, *After Paul*, 164–83.

2. Annas and Caiaphas were usually pictured as permanent dwellers in hell because they were instrumental in Jesus's crucifixion.

3. For a wealth of examples like these, see Emmel et al., "Curses."

4. In Greek the alpha (*a-*) functions as a negative prefix like, for example, the English "un-" or "in-" (e.g., uneducated, incomplete).

5. See the "Historical and Cultural Background" section above.

6. Thiselton, *First Epistle*, lists ten or more attempts.

7. The statement that "no one can say, 'Jesus is Lord,' except by the Holy Spirit" (12:3) obviously does not refer to the ability to speak out this sentence, as if these words were "unpronounceable" for non-Christians. Paul does not suggest that the mere ability to formulate the two Greek words *Kyrios Iēsous* gave evidence of Spirit endowment.

8. Cullmann, *Christology of the New Testament*, 218–20.

9. Did Paul's phrase also refer to a feud between patrons of different house churches (cf. chaps. 1–4)? Is it possible that one Christian patron tried to use Jesus's name to curse another Christian patron with whom he or she had secular disputes (cf. 6:1–11)?

10. The three statements also may function as an outline for his subsequent discussion. Verses 7–11 focus on the Spirit, verses 12–14 on the body of Christ, and verses 15–31 on the interdependence of the individual body parts according to God's creation.

11. See "Grace and Patronage" in the introduction. Cf. deSilva, *Honor*, 126–56.

12. The Greek participle in 12:7 (*sympheron*), often translated as "common good," speaks to that which is beneficial. Paul uses it negatively in 6:12 and 10:23 to say that "not everything is *sympherei*."

1 Corinthians 12:7–11

1. Theological passives, designed to avoid misusing God's name, are exceedingly common in Scripture. An English parallel would be "I'm blessed!" meaning "God blessed me!"

2. For example, compare the two lists of this chapter: 12:8–10 and 12:28–30.

3. For example, Kistemaker, *First Epistle to the Corinthians*, 420–21, suggests a threefold division (pedagogical, supernatural, communicative); Blomberg, *1 Corinthians*, 244, suggests an ABA pattern (word, deed, word); Ciampa and Rosner, *First Letter*, 573, suggest an ABAB pattern (speech, wonder, speech, wonder).

4. In classical Greek *allos* meant "another of the same kind" and *heteros* meant "another of a different kind." In Koine Greek, however, that distinction has been blurred. *Heterō* is used in verse 9, "to another, faith," and in verse

10, "to another, kinds of tongues." See Fee, *First Epistle*, 584–85n9.

5. Cf. Wis. 7:7–10 (NRSV): "Therefore I prayed, and understanding was given me; I called on God, and the spirit of wisdom came to me. . . . I accounted wealth as nothing in comparison with her. . . . I loved her more than health and beauty, and I chose to have her rather than light, because her radiance never ceases."

6. Carson, *Showing the Spirit*, 39.

7. For the OT connection between healing and forgiveness, see, for example, 2 Chron. 7:14; Ps. 41:4; Isa. 53:5; Jer. 30:17; Hosea 6:1; Mal. 4:2.

8. See Ellis's helpful study on prophecy and scriptural exposition in "'Wisdom' and 'Knowledge' in 1 Corinthians," esp. 57–62.

9. Although some have suggested that "tongues" refers to human language in this context, Johnson ("Tongues," *ABD* 6:597) helpfully highlights that Paul "could hardly make clearer his conviction that tongues are an intrinsically noncommunicative form of utterance (1 Cor. 13:1; 14:2, 4, 7–9, 16–17, 23)." "Noncommunicative" does not necessarily mean "nonlanguage." Paul may well, as some commentators argue, think of it as a language of angels (13:1). In the first-century *Testament of Job*, for example, Job's daughter "sang angelic hymns in the voice of angels" and "spoke in the language of those on high; for her heart was transformed, being lifted above the worldly things. She spoke in the dialect of the Cherubim" (*T. Job* 11.24, 27–28 [Kohler, "Testament of Job," 336–37]).

10. See "Acts," in Pate, *Story of Israel*, esp. 192–94.

1 Corinthians 12:12–30

1. Paul's phraseology in this verse has resulted in extended conversations about its precise meaning. For example, what is the Spirit's relationship to "baptism" (cf. Gal. 3:27–28)? Does Paul say that believers are baptized in, by, or with the Spirit? How do the two parallel statements relate—we were all baptized in/by/with one Spirit and we were all given the one Spirit to drink? Sorting this out is clearly no easy matter, but it seems reasonable to conclude that 12:13 is parallel in meaning to 10:2–4 ("all were baptized into Moses" and "all drank the same spiritual drink").

2. As both Mitchell (*Rhetoric of Reconciliation*, 68–83) and D. B. Martin (*Corinthian Body*, 38–63) have clearly shown, Paul's rhetoric follows the common pattern of Greco-Roman unity, or concord, speeches (*homonoia*).

3. Paul employs here a third-class condition (12:15), which means that the condition carries no anticipation that the statement is true or false. We might have expected a second-class condition, which anticipates the condition to be false ("if the foot should say" [which, of course, it does not]). The use of a third-class condition, then, more than hints that Paul has some actual examples in mind. For rhetorical reasons, he avoids using a first-class condition, which expects the condition to be true ("if the foot should say" [which indeed it does]). That would have been too direct.

4. Fitzmyer suggests "feet" is a metaphor for slaves and laborers (*First Corinthians*, 480). Notice also the comments by Clement of Rome in his first letter to the Corinthians

(*1 Clem.* 37–38; written in the mid-90s, the earliest Christian writing outside the NT).

5. Witherington, *Conflict and Community*, 259–60: "The Romans divided society into two groups with regard to honor: the *honestiores*, or privileged, and the *humiliores*, who did not qualify . . . to be among the elite."

6. In Greek, 12:25 is a purpose clause (introduced by *hina*), meaning "God's purpose in creating the body this way is this . . ."

7. As Calvin comments, the body is concerned with the dishonored parts because "their shame would be the common disgrace of the whole body" (*Commentary*, 411).

8. "You yourselves"; Paul's unnecessary inclusion of a pronoun makes it emphatic.

9. Dunn, *Jesus and the Spirit*, 273. Dunn gives three characteristics of apostles: (1) they were personally commissioned at a resurrection appearance; (2) they were missionaries and church founders; (3) they had a distinctive eschatological role.

10. Thiselton, *First Epistle*, 1018.

11. Thiselton, *First Epistle*, 1017.

12. John Chrysostom calls it "aptness for a patron's office" (*Hom. 1 Cor.* 32.3 [*NPNF*[1] 12:187]).

13. The verbal form of the word *kybernaō* originally meant to steer a ship. A *kybernētēs* could be a captain of a ship (cf. Acts 27:11; Rev. 18:17).

14. See also Theissen, *Psychological Aspects*, 292–303.

Additional Insights, pages 178–79

1. Cf. Hicks, "Body Political," 30.

2. Mitchell, *Rhetoric of Reconciliation*, 158–60; Dio Chrysostom, *Disc.* 1.32; 3.104–7; 17.19; 34.23; 50.3.

3. Seneca, *Anger* 2.31.7 (LCL).

4. Käsemann, *Perspectives on Paul*, 102–21.

5. Hicks, "Body Political," 34.

1 Corinthians 12:31–13:13

1. The discussion of spiritual gifts draws on my article "Spiritual Gifts," in *BIBD*, 1572–74.

2. When Paul calls love a most excellent "way," his thinking likely centers on the OT theme of walking with God and following his way (see the sidebar "Walking in the Way of God" in the unit on 3:1–15). What follows in chap. 13, then, is a description of the very life pattern of the Christian community.

3. Harris, "'Sounding Brass' and Hellenistic Technology."

4. "Mysteries" (*mystēria*) is a common word for Paul. It usually refers to that which humans cannot discover on their own and only God can reveal (e.g., 2:1, 7; 4:1; 14:2; 15:51).

5. The word *psōmizō* ("give away") carries the notion of feeding (Rom. 12:20). The mental picture Paul draws, then, is one of feeding the poor.

6. Ancient manuscripts hold two well-attested readings of this text that make it difficult to determine with certainty which was original to Paul. The alternative reading is "If I should give my body to be burned." If this indeed was original to Paul, he probably had in mind a Corinthian celebration that commemorated how two young sisters threw themselves into the burning temple of Athena rather than

surrender to the Dorians (ca. 1000 BC). See Malina and Pilch, *Social-Science Commentary*, 117.

7. English translations generally treat these as adjectives, suggesting Paul's primary purpose is to describe the timeless qualities of love. Paul's target, however, is not love itself but the Corinthians, whose character and actions should have been transformed by love.

8. The verb (*chrēsteuetai*) is somewhat rare and occurs only here in the NT, whereas the adjectival form of this verb, *chrēstos* ("kind," "good," "useful," "generous"), is common. Tertullian describes how pagan opponents, in an attempt to give Christians a nickname, changed *Christianus* to *Chrestianus* (one showing kindness): "But Christian, so far as the meaning of the word is concerned, is derived from anointing. Yes, and even when it is wrongly pronounced by you 'Chrestianus' (for you do not even know accurately the name you hate), it comes from sweetness and benignity" (Tertullian, *Apol.* 3 [*ANF* 1:60]).

9. Paul does not suggest that love cannot cause righteous anger; that would militate against numerous biblical descriptions of God. In Acts 17:16 Paul himself is provoked to anger because of the idols.

10. Paul's terminology here is borrowed from the world of finance and paints the image of someone tallying numbers to be able to pay back in full.

11. For more on wealth and the justice system, see the "Historical and Cultural Background" in the unit on 6:1–6.

12. Paul is the only NT author to use the verb (9:12b; 1 Thess. 3:1, 5). His use of the verb here does not include the negative sense of concealing truth or keeping things hidden that should have been revealed.

13. Paul's use of the theological passive should not be overinterpreted (see the comments on 12:7). Here it simply expresses that God is the active agent who brings the purpose of the gifts to their end.

14. For an argument that faith and hope are eternal qualities, see Barrett, *Commentary*, 308–11.

1 Corinthians 14:1–19

1. Ellis, "'Spiritual' Gifts," 24, suggests *pneumatika* narrows the broader *charismata* and is used only for "gifts of inspired perception, verbal proclamation and/or its interpretation."

2. See comments on 12:10b. Cf. Ellis, "Role of the Christian Prophet."

3. Whether the "mysteries" were spoken "in" or "by" the Spirit (*pneumati*) makes no difference to the meaning of Paul's contrast.

4. *Meizōn* ("greater"; a comparative adjective) speaks not to status but to significance in relation to edification.

5. See comments on 12:28. See also Dunn, *Jesus and the Spirit*, 236–38.

6. Just as a beautiful piece of music, an incredible piece of artwork, a moving poem, or a spectacular sunrise would lift the soul.

7. The English word "evangelism" comes from the Greek *euangelion*, which we translate "gospel"—a connection that unfortunately can get lost in the English language. Put differently, evangelism = gospelizing.

1 Corinthians 14:20–40

1. The Greek word *phrēn* refers to "sense," "insight," "deliberation," "thoughtful planning," "judgment calls" (e.g., Prov. 7:7; 9:4 LXX). It speaks to thinking that has moved from the head to the heart and become the normal (daily) pattern of consideration.

2. The word *teleios* means "perfect," "complete," "mature" (NIV: "adults"), pointing to those who have reached the goal. In contrast to children, who chase the latest and most exciting noisemaking device, the mature can distinguish the good and meaningful from what is merely a thrill for self-enjoyment. Children are guided by immediate emotion, mature adults by deliberate discernment.

3. The reason Paul does not repeat the word "sign" in 14:22b may simply be to highlight parallels between God's nonlinguistic action through the Assyrians and the "nonlinguistic" quality of tongues. Contrary to prophecy, tongues are only signs, not "speeches."

4. Paul does not suggest tongues have a different origin than prophecy. Both are "signs" from God. Cf. Ciampa and Rosner, *First Letter*, 697–723. Ralph P. Martin (*Spirit and the Congregation*, 72) argues that Paul refers to a small, faithful remnant that benefited from trusting the prophecy the others rejected.

5. For further comments on Luke's list, see my article "Acts," in Pate et al., *Story of Israel*, 177–205 (esp. 192–94).

6. Collins, *First Corinthians*, 522.

7. Cf. Witherington, *Women in the Earliest Churches*, 98. Also Fee, *First Epistle*, 710.

8. Garland, *1 Corinthians*, 674.

9. See Green's helpful list of points to consider when evaluating a prophecy: (1) Does it glorify God rather than the speaker, church, denomination? (2) Does it accord with Scripture? (3) Does it build up the church? (4) Is it spoken in love? (5) Does the speaker submit to the judgment and consensus of others? (6) Is the speaker in control of him- or herself? (7) Is there a reasonable amount of instruction, or does the messenger ramble? (*To Corinth with Love*, 84).

Additional Insights, pages 198–99

1. Witherington, *Conflict and Community*, 287–88.

2. Boring, "Prophecy," *ABD* 5:496–97.

3. Dunn, "Responsible Congregation," 227.

1 Corinthians 15:1–11

1. Paul's use of the Corinthians' catchphrase *gnōrizō* ("I make known"; NIV: "I want to remind you") should not be missed. They pride themselves as people of *gnōsis* ("knowledge"), yet Paul has to speak to them about foundational things as if they have no *gnōsis*.

2. For further explanation of conditional sentences, see note 3 in the comments on 12:12–30.

3. The Greek *prōtois* can be both temporal and qualitative: "first and most important."

4. "Midrash" is the general name for rabbinical approaches to biblical interpretation.

5. See BDAG, 311; *EDNT* 1:423.

6. The title "church of God" is common to Paul (e.g., 1:2; 10:32; 11:16, 22; 2 Cor. 1:1; Gal. 1:13; 2 Thess. 1:4; 1 Tim. 3:5).

7. Timothy Keller, *The Reason for God: Belief in an Age of Skepticism* (London: Penguin, 2008), 202.

1 Corinthians 15:12–34

1. See, for example, Plutarch, *Rom.* 28.6 (Clough, *Plutarch's Lives*, 1:74): "Let us believe with Pindar that 'All human bodies yield to Death's decree, the soul survives to all eternity.' For that alone is derived from the gods, thence comes, and thither returns; not with the body, but when most disengaged and separated from it, and when most entirely pure and clean and free from the flesh." See also Wright, *Resurrection of the Son of God*, 316: "Everybody knew dead people didn't and couldn't come back to bodily life."

2. The depth of Paul's statement about being false witnesses (*pseudomartyres*) should not be missed. It goes to the core of the Ten Commandments (Exod. 20:16; Deut. 5:20; cf. Mark 10:19) and carries punishment (Prov. 19:5, 9). Paul may even have the fate of false prophets (*pseudoprophētai*) in mind (cf. Deut. 13:5; Ezek. 13:3, 9; Matt. 24:11, 24; Rev. 19:20; 20:10). To be called a false witness is no small matter.

3. As the context shows, the comparative adjective has a superlative meaning. Paul's point is not merely psychological—that nonbelievers are in the right to smile overbearingly at these Christians who cling to a hope that is empty; rather, his point is to bring a devastating refutation of those who reject resurrection. If they were right, God would have sent Christ for nothing.

4. That Paul does not attempt to draw a direct parallel between Adam and Christ, so as to suggest that "all" has the same referant in both clauses ("every human sins because of Adam, and every human is raised to eternal life because of Christ"), becomes clear from the context and from the structure of his sentence. Those who are to be raised are those who are in Christ. Paul is keenly aware that some will remain outside the Christ community and therefore not be part of the resurrection (1:18).

5. The present tense of this verb suggests that Paul sees this as a done deal.

6. The Greek *panta en pasin* may also be translated "everything to everybody."

7. Paul quotes from the Septuagint but replaces the second-person singular ("you") in the OT text with a third-person singular ("he") in order to apply it to Christ, an application also used by later NT authors. Cf. Matt. 22:44; Mark 12:36; Luke 20:42–43; Acts 2:34–35; Heb. 1:13.

8. Did he think of a Corinthian practice where the living hoped to rescue dead relatives from God's wrath through baptism? Were Christians baptized for people who had died before being baptized? Were some baptized on behalf of people who were dying? Given the plethora of issues Paul has addressed throughout this letter, however, it seems difficult to imagine Paul would gloss over a practice of vicarious baptism without further comment.

9. See also chapter 3 of C. S. Lewis's *The Great Divorce* (London: G. Bles, 1945), in which he uses a great metaphor to depict the solidity and substance of heaven.

1 Corinthians 15:35–49

1. Although claiming a specific meaning for the aorist tense always proves somewhat problematic, Paul's deliberate switch from present ("gives") to aorist ("determined") in the same clause clearly suggests he has God's final work of creation in mind. God gives at the end what he planned at the beginning.

2. As becomes clear from 15:41, the reference here is to planets, not to spiritual beings. For more, see Wright, *Resurrection of the Son of God*, 346.

3. Paul's ability to play on the two major meanings of *doxa*, "splendor/brightness" and "glory" (God's reputation and honor; this Greek term is used to translate the Hebrew *kabod*), gives him the opportunity to contrast flesh and glory. "Flesh" refers to the realm of the fallen, where mortality and weakness reign; "glory" refers to the divine realm, where God dwells in immortality and reigns in power (cf. Rom. 1:22–23; 2 Cor. 4:4). Cf. Garland, *1 Corinthians*, 731.

4. The Septuagint (LXX) is the Greek translation of the OT used by the early Greek-speaking Christians and Jews. It dates back to the third century before Christ.

5. Paul's contrast is between *psychē* ("soul," "natural life") and *pneuma* ("spirit"), not *sarx* ("flesh") and *pneuma*. It is designed to give the broadest statement possible and to transition into the following discussion on Adam and Christ.

1 Corinthians 15:50–58

1. E.g., Gen. 15:4; 29:14; 37:27; Judg. 9:2; 2 Sam. 5:1; 7:12; 1 Kings 8:19; 1 Chron. 11:1; Isa. 39:7; 58:7. Cf. Sir. 14:18.

2. The emphasis is on receiving into one's possession the promised blessings of God (see, e.g., Gen. 15:7; 28:4; Exod. 23:30; Num. 18:20; 34:17; Deut. 1:8; 6:18; 31:13; Josh. 1:15; Judg. 18:9; 1 Chron. 28:8; Pss. 25:13; 37:9; Isa. 49:8; 60:21).

3. O'Brien, "Mystery."

4. The Greek term is *allassō*, meaning "broad sweeping change" (NIV: "we will . . . be changed"). Cf., e.g., Acts 6:14; Rom. 1:23, 26; Gal. 4:20; Heb. 1:10–12; see also Jer. 2:11.

5. The Greek *atomos*, from which English gets the word "atom," refers to the smallest unit, something that cannot be cut into any smaller pieces. See BDAG, 149.

6. See also Matt. 22:11; Acts 1:10; Rev. 3:5; 7:14, along with Paul's own use of "new clothing" as a metaphor of transformation (e.g., 2 Cor. 5:2, 4; Gal. 3:27; Eph. 4:24; Col. 3:10, 12, 14).

7. The Greek *kentron* refers to the sting of a poisonous animal.

8. The Greek prefix of negation "*a-*" brings here the meaning that they are not to change back to the ways of paganism.

1 Corinthians 16:1–11

1. Garland, *1 Corinthians*, 751n1. Fee (*First Epistle*, 812) suggests Paul uses this term to speak of the actual "collecting" of the money. In other places, Paul refers to the collection as an act of grace (*charis* [16:3; 2 Cor. 8:7]), of service (*diakonia* [2 Cor. 8:4; 9:1, 12, 13; Rom. 15:25, 31]), or of fellowship (*koinōnia* [Rom. 15:26]).

2. In Greek, the present tense expresses a continuous aspect or repeated action. The default tense is aorist, so Paul's switch from "you should do" in verse 1 to "one should be putting aside" in verse 2 is a deliberate underscoring of the repeated basis on which this must occur.

3. The Greek verb used here (*euodoō*) originally meant "to travel a good path" but was used metaphorically for doing well in life. So Paul is exhorting to give in accordance with how well one is doing, that is, according to one's means.

4. In 2 Cor. 1:15–2:11 Paul refers to a painful visit different from the one he plans to make here. Most likely that was an unplanned visit he made by sailing directly from Ephesus to Corinth. Since he repeats his plans concerning the collection in 2 Cor. 8–9, it seems reasonable to conclude that he did not accomplish this task during the painful visit.

5. From Acts 18:11, we know that Paul likely spent about eighteen months in Corinth during his second missionary journey.

6. Paul's reference to Pentecost may indicate a desire to celebrate the church's "birthday," God's initiation of the age to come through the outpouring of the Holy Spirit (Acts 2). It is just as likely, though, that it is a simple reference to the time of year when travel became easier and less dangerous.

7. In Koine Greek, the perfect tense expresses a completed action with ongoing results.

8. 1:28; 6:4; see also Luke 18:9; 23:11; Acts 4:11; Rom. 14:3, 10; 2 Cor. 10:10; Gal. 4:14; 1 Thess. 5:20; cf. Mark 9:12.

1 Corinthians 16:12–24

1. See Ellis, "Paul and His Co-workers," 183.

2. The absence of a greeting from Apollos, parallel to the one from Aquila and Priscilla (16:19), may be due either to a strained relationship between Apollos and some Corinthians or to a concern on Apollos's part that his oratory skills had given him a "personal following" he wanted to discourage. If so, it speaks to a tension in Corinth that some preferred a visit from the eloquent Apollos (Acts 18:24, 27) rather than the timid Timothy (2 Tim. 1:7).

3. This is Paul's only reference in any of his letters to all the churches in a province. He does not spell out how many churches that includes, but Ephesus functioned as the capital and financial headquarters for the whole western part of Asia Minor (cf. Acts 19:10, 26).

4. For a reconstruction of Aquila and Priscilla's life, see Murphy-O'Connor, *Paul*. The Christian couple likely was Jewish; they were former slaves who now enjoyed freedman status. They came to faith in Rome, which they were forced to leave because of Claudius's edict in AD 49 to expel all Jews from Rome (Acts 18:2). They fled to Corinth, where they established a leather business that Paul joined when he came to Corinth (18:3). From there they moved to Ephesus.

5. Paul's Letter to the Romans suggests they went back to Rome from Ephesus (Rom. 16:3). The last we hear about them, they have returned from Rome to Ephesus (cf. 2 Tim. 4:9).

6. The Greek plural *adelphoi* ("brothers and sisters") is inclusive and refers to both males and females.

7. See Richards, *Paul and First-Century Letter Writing*. In Romans, the scribe, Tertius, is a fellow Christian (Rom. 16:22). It is possible Luke was Paul's scribe for the pastoral letters (2 Tim. 4:11).

8. In light of other Greco-Roman letters, however, it is not impossible that Paul intended (or the audience understood) an imperative—"let it be . . ." or "make certain that the grace of . . ." God's grace is the basis of their very existence as a community of believers (1:4–9). On the significance of this ending, see also Weima, *Neglected Endings*, 78–87.

Bibliography

Recommended Reading

Blomberg, Craig L. *1 Corinthians*. NIV Application Commentary. Grand Rapids: Zondervan, 1994.

Collins, Raymond F. *First Corinthians*. Sacra Pagina. Collegeville, MN: Liturgical Press, 1999.

Ellingworth, Paul, and Howard Hatton. *A Handbook on Paul's First Letter to the Corinthians*. UBS Handbook Series. New York: United Bible Societies, 1995.

Fee, Gordon D. *The First Epistle to the Corinthians*. New International Commentary on the New Testament. Grand Rapids: Eerdmans, 1991.

Garland, David E. *1 Corinthians*. Baker Exegetical Commentary on the New Testament. Grand Rapids: Baker Academic, 2003.

Malina, Bruce, and John Pilch. *Social-Science Commentary on the Letters of Paul*. Minneapolis: Fortress, 2006.

Thiselton, Anthony C. *The First Epistle to the Corinthians*. New International Greek Testament Commentary. Grand Rapids: Eerdmans, 2000.

Winter, Bruce W. *After Paul Left Corinth: The Influence of Secular Ethics and Social Change*. Grand Rapids: Eerdmans, 2001.

Witherington, Ben, III. *Conflict and Community in Corinth: A Socio-Rhetorical Commentary on 1 and 2 Corinthians*. Grand Rapids: Eerdmans, 1995.

Select Bibliography

Aristotle. *The Art of Rhetoric*. Translated by John Henry Freese. LCL. Cambridge, MA: Harvard University Press, 1926.

Barbour, R. S. "Wisdom and the Cross in 1 Corinthians 1 and 2." Pages 57–71 in *Theologia Crucis—Signum Crucis: Festschrift für E. Dinkler*. Edited by C. Andresen and G. Klein. Tübingen: Mohr, 1979.

Barré, Michael L. "To Marry or to Burn: *Purousthai* in 1 Cor. 7:9." *Catholic Biblical Quarterly* 36.2 (1974): 193–202.

Barrett, C. K. "Cephas and Corinth." Pages 28–39 in *Essays on Paul*. London: SPCK, 1982.

———. *A Commentary on the First Epistle to the Corinthians*. Black's New Testament Commentary. London: A & C Black, 1968.

———. "*Shaliaḥ* and Apostle." Pages 88–102 in *Donum Gentilicium: New Testament Essays in Honour of David Daube*. Edited by E. Bammel, C. K. Barrett, and W. D. Davies. Oxford: Clarendon, 1978.

Beasley-Murray, George R. "Baptism, Wash." Pages 143–54 in vol. 1 of *New International Dictionary of New Testament Theology*. Edited by C. Brown. Grand Rapids: Zondervan, 1965.

Bjerkelund, Carl J. *Parakalō: Form, Funktion und Sinn der parakalō Sätze in den paulinischen Briefen*. Oslo: Universitetsforlaget, 1967.

Blasi, Anthony J. *Early Christianity as a Social Movement*. Toronto Studies in Religion 5. New York: Peter Lang, 1988.

Boring, Eugene. "Prophecy (Early Christian)." Pages 495–502 in vol. 5 of *Anchor Bible Dictionary*. Edited by D. N. Freedman. New York: Doubleday, 1992.

Bradley, Keith R. *Discovering the Roman Family: Studies in Roman Social History*. New York: Oxford University Press, 1991.

Brown, Raymond E., Joseph A. Fitzmyer, and Roland E. Murphy. *The Jerome Biblical Commentary*. Englewood Cliffs, NJ: Prentice-Hall, 1996.

Buckland, W. W. *A Text-Book of Roman Law from Augustus to Justinian*. 3rd ed. Cambridge: Cambridge University Press, 1963.

Calvin, John. *Commentary on the Epistles of Paul the Apostle to the Corinthians*. Grand Rapids: Baker, 2005.

Carson, D. A. *Showing the Spirit*. Grand Rapids: Baker, 1987.

Castelli, Elizabeth A. *Imitating Paul: A Discussion of Power*. Louisville: Westminster John Knox, 1991.

Ciampa, Roy E., and Brian S. Rosner. *The First Letter to the Corinthians*. Pillar New Testament Commentary. Grand Rapids: Eerdmans, 2010.

Clarke, A. D. *Secular and Christian Leadership in Corinth: A Socio-Historical and Exegetical Study of 1 Cor. 1–6*. Leiden: Brill, 1993.

Clough, A. H. *Plutarch's Lives: The Translation Called Dryden's*. 5 vols. Boston: Little, Brown, 1906.

Cohick, Lynn. "Marriage, Divorce, and Discipleship: Jesus' Encounter with the Samaritan Woman." *International Reference Library of Biblical Research* 8 (2010): 20–36.

Conzelmann, Hans. *1 Corinthians*. Hermeneia. Philadelphia: Fortress, 1975.

Copan, Victor A. *Saint Paul as Spiritual Director: An Analysis of the Concept of the Imitation of Paul with Implications and Applications to the Practice of Spiritual Direction.* Paternoster Biblical and Theological Monographs. London: Paternoster, 2007.

Cullmann, Oscar. *The Christology of the New Testament.* Philadelphia: Westminster, 1963.

deSilva, David. *Honor, Patronage, Kinship and Purity: Unlocking New Testament Culture.* Downers Grove, IL: InterVarsity, 2000.

Dunn, James D. G. *Jesus and the Spirit: A Study of the Religious and Charismatic Experience of Jesus and the First Christians as Reflected in the New Testament.* London: SCM, 1975.

———. "The Responsible Congregation (1 Co 14, 26–40)." Pages 201–36 in *Charisma Und Agape (1 Ko 12–14).* Edited by Lorenzo De Lorenzi. Rome: Patriarcale Basilica di S. Paolo, 1983.

Ellis, E. Earle. "Coworkers, Paul and His." Pages 183–89 in *Dictionary of Paul and His Letters.* Edited by G. F. Hawthorne and R. P. Martin. Downers Grove, IL: InterVarsity, 1993.

———. *Prophecy and Hermeneutic in Early Christianity: New Testament Essays.* Grand Rapids: Eerdmans, 1978.

———. "The Role of the Christian Prophet in Acts." Pages 129–44 in Ellis, *Prophecy and Hermeneutic.*

———. "'Spiritual' Gifts in the Pauline Community." Pages 23–44 in Ellis, *Prophecy and Hermeneutic.*

———. "'Wisdom' and 'Knowledge' in 1 Corinthians." Pages 45–62 in Ellis, *Prophecy and Hermeneutic.*

Emmel, Stephen, et al., trans. "Curses." Pages 183–86 in *Ancient Christian Magic: Coptic Texts of Ritual Power.* Edited by Marvin W. Meyer and Richard Smith. Princeton: Princeton University Press, 1999.

Engberg-Pedersen, Troels. "Proclaiming the Lord's Death: 1 Corinthians 11:17–34 and the Forms of Paul's Theological Argument." Pages 103–32 in *Pauline Theology: 1 and 2 Corinthians.* Edited by D. M. Hay. Minneapolis: Fortress, 1993.

Esler, Philip F. "Jesus and the Reduction of Intergroup Conflict: The Parable of the Good Samaritan in the Light of Social Identity Theory." *Biblical Interpretation* 8.4 (2000): 325–57.

Fantham, Elaine, Helene Peet Foley, Natalie Boymel Kampen, Sarah B. Pomeroy, and H. Alan Shapiro. "The 'New Woman.'" Pages 280–93 in *Women in the Classical World: Image and Text.* New York: Oxford University Press, 1994.

Fitzmyer, Joseph. *First Corinthians.* Anchor Bible. New Haven: Yale University Press, 2008.

George, Timothy. *Theology of the Reformers.* Nashville: Broadman, 1988.

Gill, David W. J. "Erastus the Aedile." *Tyndale Bulletin* 40.2 (1989): 293–301.

———. "The Importance of Roman Portraiture for Head-Coverings in 1 Corinthians 11:2–16." *Tyndale Bulletin* 41.2 (1990): 245–60.

———. "The Meat-Market at Corinth (1 Corinthians 10:25)." *Tyndale Bulletin* 43.2 (1992): 389–93.

Green, Michael. *To Corinth with Love.* Waco: Word, 1988.

Hall, David R. *The Unity of the Corinthian Correspondence.* New York: T&T Clark, 2003.

Halperin, David M. "Homosexuality." Pages 720–23 in the *Oxford Classical Dictionary.* Edited by S. Hornblower and A. Spawforth. 3rd rev. ed. Oxford: Oxford University Press, 2003.

Harris, William. "'Sounding Brass' and Hellenistic Technology: Ancient Acoustical Device Clarifies Paul's Well-Known Metaphor." *Biblical Archaeologist Review* 8.1 (1982): 38–41.

Hengel, Martin. *The Pre-Christian Paul.* London: SCM, 1991.

Hicks, Ruth I. "The Body Political and the Body Ecclesiastical." *Journal of the Bible and Religion* 31.1 (1963): 29–35.

Hock, R. F. *The Social Context of Paul's Ministry.* Philadelphia: Fortress, 1980.

Hodgson, R. "Paul the Apostle and First Century Tribulation Lists." *Zeitschrift für die neutestamentliche Wissenschaft und die Kunde der älteren Kirche* 74 (1983): 59–80.

Holmes, Michael W. *The Apostolic Fathers: Greek Texts and English Translations.* Updated ed. Grand Rapids: Baker, 1999.

Horsley, Richard A. "Gnosis in Corinth: 1 Corinthians 8.1–6." *New Testament Studies* 27 (1980): 32–51.

Hubbard, Moyer V. "2 Corinthians." Pages 194–263 in *Zondervan Illustrated Bible Background Commentary,* vol. 3: *Romans to Philemon.* Grand Rapids: Zondervan, 2002.

Isenberg, M. "The Sale of Sacrificial Meat." *Classical Philology* 70.4 (1975): 271–73.

Jenkins, Philip. *The New Faces of Christianity: Believing the Bible in the Global South.* Oxford: Oxford University Press, 2006.

Johnson, Luke Timothy. "Tongues, Gift of." Pages 596–600 in vol. 6 of *Anchor Bible Dictionary.* Edited by D. N. Freedman. New York: Doubleday, 1992.

Käsemann, Ernst. *Perspectives on Paul.* Translated by Margaret Kohl. Philadelphia: Fortress, 1971.

Kaster, Robert A. "The Shame of the Romans." *Transactions of the American Philological Association* 127 (1997): 1–19.

Kennedy, George A. *Aristotle: On Rhetoric, A Theory of Civic Discourse.* 2nd ed. New York: Oxford University Press, 2007.

Kinneavy, James L. *Greek Rhetorical Origins of Christian Faith: An Inquiry.* Oxford: Oxford University Press, 1987.

Kistemaker, Simon J. *Exposition of the First Epistle to the Corinthians*. New Testament Commentary 18. Grand Rapids: Baker, 1993.

Kohler, K. "The Testament of Job: An Essene Midrash on the Book of Job." Pages 264–338 in *Semitic Studies in Memory of Rev. Dr. Alexander Kohut*. Edited by G. A. Kohut. Berlin: S. Calvary, 1897.

Longenecker, Richard N. *Biblical Exegesis in the Apostolic Period*. 2nd ed. Grand Rapids: Eerdmans, 1999.

MacDonald, Margaret Y. "Women Holy in Body and Spirit: The Social Setting of 1 Corinthians 7." *New Testament Studies* 36 (1990): 161–81.

Martin, Dale B. *The Corinthian Body*. New Haven: Yale University Press, 1995.

Martin, Ralph P. *The Spirit and the Congregation: Studies in 1 Corinthians 12–15*. Grand Rapids: Eerdmans, 1984.

Meeks, Wayne A. *The First Urban Christians: The Social World of the Apostle Paul*. New Haven: Yale University Press, 1983.

Metzger, Bruce M. *A Textual Commentary on the Greek New Testament*. New York: United Bible Societies, 1994.

Mitchell, Margaret M. *Paul and the Rhetoric of Reconciliation*. Tübingen: Mohr Siebeck, 1991.

Mitton, C. Leslie. "New Wine in Old Wine Skins: IV. Leaven." *Expository Times* 84 (1973): 339–43.

Mommsen, Theodor, and Paul Krueger, eds. *The Digest of Justinian*. Vol. 4. Translated by Alan Watson. Philadelphia: University of Pennsylvania Press, 1985.

Moores, John D. *Wrestling with Rationality in Paul*. Society for New Testament Studies Monograph Series 82. Cambridge: Cambridge University Press, 1995.

Murphy-O'Connor, Jerome. "Corinthian Slogans in 1 Cor. 6:12–20." *Catholic Biblical Quarterly* 40 (1978): 391–96.

———. "The Divorced Woman in 1 Corinthians 7:10–11." Pages 32–42 in *Keys to First Corinthians: Revisiting the Major Issues*. Oxford: Oxford University Press, 2009.

———. *Paul: A Critical Life*. Oxford: Oxford University Press, 1997.

———. "Sex and Logic in 1 Corinthians 11:2–16." *Catholic Biblical Quarterly* 42.4 (1980): 482–500.

———. "Works without Faith in 1 Corinthians 7:14." Pages 43–57 in *Keys to First Corinthians: Revisiting the Major Issues*. Oxford: Oxford University Press, 2009.

O'Brien, Peter T. "Mystery." Pages 621–23 in *Dictionary of Paul and His Letters*. Edited by G. F. Hawthorne, R. P. Martin, and Daniel G. Reid. Downers Grove, IL: InterVarsity, 1993.

Pate, C. Marvin, J. Scott Duvall, J. Daniel Hays, E. Randolph Richards, W. Dennis Tucker Jr., and Preben Vang. *The Story of Israel: A Biblical Theology*. Downers Grove, IL: InterVarsity, 2004.

Pogoloff, Stephen M. *Logos and Sophia: The Rhetorical Situation of 1 Corinthians*. Atlanta: Scholars Press, 1992.

Quesnell, Q. "'Made Themselves Eunuchs for the Kingdom of Heaven' (Mt 19:12)." *Catholic Biblical Quarterly* 30 (1968): 335–58.

Richards, E. Randolph. *Paul and First-Century Letter Writing*. Downers Grove, IL: InterVarsity, 2004.

———. *The Secretary in the Letters of Paul*. Tübingen: Mohr Siebeck, 1991.

Rousselle, Aline. "Body Politics in Ancient Rome." Pages 296–336 in *A History of Women in the West*, vol. 1, *From Ancient Goddesses to Christian Saints*. Edited by Pauline S. Pantel. Cambridge, MA: Harvard University Press, 1992.

Scott, S. P., trans. *The Civil Law*. 17 vols. Cincinnati: Central Trust, 1932.

Shanor, J. "Paul as Master Builder: Construction Terms in First Corinthians." *New Testament Studies* 34 (1988): 461–71.

Theissen, Gerd. *Psychological Aspects of Pauline Theology*. Translated by John P. Galvin. Philadelphia: Fortress, 1987.

Thiselton, Anthony C. "The Supposed Power of Words in the Biblical Writings." *Journal of Theological Studies* 25 (1974): 283–99.

Thomas à Kempis. *The Imitation of Christ*. Oak Harbor, WA: Logos Research Systems, 1996.

Verbruggen, Jan L. "Of Muzzles and Oxen: Deuteronomy 25:4 and 1 Corinthians 9:9." *Journal of the Evangelical Theological Society* 49 (2006): 699–711.

Watson, John Selby, trans. *Quintilian's Institutes of Oratory; or, Education of an Orator*. Vol. 1. Bohn's Classical Library. London: Bohn, 1856.

Weidemann, Thomas. *Greek and Roman Slavery*. Baltimore: Johns Hopkins University Press, 1981.

Weima, Jeffrey A. D. *Neglected Endings: The Significance of the Pauline Letter Closings*. Journal for the Study of the New Testament Supplement Series 101. Sheffield: Sheffield Academic Press, 1994.

Whiston, William, trans. *The New Complete Works of Josephus*. Rev. ed. Grand Rapids: Kregel, 1999.

Winter, Bruce W. *Philo and Paul among the Sophists*. Cambridge: Cambridge University Press, 1997.

———. "Secular and Christian Responses to Corinthian Famines." *Tyndale Bulletin* 40.1 (1989): 86–106.

Wire, Antoinette Clark. *The Corinthian Women Prophets: A Reconstruction through Paul's Rhetoric*. Minneapolis: Fortress, 1990.

Witherington, Ben, III. *Women in the Earliest Churches*. Cambridge: Cambridge University Press, 1988.

Wright, N. T. *The Resurrection of the Son of God*. Minneapolis: Fortress, 2003.

Yonge, Charles D., trans. *The Works of Philo*. 1854–90. Repr., Peabody, MA: Hendrickson, 1993.

Bibliography

Image Credits

Unless otherwise indicated, photos, illustrations, and maps are copyright © Baker Photo Archive.

The Baker Photo Archive acknowledges the permission of the following institutions and individuals.

Photos on pages 66, 92, 170, 193, 195 © Baker Photo Archive. Courtesy of the British Museum, London, England.

Photos on pages 12, 18, 37, 42, 49, 56, 70, 110, 144, 156, 164, 198, 230 © Baker Photo Archive. Dr. James C. Martin, courtesy of the Greek Ministry of Antiquities.

Photos on pages 14, 68, 82, 121, 147, 149, 162, 172, 176, 196 © Baker Photo Archive. Dr. James C. Martin, courtesy of the Greek Ministry of Antiquities and the Ancient Corinth Archaeological Museum, Ancient Corinth, Greece.

Photo on page 8 © Baker Photo Archive. Dr. James C. Martin, courtesy of the Greek Ministry of Antiquities and the Delphi Archaeological Museum, Delphi, Greece.

Photos on pages 131, 150 © Baker Photo Archive. Dr. James C. Martin, courtesy of the Greek Ministry of Antiquities and the National Archaeological Museum, Athens, Greece.

Photo on page 233 © Baker Photo Archive. Dr. James C. Martin, courtesy of the Greek Ministry of Antiquities and the Thessaloniki Archaeological Museum, Thessaloniki, Greece.

Photo on page 52 © Baker Photo Archive. Courtesy of the Egyptian Museum, Cairo.

Photo on page 136 © Baker Photo Archive. Courtesy of the Eretz Israel Museum, Tel Aviv.

Photo on page 46 © Baker Photo Archive. Courtesy of the Holyland Hotel. Reproduction of the City of Jerusalem at the time of the Second Temple, located on the grounds of the Holyland Hotel, Jerusalem, 2001. Present location: The Israel Museum, Jerusalem.

Photos on pages 35, 78, 87, 97, 174, 204 © Baker Photo Archive. Courtesy of the Musée du Louvre; Autorisation de photographer et de filmer. Louvre, Paris, France.

Photos on pages 40, 128 © Baker Photo Archive. Courtesy of the Turkish Ministry of Antiquities and the Antalya Museum, Turkey.

Photo on page 208 © Baker Photo Archive. Courtesy of the Turkish Ministry of Antiquities and the Bergama Museum, Turkey.

Photo on page 210 © Baker Photo Archive. Courtesy of the Turkish Ministry of Antiquities and the Ephesus Archaeological Museum, Turkey.

Photo on page 185 © Baker Photo Archive. Courtesy of the Turkish Ministry of Antiquities and the Hierapolis Museum, Turkey.

Photos on pages 85, 114 © Baker Photo Archive. Courtesy of the Turkish Ministry of Antiquities and the Istanbul Archaeological Museum.

Photos on pages 135, 154, 187, 188, 220 © Baker Photo Archive. Courtesy of the Vatican Museum.

Additional image credits

Photo on page 138 © Catacomb of Via Latina, Rome, Italy / De Agostini Picture Library / The Bridgeman Art Library.

Photo on page 104 © Dr. James C. Martin and the Israel Museum (Shrine of the Book). Collection of the Israel Museum, Jeruslaem, and courtesy of the Israel Antiquities Authority, exhibited at the Shrine of the Book, the Israel Museum, Jerusalem.

Photo on page 26 © J. Albert Cole. Prints & Photographs Division, Library of Congress, LC-USZ62-77142.

Photo on page 216 © Jebulon / Wikimedia Commons, CCO-1.0 Universal, http://commons.wikimedia.org /wiki/File:Temptation_Adam_Eva.jpg.

Photos on pages 17, 38, 44, 73, 142, 158, 182, 201, 207, 227 © Kim Walton.

Photo on page 167 © Kim Walton, courtesy of the Greek Ministry of Antiquities and the Corinth Archaeological Museum.

Photo on page 103 © Kim Walton, courtesy of the Greek Ministry of Antiquities and the Delphi Archaeological Museum, Delphi, Greece.

Photos on pages 30, 54 © Kim Walton. Courtesy of the British Museum, London, England.

Photos on pages 160, 219 © Kim Walton. Courtesy of the Capitoline Museums, Rome.

Photo on page 23 © Kim Walton. Courtesy of the Metropolitan Museum of Art, New York.

Contributors

General Editors
Mark L. Strauss
John H. Walton

Associate Editors, Illustrating the Text
Kevin and Sherry Harney

Contributing Authors, Illustrating the Text
Joshua Blunt
Rosalie de Rossett

Series Development
Jack Kuhatschek
Brian Vos

Project Editor
James Korsmo

Interior Design
Brian Brunsting

Visual Content
Kim Walton

Cover Direction
Paula Gibson
Michael Cook

Index

www.ingramcontent.com/pod-product-compliance
Lightning Source LLC
Chambersburg PA
CBHW061228150426
42812CB00054BA/2547